The Globalisation Challenge for European Higher Education

HIGHER EDUCATION RESEARCH AND POLICY (HERP)

VOLUME 4

The *Higher Education Research and Policy* (HERP) series is intended to present both research-oriented and policy-oriented studies of higher education systems in transition, especially from comparative international perspectives. Higher education systems worldwide are currently under multi-layered pressures to transform their funding and governance structures in rapidly changing environments. The series intends to explore the impact of such wider social and economic processes as globalization, internationalization and Europeanization on higher education institutions, and is focused on such issues as the changing relationships between the university and the state, the changing academic profession, changes in public funding and university governance, the emergent public/private dynamics in higher education, the consequences of educational expansion, education as public/private goods, and the impact of changing demographics on national systems. Its audience includes higher education researchers and higher education policy analysts, university managers and administrators, as well as national policymakers and the staff of international organizations involved in higher education policymaking

PETER LANG
EDITION

Pavel Zgaga/Ulrich Teichler/John Brennan (eds.)

The Globalisation Challenge for European Higher Education

Convergence and Diversity, Centres and Peripheries

Second Revised Edition

PETER LANG
EDITION

Bibliographic Information published by the Deutsche Nationalbibliothek
The Deutsche Nationalbibliothek lists this publication in the Deutsche Nationalbibliografie; detailed bibliographic data is available in the internet at http://dnb.d-nb.de.

ISSN 2193-7613
ISBN 978-3-631-67299-0 (Print)
E-ISBN 978-3-653-06508-4 (E-Book)
DOI 10.3726/978-3-653-06508-4

© Peter Lang GmbH
Internationaler Verlag der Wissenschaften
Frankfurt am Main 2013
Second Revised Edition 2016
All rights reserved.
Peter Lang Edition is an Imprint of Peter Lang GmbH.

Peter Lang – Frankfurt am Main · Bern · Bruxelles · New York · Oxford · Warszawa · Wien

This publication has been peer reviewed.

www.peterlang.com

Contents

Foreword 7

Introduction
Pavel Zgaga, Ulrich Teichler and John Brennan
Challenges for European Higher Education: 'Global' and 'National',
'Europe' and 'sub-Europes' 11

Part 1
Front Issues: Quality and Mobility, Convergence and Diversity,
Policy Ideas 31

Janja Komljenovič and Klemen Miklavič
Imagining Higher Education in the European Knowledge Economy:
Discourse and Ideas in Communications of the EU....................................33

Ulrich Teichler
The Event of International Mobility in the Course of Study
– The European Policy Objective 55

Ellen Hazelkorn and Martin Ryan
The Impact of University Rankings on Higher Education Policy in
Europe: A Challenge to Perceived Wisdom and a Stimulus for Change 79

Elsa Hackl
Diversification in Austrian Higher Education: A Result of European
or National Policies? 101

Manja Klemenčič
The Effects of Europeanisation on Institutional Diversification
in the Western Balkans..117

Part 2
Massified and Internationalised Higher Education: Equity,
Values, Societal Issues...139

Voldemar Tomusk
The Monolithic Un-intentionality of Higher Education Policies:
On the Continuing Importance of Karl Marx, Joseph Stalin
and the Minor Classics Less Known...141

6 Contents

Susan L. Robertson
"Hullabaloo in the Groves of Academe": The Politics of 'Instituting' a
Market in English Higher Education..161

John Brennan
Higher Education Differentiation and the Myth of Meritocracy:
The Case of the UK...185

Leon Cremonini
The Recognition of Prior Learning and Dutch Higher Education
– At cross-purposes? 201

Marek Kwiek
From System Expansion to System Contraction. Access to Higher
Education in Poland 233

Part 3
Higher Education in Eastern and South-east Europe:
New Trends, New Challenges..259

Martina Vukasović and Mari Elken
Higher Education Policy Dynamics in a Multi-level Governance
Context: A Comparative Study of Four Post-communist Countries...........261

Jana Baćević
What Kind of University for What Kind of Society? Nation-States,
Post-National Constellations, and Higher Education in the
Post-Yugoslav Space...287

Tatjana Sekulić
The Bosnian Puzzle of Higher Education in the Perspective
of the Bologna Process..309

Danijela Dolenec and Karin Doolan
Reclaiming the Role of Higher Education in Croatia: Dominant and
Oppositional Framings 325

Pavel Zgaga
Reconsidering Higher Education Reforms in the Western Balkans:
'Policy Colonies' or 'Policy Autarchies'? 347

Editors 371
Contributors..373
Index..381

Foreword

Pavel Zgaga, Ulrich Teichler and John Brennan

In this monograph, 19 authors – from different parts of Europe and of different ages – consider in 15 chapters some crucial aspects of higher education dynamics over the past decade or two. Different perspectives and experiences are therefore involved. This has been one of the objectives from the outset of our joint work: during the last two decades, the 'globalisation challenge' for European higher education has been continuously discussed and these discussions have most often led to identifying common features, trends, issues and policy directions. Also here, one of the objectives is to focus on major issues such as e.g. mobility, quality, diversification, access etc. as they appear within the contemporary European higher education discourse. Further, some social implications of higher education change and equity issues are elaborated, mainly through 'national lenses' and case studies. However, the aim has also been to present some 'hidden' or 'alternative stories' which speak about European policy transfer issues within specific and problematic regional and/or national environments. Therefore, the intention has been to discuss commonalities as well as differences within contemporary European higher education.

At the beginning, it is necessary to briefly sketch the context in which this monograph was formed. The story began with a research project proposal under the EUROCORES scheme of the European Science Foundation (ESF) a few years ago. Within this scheme, a theme proposal on *Higher Education and Social Change* (EuroHESC) had been selected in 2007 for further development. One of the research project proposals, developed by a consortium of research centres and institutes from seven universities,[1] was entitled *Differentiation, equity, productivity: The social*

---

1   These institutions are: The Open University, Centre for Higher Education Research and Information (CHERI), London, UK; Dublin Institute of Technology, Graduate Research School, Dublin, Ireland; University of Twente, Centre for Higher Education Policy Studies (CHEPS), Enschede, the Netherlands; Poznan University, Centre for Public Policy, Poznan, Poland; Kassel University, International Centre for Higher Education Research (INCHER), Kassel, Germany; Karlstad University and Göteborg University, Centre for Public Sector Research, Sweden; University of Ljubljana, Centre for Educational Policy Studies (CEPS), Ljubljana, Slovenia.

and economic consequences of expanded and differentiated higher education systems (DEP). The project proposal was positively evaluated (2009), but unfortunately for various – formal and financial – reasons it was impossible to establish a consortium with a sufficient number of consortium members (i.e., 70 percent of all) and funded by all the respective national research agencies.

It was during this period that the Slovenian Research Agency (ARRS) joined the ESF and it took the decision to fund all research groups from domestic institutions that had been involved in projects evaluated positively by ESF peer reviewers, regardless of the possibility of establishing an international project consortium to undertake comparative European research, which turned out to be the situation facing the DEP project. Of course, in this case it was necessary to modify the original project for it to be viable in the new conditions, but it was also necessary to maintain cooperation with the international partners. In the original DEP project proposal, the Slovenian partner (CEPS) was in charge of the transversal issues and thus in the process of modifying the project the accent was placed on the internationalisation processes in higher education while some elements of the original proposal – too ambitious under the new conditions – were omitted.

From the start of 2010 to the end of 2012 a six-member research team at the University of Ljubljana implemented the modified DEP project, while also working closely not only with five partner institutions of the original project (unfortunately, contacts were abandoned with the Karlstad and Göteborg universities as the Swedish principal investigator Susan Marton suddenly passed away), but also with researchers from other institutions, mostly but not only in Central and South-east Europe. In addition, the modified project was linked in one of its dimensions to another joint project entitled *Enhancing access through a focus on equity* (EQUNET) financed through the Life Long Learning programme of the European Commission.[2]

Thus, a network was created and the fruitful cooperation of researchers from several institutions began. On one hand, the Ljubljana team was working on its own research agenda (much broader than the structure of this

---

2   The consortium was led by the Menon network (Brussels) and made up of eight associations and four umbrella organisations bringing stakeholder groups together from across Europe, including four research institutes and centres from Bologna, Hanover, Vienna and Ljubljana.

monograph); on the other, it was also organising colloquia and seminars with invited participants: so-called *idyllic meetings* in spring and *symposion* events in autumn. The first type of event was designed as a colloquium in a relatively small circle (20 – 25 people) allowing for a detailed discussion of particular themes while the second was conceived as a small-scale conference. The series of events started by discussing a broad theme of the future of European higher education, followed by a discussion on more detailed themes, such as e.g. equity in European higher education (co-organised by the EQUNET project team), the differentiation of higher education in an internationalised and globalised context, internationalisation and/or globalisation processes and their general impact on national higher education systems (with a particular focus on convergence and divergence as well as on centres and peripheries) and, finally, with an anniversary conference on "the past, present and future of higher education research: between scholarship and policy making" which marked the 25 years of the Consortium of Higher Education Researchers (CHER) after its annual conference in 2012.

As mentioned, a special feature of this network was its geographic and, in particular, generational diversity: senior researchers alongside early-stage researchers and PhD students. Several of them had experience from working for national student unions as well as for the European Students Union (ESU), thus being involved in European higher education reforms of the last decade in quite a direct way. Some participants were also professionals working for relevant European and/or national institutions and associations – or simply people with long and valuable experience in higher education. From the geographic point of view, almost all European regions were represented. In particular, participation from South-east Europe was emphasised, as a region which has not been appropriately represented, either within the contemporary circle of European higher education researchers or as an object of focused research. It is obvious that a generation of higher education researchers is growing today in this region who will have much to say in the future!

Such a network definitely sets up the potential for originality and novelty and has a special value-added: certain themes have been discussed in ways that open up new perspectives as well as dilemmas, allow for new insights and perhaps indicate some new solutions. It also provided a contribution that went beyond the basic horizons of the modified DEP project. It was therefore no surprise that an idea matured in the spring of

2012 that a core group of participants at these events would write a monograph based on some materials discussed and considered at previous events. The results can now be read in this book. It is made up of three parts: the first part focuses mainly on 'global narratives' in European higher education and specifically in relation to diversification, while the second elaborates on some particular aspects of equity and related issues in higher education. The third part pays attention to higher education reforms and developments in South-east Europe and provides a reminder that 'global narratives' are not dominant everywhere and that attention should also be paid to 'regional and/or local narratives' so as to see the whole picture.

Foreword to the second edition

The news that a book is sold out is always good news and an important recognition for authors, editors and the publisher. It means that with the themes and issues addressed in this book we have attracted considerable attention and also that the publisher has successfully promoted the book. We are delighted therefore that the publisher has decided to publish a second edition, and we hope that it will continue to mobilize the attention of the reading public. The new edition is unchanged except for minor editing.

Kassel, Ljubljana and London, November 2015

Editors

Introduction

Challenges for European Higher Education: 'Global' and 'National', 'Europe' and 'sub-Europes'

Pavel Zgaga, Ulrich Teichler and John Brennan

This book addresses the globalisation and/or internationalisation challenge for European higher education from two cross-cutting perspectives: convergence and diversity, centres and peripheries. At this point, we cannot enter into the complex relationship between the concepts of globalisation and internationalisation; instead, we will focus on the double meaning the globalisation and/or internationalisation challenge for European higher education has had over the last two decades: as 'globalisation in the true sense' on one hand and as 'Europeanisation', i.e. "the regional version of internationalisation or globalisation" (Teichler 2004: 4) on the other. In this book, this "regional version" is brought to forefront without forgetting the former. However, we also do not forget that even 'Europeanisation' has a double meaning: Europe as a 'global region' (i.e., a perspective of 'looking out') vs. Europe as 'European regions' (i.e., a perspective of 'looking within').

I

A review of the state of the research field which formed the basis for the EuroHESC programme (Higher Education Looking Forward: An Agenda for Future Research – HELF) found that "there is limited comparative research on the extent of the differences between countries and the possibility of convergence via globalisation" (Brennan et al. 2008: 11). Research on these issues is therefore strongly needed; however, its approaches should be carefully reconsidered. First of all, new research should begin by recognising that "a single narrative or 'idea' cannot any longer capture the complex and often contradictory nature of higher education" today as it exists across different countries, "variations reflect different traditions and contemporary circumstances and contexts". Further, the HELF report warned that these variations should not become "an excuse to descend into praise of the particular and the unique"; on the contrary, "An understanding of the different things that higher education does is extremely important but the range of differences is not infinite, differences are bounded and they can be typologised in relation to both internal and external variables. And we should not rule out the possible existence of some unifying concept or concepts. A focus on difference may be a key route towards identifying and better understanding such concepts" (ibid.). This idea is shared by the authors of this monograph.

The relationship between 'unity' and 'diversity' – or 'diversity' and 'unity' – has been in the very front of contemporary debates on the 'Europeanisation' processes: both at a general level (e.g., as "a 'European way' to manage unity and diversity", Olsen 2005) and in its particular dimensions, one of which affects and/or manifests in higher education (e.g. Haanes 2006, Amaral et al. 2009). Particularly after 1990, the general processes of 're-uniting Europe' importantly challenged national higher education systems: in the given historical circumstances it seemed that parallel to the 'national systems' of higher education rooted in the 19th century there is a need for a 'European system'[1] at the turn of the millennium.

The policy dilemma – either a 'united' ('harmonised') 'European system' or 'European systems' as a 'unity in diversity' – was constantly reproduced over the next two decades, in one form or another and either consciously or unconsciously. Already at its inception it was not an easy dilemma. On one hand, it was provoked by the rapidly penetrating 'globalisation' and a fear of losing "a world-wide degree of attraction" or "international competitiveness"; on the other hand, it was an inner result of the ongoing "European process" and its "extraordinary achievements of the last few years" (Bologna Declaration 1999). The dichotomy of convergence and diversity, if we use other words to denote more or less the same issue,

---

1   In paragraph 8, in the context of "international competitiveness", the Bologna Declaration addressed "the European systems of higher education". It is less known that a draft of the Declaration of 9 June 1999 contained at this point the term "the European system of higher education". During the last round of negotiating the text, the singular was replaced by the plural in the first sentence of this paragraph; however, the plural remained unchanged in its third sentence. Interestingly, a wrong (i.e. draft) version   is   given   at   http://www.ehea.info/Uploads/about/BOLOGNA_ DECLARATION1.pdf (the official 'Bologna website'; last accessed 18 January 2013); this link is also replicated today on other websites, including the European Commission. For a proper reading the reader needs to look back to archives today.

has already been inscribed, e.g. upon the foundation of the Erasmus Programme (1986). The fall of the Berlin Wall a few years later, followed by deep political, economic and social changes in Eastern Europe, spread it further to the Tempus Programme (1990) which was established to extend the new European strategy in higher education across the former Iron Curtain. The *Zeitgeist* called for the creation of more 'unity' in the European 'diversities'; it was in this context that the political momentum was accumulated to establish the European Higher Education Area (EHEA).

The process of 'Europeanisation' – understood here as a 'European way' to manage unity and diversity in higher education – has encountered a number of interpretations. Basically, they can be divided into two groups: conditionally speaking, they depend on approaching and observing 'Europeanisation' either as 'globalisation' or as 'internationalisation'. From the point of view of 'globalisation' as the 'levelling of the diverse', higher education is considered as part of a global market system; within this perspective, there is no necessary connection between higher education and national development. In contrast, 'internationalisation' can only be considered as a process *inter* nations. Yet, the discussion on 'globalisation' has proven that the issue is not so simple as the solution cannot simply lie in 'joining the right side'. This levelling leads to eliminating all differences (and thus quality), while the difference in itself leads to autarchy. For example, international cooperation remains pure rhetoric if some convergence is not established between parties and a discussion remains a monologue until some 'unifying concepts' are set up. The relationship of convergence and diversity is driven by a specific dialectic. We need to establish 'unifying concepts' but – as mentioned above – only a focus on difference helps us to identify and better understand these concepts.

After two decades, European higher education still consists of national higher education systems; yet, some of them are more 'globalised' than others. Today, European national higher education systems look much more convergent than ever before but a cluster of new challenges is emerging: questions about the nature of the true potential of the EHEA and about the real impact of recent reforms across countries; questions about the aims and near future of European higher education etc. There is also enough evidence that a tension between 'European' convergence and 'national' diversities persists – and is perhaps even becoming exacerbated with its sharpening economic as well as political problems. The *Zeitgeist* has obviously changed and today it seems to be closer to rehabilitating the European 'diversities' aspect than strengthening a perspective of European 'unity'. Of course, this general change cannot remain without consequences for higher education. For example, the reduced funding for the Erasmus Programme – for the first time in its 25-year history – is just one of the signs of the depth of this change.

Different interpretations of the formerly 'concerted' pan-European policy (either in Bologna 1999 or in Lisbon 2000, or both) as well as diverse implementation processes at the national and/or regional level – enhanced by a mix of different discourses and the 'local' political and ideational pressures behind these processes – are now producing a new kind of European 'divergence'. Here we come across another dichotomy, the dichotomy of centres and peripheries. It has not received much attention during the discussions of the last two decades; nevertheless, it seems that it can open up some new perspectives in understanding the higher education dynamic of the present decade.

It is obvious that today the EHEA is not a homogenous area – and that it cannot be. Changes in individual national systems influenced by the 'Europeanisation' and 'globalisation' processes, and the Bologna Process in particular, are having quite different impacts in various European countries and/or regions. On one hand, different qualities of e.g. 'big' and 'small' higher education systems demand adapted policies and specific actions. This cannot be interpreted as a necessary and inevitable contradiction of the 'common policy'; only focusing on differences may help to identify and understand what is common. Moreover, the 'common higher education space' that was declared in 2010 after 10 years of 'harmonised' reforms in 49 countries of the continent is producing certain new tensions: e.g. in organisation of the system and its support institutions;[2] the large imbalances in incoming and outgoing mobile students and staff; the 'attractiveness' of national universities in various countries etc.

On the other hand, it looks like an 'invisible hand' is pushing European countries to either accept roles of 'policy exporters' or 'policy importers'. There is a strange incapability on the part of 'peripheral' countries to design their own national policies; instead, they are adopting and implementing recommended 'common policies' developed in 'policy centres' without taking the specifics of the 'peripherals' into account. Of course, there are

---

2   E.g., quality assurance agencies in 'small' higher education systems can never achieve
      the critical mass that agencies in 'large' countries have.

many reasons for this; one of them is likely to be located in the very nature of the formation of the EHEA: the domination of the 'common policy' focus has led to "Bologna omnipresence" or "pan-Bolognisation" in contemporary European higher education discourses (Zgaga 2012: 30). This is just one of the reasons it is necessary to focus on differences again in order to reconceptualise a 'unifying concept' or 'concepts'.

II

The chapters in this book are organised in three parts, with each part consisting of five chapters. *Part 1* addresses some 'front issues': quality and mobility, convergence and diversity and policy ideas.

In claims about global challenges, the term 'knowledge economy' tends to be put forward to suggest that higher education across all countries is bound to be more strongly shaped by economic imperatives. Janja Komljenovič and Klemen Miklavič depict the European Union as a strong advocate of a common European higher education policy in their article "Imagining Higher Education in the European Knowledge Economy: Discourse and Ideas in Communications of the EU". Higher education policy statements by the European Commission have emphasised the importance of higher education for the economic future of Europe from the outset of the EU's involvement in higher education policies since the 1970s, but the biggest policy early initiatives such as establishing the ERASMUS programme of student mobility in the 1980s and efforts to create a convergent pattern of study programmes and degrees in the Bologna Process – led by national governments since the late 1990s – have obviously pursued a relatively broad range of objectives without calling for a single and convergent major set of policy objectives.

The authors point out that the Lisbon Strategy was the major EU initiative of placing knowledge, and in this framework higher education, in the core of economic policy. In their critical discourse analysis of documents and their analysis of expert interviews undertaken, they argue that the EU aims at "causing the approximation of the academic sphere and the economic sector": Europe's answer to the global 'knowledge economy' should be an increase of expenditures on knowledge and greater efficiency, quality and 'competitiveness' in higher education. In the various EU statements ('Communications' etc.) since the year 2000, the "hitherto unfitness of European universities" is deplored: "They are portrayed as ossified institutions that function in an old and outdated fashion rooted in the ideas and context of the 19th century". The EU has advocated in its statements an increase in the institutional autonomy of universities that, if led by strong professionalised management and the desire to be responsive to external expectations, would enhance efficiency within the framework of economic rationales. The EU obviously considers the knowledge economy as a "central integrative paradigm", generally being viewed as persuasive and inevitable, that is likely to create a widespread consensus among most actors involved. The "normative convergence" was viewed as being so strong that all national prerogatives and all alternative norms could be "elegantly circumvented".

While the EU higher education policy in the framework of the Lisbon Agenda pursues a strong, controversial normative rationale of gearing higher education to 'economic competitiveness', a second internationally widespread objective of higher education is operational in its nature. An increase in international activities of higher education is generally held as inevitable and desirable, whereby a rise in international student mobility is the most widely shared operational objective in Europe and beyond. As Ulrich Teichler points out in "The Event of International Mobility in the Course of Study – the European Policy Objective" (i.e., the second chapter of *Part 1*), quantitative growth of student mobility is the single most widely shared and most popular aim in the discourse on improving higher education across Europe. Quantitative targets became more ambitious in this respect with the ministers involved in the Bologna Process calling for an average rate of 20 percent of students across European countries spending at least a semester of study or study-related work experience in another European country by the year 2020. This quantitative target implicitly suggests that outbound mobility for the purpose of acquiring first-hand international experience of life and study in another country is the highest aim in Europe – more important than maximum figures on the hosting of students from other countries.

The great popularity of increasing border-crossing student mobility seems to be based on the belief that student mobility is beneficial with regard to a broad range of educational and societal goals. The value of study in another country might comprise 'learning from contrast', a more reflective personality, successfully taking up visible international work tasks and generally the enhancement of professionally relevant competencies which lead to more successful careers. Surprisingly, though, as Teichler points out, this widely shared objective is not accompanied by concerted efforts even to create basic statistics in order to identify the magnitude of student mobility. For example, the figures on foreign students and study abroad have served as approximations for estimating mobility, i.e. border-crossing for the purpose of study, and many countries continue not to register short-term mobility, i.e. the most widespread mode of intra-European student mobility. The author points out that inward mobility to Europe from other regions of the world has grown substantially in recent years – often for the whole degree programme and often motivated to experience a higher quality of teaching and learning abroad than at home and to enhance one's academic competencies. Intra-European mobility, in contrast, seems to be growing moderately, is undertaken predominantly for a period of study and to partner universities of a similar quality as that at home, whereby inter-cultural understanding and 'learning from contrast' is more likely to be expected than superior academic quality.

Competition for the establishment and preservation of select high-quality universities is widely held as the third global imperative for higher education. Ellen Hazelkorn and Martin Ryan point out in their article "The Impact of University Rankings on Higher Education Policy in Europe: A Challenge to Perceived Wisdom and a Stimulus for Chance" that the higher education policy discourse in Europe has substantially changed since 'global rankings' of universities have been published. While criticism of the methods and validity of information was widely voiced, concern spread notably among advocates of the Lisbon Agenda to strengthen higher education and research in order to make Europe economically most 'competitive'.

One tended to believe that too few higher education institutions in Europe "are recognized as world-class in the current environment of research-oriented global rankings". The view spread that the quality of a higher education system largely depends on the concentration of potential in a few top institutions, whereas earlier higher education policies, based on the belief of higher education as a public good serving broad cultural and social objectives, had favoured a similar level of quality among most higher education institutions. Hazelkorn and Ryan analyse policies in France, Germany and the United Kingdom; they note a smaller impact of the ranking discourse in the United Kingdom because substantial quality differences between institutions had already existed and were widely accepted. The authors argue that rankings did not trigger a completely new debate but "accelerated and intensified" what was often called a "modernisation agenda" of higher education. Finally, they point out that measures taken to support the outstanding situation of a few top universities cannot lead to rapid changes and that their impact can only be measured validly after a while.

The European discourse on "world-class universities" can be viewed as one of the various calls for the diversification of higher education systems. In the fourth chapter of this section, in her article on "Diversification in Austrian Higher Education: A Result of European or National Policies?" Elsa Hackl shows that this only addresses one feature of diversification. Over the years, "the need to diversify European higher education has been one of the persistent topics of European policy makers" and, in this framework, a broader range of possible dimensions of diversity has been addressed.

Diversification has been a topic across European countries since the 1960s, whereby differentiation among institutional types was advocated and often implemented initially while the focus shifted over the years towards diversification among individual universities of higher education. In her case study of Austria, Hackl shows that national policies were justified as following European trends and imperatives even if they did not closely follow the dominant trends. The establishment of *Fachhochschulen* and thus "differentiation for practice relevance" was not realised in Austria before the 1990s. "Diversification for competitiveness" was not pursued through policies directly shaping the patterns of higher education, but via reforms of governance starting in 2002: "Through detachment from the federal administration and legal autonomy the universities ought to be provided sufficient scope of action and entrepreneurship". Finally, the third policy step, that of "diversification for excellence" has for a few years appeared more in tune with policies in other European countries; yet it seems too premature to ascertain that the newly established "Institute of Science and Technology – Austria" is on its way to becoming a "world class university". Thus, the author convincingly shows that European policy discourses on higher education are influential in individual European countries even though the European countries are not clearly headed towards convergent solutions.

The fifth chapter of the first part of this book also addresses the impact of European policy discourses as regards the need for more diversified higher education systems on national policies and actual developments. Manja Klemenčič analyses in her article "The Effects of Europeanisation on

Institutional Diversification in the Western Balkans" the situation in four Western Balkan countries: Albania, Croatia, Serbia and Slovenia. In the initial review of "European positions", she shows that the European Commission is increasingly extending its Lisbon Agenda to the interpretation of the Bologna Process and ever more advocating greater quality differences between European universities in Europe. When turning to Western Balkan countries, she points out that "voluntary cooperation" is typical for higher education policy in the European Union and that "persuasion- and incentive-based mechanisms prevail". In contrast, the "Western Balkan countries are all subject to intensive EU intervention in terms of financial and expert support". Actually, "all countries have been working on consolidating a binary structure". In contrast to the majority of Western European countries, "all the countries have made legislative changes for the emergence (and expansion) of private higher education".

Moreover, all the Western Balkans countries have tried to follow the general European "standards" of accreditation and quality assurance and understood this as a tool for creating similar characteristics of their higher education system as in other European countries. Yet they have differed from other regions by not emphasising diversity between individual institutions and "institutional profiling". Klemenčič is convinced, however, that the Western Balkan countries are on the move towards increasing vertical diversity, whereby "research quality" is "the single most powerful element of diversification". She concludes: "there is a danger that the already existing vertical differentiation will become even steeper, leading to the imitation of top-ranking universities and thus the weakening of horizontal diversity".

III

Part 2 addresses equity, values and societal issues in the context of massified and internationalised higher education. The five chapters deal with a series of difficult and controversial issues. As universities become 'businesses' and students become 'consumers', questions about the central functions of universities, the relationships between the academic and the social, the different forms of knowledge and their value to both individuals and societies must be asked, although answers to them may vary at different times and in different places. And the answers may be uncomfortable, not least to those of us who work in higher education.

The chapter by Voldemar Tomusk examines the social and knowledge functions of expanded higher education systems and describes the forms and agendas of social engineering which have lain at the heart of the transitions from 'elite' to 'mass' to 'universal' higher education systems, using Martin Trow's terminology (Trow 1974). The chapter's title, "Monolithic Un-Intentionality of Higher Education Policies: On the Continuing Importance of Karl Marx, Joseph Stalin and the Less Well-known Minor Classics" offers a tantalising promise of the analysis to follow!

In the process of higher education's expansion, the sense of benefits to the individual from higher education credentials shifts from an emphasis on the 'gain' from the possession of credentials to an emphasis on the avoidance of 'loss' from the absence of credentials. Higher education is increasingly becoming a 'consumption' good, conferring some social status but little else and essentially performing a function of social reproduction. Tomusk poses some uncomfortable questions about the nature of knowledge within so-called knowledge societies and argues that "knowledge has been relativised to the extent that learning is disappearing from higher education". The social justifications for the expansion of higher education risk, in the view of Tomusk, undermining the true value of learning for the individual (and for society).

In the following chapter, "'Hullabaloo' in the Groves of Academe": The Politics of 'Instituting' a Market in English Higher Education, Susan Robertson examines the processes of privatisation and marketisation in higher education by focusing on the English case where these processes have been stimulated by the arrival of a new government in 2010, a government strongly committed to a neo-liberal ideology. For higher education in England, the costs of delivering the teaching function in higher education have largely been transferred from the state to the student by the introduction in most academic fields of full-cost fees, the levels of which are set by the higher education institutions themselves, thus instigating a competitive market in relation to price.

Robertson focuses in particular on the arrival and role of new private for-profit providers of higher education. Her argument is that the creation of a market is a highly political process which must inevitably challenge existing interests and values, creating a "major disturbance" to the life and work of all institutions of higher education. The new private providers in the UK include firms and branch campuses of foreign universities. The government's intention is that the greater competition provided by the new higher education providers (which generally do not include a research function) will reduce costs and thus benefit the consumer. Robertson presents a list of "legitimation claims", the first of which is "savings" with others including a more "efficient and sustainable system", "fairer access" and a "more level playing field" for institutional competition. The validity of the claims remains to be tested.

The next chapter by John Brennan, "Higher Education Differentiation and the Myth of Meritocracy: The Case of the UK", continues the British case study theme, this time focusing on social equity issues and the part being played by a highly stratified higher education system in maintaining the high levels of inequality and declining opportunities for upward social mobility which characterise contemporary Britain. Central to the argument is the concept of meritocracy as set out by the British sociologist Michael Young in the 1950s. Young's largely satirical book used the concept of meritocracy to explain how social inequality could be legitimised by implying that the socially advantaged attain and deserve their advantages through 'merit', i.e. through their ability and hard work. The attainment of educational credentials was taken as a good measure of 'merit'. Similarly, the socially disadvantaged deserve their disadvantages because they reflect a lack of merit, little ability and no willingness to work hard.

Brennan applies these concepts to the highly differentiated system of higher education present in Britain today, a system of "vertical differentiation" which enables a 'mass' system of higher education to continue to perform functions of elite reproduction. He notes that, compared with the labour markets of many other European countries, graduate success in the British labour market is a function of 'where' you studied rather than 'what' you studied. And 'where' you study is in large part a function of social background. For the meritocratic argument to work in these circumstances, it is necessary for some institutions to be regarded as better than others, this being a central feature of British higher education. However, Brennan describes some recent British research which suggests that the quality and standards of student learning in high status 'top' universities may actually be lower than it is in other more 'mass' institutions, thus undermining the meritocracy argument.

The next chapter in *Part 2* moves us to the Netherlands and takes us beyond higher education in the sense that it focuses on knowledge acquired outside higher education and considers the extent to which this is recognised and valued within higher education. In his chapter "The Recognition of

Prior Learning and Dutch Higher Education – At Cross-purposes?", Leon Cremonini explores the role of Dutch arrangements for the recognition of prior learning (RPL) in both meeting manpower needs in the labour market and achieving greater social equity in accessing higher education. His conclusion seems to be that it is more effective in achieving the former than in achieving the latter.

Cremonini sets out the Dutch arrangements for RPL both within the theoretical literature on the social reproductive functions of higher education and within policy frameworks at both European and Dutch national levels. Within the Dutch education system, children are channelled into different educational pathways at an early age. These pathways reflect different social origins and point towards different social and economic destinations with a university education coming towards the end of the pathway leading to a good job and 'success' in life. The promise of RPL is to shift the focus onto outcomes rather than the pathways to achieving them. Thus, RPL permits the recognition of an individual's knowledge wherever and however it is acquired. However, the emphasis on knowledge in terms of competencies and learning outcomes means that RPL in the Dutch system is mainly an employment tool which, if it leads into higher education at all, leads into the vocational side of the Dutch binary system.

In the final chapter of *Part 2*, several of the themes explored in earlier chapters are revisited with respect to the interesting case of Poland, interesting in part for its post-Communist legacy but also because for its changing demographics, with the country facing one of the steepest demographic declines in Europe. Marek Kwiek, in "From System Expansion to System Contraction: Access to Higher Education in Poland", reviews the expansion of Polish higher education over the last 20 years and considers the possible consequences for Polish higher education of the shift into a period of major demographic contraction. In so doing, he considers the implications for public and private providers of higher education, for institutional differentiation more generally and for social stratification and mobility within Polish society.

Kwiek notes the existence of high probabilities of the inter-generational "inheritance" of higher education in Poland. Compared with other European countries, a bigger proportion of Polish students have parents who also attended higher education. Using international data from the European Union Survey of Income and Living Conditions, he finds lower rates of intergenerational mobility in Poland than in most other countries. The key question then to be considered, for Poland and for several other Eastern European countries, is whether the forthcoming period of demographic decline will bring any change in these patterns. In so doing, he considers the prospects for private providers of higher education, the possibility of the greater 'homogenisation' of higher education (as opposed to continuing differentiation), and the implications for social diversity in terms of age, gender, sector (public/private) and modes of study (part-time or full-time).

Taken as a whole, the five chapters in *Part 2* consider the multiple and changing interconnections between change in higher education and wider social changes. Some general trends can be discerned but there are also particularities to be found in different places, reflecting different histories and different locations within the 'globalised knowledge society'. The importance of history and location is further explored in *Part 3*.

IV

Part 3 addresses new trends and new challenges in higher education in Eastern and, in particular, South-east Europe. The main focus is given to countries of the Western Balkans – a region often in the headlines during the last two decades but which has largely remained *terra incognita* both regarding information and research on higher education.

In the dominant global discourses – and the discourse on higher education is just one of them – the countries of 'Eastern Europe'[3] usually appear as 'the former Communist countries'. This is a highly generalised term. Today, this term falls far too short. Its main deficiency is the inherent illusion of the 'total uniformity' which supposedly reigned after 1917 and/or 1945 in all of these countries without distinction, that is, the loss of both an insight into and an understanding of the differences. This deficiency makes it almost impossible to grasp similarities and commonalities. Not only were there substantial differences between the distinctive types of 'Communism' which one should recognise (e.g., the Soviet 'real socialism' on one side and

---

3   Eastern Europe may appear to be a clear geographical term if one observes Europe e.g. from North America. However, Czech Republic, for example, would understand looking from its particular *Central European* perspective that Eastern Europe is Belarus, Russia or Ukraine, as well as, for example, Montenegro looking from its particular *South-east European* perspective. These terms are far from being 'clear geographic terms' if one does not recognise that they are heavily loaded with essentially cultural contents.

Yugoslav 'self-governmental socialism' on the other); significant differences – neutral or latently conflicting – also existed at sub-regional levels. Developments after 1990, in particular in the newly independent states, have taken quite diverse paths, although they had common constitutional foundations as in the case of the former Yugoslavia. Therefore, from today's point of view – a point of view "of convergence via globalisation" – differences are a more important subject of research than similarities of the political orders which were abandoned more than two decades ago.

In their chapter "Higher Education Policy Dynamics in a Multi-level Governance Context: A Comparative Study of Four Post-communist Countries", Martina Vukasović and Mari Elken aim to draw a comparative picture of higher education reforms in a sample of small 'ex-Communist' countries of the Baltic Sea and the Western Balkans. Their main concern is not "patterns of convergence and divergence"; instead, they put these countries in the context of 'Europeanisation' and policy transfer. Four countries – Croatia, Estonia, Serbia and Slovenia – form a sample which was "chosen due to the unique mix of similarities and differences" and which the authors find "useful for exploring the differences between policy transfer and Europeanisation". Among many differences their analysis identifies a *'file rouge'*: national policy changes prior to the Bologna Process are characterised more by policy transfer and particular national policy concerns than by Europeanisation; later this relationship was turned around. Nevertheless, beyond the 'Bologna' milestone in all four countries "idiosyncratic policy concerns were also addressed"; yet often in a way that controversial national policy reforms were presented as an integral part of the 'Bologna umbrella'. In conclusion, the authors draw attention to the "limited influence these countries have had on the shaping of European preferences" as a background with the result "that in these countries the European initiatives are taken more on face value than might be the case in some Western or Northern European countries". At this point, they identify some issues worth research attention in the future.

The next chapter is entitled "What Kind of University for What Kind of Society? Nation-States, Post-National Constellations, and Higher Education in the Post-Yugoslav Space". Jana Baćević addresses the issue of the transformation of higher education following the dissolution of Yugoslavia and connects the topic with the question of the "changing concept of political communities that universities 'belong' to". In other words, at a general level changes in higher education are considered with a focus on the role of higher education in a society; on a particular level they are analysed within the context of 'post-conflict' societies and universities in four successor states of the former Yugoslavia: Bosnia and Herzegovina (B&H), Kosovo, Macedonia and Sandžak (an ethnically mixed region within Serbia).

Baćević aims to show how policy developments in these countries can be understood in the broader context of political transformations of the region and how these developments relate to political communities and entities that have arisen during the last two decades from the ashes of the previous common state. In this perspective, she draws attention to the different facets the "transnationalisation of higher education" has in the Western Balkans. Like we saw in the previous chapter, this story does not end with 'Europeanisation': "transnationalisation, globalisation, and European integration are not the only relevant political processes" shaping these societies – and their universities – today. A special emphasis is put on social processes connected to fragmentation or diversification along ethnic, linguistic and similar lines. Following this path, the author comes to an important conclusion: "not only are political communities no longer defined by the boundaries of the nation-states, but multiple political communities exist within the boundaries of nation-states".

Baćević also stresses that the majority of the research on higher education in the Western Balkans has so far focused on "the processes of [the European] integration" but "largely ignoring the parallel processes of fragmentation" which have taken place everywhere. With the increasingly fragmented social and political framework, universities intend "to serve education of one particular group" and this shift "is in fact not entirely different from the times when higher education was reserved for the members of particular social groups, that is, the elites". The problem is not exclusion from exclusion, but "identity-based higher education" which poses problems "for those who do not belong to one of the dominant groups".

The third chapter, "The Bosnian Puzzle of Higher Education in the Perspective of the Bologna Process", focuses on a specific case of B&H, a country that has suffered much during the wars of the 1990s. Those wars ended with the Dayton Peace Agreement (1995) and by establishing an unusual form of government (a country administratively divided into the Federation of B&H with 10 cantons, the Republic of Srpska and the Brčko

District) imposed by the international community. Today, this form raises a number of concerns, including several in the area of higher education. Tatjana Sekulić, the author who originated in this country but lives and works in Italy, finds B&H "under-researched compared to other former Yugoslav successor countries" as well as a special country case within the context of 'post-conflict' societies and 'Europeanisation' processes in the Western Balkans.

Her chapter gives a short historical overview of the development of higher education after 1945 and describes a process of institutional fragmentation and multiplication as a result of the civil war and ethnic conflict of the 1990s. Addressing changes in the structure of B&H's higher education system, she stresses "a kind of paradox" of the socialist period: while the higher education system of the former Yugoslavia was under the political control of the political centres at the federative as well as 'republic'[4] levels, its internal organisation was completely decentralised and sometimes produced "more liberal practices within independent faculties" than one could imagine. In the last two decades, this picture has changed immensely. Within the totally 'decentralised' country of today, i.e. a country with no 'central' ministry responsible for higher education (all responsibilities are with canton ministries etc.), the key higher education policy concept seems to be the construction of a "re-integrated model of university governance". Sekulić concludes: "The same authoritarian control pattern, applied on the level of these 'statelets', continuously slows down and obstructs the decision-making process at both the single university and on the state level." It should be noted, however, that the "absurdity of the Bosnian fragmented context" is not a purely 'national' invention: it is a result of the war – and the involvement of the 'international community'.

The fourth chapter, "Reclaiming the Role of Higher Education in Croatia: Dominant and Oppositional Framings", presents another country-specific case. However, Danijela Dolenec and Karin Doolan do not attempt to outline a general trend of developments in Croatian higher education over the last decade or two; rather they outline the "development of the neoliberal doctrine in higher education" and analyse how it has influenced the official discourse. Lots has been said in contemporary international discussion about the 'neoliberal turn' but not much has been said from the specific context of

---

4   In the former Yugoslavia a federal unit was called a *Socialist Republic*.

'(post-)transitional' and 'post-conflict' countries. This point makes their contribution fresh and challenging.

As in almost all countries of the region, since the mid-1990s the growth of the student population in Croatia has been based on the rising number of self-financed students. For quite a long time, this change encountered no significant public opposition. National policy documents continued to refer to the European welfare state – but "adjusted to the conditions of the 21st century". This is a point which calls for interpretation; yet not only the neo-liberal one. At the end of the previous decade, a strong student protest movement (also) appeared in Croatia; its manifesto and documents testify to a possible different interpretation. Helped by Nancy Fraser's concept of justice, Dolenec and Doolan "interpret the student protest movement in Croatia as the initial site of resistance to the spread of the neoliberal doctrine" and conclude that "constructions of higher education in official state documents predominantly reflect the neoliberal model" while "the student protests in Croatia construct higher education along the counter-hegemonic humanist tradition".

In the last chapter of this book, Pavel Zgaga reconsiders "Higher Education Reforms in the Western Balkans" with regard to a dichotomy of "Policy Colonies" and "Policy Autarchies". His focus is on higher education reforms in the Western Balkans which are put in the light of progressing Europeanisation, internationalisation and globalisation. Among the richness of regional diversities the author identifies some common trends of reforms in the past two decades. Thus, substantial reforms started almost everywhere only after 2000; reforms of the 1990s were mainly adaptations of the 'traditional' system to challenges brought by the political upheaval of 1990–1991. With these substantial reforms, the politicisation and privatisation of higher education came to the fore.

Privatisation proved to be "a Pandora's box in the Western Balkans": there were no such institutions before 1991 but today there are about 250 private institutions in a region of about 25 million people. Were they 'imported'? This question opens another one: a question which this part of the book starts with – i.e., policy transfer. Analysing the 'Bologna' implementation in the region, the author comes to the conclusion that reforms have been run "in formal rather than substantive terms". In public, there is often an observation that the 'Bologna' reforms have 'failed in implementation' but not as an 'idea'. In other words, there has been the European 'Bologna' and there have been regional 'Bolognas' – as "adjustments to local circumstances". Zgaga identifies the key problem of the 'failed' reforms in the region as follows: "The normative dimension of the system has been changed fundamentally while the axiological dimension has remained largely unchanged". This finding leads to a further question of the relationship between 'policy centres' and 'policy colonies' which is briefly discussed in the concluding part of the chapter.

V

The chapters in this volume present a mix of theoretical, policy, empirical and regional perspectives on the roles played by higher education systems and institutions in their changing social, political and economic contexts. While a 'European' story is offered, particularly in *Part 1*, it is a story set within an increasingly global context, where universal 'drivers' of change are emphasised and reflect increasingly dominating and universal distributions of power and authority. A neo-liberal agenda is frequently central to the story and is seen as globally directed, often constituting a new form of colonialism which entails the dismantling of the welfare state, an emphasis on competitiveness – whether between nation-states, regions or individuals – an emphasis on deregulation, a minimal role for the state, a celebration of the private over the public, and of the economic over the social, cultural or political.

In the neo-liberal world, higher education is assigned a key role in driving economic progress and in achieving individual, national and regional economic interests. In this sense, higher education is increasingly required to respond effectively and efficiently to externally-set pressures, whether or not these are set within the processes and mechanisms of the regulative state or of the consumerist pressures of the marketised 'knowledge economy' – global, local and regional. While there are common strands to this responsiveness, there are also differences – between individual higher education institutions, individual nation-states and regions of various kinds, both economic and political. And there are large implications for the part played by higher education in shaping the levels and processes of social equity and mobility, issues explored in particular in some of the *Part 2* chapters.

In attempting a 'European' perspective on these trends, the concept of 'region' assumes an interestingly problematic status. Depending on the context, it can be both 'super'-national and 'sub'-national. We can find a

'Europe' of the European Commission, of the Bologna Process, with an expanding membership of nation-states, which can be set against a series of mainly geographically defined 'sub-Europes' of which the 'Western Balkans' provides the central focus for the chapters contained in *Part 3*.

While it is tempting to see sub-regions such as the Western Balkans as interesting illustrations of global trends being developed and driven from far away, it is perhaps more instructive to see them as alternative stories, of reminders of counter hegemonies and indeed possibly of potential 'policy transfers' in directions different from those which are currently regarded as dominant. Their stories reflect both history and location, of the arbitrariness of local conditions but also of the long-term nature of their effects and impacts.

Some of the interesting alternative stories on offer here provide reminders of the traditions of universities as 'troublesome institutions' which exist as much to critique and transform as to confirm and reproduce their host societies. In particular, they provide useful reminders of important 'public goods' which higher education can provide to the potential benefit of all, but which may need protection against the pressures of private interests and consumer demand. The question then arises as to where this protection will come from. But, similarly, there may also be some 'public bads' generated by higher education from which the rest of society needs some protection. Again the question arises as to where the protection will come from. 'State versus market' provides easy answers but it may be that the important and more difficult answers lie in the details of funding, regulation and accountability arrangements. And the space allowed for the notions of autonomy and academic freedom within higher education may be an increasingly contested space, whatever the forms of funding and regulation.

Much has been made in the higher education literature of the idea of the 'entrepreneurial university' within increasingly knowledge-based economies and societies. But many of the above chapters, especially in *Part 3*, are perhaps more suggestive of the idea of the 'transformative university' and it may be especially the latter which can be found in the transformative contexts provided by nation-building conditions such as those witnessed in the Western Balkans in recent years. More generally, the relationship between the transformation of universities and the transformation of the wider societies of which they are form part constitutes a central question for future social science research into higher education. Social transformation or social reproduction provide a further refinement of the question. Different answers may be found in different locations and indeed transformation and reproduction may both be found to be happening within increasingly diverse societies and increasingly differentiated higher education systems.

The chapters in this book provide many examples of the ways in which universities are changing as a result of changes in the wider societies of which they are part. But the changes are not occurring everywhere in the same direction. And there remains at least some evidence to suggest that universities can, in some contexts and circumstances, still be their own drivers of change and social transformation. Comparative research on the functioning of universities matters because universities matter, and universities matter because knowledge matters (Rhoten and Calhoun 2011). We look forward to learning about further episodes in the relationships between universities and social change, in Europe and beyond.

References

Amaral, A., G. Neave, Ch. Musselin, P. Maassen, eds. (2009). *European Integration and the Governance of Higher Education and Research*. Dordrecht: Springer.

Brennan, J., J. Enders, Ch. Musselin, U. Teichler, J. Välimaa (2008). *Higher Education Looking Forward: An Agenda for Future Research*. Synthesis report of the European Science Foundation's Forward Look on Higher Education in Europe Beyond 2010: Resolving Conflicting Social and Economic Perspectives. Strasbourg: European Science Foundation.

The European Higher Education Area [Bologna Declaration]. Joint Declaration of the European Ministers of Education Convened in Bologna on 19 June 1999.

Haanes, V. L. (2006). "Unity in Diversity and Diversity in Unity: The Role and Legitimacy of European Universities". *Higher Education in Europe*. Vol. 31. No. 4. 443-448.

Olsen, J. P. (2005).*Unity and Diversity – European Style*. Working Paper. No. 24, September 2005. Oslo: University of Oslo, Centre for European Studies.

Rhoten, D., C. Calhoun, eds. (2011). *Knowledge Matters: The Public Mission of the Research University*. New York: Columbia University Press.

Teichler, U. (2004). "The Changing Debate on Internationalisation of Higher Education". *Higher Education*. Vol. 48. No. 1. 5-26.

Trow, M. (1974). "Problems in the Transition from Elite to Mass Higher Education". In: *General Report on the Conference on Future Structures of Post-Secondary Education*. Paris: OECD. 55-101.

Zgaga, P. (2012). "Reconsidering the EHEA Principles: Is There a 'Bologna Philosophy'?" In: Curaj, A., P. Scott, L. Vlasceanu, L. Wilson, eds. *European Higher Education at the Crossroads: Between the Bologna Process and National Reforms*. Dordrecht: Springer. 17-38.

Part 1

Front Issues:
Quality and Mobility,
Convergence and Diversity,
Policy Ideas

Imagining Higher Education in the European Knowledge Economy: Discourse and Ideas in Communications of the EU

Janja Komljenovič and Klemen Miklavič

Abstract

The paper focuses on the role of EU institutions in European higher education. Following the outset of the EU Lisbon Strategy (2000), the EU Commission positioned itself as an influential venue for generating, coordinating and communicating discourse on higher education (within the Bologna Process and beyond). Gradually, the scattered ideas converged into a relatively detailed set of policy proposals on the systemic and institutional reforms needed to engage higher education in the regional economic project. The ideas evolved within the imagined knowledge economy. The dominance of this political rationale has resulted in the steady advance of the Europeanisation of higher education, including the incremental tendency to transfer national competencies to supranational arenas – so far limited to soft instruments such as recommendations, guidelines, reporting and common actions.

Key words: higher education, EU policy, EU institutions, knowledge economy, ideas, discourses, Europeanisation, university

Introduction

The policy initiatives and strategies, based on the new emerging political and economic imaginaries, have taken the contemporary (massified) higher education policy beyond the nation-state boundaries, thereby creating new arenas of policy making. This is occurring in an era of a general shift in economic and social governance – increasingly dispersed between Europe's nation-states and other levels or scales. The new context for developing and communicating ideas, discourses and political rationales is affecting the course of European higher education.

The institutions of the European Union (EU) are indeed an important source of such ideas and programmes within and beyond the Bologna Process, inspiring the reforms of higher education to serve the present and future of European society. This paper aims to analyse the discourse of EU institutions and shed light on the underlying ideas and ideologies. The central question is which ideas and discursive meanings about higher education are presented by this EU discourse. The analysis focuses on the role of the European Commission (EC) in relation to other EU institutions (especially the Council of the EU) and on frictions between the supranational level and the nation-states, whereby the nature of ideas and their broader implications will be investigated.

This paper is an attempt to contribute some empirically based findings and theoretical reflections to the existing literature on the EU's role/position in the Europeanisation of higher education with particular attention to the meaning of higher education in the European political and socio-cultural setting.

Approaches and methods

In this analysis, we have integrated several approaches and tried to relate them as closely as possible. A good share of our empirical work addresses the written trail of the European institutions' involvement with higher education. We examine the main higher education related documents of the EC and the Council of the EU released since 2000. The selected documents were viewed as relevant and directly addressing higher education. We disregarded documents that address particular subfields (e.g. mobility) or were dedicated to other policy areas, thereby treating higher education only as a secondary field.

Table 1.   Types and number of EU policy documents included in the analysis

Institution	Type of document	Number of documents
Council of the EU	Resolution	2
	Recommendation	1
	Conclusion	3
European Commission	Communication	7
	Report	4
	All	17

The empirical part of this study also includes nine interviews with various officials ranging from civil servants to external experts responsible for higher education or involved in the creation of the texts in the EC and the Council of EU.

We primarily analysed the discourses and only to a modest extent their materialisation or institutionalisation. Engaging the *Discourse-Historical Approach (DHA)* and more broadly *Critical Discourse Analysis (CDA)* (Wodak 2001, Fairclough 2003, Fairclough and Wodak 2008, Wodak 2008, Krzyzanowski 2010, Krzyzanowski and Wodak 2011) the analysis is context-sensitive and relies on a multi-level definition of context encompassing the influence of changing socio-political conditions on the dynamics of discursive practices – especially policy documents and the processes leading to them. In our endeavour to outline the social and normative context, we found it appropriate to combine the CDA/DHA with the framework of the *cultural political economy* (Jessop 2008) that we present in the next chapter. We refer to the concepts of semiosis, political rationale, (hegemonic) policy and economic imaginaries (Jessop 2008, Robertson 2008, Robertson 2010). Within the CDA/DHA we were sensitive to the development of concepts over time and referred to analytical categories such as *discursive strategy, discursive topic, narratives, legitimating strategies, arguments, argumentative devices or topoi* and *intertextuality*.

We were interested in the connection between ideas and action and their prevailing institutional contexts. We thus introduced the aspect of agency into our study for which we used the *discursive institutionalism* framework (Radaelli and Schmidt 2004, Schmidt 2008, Schmidt 2010). This approach helped us see the discourse through the following analytical categories:

– we observed: a) *cognitive activity* whereby actors make sense of reality and seek solutions to identified/defined problems; and b) *normative activity* whereby actors try to fit the policies and ideas to the prevailing normative/value setting;

– in the *interactive dimension* of the discourse we distinguished between: a) the *coordinative sphere* where policy actors are involved in the process of coordinating agreement on policy ideas and creating coordinative discourse; and b) the *communicative sphere* where the coordinative discourse is carried over into the communicative discourse with the aim of presenting, deliberating and legitimating political ideas;

– in the fashion of discursive institutionalism we also looked into the levels of generality and types of ideas that appear in the texts, communications or other sources of ideas. There are three levels of generality: *policy, programmatic and philosophical* ideas.

However, some space was left for inductive approaches, especially when examining the interviews. Therefore, the theoretical framework outlined above was not adopted in an orthodox manner.

The context – imaginaries and political rationales

The ideas expressed through the 'knowledge economy' are rooted in the history of the last few decades. It gradually replaced the notion of industrial competitiveness when technological progress affected the economic indicators of leading industrial countries in the 1980s. The policy response in, e.g. the USA, was to encourage talented people to acquire skills and generate innovative technologies to keep the economy strong (Jessop 2008: 23). Knowledge gradually reinforced itself in a large number of discourses along with forming what Jessop (2008) calls the *hegemonic economic imaginary* – discursively constructed imagined economies. Specialised international organisations and think-tanks, like the OECD, took over the provision of theoretical and policy paradigms to support a specific structure of thinking in which various social actors operate and favour the enhancing of this imaginary. The knowledge economy imaginary sits well alongside the ideological shifts in the 1970s and 1980s: e.g. Keynesian full employment switched to the idea of individual responsibility for the employability of a qualified labour force and the post-Fordist flexible labour market where skills and competencies are the main currency (ibid.). It progressed as a social process integrating ideational, material institutional and relational moments (Robertson 2008: 91), eventually also representing the nodal strategy and discourse in modern Europe (Fairclough and Wodak 2008: 114).

In this imagined knowledge economy the role of higher education has experienced a substantial ideational and representational shift (Robertson 2008: 92). The driving force behind economic growth is supposed to be technological change, thus public policy focuses on disciplines such as science and technology (Olssen and Peters 2005) which are economic in their nature (Skulasson 2008). Higher education is rapidly altering its position in the newly constructed policy realm, including two main role changes: 1. higher education became an industry per se providing skills and competencies to customers; and 2. higher education became largely subdued to economic necessities, especially supporting the economy with skilled labour, research and innovation (Jessop 2008).

Positioning the EU in European higher education

Education policy was not on the European Community's agenda until the 1970s and since then it has been a very sensitive topic since it has been understood to be a matter of national sovereignty. There were attempts to raise the competence over higher education to the EU level, although they were never far-reaching. The most important action was the Erasmus Programme established in 1987 (Corbett 2006). Activities related to higher education in this period were intertwined with idea of Mitterand and Delors to further European integration in the field of the market and economy, which also implied the free movement of labour (mobility) and recognition of professional qualifications. The idea gained momentum in the early 1990s with Jacques Delors' call to modernise education and training systems connected to the challenges of employment (Pépin 2011: 25). This was accompanied by the general view that Europe needed to exploit its higher education systems better, if not improve them, as part of contemporary EU structural shifts towards the imagined knowledge economy (Corbett 2005). We will return to this in the next section.

The member states had considerable reservations in letting the EC take the initiative in the field of education, which were a reflection of the strong meaning ascribed to education and higher education in the national normative and value settings. For instance, the *Memorandum on Higher Education* (European Commission 1991) underscored the dramatic importance of higher education for the economic future of the Community and triggered a heated reaction in the higher education sector as the memorandum was criticized as merely economy-oriented and neglecting the nature of higher education (Corbett 2011). Thereafter, the EC moved to the fringes of European higher education policymaking until the turn of the century, thus leaving a policy vacuum in the higher education field. The first serious political attempt to fill this vacuum was initiated with the Sorbonne Declaration (1998), signed by the ministers of the four largest EU countries, and followed by the Bologna Declaration (1999). The EC was caught by surprise, was left out and then only allowed to fully enter the process in 2001 when the first evaluation showed that the Bologna Process had been too fragile and lacking support the EC could offer (Corbett 2011).

Once the EC became an official partner at the Bologna table, the Bologna Process represented a back door for it to enter higher education policy. The implementation of the Bologna policies in the member states has been underpinned by the substantial share of funds dedicated to support the projects that involved governments, their agencies and (notably) higher education institutions (Batory and Lindstrom 2011). One of the interviewees argued that the Bologna Process was a project without a vision or strategy. In contrast, they were offered by EU policy:

> Bologna has no goals, no policy goals. Bologna is a tool to achieve something, but it has no goals of its own. The European Union had with Lisbon these ambitious goals in the area of – well, about the Europe of Knowledge in the world. And this has obvious consequences or it entails obvious actions in the area of high education, education, training, research etc. (Interview 8; 29/06/2012).

This leads us to another important decision taken in 2000, namely the Lisbon Strategy (Council of the European Union 2000) whereby the EU set clear policy goals ultimately leading to the EU's global competitiveness and the strategy to achieve them. The knowledge economy and society were brought into the centre of the policy discourse. The new programmatic initiative gave a decisive impetus to the enforcement of this economic and political imaginary, affecting the economic, political, social, historical and cultural conditions in the EU including the region of members to the east. The open method of coordination came as a new and effective regulatory tool at the supranational level of governance. Higher education moved onto the agenda of EU institutions, which will be dealt with extensively later.

Despite the persisting tension regarding subsidiarity, the EC managed to gradually institutionalise higher education in the subsequent years and created a self-standing policy domain. Thereby, direct confrontation with the member states on the competence in the field was circumvented. From its marginal role in the 1990s, the EC became a major actor on the European higher education policy stage in the 2000s, especially through new modes of governance (such as the open method of coordination) and new institutionalised governance structures (Gornitzka and Ravinet 2011).

The path of evolution and nature of the normative context for the Europeanisation of higher education was closely linked to the knowledge economy hegemonic imaginary. Our findings can be synthesised into three unequivalent categories in an attempt to explain the ideational and discursive practice of the EU. They are:

1. instrumentalisation of higher education for economic goals;
2. ideating the new governance and steering of higher education; and
3. ideational and normative convergence – towards new constitutionalism.

The instrumentalisation of higher education for economic goals

As mentioned above, the decisive signal for the EU's intervention in the sector came when higher education was recognised as one of the most important policy fields for realising the knowledge society envisaged in the Lisbon Strategy (Council of the European Union 2000). The underlying idea of the Lisbon Strategy is to boost the European economy and guarantee strong economic competitiveness by placing knowledge in the core of the economic activities (Nokkala 2007). Thus, higher education was no longer treated as untouchable due to the subsidiary principle. Instead, it transformed into an instrumental field for managing the knowledge and society. In other words, it turned out to be an essential means for reaching wider European objectives.

Already since the communication of 2003 (EC 2003), *Europe of knowledge* appears as an abstract narrative oriented towards a better future and an ideational project in which universities are the essential and central instruments. Intervention into the hitherto protected status of the university is justified as [the universities] *"live thanks to substantial public and private funding"*. Serving society is understood as propelling the economic competitiveness, thus contributing to the Lisbon Strategy. The flow of (applied) *knowledge from universities into business and society* is the dominant discursive topic. The idea of approximating *industry* or *enterprise* and university is strongly exposed throughout the text and proposed in various modes (spin offs, start-up companies, attracting talents from other regions, more and employable graduates, innovation).

In the following document of 2005 entitled Mobilising the brainpower of Europe: Enabling universities to make their full contribution to the Lisbon strategy (EC 2005), the universities are said to be "motors of the new, knowledge-based paradigm". It is obvious from this document that there is agency and cognitive/instrumental logic in the constructing of ideas. There is a notable inclination towards more economistic key terminology (e.g. knowledge sector, knowledge industry, investment, competitiveness, human capital). The discursive topic of university–industry approximation is reiterated and refined with an upgrading of the topos of the need to serve industry with: a) applied knowledge; and b) the employability of graduates. There is a gradual advance in the policy proposals crossing into the academic domain, notably addressing the organisation of learning, arguing for output-based curricula, interdisciplinarity, emphasising transversal skills, calling for entrepreneurialism etc.

Both of the above mentioned communications (EC 2003 and 2005) extensively elaborate on the many problems within European higher education and give the contextual legitimacy for the presented policy and programmatic ideas. The topos of the need for the EU to compete with other world regions underlies the discourse. The basic conditions that call for a solution are presented through the changing world and the implied assumptions on the poor state of European universities. This can be partly explained as an attempt to build a normative background in order to present the ideas as appropriate, but the cognitive/instrumental component of the discourse is much stronger, justifying the presented course of action as a rational and feasible solution to the outlined challenges:

> Universities failing to undertake these changes – for want of drive, power to act or available resources – will create a growing handicap for themselves, their graduates and their countries (EC 2005).

Following this assertion, the EU decided to strengthen the role of higher education in reaching the Lisbon objectives. Another communication on higher education followed swiftly (EC 2006b). The previously introduced knowledge triangle appeared already in the title. The attractiveness of European higher education became the central concept used in the topos of competing with other higher education systems and institutions in order to improve the European ones. The discursive construction of the argument is completed by the key word *excellence* which emerges from *competition* and ensures *attractiveness*.

By using the term *relevance* as a new discursive element, a strategic interlinking was presented of the concept of *public interest* with the responsiveness of universities to the demands of the economy. It is assumed that "*their* [universities] *relationship with the business community is of strategic importance and forms part of their commitment to serving the public interest*" (EC 2006b). One of the authors presented the core idea with the following thoughts:

> […] higher education is not something that functions in an abstraction of society. Higher education needs to function within society and to make its contribution to society, not just expect support from society for professors to do whatever they want without any reference to society (Interview 8; 29/06/2012).

In the same communication, the EC further advanced the policy proposals (the modernisation agenda) aiming at the academic domain and micro level, which have traditionally been the autonomous responsibility of the academic community:

> in order to overcome persistent mismatches between graduate qualifications and the needs of the labour market, university programmes should be structured to enhance directly the employability of graduates and to offer broad support to the workforce more generally. [...] development of entrepreneurial, management and innovation skills should become an integral part of graduate education, research training and lifelong learning strategies for university staff (EC 2006b).

It emerged from the interviews that this formed part of a continuous attempt to strengthen the communicative discourse and break through the established academic insulation from the interests of business and industry.

> In terms of is it a more instrumentalist or is it a – I don't like the term instrumentalism. Perhaps I – is it more – Is it more tied to education's role in driving economic growth and the regeneration of our societies, more plainly, more concretely, more overtly? Absolutely. Absolutely yes. And I don't think we should be ashamed of that. I don't think it's a bad thing. And I don't think it then means that everyone has to become engineers, for example (Interview 2; 28/06/2012).

The idea extended to the economic needs of individuals:

> The university has the main role which students expect – the universities to perform for them is to give them the key to society. And the key to society passes through an economic activity (Interview 8; 29/06/2012).

Among other things, here the controversy regarding use of the concept of autonomy is visible, which in the EC's case was devised for reasons other than protecting the academic world from external pressures (see the next section).

A more substantial discursive evolution can be found in the 2011 communication (EC 2011). Jobs became a central discursive item, appearing in syntaxes like *job creating, high qualification jobs, knowledge intensive jobs, growth and jobs, research jobs, matching skills and jobs*. The genre lost a little of its academic character by moving towards the more political and apparently aiming at a system instead of institutions. Human capital theory seems to particularly strongly underpin this text with the argument of more graduates (more knowledge workers) for more knowledge jobs.

The above analysis shows the strong drift of higher education and research to the centre of the European integration project as one of Europe's answers to the challenges of the global knowledge economy. Gornitzka (2010: 545) refers to the *horizontal dynamics of the Lisbon strategy* as causing the approximation of the academic sphere and the economic sector. In a later phase, the first became discursively almost entirely subdued to the second. According to sociological institutionalists, this phenomenon accompanies the change of structures, norms, practices and identities eventually resulting in a redefinition of the purpose of the policy field (Gornitzka 2010).

Ideating a new governance model and the steering of higher education

The modernisation of the governance structure and financing in conjunction with the revision of the concept of autonomy have emerged as salient issues in the reform discourse. Our analysis illuminates the discourse and ideas on restructuring universities which involve a mix of a cognitive ideational line offering solutions to the identified problems, and the normative one stemming from the increasingly powerful economic imaginary gradually setting the normative conditions.

The discursive strategy is built on providing legitimacy and substantiating the notion of inevitability and urgency as well as advocating the hitherto unfitness of European universities. They are portrayed as ossified institutions that function in an old and outdated fashion rooted in the ideas and context of the 19th century (EC 2003). Further on, the characterising of the outdated situation presents the egalitarian principle as an obstacle to delivering excellence by keeping the institutions in mediocrity (EC 2005). Especially in the first half of the decade, the term *excellence* became the key word – an undefined concept that stood for the ultimate direction of the reforms. In this narrative, the reference to US universities is a constant discursive element.

As hinted at in the previous section, the argumentative device culminated in the normative assertion about the duty and obligation of the university towards society which persists and upgrades throughout the analysed paper trail:

> After remaining a comparatively isolated universe for a very long period, both in relation to society and to the rest of the world, with funding guaranteed and a status protected by respect for their autonomy, European universities have gone

through the second half of the 20th-century without really calling into question the role or the nature of what they should be contributing to society (EC 2003).

The leading idea in terms of responding to the presented problems is to diversify the European higher education system; there should be different higher education institutions with regard to the focus on the groups of potential students, the study offer, the way of teaching etc. More importantly, each university is to find its own strength and focus on it, thus specialising in the identified fields. There should be a smaller number of renowned, excellent research universities. Not all universities are encouraged to do research. This idea was developed over time so that it starts by saying that not all institutions are expected to do research at the same level.

Besides diversification, vertical differentiation (hierarchy) seems accepted as the necessary way to develop the system. In the second half of the decade, the egalitarianism (previously seen as an obstacle resulting in mediocrity) was overtaken by the idea of vertical diversification and categorisation. The relevance of the institutions was divided between global research-oriented universities and regional teaching and professionally-oriented ones. This solution is normatively reinforced with the recognition that Europe has too few universities excelling at the global level. The topoi of competitiveness are grounded in the arguments of the poor positioning of European universities in world rankings and lagging behind their US counterparts.

The EC was not hesitant in advancing far-reaching policy proposals in the fields of funding and quality assurance – the two strongest steering mechanisms of the higher education system. Integral to rearranging the system, the funding mechanisms are suggested to be changed in a way so as to help diversification, i.e. to concentrate funding on a chosen institution and/or fields, as well as to move towards greater *efficiency, quality* and *competitiveness*. For this, the funding should be based on multiyear contracts setting out agreed strategic objectives. Thus, the funding system is suggested to change from basic funding towards outcomes-based, competitive and relevance rewarding:

> Encourage the use of skills and growth projections and graduate employment data (including tracking graduate employment outcomes) in course design, delivery and evaluation, adapting quality assurance and funding mechanisms to reward success in equipping students for the labour market (EC 2011).

The funding of higher education should increase, notably from private sources (i.e. industry and students). The reason is said to be that in Europe the level of public funding is comparable and even slightly higher than in the compared countries (USA, Canada, and Japan). In advocating tuition fees, the EC brings forward the ideas of retracting public funding in favour of private funding which fits with the neoliberal grand idea of reforming the state (Harvey 2005, Hill 2007).

Institutional autonomy is a strongly present concept with a specific discursive role and meaning. In the earliest of the analysed EU documents (EC 2003), the strong ideational stream on reforming the institutional governance emerged. It was characterised by the use of the topos of accountability as counterbalancing the relative autarchic state of European universities. In this phase, autonomy still appeared as an ambiguous concept. Two years later, institutional autonomy became: "*a pre-condition for universities to be able to respond to society's changing needs*" (EC 2005). The idea was communicated with a persuasive strategy of portraying the national regulations as exaggerated and inappropriate interference with the universities' ability to make the necessary changes, manage funds and especially enable the process of diversification. Thus, the concept of autonomy is coupled with the topos of the need to deregulate the higher education systems.

The concept of autonomy was clearly seen by the EC as an essential element of the communicative discourse bringing forward the cognitive idea of new governance. The governance structure was explained in ever more detail:

> This requires new internal governance systems based on strategic priorities and on professional management of human resources, investment and administrative procedures. It also requires universities to overcome their fragmentation into faculties, departments, laboratories and administrative units and to target their efforts collectively on institutional priorities for research, teaching and services. Member States should build up and reward management and leadership capacity within universities (EC 2006a).

Reformers conceptualise *autonomy* as a management tool for achieving *efficiency* (Olsen 2009). In the EC discourse, autonomy refers to professionalised central management strategically running an integrated institution rather than autonomy as the protection of academic freedom and critical thought. It is possible to observe a shift in external dependency from one field (political or legal) to another (markets, stakeholders, ranking entities etc.). Universities are expected to change in line with the New Public Management principles to become more efficient, productive and economically relevant (Bleiklie and Lange 2010). In its communication, the EC also tries to balance its discourse of managerial shift by keeping references to the concept of autonomy as autonomy from the state and politics, thereby attempting to resuscitate something traditional or symbolic about the European university and introducing an appropriateness (normative) tone.

The conceptualisation of autonomy represents an integral part of the hegemonic economic imaginary containing reforms in line with a trend often referred to as the *neoliberal project* (Hartmann 2008, Hill 2007). A new kind of *social contract* emerged, shifting the focus to the strategic orientation of the system as a whole, evaluating the outcomes and avoiding micro-management and over-regulation. The idea of governance is thus embedded in a general trend which echoes the imagined global knowledge society and the related growing supranational note. In the next section, we will explore this trend further and present the broader transnational impact of the discursive and material shifts in higher education in the EU.

Ideational and normative convergence – towards new constitutionalism

As above, the ideas pertaining to the knowledge economy hegemonic imaginary indicate a tendency to shift power to the supranational level which the EC documents do not explicitly announce. It is communicated through the argument that the global/regional level of social and economic problems (notably economic growth and global competitiveness) requires regional (supranational) solutions:

> The nature and scale of the challenges linked to the future of the universities mean that these issues have to be addressed at European level. More specifically, they require a joint and coordinated endeavour by the Member States and the candidate countries, backed up and supported by the European Union, in order to help to move towards a genuine Europe of knowledge (EC 2003).

In addition, higher education is compared to other economic sectors:

> The EU has supported the conversion process of sectors like the steel industry or agriculture; it now faces the imperative to modernise its 'knowledge industry' and in particular its universities (EC 2005).

During the years of the increasing Europeanisation of higher education, one can observe the tendency to shift some regulatory competencies for higher education to the supranational level. The result of these activities and initiatives is increasing supranational soft regulation such as harmonising criteria/standards, setting guidelines and producing comparative figures. In other words, it is up to nation-states and single higher education institutions to regulate and govern higher education reform on their territory, but they do so in accordance with the guidelines, objectives and procedures that are regulated on the European level (Fairclough and Wodak 2008: 113).

Moreover, the already mentioned open method of coordination used in the Lisbon Strategy was also transferred into the practice of the Bologna Process (Ravinet 2008). With its expertise and financial resources, the EC accelerated its advance into higher education policy field – both through the Bologna Process and parallel to it. Namely, the EC had a substantial budget available to incentivise the domestic actors and thereby turn them into agents of its policy and programmatic proposals, causing the leapfrogging of national governments in complying with the EC's requirements (Batory and Lindstrom 2011: 311). It has gradually developed policy making and policy implementation networks formed by national and independent experts, civil servants, various agencies on the national and international level, which has led to the diluting of individual state power over policy outcomes in higher education (Gornitzka 2009).

As an exemplar initiative in this sense, quality assurance has been present as the EC's central policy stream in the field of higher education since the second half of the 1990s (Gornitzka 2009). The establishment of the European network of quality assurance agencies (ENQA) was an EC idea and represented a front-running initiative for the essential role of the concept of quality assurance in the Bologna Process. The idea evolved through the adoption of European standards and guidelines in quality assurance (2005) and later culminated in the European register for quality assurance (EQAR). The latest of the Bologna communiqués (Bucharest 2012) favours the agencies listed in the EQAR to perform activities across the EHEA.

The quality assurance policy evolution in the EU and the Bologna Process indicates a transition from soft law to supranational provisions with strong enforcement mechanisms continuously enhancing the consensus among governments and stakeholders – a clear case of a trajectory leading towards the transnationalisation of the evaluative state (Hartmann 2008: 82).

Even though the idea was limited to the policy level and addressed concrete problems, the interviews reveal the temptation of the authors to push the topos of the need for an international referee:

> We wanted something outside the country but within a quality assurance framework that was capable of saying to the Greeks or the Italians or whoever. 'You aren't doing these well enough, you should be tougher with people because they are not actually producing what they should.' No, we didn't get that because of course the member states didn't want it. But that's what lies behind it, an attempt to assure the quality of the quality assurance agencies (Interview 5; 09/06/2012).

The same logic revolved around the so-called transparency and information tools. The first outstanding one was the qualification framework, which followed the logic of supporting the integrating EU labour market by informing employers about the learning outcomes of graduates and easing students' choice of learning paths. A similar motive can be found in another, more recent example: the classification of universities and the multidimensional transparency tool (called *U-Multirank*) devised to respond to the growing popularity and influence of global university ranking initiatives. Grounded in this problem, the communication of U-Multirank is very refined and well placed in a series of arguments:

> It is essential to develop a wider range of analysis and information, covering all aspects of performance – to help students make informed study choices, to enable institutions to identify and develop their strengths, and to support policy-makers in their strategic choices on the reform of higher education systems (EC 2011).

The interviewees who have been involved in the DG EAC work since the late 2000s to the present all master a very well-developed persuasive discursive strategy based on rational arguments supporting the cognitive idea of this policy instrument (Interview 6; 14/05/2012, Interview 2; 28/06/2012 and Interview 3; 02/07/2012). They have used consistent argumentative devices and brought about the reasoning whereby the U-Multirank appears as a well-considered solution to a discursively created reality where there is an obvious need for transparency and information which only can be achieved by transferring the regulatory power to the supranational level. On the other side, the interviewed members of the permanent representations did not show signs of scepticism and did not remember any serious resistance among the other member states against the U-Multirank initiative (Interview 7; 05/06/2012, Interview 4; 28/06/2012 and Interview 9; 01/06/2012). From the late 1990s to date the EC has learned the methods and ways to circumvent confrontation with the member states, especially those which bring up the subsidiarity argument – notably Germany and the UK (Interview 4; 28/06/2012 and Interview 9; 01/06/2012).

The trend (Gornitzka 2009) characterised as ideational and normative convergence is opening ground to a de facto regulatory integration. This can be observed in the case of some other organisations like the WTO, World Bank and OECD. Some authors use the term *new constitutionalism* – a process whereby governments abdicate some of their regulatory powers in order to facilitate the implementation of policies and institutional change (Scherrer 2005, Hartmann 2008). This is supposed to promote competitiveness, more accountability of the state regarding market needs and aims at facilitating further commodification of social relations in the adhering states (Hartmann 2008: 67). As we concluded above in the case of the EU's higher education policy involvement, there is an obvious shift of sovereignty towards the supranational level. It is possible to conclude that European integration is paving the way to a new institutional arrangement that takes up the state functions important for establishing ideational hegemony (Hartmann 2008: 81), creating a new constellation of regulatory powers especially in relation to the global market and competition.

Conclusion

EU institutions gradually entered higher education policy in the name of pursuing the economic integration agenda. The idea of economic and labour market integration in the late 1980s and early 1990s created the necessity to address vocational/professional education and qualifications. *The knowledge economy* took over the role of the central integrative paradigm (Lisbon Strategy of 2000) and made higher education subordinate to economic goals which resulted in higher education becoming a de-facto EU policy area. The legal barriers that had hitherto prevented the European Commission taking decisive steps forward were elegantly circumvented.

The EU discourse on modernising European higher education was coordinated and communicated throughout the 2000s through reports, communications and other documents. The fundamental ideational characteristic of this discourse implied imagining universities as central instruments for regional economic growth. The devised communicative discourse illustrates cognitive ideas on how to reform the ossified and outdated higher education in order to restore the fading competitiveness of the European economy. Cooperating with business, assisting industry with research, innovation and human capital and focusing on individual preparedness for the labour market became the guiding policy imperatives.

The scattered ideas gradually converged into a relatively detailed model of the desired higher education system and institutions: the reforms should lead to more efficiency through integrating (centralising) the organisational units of the university and granting a greater degree of autonomy to professionalising management. This would in turn facilitate the competition and diversification of universities in order to address the diversified needs of society and the economy. One of the essential goals is to enable the emergence of excellent (world-class) universities – leaders in research and innovation. The new, autonomous managerial structures are also expected to bring about greater financial efficiency in managing funds, increasingly originating from private sources (including tuition fees). Education as a payable service is an implicit part of the idea of the financial reform, whereas the state should take care of the economically weaker social groups for competitive purposes.

Gradually, the discourse has acquired a normative accent characterised by socialising into the powerful and hegemonic imaginary of the knowledge economy. All decision-making levels from national governments to EU institutions have subscribed to this political rationale. At the EU level, the European Commission has established itself as the central venue for generating and coordinating the discourse.

The normative convergence under the umbrella of the political rationale of the knowledge economy permits the advancement of the phenomenon of supranational soft governance in the higher education field. Under the topoi of the need to establish *transparency* and *comparability* and accelerated by the *open method of coordination,* the set of policy ideas and ideational trends conveyed by the EU discourses (in the form of recommendations, guidelines etc.) indicate a slow but steady relinquishing of national competencies in the field of higher education in favour of the supranational level (notably quality assurance, qualification framework, recognition). This can be characterised as a sort of *new constitutionalism* – a new constellation of regulatory powers especially in relation to the global market and competition.

It was not possible to find any broader programmatic ideas behind the tendency towards new constitutionalism. Therefore, it is impossible to claim there is an intentional master plan behind the phenomenon. It can instead be attributed to this overall direction of the change, embedded in the hegemonic economic imaginary and dominant ideologies and brought about by the structural dimension of a variety of narratives, constructed realities/problems, and as a collateral result of proposed *obvious* and *appropriate* courses of action.

Acknowledgments

The authors gratefully acknowledge the support of the Slovenian National Agency for Research through its grant DEP-08-EuroHESC-OP-016.

References

Batory, A., N. Lindstrom (2011). "The Power of the Purse: Supranational Entrepreneurship, Financial Incentives, and European Higher Education Policy". *Governance: An International Journal of Policy, Administration and Institutions*. Vol. 24. No. 2. 311-329.

Bleiklie, I., S. Lange (2010). "Competition and Leadership as Drivers in German and Norwegian University Reforms". *Higher Education Policy*. Vol. 23. No. 2. 173-193.

Corbett, A. (2005). *Universities and the Europe of Knowledge: Ideas, Institutions and Policy Entrepreneurship in European Union Higher Education Policy, 1955-2005*. New York and Basingstoke: Palgrave Macmillan.

Corbett, A. (2006). "Key Moments of the European Political Debate on Higher Education". In: *The Politics of European University Identity. Political and Academic Perspectives. Proceedings of the Seminar of the Magna Charta Observatory, 14 September 2006*. Bologna: Bononia University Press. 63-106.

Corbett, A. (2011). "Ping Pong: Competing Leadership for Reform in EU Higher Education 1998–2006". *European Journal of Education*. Vol. 46. No. 1. 36-53.

Council of the European Union (2000). *Lisbon European Council 23 and 24 March 2000 Presidency Conclusions*. Brussels: Council of the European Union.

European Commission (1991). *Memorandum on Higher Education in the Community. COM(91) 349 final*. Brussels: European Commission.

Fairclough, N. (2003). *Analysing Discourse: Textual Analysis for Social Research*. Milton Park: Routledge.

Fairclough, N., R. Wodak (2008). "The Bologna Process and the Knowledge-based Economy: a Critical Discourse Analysis Approach". In: B. Jessop, N. Fairclough, R. Wodak (eds.), *Education and the Knowledge Based Economy in Europe*. Rotterdam: Sense. 109-126.

Gornitzka, Å. (2009). "Networking Administration in Areas of National Sensitivity: The Commission and European Higher Education". In: A. Amaral, G. Neave, C. Musselin, P. Massen (eds.), *European Integration and the Governance of Higher Education and Research*. Dordrecht, Heidelberg, London, New York: Springer. 109-131.

Gornitzka, Å. (2010). "Bologna in Context: A Horizontal Perspective on the Dynamics of Governance Sites for a Europe of Knowledge". *European Journal of Education*. Vol. 45. No. 4. 535-548.

Gornitzka, Å., P. Ravinet (2011). "Inception and Institutionalization of the OMC Education, the Bologna Process and the OMC Research: From Coordination Templates to New Policy Arenas?" Paper presented at the Congrès AFSP Strasbourg 2011. Universités et recherche face à la réforme. Strasbourg.

Hartmann, E. (2008). "The EU as an Emerging Normative Power in the Global Knowledge-based Economy? Insights from the Emerging Recognition for Higher Education Qualifications". In: B. Jessop, N. Fairclough, R. Wodak (eds.), *Education and the Knowledge-based Economy in Europe*. Rotterdam: Sense. 63-88.

Harvey, D. (2005). *A Brief History of Neoliberalism*. Oxford: Oxford University Press.

Hill, D. (2007). "Educational Perversion and Global Neoliberalism". In: E. W. Ross, R. Gibons (eds.), *Neoliberalism and Education Reform*. Creskill, NJ: Hampton Press.

Jessop, B. (2008). "The Cultural Political Economy of the Knowledge-based Economy and Its Implications for Higher Education". In: B. Jessop, N. Fairclough, R. Wodak (eds.), *Education and the Knowledge-based Economy in Europe*. Rotterdam: Sense. 13-39.

Krzyżanowski, M. (2010). "Discourses and Concepts: Interfaces and Synergies between Begriffsgeschichte and the Discourse Historical Approach in CDA". In: R. de Cilia, H. Gruber, M. Krzyżanowski, F. Menz (eds.), *Diskurs-Politik-Identität /Discourse – Politics – Identity*. Tübingen: Stauffenburg Publishers. 125-137.

Krzyżanowski, M., R. Wodak (2011). "Political Strategies and Language Policies; the European Union Lisbon Strategy and its Implications for the EU's Language and Multilingualism Policy". *Lang Policy*. Vol. 10. No. 2. 115-136.

Nokkala, T. (2007). Constructing the Ideal University: The Internationalisation of Higher Education in the Competitive Knowledge Society. Dissertation. Tampere University Press, Tampere.

Olsen, J. P. (2009). *Democratic Government, Institutional Autonomy and the Dynamics of Change*. ARENA Working Paper. No 1. Available at http://www.arena.uio.no (accessed 23 October 2012).

Olssen, M., M. A. Peters (2005). "Neoliberalism, Higher Education and the Knowledge Economy: from the Free Market to Knowledge Capitalism". *Journal of Education Policy*. Vol. 20. No. 3. 313-345.

Pépin, L. (2011). "Education in the Lisbon Strategy: Assessment and Prospects". *European Journal of Education*. Vol. 46. No. 1. 25-35.

Radaelli, C. M., V. A. Schmidt (2004). "Conclusions". *West European Politics*. Vol. 27. No. 2. 364-379.

Ravinet, P. (2008). "From Voluntary Participation to Monitored Coordination: Why European Countries Feel Increasingly Bound by Their Commitment to the Bologna Process". *European Journal of Education*. Vol. 43. No. 3. 353-367.

Robertson, S. (2008). "Embracing the Global: Crisis and the Creation of a New Semiotic Order to Secure Europe's Knowledge-based Economy". In: B. Jessop, N. Fairclough, R. Wodak (eds.), *Education and the Knowledge-based Economy in Europe*. Rotterdam: Sense. 89-108.

Robertson, S. (2010). "The EU, 'Regulatory State Regionalism' and New Modes of Higher Education Governance". *Globalisation, Societies and Education.* Vol. 8. No. 1. 23-37.

Scherrer, C. (2005). "GATS: Long-term Strategy for the Commodification of Education". *Review of International Political Economy.* Vol. 12. No. 3. 484-510.

Schmidt, V. A. (2008). "Discursive Institutionalism: The Explanatory Power of Ideas and Discourse". *The Annual Review of Political Science.* Vol. 11. 303-326.

Schmidt, V. A. (2010). "Taking Ideas and Discourse Seriously: Explaining Change Through Discursive Institutionalism as the Fourth 'New Institutionalism'". *European Political Science Review.* Vol. 2. No. 1. 1-25.

Skulasson, J. (2008). Autonomy and Governance in European Universities. Lecture in Hanoi 25 November 2008.

Sorbonne Declaration. (1998). *Joint Declaration on Harmonisation of the Architecture of the European Higher Education System.* Paris, Sorbonne. Available at http://www.bologna-berlin2003.de/pdf/Sorbonne_declaration.pdf (accessed 23 October 2012).

Wodak, R. (2001). "The Discourse – Historical Approach". In: R. Wodak, M. Mayer (eds.), *Methods of Critical Discourse Analysis.* London: Sage Publishers.

Wodak, R. (2008). "Introduction: Discourse Studies – Important Concepts and Terms". In: R. Wodak, M. Krzyżanowski (eds.), *Qualitative Discourse Analysis in the Social Sciences.* Basingstoke: Palgrave Macmillan. 1-29.

List of analysed policy documents:

Council of the European Union (2005). *Resolution of the Council and of the Representatives of the Governments of the Member States Meeting Within the Council, on Mobilising the Brainpower of Europe: Enabling Higher Education to Make its Full Contribution to the Lisbon Strategy.* Brussels: Council of the European Union.

European Parliament and Council of the European Union (2006). *Recommendation of the European Parliament and of the Council of 15 February 2006 on Further European Cooperation in Quality Assurance in Higher Education.* Brussels: European Parliament and Council of the European Union.

Council of the European Union (2007). *Council Resolution on Modernising Universities for Europe's Competitiveness in a Global Knowledge Economy.* Brussels: Council of the European Union.

Council of the European Union (2009). *Conclusions of the Council and of the Representatives of the Governments of the Member States, Meeting Within the Council on Developing the Role of Education in a Fully-Functioning Knowledge Triangle.* Brussels: Council of the European Union.

Council of the European Union (2010). *Council Conclusions of 11 May 2010 on the Internationalisation of Higher Education.* Brussels: Council of the European Union.

Council of the European Union (2011). *Council Conclusions on the Modernisation of Higher Education.* Brussels: Council of the European Union.

European Commission (2001). *Communication from the Commission to the European Parliament and the Council on Strengthening Cooperation with Third Countries in the Field of Higher Education.* Brussels: European Commission.

European Commission (2003). *Communication from the Commission. The Role of the Universities in the Europe of Knowledge*. Brussels: European Commission.

European Commission (2004). *Report from the Commission to the European Parliament, the Council, the European Economic and Social Committee and the Committee of the Regions on the Implementation of Council Recommendation 98/561/EC of 24 September 1998 on European Cooperation in Quality Assurance in Higher Education.* Brussels: European Commission.

European Commission (2005). *Communication from the Commission. Mobilising the Brainpower of Europe: Enabling Universities to Make Their Full Contribution to the Lisbon Strategy.* Brussels: European Commission.

European Commission (2006a). *Communication from the Commission to the Council and to the European Parliament of 8 September 2006 on Efficiency and Equity in European Education and Training.* Brussels: European Commission.

European Commission (2006b). *Communication from the Commission to the Council and to the European Parliament. Delivering on the Modernisation Agenda for Universities: Education, Research and Innovation.* Brussels: European Commission.

European Commission (2008a). *Commission Staff Working Paper Accompanying Document to the Report from the Commission to the Council on the Council Resolution of 23 November 2007 on Modernising Universities for Europe's Competitiveness in a Global Knowledge Economy.* Brussels: European Commission.

European Commission (2008b). *Report from the Commission to the Council on the Council Resolution of 23 November 2007 on Modernising Universities for Europe's Competitiveness in a Global Knowledge Economy.* Brussels: European Commission.

European Commission (2009a). *Communication from the Commission to the European Parliament, the Council, the European Economic and Social Committee and the Committee of the Regions. A New Partnership for the Modernisation of Universities: The EU Forum for University Business Dialogue.* Brussels: European Commission.

European Commission (2009b). *Report from the Commission to the Council, the European Parliament, the European Economic and Social Committee and the Committee of the Regions. Report on Progress in Quality Assurance in Higher Education.* Brussels: European Commission.

European Commission (2011). *Communication from the Commission to the European Parliament, the Council, the European Economic and Social Committee and the Committee of the Regions. Supporting Growth and Jobs – an Agenda for the Modernisation of Europe's Higher Education systems.* Brussels: European Commission.

List of interviews:

Interview 1. A high ranking official responsible for higher education in an EU member state throughout the 1990s and 2000s, also representing a member state in the Council of the EU and other international fora dedicated to higher education

Interview 2. An EC DG EAC officer working in the field of higher education since 1996 and for EC DG EAC since 2008

Interview 3. A seconded expert at the EC DG EAC between 2006 and 2009

Interview 4. A seconded expert to the EC DG EAC since 2011, formerly responsible for education issues at a member state's permanent representation to the EU

Interview 5. The EC head of a unit responsible for higher education between 2000 and 2006

Interview 6. A high ranking official at the EC DG EAC working in the field of higher education between 2000 and 2006

Interview 7. A member state official responsible for education at a permanent member state representation to the EU

Interview 8. An EC expert working for the EC DG EAC between 2002 and 2006

Interview 9. A member state official responsible for education issues at a permanent representation to the EU, formerly an official at the EC DG EAC

The Event of International Mobility in the Course of Study – The European Policy Objective

Ulrich Teichler

Abstract

The strong political efforts to enhance – the predominantly short-term – student mobility within Europe have for a long time not even triggered any efforts to measure the magnitude of mobility. Until recently, international statistics have only provided information on foreign students and study abroad, and the intention was even to exclude temporary mobility. On the basis of incomplete information, it is possible to estimate that three-quarters of foreign students are not mobile, but have instead lived and learned in the country of study already prior to study. About one-tenth of mobile students have lived and learned somewhere else and study in the country of their citizenship. The weakness of statistics has partly been due to the vague policy criteria. In the meantime, it is clear that the experience of having studied in another country during the course of one's study is the major European policy objective. Accordingly, one can estimate that more than 10 percent of recent graduates have been mobile during the course of their study, more than twice as many by means other than those by ERASMUS, and several times as many through short-term mobility than through studying a whole study programme abroad. Information on the impact of the outwards mobility of European students is more solid. Notably, evaluation studies show that former ERASMUS students are only slightly superior in general and specific academic competencies and in their general career, but clearly better prepared for visibly international tasks and for international professional mobility. In order to enhance the information base on the magnitude and impact of the outwards mobility of European students, regular European-wide graduate surveys are needed that include a relatively large number of respondents in order to provide the opportunity of comparing the studies and careers of mobile and non-mobile students.

Key words: student mobility, higher education statistics, graduate surveys

Increasing student mobility: A major European policy objective in search of a proper definition and database

Increasing cross-border mobility is a key policy objective in Europe in the higher education domain, and it might be characterised as the least controversial objective. Most actors and experts are convinced that there is a desirable impact of student mobility on the students themselves, the higher education institutions and the countries sending and hosting mobile students (see, for example, van der Hijden 2012).

Efforts to facilitate and actually increase student mobility have already played a role in Europe for many decades. Already since World War II, the hope that more detailed knowledge of other countries would dilute prejudices and increase sympathy for other ways of life and thinking gained momentum. In the 1950s, the Council of Europe took the lead regarding conventions regarding the recognition of study. Over the years, the aims became more ambitious and the range of countries involved broadened, as the 1997 Lisbon Convention for the recognition of studies shows, which was initiated jointly by the Council of Europe and by UNESCO in collaboration with the European Commission (see Teichler 2003). In the 1970s, when the European Union became involved in higher education policy, the promotion of temporary student mobility in Europe was chosen as a key policy area, and this led to the establishment of the ERASMUS Programme in 1987. Finally, the ministers in charge of higher education policy in many individual European countries decided in the Bologna Declaration in 1999 to establish a convergent cycle structure of study programmes and degrees (bachelor-master) in Europe with the strategic objective to increase student mobility (see Wächter 2008).

Undoubtedly, a widely shared aim of higher education policy is to *increase student mobility quantitatively*. At first glance, this seems to be a simple straightforward objective. A closer look, however, reveals there is a multitude of possible definitions and measures of student mobility and that the actual data available are hardly in tune with the policy objectives.

Moreover, the measures to expand mobility not only had overall quantities in mind, but also *the socio-biographic composition of mobile students*. For example, the financial support for temporary intra-European mobility in the framework of ERASMUS should facilitate students from a wide socio-economic spectrum to be mobile. The available information suggests that student mobility is less socially select now than in the past, when only very few students were internationally mobile and that student mobility financially supported by schemes such as ERASMUS is less socially select than student mobility outside such support programmes, but that European mobile students continue to be slightly more socially select than all European students. Views vary as to whether social selectivity can be interpreted as 'small' and more or less normal or as 'substantial' and as curable by targeted measures.

Finally, the expansion of student mobility is not a goal in its own right. It is pursued, as already pointed out, because a valuable impact of an international study experience is expected. Actually, we note that a broad range of possible effects is discussed, and there is a multitude of studies having measured the actual effects.

This article starts off from the conviction that major policy thrusts should be accompanied by systematic information in order to shed light on the problems, the actual trends and the effects of policy measures. In the case of policies in favour of student mobility, information is most important about the actual quantitative development of student mobility and the effects of study experience in another country on mobile students. And this article is based on the observation that policies such as those of promoting student mobility often start off with vague definitions and might become more precise after a while in the search for evidence. Therefore, the links between policy objectives, the characteristics of the database and the actual findings will be discussed.

Emphasis will be placed on intra-European mobility and on any outgoing mobility of European students. The mobility of students from economically less advanced countries outside Europe to Europe will not be addressed here because it follows completely different rationales and leads to very different results (cf. de Wit 2012). The subsequent analysis will focus on the definitions and trends of the quantitative development of student mobility because the policy discourse and the data available have been quite fuzzy in the past and are in need of clarification (cf. Teichler 2012). In addition, a short overview will be provided of the key information about the impact of international experience in the course of study.

As will be shown below, over the years the notion has spread that the following operational questions would be the best for capturing the spirit of policies encouraging the mobility of European students: How many European students spend at least some study time in another European country in the overall study period? How do students who have been mobile subsequently differ in their competencies and their subsequent study, work and life paths? Further, a short overview will be provided about what we know by way of a response to these questions.

'Student mobility' – A variety of meanings

The more student mobility has become a major policy goal the more a need has been felt to clarify what is meant by this term: What is included or excluded? Which distinctions have to be made as regards the purposes, operations and expected results of mobility? Altogether, what is meant if calls are made for information on mobility as well as for the expansion and enhancement of student mobility?

First, we note that three different terms are widely used: *Foreign, mobile and international students.*

– *'Foreign students' and 'study abroad'*: students with a nationality ('citizenship', 'passport' etc.) different from that of the country of study;
– *'Mobile students'*: students who cross national borders for the purpose of study; and
– *'International students'*: no clear definition (often used for either 'foreign' or 'mobile' or for various definitions without a proper explanation).

The term 'mobility' is often used misleadingly when data are provided on foreign students. Authors often consider 'foreign' and 'mobile' as synonyms; sometimes they are genuinely interested in foreign students and use 'mobility' just as a popular catchphrase, or they are interested in 'mobility' and consider data on foreign students pragmatically as the best possible 'indicator' of mobility.

Obviously, *data on foreign students increasingly lose their value as a possible 'proxy' for student mobility* because the more international societies become, the higher will be the proportion of foreign students who have lived and learned already in the country of study prior to the study period. Therefore, second, analyses really interested in mobility have to make a distinction between foreign mobile students and other foreign students.

Third, not all mobile students are foreign students: some nationals of the country of study might have lived and learned outside their country of nationality and return to the country of their nationality for the purpose of study. Others might have adopted the nationality of the country they have moved to for the purpose of study. Therefore, a distinction is preferable between foreign mobile students and mobile students holding citizenship of the country of study.

Fourth, the *direction of mobility* is always addressed. Students can be described both according to 'origin' and 'destination': on one hand, the number of 'incoming students' or *'inwards mobile'* (similarly to the number of 'foreign' students, if nationality is of interest) and, on the other, the number of 'outgoing students' or *'outwards mobile'* students (or similarly to 'study abroad', if nationality is of interest).

In the framework of the Bologna Process, attention is paid primarily to incoming students in the case of mobility between Europe and other parts of the world; the 'increasing attractiveness' of study in Europe is expected for students from other parts of the world. In contrast, intra-European mobility seems to be viewed as valuable in both directions. As will be discussed below, outgoing mobility might be understood as the prevailing target of intra-European student mobility.

Fifth, the relevance of student mobility varies substantially according to the *period of mobility*: Students might go to another country to spend *the whole study period* there ('diploma mobility', 'degree mobility', 'programme mobility' etc.), or they spend some part of a whole study period in another country ('credit mobility', 'student exchange', *'short-term mobility',* or 'temporary mobility' etc.). As will be discussed below, this distinction is often not made in statistics. Moreover, short-term mobility is not consistently included in the available statistics even though it has the highest priority in policies promoting intra-European mobility.

Sixth, related to the previous issue, there is a debate about the *threshold period of mobility*: Should student mobility only be viewed as a meaningful experience if there is a certain minimum period of time in another country? Often, a semester or a trimester is considered to be such a minimum.

Seventh, the definition of student mobility might vary according to the *purpose of the stay abroad*: regular study, internships, language courses, summer schools, work on a thesis, self-learning etc. No general consensus in this respect has emerged apart from the obvious one that regular study for a least a typical period of study (e.g. a semester) is understood as student mobility.

Eight, a crucial question is whether to focus on the frequency of *mobility at a certain moment in time or the 'event' of mobility during the course of study*. Most reports on student mobility address the frequency of studying in another country at a certain moment in time ('current mobility' with reference to an academic year or a certain month). The difference is striking: For example, less than 1 percent of students in all ERASMUS-eligible countries are mobile within an academic year with ERASMUS support but, since the average period of study in Europe is at least four years, we estimate that more than 3 percent of students from these European countries are mobile with ERASMUS support during the overall period of study. We might define the latter as the 'event of student mobility' during the course of study.

Beyond this, the practice varies concerning whether data reports include: (a) all tertiary students (in UNESCO terms including ISCED 5b); or (b) only higher education students in programmes equivalent to a bachelor and master (ISCED 5a), or also doctoral students or students of similar programmes (ISCED 6) whereby data on the ISCED 5b and ISCED 6 levels tend to be incomplete. There are also different ways of handling distance students and students on foreign branch campuses.

In sum, 'student mobility' is not an obvious concept and is not defined more or less homogeneously. Those advocating increasing mobility should clarify which mobility they have in mind; those calling for evidence and for data improvement similarly have to clarify the concepts and definitions. And those reporting and analysing the frequency of student mobility ought to make clear which concepts and operational definitions they are referring to.

The state of international statistics

Europe-wide statistics relevant for understanding the frequency of international mobility are jointly collected by the UNESCO Institute for Statistics (UIS), OECD and EUROSTAT (the statistical agency of the European Union) (see, for example, UNESCO Institute for Statistics 2009, OECD 2009, Eurostat and Eurostudent 2009). These three supranational agencies, called *UOE* in short form, ask the agencies in charge of the national collection of educational data to deliver data (possibly collecting from individual institutions of higher education) according to a common set of definitions and operational guidelines that are updated annually. UOE will eventually decide whether the data delivered follow the definitions and operational guidelines sufficiently to be included in the international statistics.

Until recently, UOE aimed to collect data on *foreign students*, subdivided by country of nationality, gender, field of study and programme level (ISCED 5b, 5a and 6). Moreover, by aggregating the information for an individual country of origin, it calculated the number of students from each country who *study abroad*. However, if individual countries, notably the UK, delivered data on foreign mobile students, they were included in the tables in the same way as data for other countries on foreign students.

When the Bologna Process gained momentum, the conviction grew among actors and experts that this traditional body of statistical information was no longer appropriate. Three studies were undertaken between 2001 and 2005 that revealed major methodological *weaknesses of the international student statistics*, tried to estimate the range of errors in the available statistics and formulated proposals to improve the concepts and modes of data gathering. Two of these studies were initiated by the European Parliament and were undertaken by scholars at the International Centre for Higher Education Research of the University of Kassel (INCHER-Kassel), the latter one in cooperation with the European Institute of Education and Social Policy (EIESP) in Paris (Lanzendorf and Teichler 2003, Lanzendorf, Teichler, and Murdock 2006); the third study was funded by the European Commission and was undertaken by the Academic Cooperation Association (ACA), Brussels, in cooperation with various institutions (Kelo, Teichler, and Wächter 2006).

Five major directions of critique were voiced:
- International statistics traditionally have provided information about *foreign students and study abroad*; these data are *weak approximations for student mobility* because a substantial proportion of foreign students in various European countries has not been mobile for the purpose of study, but has already lived and been educated in the country of study. In reverse, some students have lived and learned in another country prior to study and moved to the country of their citizenship for the purpose of study.
- Many countries do *not include temporarily mobile students* – i.e. the most frequent mode of intra-European student mobility – or included them only partially in their student statistics. Some countries even count temporarily outwards mobile students as home students during the study period abroad.
- The available international statistics do *not offer any distinction between degree-mobile students*, i.e. those intending to study a whole study programme abroad, and *short-term mobile students*, i.e. those intending to study abroad for one semester or for a somewhat longer time span within a study programme.

–   There is no distinction made in the international statistics according to citizenship or mobility according to *bachelor and master* programmes.
–   No statistics or surveys across Europe are suitable for establishing the *event of student mobility*, i.e. how many students have studied abroad during the course of study – for either the whole study programme or at least some period during the course of study.

In these three studies, the supranational as well as the national data collection agencies were asked to provide detailed information as regards the diversity of national data, details of definitions and data-handling. This helped show not only how often the national data collection deviated from the norm set by the UOE; thus, it often revealed that the statistics are not as reliable as the reader might believe. But it also provided information for some countries, how much the figures on 'foreign mobile' differ from those of 'foreign students' and how many mobile students who are citizens of their host country (i.e. had previously lived and learned in another country) are usually not counted. These estimates will be presented in the subsequent section.

The international data collectors drew the conclusion pragmatically that they should continue to collect data on foreign students, but that data on mobility should be collected in addition, whereby the countries might provide data according to one of the two principles identified in the above named studies (see Richters and Teichler 2006: 87): according to *prior education* (those students are defined as mobile who completed secondary education in a country different from the country of study in higher education) and/or according to *residence* (those students having lived prior to study or are registered regularly in a country different from the country of study in higher education).

However, UOE did not follow the other recommended steps. They *continue to recommend that short-term mobile students (up to one year) remain excluded* from the data set of mobile students. And they proposed not to include those mobile students at all whose nationality corresponds to that of the country of study in higher education (the 'returners').

A fourth study recently undertaken on mobility data (Teichler, Ferencz, and Wächter 2011) shows that many European countries have decided in recent years to collect data on foreign mobile students – in most cases in addition to the collection of data on foreign students. Among the 32 countries addressed in the study (EU member countries as well as Iceland, Liechtenstein, Norway, Switzerland and Turkey), the number of those collecting information on foreign mobile students increased from 9 in the 2002/03 academic year to 24 in 2006/07. Among the 24 countries, 15 collect data on mobile students with home country nationality as well. About a third of the countries addressed include short-term mobile students, but even they, as a rule, do not make any clear distinction in the statistics between short-term mobile and diploma mobile students.

It should be added here that UOE has succeeded in improving the data quality of foreign mobile graduates. There might be more or less statistics in the near future on both 'foreign' and 'foreign mobile'. But, there is no move in sight to collect separate statistics on short-term mobile students, and we do not know the extent to which short-term mobile students are excluded from or included in the statistics of foreign or foreign mobile students, as suggested by UOE. Thus, it is no surprise to note that the European Commission, in creating indices on European educational objectives, still relies on UOE data on foreign students and study abroad (Commission of the European Communities 2010).

Student mobility in the Bologna Process: A cautious account

The weaknesses of the available statistical sources are so grave that it is impossible to give a convincing detailed account of how student mobility in Europe has progressed in the years of the Bologna Process. However, based on the data presented in the above named 32-country study (Bürger, Ferencz, Wächter 2011), we can present the best possible approximations (cf. also Teichler 2012).

An increase of foreign students: According to UOE data, the number of foreign students in the 32 European countries named above increased from about 827,000 in 1999 to about 1,118,000 in 2003 and eventually 1,516,000 in 2007, i.e. by more than 80 percent in eight years. As the overall number of tertiary education students in the same period grew from more than 15 million to almost 22 million, i.e. by about 40 percent, the rate of foreign students did not increase that impressively, but it rose by about three-tenths: from 5.4 percent of all students in these European countries in 1999 to 5.8 percent in 2003 and eventually to 7.0 percent in 2007.

According to another study comprising data for all 46 countries that had joined the Bologna Process by 2009, the percentage of foreign students in the EHEA increased from 3.5 percent in 1999 to 4.6 percent in 2007; the substantially lower figures are primarily due to the fact that Russia – characterised by a large absolute number of students and a low percentage of foreign students – is included in the latter data (CHEPS, INCHER and ECOTEC 2010).

A substantial increase of students from outside Europe: The number of foreign students from outside Europe slightly more than doubled in these European countries during this period. Half of this growth is due to the worldwide increase in the student population, while the other half suggests that higher education in Europe has become more attractive to students from other parts of the world wishing to study abroad. Actually, the rate of foreign students from outside Europe (and unknown nationality) increased from 2.4 percent to 3.7 percent during that period. As we have reasons to believe that the vast majority of students from outside Europe come to Europe with the intention to study the whole study programme there, we may conclude that this information is reasonably valid.

A small increase in foreign students from other European countries: According to the UOE data which only include parts of temporarily mobile students, in 2007 the number of foreign students from other European countries was in the 32 European countries about one and a half times as high as that of 1999. However, as the total number of tertiary education students rose by about 40 percent during this period, the rate of foreign students in these countries being citizens of other European countries accounting for 3.0 percent in 1999 decreased slightly up to 2003 and eventually reached 3.3 percent in 2007. Thus, we do not note any acceleration of intra-European mobility in comparison to the prior growth trend. However, we cannot exclude the possibility that short-term mobility within Europe has increased to a greater extent recently because a substantial proportion of short-term mobile students are not included in these statistics.

Enormous variations in foreign student quota by country: In disregarding the special conditions of very small countries (Luxembourg, Liechtenstein, Cyprus etc.), we note that – according to the UOE statistics – the rates of foreign students in 2007 were 15-20 percent in Switzerland, United Kingdom and Austria, about 10 percent or slightly more in Belgium, France, Germany and Sweden, a few percent in the majority of countries, and finally even less than 1 percent in Poland, Slovakia, and Turkey. It might be added here that in Europe the rates of study abroad differ to a smaller extent by country than the rates of foreign students: The former ranged in 2007 according from 1.2 percent in the case of the United Kingdom to 6.0 percent in the case of Austria.

One-quarter of non-mobile students among foreign students: According to the information provided on student mobility by 24 European countries, the overall number of foreign inwards mobile students was about 841,000 in 2007, while the total number of foreign students was about 1,132,000. Thus, the number of non-mobile students accounted for 291,000, i.e. 25.7 percent of all foreign students. Obviously, data on foreign students taken as a 'proxy' for mobile students actually over-count study mobility by about a quarter. Actually, the highest rates of foreign mobile students were 14.9 percent in the UK, 14.0 percent in Switzerland and 12.4 percent in Austria.

More than one-tenth of mobile students are not foreign: The 15 countries which have collected information on incoming home country students report that they comprise on average more than one-tenth of all inwards mobile students. The rate, however, varies substantially by country: about half of all inwards mobile students in Denmark and one-third in Finland, one-tenth or more in Iceland, Switzerland and Norway, but less than one-tenth in two-thirds of these countries. This rate might be viewed as small, but it is interesting to note that overall more than 100,000 students in Europe moved to the country of their citizenship for the purpose of study after having lived and learned in another country prior to study.

Finally, we have to underscore that even the improved international data collection on student mobility does not provide any information on three highly important issues: *The numbers of outwards mobile students cannot be established.* Moreover, *no information is collected systematically in this framework on temporary mobility.* Finally, they are *not suitable at all to make any estimate on the event of student mobility during the course of study.* As we do not see moves underway to counteract the second and third information gaps within official statistics, a search for other sources of information seems appropriate.

The event of student mobility during the course of study – the key objective of temporary mobility in Europe

All three European policy campaigns of stimulating intra-European student mobility have put a *strong weight on temporary, short-term mobility.*

- The first initiative in favour of conventions aimed at recognising study achievements across borders by the Council of Europe in the 1950s with the help of *conventions* addressed the recognition of prior learning for admission to higher education, the recognition of the prior study of temporarily mobile students, and the recognition of degrees for persons transferring to advanced academic programmes or to the world of work.
- The second major initiative, the EU-supported *ERASMUS programme*, was announced in 1987 as a contribution to the long-term aim to reach a 10 percent rate of students in Europe spending a period of study in another European country. Also the major evaluation studies focused on the conditions of study in another country and on the value of the experience in another country on the subsequent study, on the development of competencies and on career and life paths after graduation.
- The *Bologna Declaration* of 1999 and the subsequent declarations emphasised the aim to increase the attractiveness to students from outside Europe, i.e. inwards mobility from other regions of the world and more or less mutual intra-European – mostly short-term – mobility. The 2009 Leuven Communiqué of the ministers involved in the Bologna Process specified measurable targets and in this framework called for a 20 percent margin of European students who have studied in another country during their course of study for the year 2020 (Leuven Communiqué 2009). And some European countries set even more ambitious targets (see Eurydice 2010).

In fact, the real aim of temporary student mobility is not to realise that a certain rate of students has to be in another country at a certain moment in time. Rather, a certain rate of students should have the event of study for a while in another country during their overall course of study. And the Leuven Communiqué states more clearly than previous key documents of the Bologna Process that *the main aim of temporary student mobility within Europe* is neither to increase the rate of foreign students in individual higher education institutions or individual European countries nor to let non-mobile students experience the company of inwards mobile students from other countries. Instead, *an increase in outbound mobile students* is the key objective: one's own students should have broader experience than the home institution of higher education and the home country is likely to offer.

Measuring the frequency of the event of student mobility during the course of study

According to the logic of European policies promoting intra-European student mobility, the best possible indicator of the success or failure of such a policy is not a high rate of mobile students at any moment in time, but the rate of students who were mobile during the course of study. This might be called the *rate of the event of mobility during the course of study*. The event of mobility during the course of study, by definition, can only be gathered from students who have completed or are close to completing their study programme. They have to provide retrospective information.

Statistical systems as a rule only collect a limited range of information per person. Therefore, they are suitable for covering the complexity of retrospective analyses of student mobility: whether they spent the whole study programme abroad or only a period, in which cycle they were (in the case of a master graduate), whether they were mobile more than once etc. Therefore, *questionnaire surveys* seem to be the *best possible source* even though it is the handicap of surveys that they only provide information on about half or even less than half of the persons addressed who are willing voluntarily to respond and provide the respective information.

Three approaches to providing survey data on the event of student mobility have been chosen in recent years. First, *retrospective reporting by students*: In the so-called EUROSTUDENT III 2005-2008 study, comprising 23 European countries, information is provided about the proportion of students having previously studied abroad (a country mean of about 5 percent) and about the proportion of students having study experience and/or other study-related experience (a country mean of about 10 percent; see Orr 2008: 132). Yet this approach is bound to under-count short-term student mobility substantially because students surveyed in early stages of their study might be mobile at later stages of their course of study.

Second, *retrospective reporting by students close to graduation*: Approaches to identify mobility retrospectively by surveying students close to graduation have been chosen in some national surveys. For example, the rate of having studied abroad or having followed study-related activities was provided in a representative German survey undertaken every third year (*"Das soziale Bild der Studentenschaft"*). In this case, information on mobility was extracted only for students of advanced semesters who can be considered as being close to graduation. In the Italian *AlmaLaurea* system of surveying final-year students and graduates from a large number of Italian universities, the publication of the retrospective reports of final-year students – including international mobility in the course of study – only comprises the responses of those persons who could be validated shortly afterwards as graduates. While both approaches are convincing options, even they cannot fully exclude the possibility that students are mobile even later during the course of study.

Third, *retrospective reporting by graduates*: Several graduate surveys have elicited information from former students about whether they had been mobile during the course of their study. This certainly includes all possible mobility up to the degree level which is the basis for tracing graduates. However, by definition, this does not include the mobility of students who eventually did not graduate ('drop-outs' or students not intending to graduate). Graduate surveys seem to be the *best possible option to collect information on the event of student mobility* during the course of study because they not only cover well the information which student surveys close to graduation cover, but they can also address mobility shortly after graduation and the relationship between mobility during the course of study and after graduation.

Yet one has to bear in mind that there does not exist any comprehensive system of graduate surveys across European countries. Two comparative graduate surveys have been undertaken in the past. First, in the so-called *CHEERS study* ("Careers after Higher Education: A European Research Survey") supported by the European Union, scholars from 11 European countries and Japan surveyed altogether about 35,000 persons of their respective countries three to four years after their graduation in the 1994/95 academic year (Schomburg and Teichler 2006). Second, the so-called *REFLEX study* ("The Flexible Professional in the Knowledge Society"), supported by the European Union, was a follow-up study to the CHEERS project with various new accents (Allen and van der Velden 2011). More than 40,000 graduates of the 1999/2000 academic year from 14 European countries and Japan were surveyed five years after graduation.

Both surveys turned out to be valuable instruments for showing the frequency of different forms of migration and mobility in the life-course up to a few years after graduation. For example, an analysis of the home country graduates of 10 European countries participating in the CHEERS project showed that about one-third as many graduates had been mobile while in school as those who had been mobile during the course of study.

Professional mobility in the first few years after graduation is about as widespread as mobility during the course of study, if not only those are counted who were employed abroad by a foreign employer, but also those who are sent abroad for a considerable time by their home country employer (Jahr and Teichler 2007). The REFLEX study shows that altogether more than 40 percent of graduates on average across the European countries surveyed had extended periods of experiencing other countries in their life course up to five years after graduation, i.e. migration, mobility while in school, mobility in the course of study as well as professional mobility. This varied between the countries surveyed from 26 percent in Spain to 61 percent in Switzerland (Teichler 2011a).

No similar European graduate survey has been undertaken more recently, i.e. at a time when the effects of the Bologna Process could already be observed. However, a secondary analysis of *recent national graduate surveys in 10 European countries* was published in 2011 (Schomburg and Teichler 2011). Thereby, information was provided on the rate of graduates who had been mobile during the course of study in nine countries.

Table 1 provides an overview of the share of Bachelor graduates (and in some countries also the share of Master graduates) who had been temporarily outward mobile for the purpose of study whereby, as a rule, study abroad for at least one semester is referred to (for more detailed information, see Schomburg 2011). Accordingly, the *proportion of those having studied temporarily abroad during the course of study* varies substantially by country. In three countries – the Netherlands, Austria and Norway – the target set in the Leuven Communiqué of 2009 – i.e. a quota of 20 percent in the year 2020 – has already been reached or exceeded for Bachelor graduates. In Germany, it is about 15 percent. One can argue that the 20-percent target is already reached in Germany as well if one takes into consideration the transition from Bachelor to Master programmes and those German graduates who had studied abroad for their whole study period. However, the share of Bachelor graduates having spent a study period abroad is only about 5 percent or less in the other countries – Czech Republic, France, Italy, Poland, and the United Kingdom.

Table 1.   *Periods abroad during the course of study of graduates from selected European countries (in percent)*

Country	Bachelor graduates			Master graduates			Single-cycle/ traditional degrees		
	Univ.	Other HEIs	All	Univ.	Other HEIs	All	Univ.	Other HEIs	All
Austria									
Study	16	22	18	•	•	•	22	23	22
Various activities	24	33	27	•	•	•	37	40	37
Czech Republic									
Study	•	•	6	•	•	18	•	•	•
Work	•	•	6	•	•	15	•	•	•
Germany									
Study	16	14	•	17	9	•	19	9	•
Various activities	28	27	•	35	22	•	37	20	•
France									
Study	6	2	•	12	22	•	11	•	•
Various activities	20	22	•	29	54	•	32	•	•
Italy									
Study	5	•	5	15	•	15	10	•	10
The Netherlands									
Study	28	21	•	28	•	28	35	16	•
Norway									
Study	20	•	•	25	•	•	•	•	•
Poland									
Study	•	•	2	•	•	3	•	•	3
United Kingdom									
Study	4	•	•	•	•	•	•	•	•

Univ. = University, Other HEIs = Other higher education institutions (e.g. Fachhochschulen, Hogescholen, Grandes Écoles etc.)
Source: Data from national surveys reported in Schomburg 2011

Although the data are by no means perfect (e.g. as regards the definition of 'student mobility' and the counting of mobility over the cycles of study programme), they allow us to estimate that, on average of the ERASMUS-eligible countries, more than 10 percent of the students spent a period of study of at least three months in another country during the course of their study. Thereby, the rates seem to vary from about 30 percent to clearly less than 5 percent. Thus, the target of 20 percent for 2020 strived for in the Leuven Communiqué has a different meaning for the various European countries: Some of them have already exceeded that rate, others might view it as a realistic target and, finally, other countries might consider this target as completely out of reach for the near future.

Measuring the value of the outwards mobility of European students

The general public discourse on the role of student mobility in European higher education as well as the discourse on the best ways of measuring the frequency of mobility has come to the conclusion, as shown above, that the event of outwards mobility during the course of study is the key criteria of success of 'quantitative' policies to encourage and facilitate the mobility of students of European countries. Consequently, information on the impact of student mobility is most valuable for assessing the 'quality' of the policies in favour of student mobility that shows the subsequent educational paths, the competencies and the careers after graduation of formerly outwards mobile students from European countries.

The most comprehensive analyses of that kind concentrate on the ERASMUS programme. Four major evaluation studies have been undertaken in this area, comprising surveys of former ERASMUS students, their teachers, programme coordinators, employers etc.: The ERASMUS Evaluation study of the first seven years (Teichler and Maiworm 1997), the study on SOCRATES in the framework of the ERASMUS programme (Teichler 2002), the analysis of the professional value of study abroad undertaken in 2005 (Janson, Schomburg, Teichler 2009), and the study "ERASMUS and quality, openness and internationalisation in higher education" undertaken in 2007 (CHEPS, INCHER and ECOTEC 2010, Bürger and Lanzendorf 2010).

Certainly, the major ERASMUS evaluation studies are by no means an ideal way of measuring the impact of outwards mobility.

–   The number of students made mobile with ERASMUS support is quite impressive. It has increased from a few thousand at the beginning to more than 200,000 annually. Yet, as already pointed out, even now less than 1 percent of European students study annually with ERASMUS support, and only slightly more than 3 percent of students annually graduating in Europe have been in another European country with ERASMUS support. The incomplete data available allow us to estimate that *the number of outward mobile students in Europe is at least three times as high as that of ERASMUS students*. A study comparing ERASMUS students and other mobile students came to the conclusion that other formerly mobile students are more successful afterwards on average than ERASMUS students – a result that does not come as a surprise because ERASMUS was created to mobilise those who would not be mobile anyway. This finding suggests that analyses of former ERASMUS students do not exaggerate the value of outward mobility on average in Europe.

–   Second, the ERASMUS evaluation studies, as the authors point out themselves, have *methodological limitations*: For example, the self-ratings of impacts might be biased. Retrospective ratings of competencies prior to the study period in another country might lead to over-estimations of the value of mobility. In various studies, comparison groups of non-mobile students are missing for examining the add-on effects of mobility and, if comparison groups are available, it remains difficult to find out the extent to which differences between mobile and non-mobile students are due to mobility or are "selection effects", i.e. they can be explained by the different composition of mobile students and non-mobile students.

–   Third, many *other studies* on student mobility in Europe are available that are *more sophisticated* in addressing issues such as teaching and learning process, intercultural experiences, students' motives, curricula and competence enhancements etc. However, these studies are less valuable in assessing the impact of student mobility altogether because they *cannot provide a representative picture*.

Thus, most experts and actors are convinced that the information provided by the ERASMUS evaluation studies provide a more solid information base on the 'qualitative' value of the outward mobility of European students than the available statistics and surveys on the 'quantity' of student mobility. We might summarise the results of studies on the value of the mobility of European students as follows (see Teichler 2011b).

Former ERASMUS students express an enormously *high degree of satisfaction* as regards their study period abroad, even though problems are frequently named such as insufficient financial support, late provision of financial support, administrative problems in the host country and notably with the administration of the host institution, accommodation problems and – somewhat surprisingly – too much contact with home country nationals during the study period abroad.

Obviously, the mobile students most highly appreciate that they have experienced eye-opening contrasts during the period in another European country. *'Learning from contrast'* is the major result of short-term student mobility in Europe. The result is a new way of thinking which embeds comparative reasoning and the conviction that there are more possible solutions for any issue than one tends to imagine if one has not been internationally mobile. This is an impact that cannot be separated into distinct categories of the academic and cultural impact of mobility.

There is a discrepancy between the conviction of mobile students that their *academic progress has been higher* on average during the period of study in another country than during a corresponding period at home on one hand, and an *incomplete recognition* of the study achievements abroad upon return on the other. This reflects the facts that on the one side students might absorb somewhat less of the typical knowledge abroad as a consequence of various factors. On the other side, students are convinced that this is more than outweighed by the value of learning from contrasts.

Actually, the extent of recognition of study achievements abroad – a major criteria underscored by the European Commission – can be measured differently and will be assessed differently according to underlying concepts of those taking the results of evaluation studies into account. In counting the number of courses and credits, one could come to the conclusion that recognised study achievements abroad correspond to about three-quarters of regular study at home. But students report on average that the overall study period will be prolonged by about half of the study period abroad. Obviously, some of the seemingly recognised achievements will not count eventually because they are not really accepted as corresponding to required courses at home.

As a result, former ERASMUS students from Western European countries view themselves as *only slightly superior* to other students and are similarly viewed by their teachers and by employers as far as *specific academic knowledge and general study-related competencies* are concerned. However, they clearly feel *superior in competencies directly linked to international experiences*, e.g. foreign language proficiency as well as knowledge and understanding of various countries and comparative thinking.

It should be added that ERASMUS seems to hold a clearly *higher value for students from Central and Eastern European countries* than for those from Western European countries. The former report higher achievements and competencies as compared to non-mobile students and rate the professional impact of temporary study abroad clearly more positively than their fellow students from Western European countries.

In looking beyond graduation, we note that student mobility *reinforces the students' interest in further learning*. Formerly mobile students are more likely to continue study upon or sometime after graduation.

Former ERASMUS students are convinced that temporary mobility during the course of study has *helped them in the transition process to employment*. Having studied in another country seems to be a positive signal for employers in their choice among candidates. The period of job search is below average for formerly mobile students, and also unemployment in early career stages is lower on average for formerly mobile students than for formerly non-mobile students.

However, graduate surveys suggest that international mobility during the course of study or shortly after graduation *does not lead to clearly more successful employment and work* during the first few years after graduation. Only small differences can be observed, for instance, as regards the occupational status in general, the utilisation of knowledge on the job and job satisfaction.

However, the biggest distinction between formerly mobile students and formerly non-mobile students is not that of general competencies and general professional success. Rather, formerly mobile students surpass formerly non-mobile students *most clearly in taking up visibly international job tasks*. The major professional impact of ERASMUS is not to enhance individual career benefits for the mobile ones, but a – macro-societal – change of the overall competencies of graduates in line with the growing internationalisation of the world of work.

The most visible difference in the careers of formerly mobile students and formerly non-mobile students finally applies to *professional mobility*. Formerly mobile students opt several times as often for employment and work in another – in most cases European – country.

The fact that formerly mobile students are only slightly superior as regards general competencies and slightly more successful in their careers than formerly mobile students but clearly as regards visibly international competencies and work tasks does not call into question the success of ERASMUS: Public funds are made available to increase the number of graduates competent to cope with the increase of visibly international work tasks, but not to provide public funds for the privileged, i.e. to those who will be rewarded by higher status and income anyway.

Yet the professional impact of temporary study in another European country has *declined in some respects over the years*, as a comparison of surveys of different cohorts of formerly mobile students has shown. This finding seems to reflect – according to the interpretation by the authors (Janson, Schomburg, and Teichler 2009) – a declining exceptionality of temporary study abroad because the study and living environment is becoming more international for students living in Europe, even if they do not study abroad.

It should be pointed out that the *surveys of teachers, coordinators, employers etc.* undertaken in the framework of evaluating the ERASMUS programme have provided results which are important for obtaining a more solid picture in various respects. By and large, these surveys *confirm the major findings of the surveys of formerly mobile students*: that temporary mobility has a moderate positive effect on subsequent learning, competencies and careers, but a clearly more striking effect on visibly international competencies, on visibly international work tasks and on international professional mobility.

Conclusion

The strong political efforts to enhance – predominantly short-term – student mobility within Europe have for a long time not even triggered any efforts to measure the magnitude of mobility. Until recently, international statistics only provided information on foreign students and study abroad, and the intention was even to exclude temporary mobility.

On the basis of incomplete information, it is possible to estimate that three-quarters of foreign students are not mobile, but have lived and learned in the country of study already prior to study. About one-tenth of mobile students has lived and learned somewhere else and study in the country of their citizenship. The weakness of statistics has been in part due to the vague policy criteria.

In the meantime, it is clear – as expressed by the ministers of the European countries involved in the Bologna Process in the Leuven Communiqué in 2009 – that the event of having studied in another country during the course of study is the major European policy objective. An average target across countries of 20 percent is envisaged for the year 2020.

Accordingly, one can estimate that more than 10 percent of recent graduates were mobile during the course of study. Among them, there are more than twice as many who had been mobile by other means than those of ERASMUS. And short-term mobility is several times more widespread than the event of student mobility through studying the whole study programme abroad.

Information on the impact of the outwards mobility of European students is more solid. Notably, evaluation studies show that former ERASMUS students are only slightly superior in general and specific academic competencies and in their general career, but clearly better prepared for visibly international tasks and for international professional mobility.

In order to enhance the information base on the magnitude and impact of the outwards mobility of European students, regular European-wide graduate surveys are needed. They have to comprise a relatively high number of respondents in order to make it possible to compare the studies and careers of mobile and non-mobile students.

References

Allen, J., R. van der Velden, eds. (2011). *The Flexible Professional in the Knowledge Society: New Challenges for Higher Education*. Dordrecht: Springer.

Bürger, S., I. Ferencz, B. Wächter (2011). "International Mobility of European Students: Comparative Overview and Trends". In: U. Teichler, I. Ferencz, B. Wächter (eds.), *Mapping Mobility in Higher Education in Europe. Volume 1: Overview and Trends*. Bonn: Academic Exchange Service. 33-88.

Bürger, S., U. Lanzendorf, eds. (2010). *Higher Education Institutions in Europe: Mobilized by Mobility*. Kassel: International Centre for Higher Education Research Kassel (Werkstattberichte, 73).

Centre for Higher Education Policy Studies, International Centre for Higher Education Research Kassel and ECOTEC (2008). *ERASMUS and Quality, Openness and Internationalisation in Higher Education in Europe*. Enschede: Twente University, CHEPS.

Centre for Higher Education Policy Studies, International Centre for Higher Education Research Kassel and ECOTEC (2010). *The First Decade of Working on the European*

Higher Education Area: The Bologna Process Independent Assessment. Volume 1. Enschede: Twente University, CHEPS.

Commission of the European Communities (2010). *Progress Towards the Common European Objectives in Education and Training (2010/2011) – Indicators and Benchmarks*. Brussels: Commission of the European Communities (SEC (2011)526; Commission Staff Working Document).

De Wit, H. (2012). "Student Mobility between Europe and the Rest of the World: Trends, Issues and Challenges". In: A. Curaj, P. Scott, L. Vlasceanu, L. Wilson (eds.), *European Higher Education at the Crossroads: Between the Bologna Process and National Reforms. Part 1*. Dordrecht: Springer. 431-439.

Eurostat and Eurostudent (2009). *The Bologna Process in Higher Education in Europe: Key Indicators on the Social Dimension and Mobility*. Luxembourg: Sogeti.

Eurydice, ed. (2010). *Focus on Higher Education in Europe 2010 – The Impact of the Bologna Process*. Brussels: Eurydice.

Jahr, V., U. Teichler (2007). "Graduates' International Experience and Mobility". In: U. Teichler (ed.), *Careers of University Graduates: Views and Experiences in Comparative Perspectives*. Dordrecht: Springer. 211-224.

Janson, K., H. Schomburg, U. Teichler (2009). *The Professional Value of ERASMUS Mobility*. Bonn: Lemmens.

Kelo, M., U. Teichler, B. Wächter, eds. (2006). *EURODATA: Student Mobility in European Higher Education*. Bonn: Lemmens.

Lanzendorf, U., U. Teichler (2003). *Statistics on Student Mobility within the European Union*. Luxembourg: European Parliament.

Lanzendorf, U., U. Teichler, J. Murdock (2006). *Student Mobility*. Luxembourg: European Parliament, Directorate-General for Internal Policies of the Union, Policy Department Structural and Cohesion Policies.

Leuven Communiqué (2009). Available at http://www.ehea.info/Uploads/Declarations/Leuven_Louvain-la-Neuve_Communiqu%C3%A9_April_2009.pdf (accessed 4 November 2012).

OECD (2009). *Education at a Glance: OECD Education Indicators 2009*. Paris: OECD.

Orr, D., ed. (2008). *Social and Economic Conditions of Student Life in Europe*. Bielefeld: W. Bertelsmann Verlag.

Richters, E., U. Teichler (2006). "Student Mobility Data: Current Methodological Issues and Future Prospects". In: M. Kelo, U. Teichler, B. Wächter (eds.), *EURODATA: Student Mobility in European Higher Education*. Bonn: Lemmens. 78-95.

Schomburg, H. (2011). "Employability and Mobility of Bachelor Graduates: The Findings of Graduate Surveys in Ten European Countries on the Assessment and Impact of the Bologna Reform". In: H. Schomburg, U. Teichler (eds.), *Employability and Mobility of Bachelor Graduates in Europe: Key Results of the Bologna Process*. Rotterdam/Taipei: Sense Publishers. 253-273.

Schomburg, H., U. Teichler (2006). *Higher Education and Graduate Employment in Europe: Results of Graduate Surveys from Twelve Countries*. Dordrecht: Springer.

Schomburg, H., U. Teichler, eds. (2011). *Employability and Mobility of Bachelor Graduates in Europe: Key Results of the Bologna Process*. Rotterdam/Taipei: Sense Publishers.

Teichler, U., ed. (2002). *ERASMUS in the SOCRATES Programme: Finding of an Evaluation Study*. Bonn: Lemmens.

Teichler, U. (2003). "Mutual Recognition and Credit Transfer in Europe: Experiences and Problems". *Journal of Studies in International Education*. Vol. 7. No. 4. 312-341.

Teichler, U. (2011a). "International Dimensions of Higher Education and Graduate Employment". In: J. Allen, R. van der Velden (eds.), *The Flexible Professional in the Knowledge Society: New Challenges for Higher Education*. Dordrecht: Springer. 165-185.

Teichler, U. (2011b). The Value of Study Abroad: The ERASMUS Experience, presentation to the Seminar Series "Higher Education in Europe: Recent Reform and Its Impact on Research, Quality and Equity", Oxford University, St. Antony's College, European Studies Centre, Oxford, 3 November 2011

Teichler, U. (2012). "Student Mobility in Europe: The Informational Value of Official Statistics and Graduate Surveys". In: A. Curaj, P. Scott, L. Vlasceanu, L. Wilson (eds.), *European Higher Education at the Crossroads: Between the Bologna Process and National Reforms. Part 1*. Dordrecht: Springer. 485-509.

Teichler, U., I. Ferencz (2011). "Student Mobility Data – Recent Achievements, Current Issues and Future Prospects". In: U. Teichler, I. Ferencz, B. Wächter (eds.), *Mapping Mobility in Higher Education in Europe. Volume 1: Overview and Trends*. Bonn: Deutscher Akademischer Austausch Dienst. 151-175.

Teichler, U., I. Ferencz, B. Wächter, eds. (2011). *Mapping Mobility in Higher Education in Europe*. 2 Volumes. Bonn: Deutscher Akademischer Austausch Dienst.

Teichler, U., F. Maiworm (1997). *The ERASMUS Experience: Major Findings of the ERASMUS Evaluation Research Project*. Luxembourg: Office for Official Publications of the European Communities.

UNESCO Institute for Statistics (2009). *Global Education Digest 2009*. Montreal: UIS.

Van der Hijden, P. (2012). "Mobility Key to the EHEA and ERA". In: A. Curaj, P. Scott, L. Vlasceanu, L. Wilson (eds.), *European Higher Education at the Crossroads: Between the Bologna Process and National Reforms. Part 1*. Dordrecht: Springer. 377-386.

Wächter, B. (2008). "Mobility and Internationalisation in the European Higher Education Area". In: M. Kelo (ed.), *Beyond 2010: Priorities and Challenges for Higher Education in the Next Decade*. Bonn: Lemmens. 13-42.

The Impact of University Rankings on Higher Education Policy in Europe: A Challenge to Perceived Wisdom and a Stimulus for Change

Ellen Hazelkorn and Martin Ryan

Abstract

The arrival of global rankings in 2003 was a clarion call for the urgent reform of European higher education. The results of the Shanghai Academic Ranking of World Universities and the Times Higher Education QS World University Ranking, first published in 2003 and 2004, respectively, challenged the perceived wisdom about the reputation and excellence of European universities. Since then, the EU and its member states have sought to reshape and modernise higher education in Europe. This paper argues that the emergence of global rankings was not only a challenge to perceived wisdom, but also a stimulus for change in European higher education policy. While it is too soon to evaluate whether new policies have made a direct impact on the performance of European countries in global rankings, it is now time for debate on the apparent influence of global rankings on higher education policy in Europe.

Key words: global rankings, European policy, higher education in France, higher education in Germany, higher education in the UK

Introduction

Speaking on behalf of the European Council at the time of the first *Shanghai Academic Ranking of World Universities* (ARWU), the Irish Minister for Education and Science said "the news is not all that good"; too few European universities are featured among the world's top 500 (Dempsey 2004). The arrival of the global rankings – the ARWU and the *Times Higher Education QS Top University Ranking* (THE-QS) in 2003 and 2004, respectively – was a game changer for higher education and research, intensifying cross-national comparisons. These rankings immediately attracted the attention of the academy and policy makers because they challenged the perceived wisdom about reputation and excellence; this was especially true for European universities when placed alongside the aim of the *Lisbon Agenda* to make Europe "the most dynamic and competitive knowledge-based economy in the world" (Lisbon European Council 2000).

Over the years, by presenting results annually as a league table (see Table 1), rankings have highlighted and tracked shifts in the competitive strengths and weaknesses of nations through the performance of their higher education institutions. Rankings for 2004 show European higher education institutions lagging behind their counterparts in the United States (USA), with the exception of the QS/THE-QS ranking, where the difference is negligible. In 2012, the pattern of European performance is largely the same, with the exception of the QS/THE-QS ranking, where European higher education institutions demonstrate a slight advantage compared to higher education institutions from the USA. Overall, it appears that there has been no catch-up for European higher education institutions since the introduction of global rankings. And despite criticism of global university rankings (Hazelkorn 2011, Rauhvargers 2011), their influence is growing.

> Europe is no longer setting the pace in the global race for knowledge and talent, while emerging economies are rapidly increasing their investment in higher education. [...] too few European higher education institutions are recognised as world class in the current, research oriented global university rankings [...] And there has been no real improvement over the past years (European Commission 2011: 2).

Table 1.   Number of higher education institutions in the global top 100: World regions in selected rankings, 2004–2012

Ranking	Yr.	North America	Europe (w/Russia)	Australia &Newz.	Asia (w/India)	Latin America	Africa	Middle East
QS/THE-QS	2012	35	38	7	20	0	0	0
	2011	35	40	7	18	0	0	0
	2008	42	35	8	13	0	0	1
	2004	38	36	12	13	0	0	1
THE-TR	2012	52	32	6	10	0	0	0
	2011	57	30	4	9	0	0	0
	2010	57	28	5	10	0	0	0
ARWU	2012	57	31	5	4	0	0	3
	2011	57	33	4	5	0	0	1
	2008	58	34	3	4	0	0	1

	2004	55	37	2	5	0	0	1
W-METRICS	2012	65	25	2	5	3	0	0
	2011	73	16	2	7	2	0	0
	2009	71	21	1	5	2	0	0
SCImago	2012	45	25	4	24	2	0	0
	2011	46	25	4	24	1	0	0
	2009	47	25	4	22	2	0	0

Key: THE-QS = Times Higher QS World Ranking; QS = Quacquarelli Symonds; ARWU = Academic Ranking of World Universities. W-Metrics = Webometrics.

Note: THE-QS (pre-2011) is combined with QS for 2011 and 2012 as the methodology is broadly similar. THE-TR was only established in 2010 and only provides data on 200 institutions. For 2011 and 2012, THE-TR provides information on 400 institutions. THE-QS for 2008 only sums to 99 due to tying institutions.

Ritzen (2010: 53 and 66) argues that European universities probably surpassed the USA at the beginning of the 20th century, but failure to invest and expand after WW2 turned the tables. In 2007, worldwide R&D expenditures totalled an estimated USD 1.107 trillion; the USA accounted for about 33 percent of this. Japan, the second-largest performer, accounted for about 13 percent, while China was third, with about 9 percent. As a bloc, the EU-27 accounted for 24 percent of global R&D in 2007 (NSF 2010). While R&D expenditures in the EU-27 are ahead of those in Japan and China, they are trailing the level of investment in the USA. OECD data on R&D expenditures (see Figure 1) show China and South Africa spending much more as a percentage of GDP over the last 10 years. South Korea's trajectory starting ten years ago is also very impressive, and it is now spending more than any other country on R&D as a percentage of GDP (see Figure 1). The EU has predicted that Brazil, Russia, India and China will dominate future R&D growth, overwhelming Europe and Japan and eventually matching the level of investment in the USA. At current levels of trend-expenditure, China will match EU-27 spending on R&D by 2018, and will match US spending on R&D by 2022 (Ritzen 2010: 37-70).

Figure 1.   Government-financed expenditure on R&D as a % of GDP

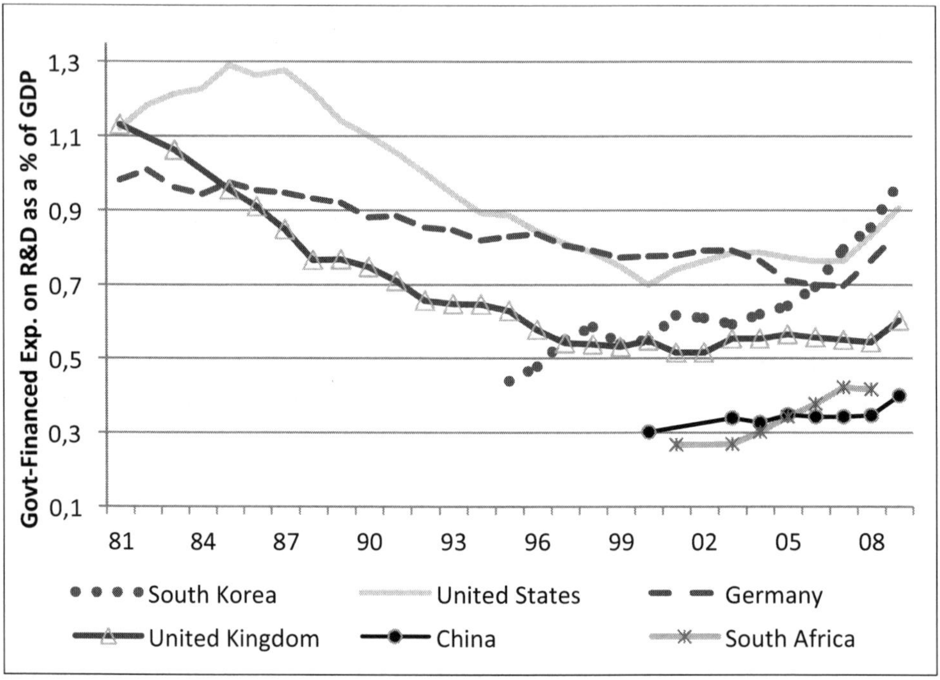

Source: OECD *Science and Technology Indicators*, 2012

Lambert and Butler (2006), Aghion et al. (2007), and Ritzen (2010), amongst others, have warned that Europe's universities are standing at a crossroads. In recent years, the EU, along with its member states, has adopted a series of policies and strategies which represent much greater government steerage of the higher education and research system (Maassen and Stensaker 2011). The next section will review recent developments in EU higher education policy. The third section looks at selective national responses in Europe, with a particular focus on France, Germany and the UK – the three largest economies in the European Union. The fourth section concludes, arguing that the emergence of global rankings was not only a challenge to perceived wisdom, but also a substantial driver for change in European higher education policy.

Overview of EU higher education policy

Higher education has been a key component of European policymaking since the early days of the European Coal and Steel Community and the decision to establish the European University in Florence in 1955 (Corbett 2003). In the early 1990s, the benefits of the 'information society' began to dominate policy discourse across Europe (Bangemann 1994) and force a new direction. Then, in the lead up to the Lisbon Strategy (Lisbon European Council 2000), European policy moved decidedly to embrace the 'knowledge economy', placing greater prominence on the production of new knowledge and knowledge management as core to economic growth rather than simply envisaging access to technological tools. Since then, and in response to growing interest in the global rankings, higher education and university-based research have become central to EU policymaking in a dramatic and significant way.

The Sorbonne Declaration, 1998, with its focus on the "harmonisation of the architecture of the European higher education system", was an initiative of four education ministers who proclaimed that "the Europe we are building is not only that of the Euro, the banks and the economy, it must be a Europe of knowledge as well" (Witte 2006: 124). That viewpoint was formalised one year later with the Bologna Declaration, 1999. While Sorbonne represented a 'quantum leap' in European higher education policy, the Bologna Process was and has remained largely voluntary, albeit international competitive pressures have effectively made it compulsory and set an international standard (Adelman 2009, ATN n.d.). Bologna anticipated the need for enhanced convergence across national systems to create a coherent system of higher education able to compete internationally (van Damme 2009: 40-41). It was predicated on the free movement of students, faculty and workers across national boundaries facilitated by "trustworthy information and with the assurance that their performance will be recognised in other parts of Europe" (Reichert 2009: 107). The process was designed to ensure comparability in the standards and quality of higher education qualifications across member states through curriculum and quality assurance changes (European Commission 2010, Sursock and Smidt 2010). While focused on enhancing cooperation, Bologna also recognised the "equal position of all institutions and systems". The vision was outward-looking, on the basis that to encourage and facilitate mobility within Europe required a system easily understood, harmonious and not constrained by parochialism – characteristics also crucial for attracting talent and investment from around the world to Europe. It set the goal of establishing the EHEA by 2010, which was officially launched by the *Vienna Declaration* (2010).

The Lisbon Strategy marked a significant change in policy direction, with its focus on European competitiveness, research investment and improving excellence (Dale 2010). The original statement made it clear that:

> Given the significant role played by research and development in generating economic growth, employment and social cohesion [...] Research activities at national and Union level must be better integrated and coordinated to make them as efficient and innovative as possible, and to ensure that Europe offers attractive prospects to its best brains.

To ensure that the desired outcomes were achieved, existing voluntary arrangements needed to "be fully exploited". This was a clear reference to the role to be played by the "open method of co-ordination", a non-binding tool which seeks to progress change without infringing national rights (Gornitzka 2005). Over the intervening years, several high-level communications have been issued stressing the importance of higher education and university-based research, with ever increasing stridency and directness (see Box 1). Broadly speaking, three main concerns have come to dominate European policy on higher education and research:

1. Too few European higher education institutions are recognised as world-class in the current environment of research-oriented global university rankings. This is because "higher education institutions too often seek to compete in too many areas, while comparatively few have the capacity to excel cross the board" (European Commission 2011: 2, Butler 2007). Compared with the USA which has only about 200 research-intensive universities, Europe has about 4,000 universities which claim or want to be research-intensive (European Commission 2011: 2).

2. European universities suffer from poor governance, insufficient autonomy and often perverse incentives. This is due to a combination of factors including the predominance of traditional decentralised organisational structures and civil service-type governance arrangements and academic contracts.

3. Public policy has favoured higher education as a public good, supporting social/cultural objectives rather than economic ones in the belief that all universities should be similar in quality rather than some being more excellent than others. As a result, public funding is spread too thinly across too many universities.

Box 1.   Selected pronouncements about European higher education competitiveness

"It is the quality of European higher education institutions, measured (among other ways) through the volume and scope of institutions' scientific – in the widest sense of the word – and technological research activities, which is crucial" (European Commission 2001, pt. 8).

"The European university world is not trouble-free, and the European universities are not at present globally competitive with those of our major partners, even though they produce high quality scientific publications" (European Commission 2003: 2).

"Universities should be funded more for what they do than for what they are, by focusing funding on relevant outputs rather than inputs" (European Commission 2006: 7).

The "challenges posed by globalisation require that the European Higher Education Area and the European Research Area be fully open to the world and that Europe's universities aim to become worldwide competitive players" (European Commission 2007: 2).

The "performance of education systems must be enhanced, and the international attractiveness of Europe's higher education reinforced" (European Commission 2010: 34).

The "potential of European higher education institutions to fulfil their role in society and contribute to Europe's prosperity remains underexploited. Europe is no longer setting the pace in the global race for knowledge and talent, while emerging economies are rapidly increasing their investment in higher education" (European Commission 2011: 2).

In one of its first communications in 2001 following publication of the Lisbon Strategy, the European Commission stressed the necessity of reaching and maintaining "an assurance of quality that is widely understood in the world" in order to ensure that Europe could compete "as well as the other leading providers of education services" (European Commission 2011). By 2006, the EU began to talk about higher education reform in terms of 'modernisation' – a theme to which it returned in its communication accompanying the launch of *Europe 2020*. This communication, *Delivering on the Modernisation Agenda for Universities: Education, Research and Innovation* (European Commission 2006: 3) openly questioned the social contract that had underpinned public support for higher education over the last number of decades, claiming that the

> pressure for uniformity has led to generally good average performance, but has increased fragmentation of the sector into mostly small national systems and sub-systems. These render cooperation difficult at national, let alone European or international, level and impose conditions which prevent universities from diversifying and from focusing on quality.

By 2007, the influence and impact of global rankings was becoming more evident. Initially, the EU's response was to highlight the diversity of European higher education, arguing this was a characteristic to be celebrated. Accordingly, a European classification system was initiated in 2005 and launched as U-Map in 2009 (van Vught 2009, van Vught et al. 2010). However, as concerns about global competition have risen, the EU has taken an increasingly more interventionist position, less concerned with diversity and more with excellence. The 2007 resolution urged European higher education to respond to "challenges posed by globalisation" (European Commission 2007: 2). The EU acknowledged that both national and European standards were no longer sufficient; rather, there was a need to enhance the international attractiveness and competitiveness of European higher education (European Commission 2011). The decision to directly challenge the dominance of global rankings by developing *U-Multirank*, the pilot of which was launched in 2011 (van Vught and Ziegele 2012), was taken in this context.

In parallel, the EU Framework Programme has been switching from encouraging the growth of research to consolidating and concentrating research in centres of excellence. The sixth framework programme, FP6, sought to encourage the formation of virtual "networks of excellence"; FP7 improved upon the concept, establishing the European Institute for Innovation and Technology (EIT), operating through knowledge-innovation communities (KICs). The European Research Council (ERC) has taken this further, on the basis that "one of the reasons for the research advantage of US universities is the concentration of research funding on less than one-tenth of degree-giving institutions". With a budget equivalent to 15 percent of overall FP7 expenditure (€7.51 billion of €50.5 billion), the ERC is putting funding directly into the hands of "excellent" researchers and not institutions. The strategy is already helping to consolidate 50 percent of the funding in just 50 universities (Myklebust 2012). FP8, due in 2014, is worth

€80 billion, and will see this process of consolidation and concentration strengthened (Maassen and Stensaker 2011).

While there are concerns about Europe's ability to harness the capacity and capability of its higher education system for economic recovery, other countries have been looking on favourably – and learning lessons – from how the EU is managing to corral and harness various national interests (see, for example, Grabert 2011, Adelman 2009, ATN n.d.). Nonetheless, the EU's role is naturally constrained because of the principle of *subsidiarity*, but its influence has been strengthened considerably in line with massive increases in its research budget. While enhanced EU "leadership" has led to allegations of "creeping competence" (Corbett 2012), the EU has been resolute in its purpose:

> The main responsibility for delivering reforms in higher education rests with member states and education institutions themselves. However, the Bologna Process, the EU Agenda for the modernisation of universities and the creation of the European Research Area show that the challenges and policy responses transcend national borders (sic).

Selective national responses

Given that the main responsibility for delivering reforms in European higher education rests with member states and education institutions themselves, it is important to examine policy responses at the national level. This section looks at selective national responses in Europe, with a particular focus on France, Germany and the UK – the three largest economies in the European Union. Of these three countries, the UK has always performed best in university rankings (see Table 2). In addition, the QS/THE-QS and ARWU rankings show Germany performing better than France. However, Germany has lost some ground in the ARWU rankings over time. Finally, the UK gained ground in the QS/THE-QS ranking between 2004 and 2012. This is arguably more important than the ground lost in the THE-TR ranking between 2010 and 2012, due to the shorter duration of the THE-TR ranking. Overall, the UK began in the strongest position in the QS/THE-QS ranking in 2004, and has also made the most gains in that ranking.

France

Higher education in France is characterised by the coexistence of two systems: universities, public institutions that have an open admissions policy – and a non-university sector, including, *grandes écoles* which have a highly selective admissions policy open only to baccalaureate holders having attended two years of (selective) classes. The *grandes écoles* are generally focused on a single subject area, such as engineering or business; they are widely regarded as prestigious, and traditionally have produced most of the scientists and executives in France.

Beginning in 2007, the French government began to introduce a series of legislative changes promoting greater institutional autonomy to encourage stronger management and better planning in higher education (Higher Education Development Association 2007).

> Concern over the global positioning of French universities within rankings has been a strong catalyst for soul-searching and change following disappointment with the performance of French universities in the ARWU (Anon 2008).

In 2008, the government launched the €8 billion *Operation Campus*, the objective of which was to establish ten regional centres of excellence by merging universities, research organisations and *grandes écoles* to enhance capacity and visibility (Landry 2010, Marshall 2010). In 2009, the government announced additional funding under the €35 billion *Investments for the Future* programme (also known as the *Big Loan* because the money was raised on the financial markets) which was launched as part of a wider stimulus package to shore up the economy after the global economic crisis.

Table 2.   Number of higher education institutions in the global top 100: France, Germany and the UK in selected rankings, 2004–2012

RANKING	YEAR	FRANCE	GERMANY	UK
QS/THE-QS	2012	2	4	18
	2011	2	4	19
	2008	2	3	17
	2004	3	5	14
THE-TR	2012	4	4	10
	2011	3	4	12
	2010	3	3	14

ARWU	2012	3	4	9
	2011	3	6	9
	2008	3	6	11
	2004	2	7	10
WEBOMETRICS	2012	0	4	4
	2011	0	2	7
	2009	0	2	5
SClmago	2012	5	4	6
	2011	5	3	6
	2009	5	2	6

Key: THE-QS = Times Higher QS World Ranking; QS = Quacquarelli Symonds; ARWU = Academic Ranking of World Universities. W-Metrics = Webometrics.

Note: THE-QS (pre-2011) is combined with QS for 2011 and 2012 as the methodology is broadly similar. THE-TR was only established in 2010 and only provides data on 200 institutions. For 2011 and 2012, THE-TR provides information on 400 institutions.

THE-QS for 2008 only sums to 99 due to tying institutions.

The flagship component of the *Big Loan* was a €7.7 billion *Excellence Initiative* (Idex) with the emphasis on creating a group of 5–10 world-class research and higher education clusters that could rival those elsewhere in Europe and the United States (Davies 2009). A year later, the French government announced plans to spend €4.4 billion to build the Paris-Saclay super-campus – with the intention of this entity achieving a place in the top ten in the world (Landry 2010). At the same time, eight research, teaching and management institutions announced plans to create the €500 million "Giant", the Grenoble Innovation for Advanced New Technologies (Prest 2010): "Our aim is quite simple: we want the best universities in the world".

While most other ministries in France have experienced spending cuts in recent years, the allocation for the higher education sector has risen. For 2013, it is due to receive an additional 2.2 percent over the previous year, totalling nearly €23 billion with priority going to student support and 1,000 new university posts (as the first stage of a five-year plan for 5,000 new posts). Universities will also benefit from increased state financing for building and renovation projects under state-region contracts. Research funding will rise by €90 million to €7.86 billion, 1.2 percent over 2012, and there will be no reduction of the 68,449 public research posts. There will also be a 'rebalancing' of research spending, with more funding allocated to research organisations and less to the Agence Nationale de Recherche whose role of selecting projects from research bids will be limited to fewer themes (Marshal 2012).

The creation of a league of five to ten major universities that would be able to attract the best researchers and students in the world has long been a key target of the French government's science and higher education policy. However, the wave of new investments in French higher education has generated anxiety and criticism; smaller universities worry they may become lower-tier educational and research outposts. As the government has said: "funds will not be distributed evenly but instead will support the government's policy of creating bigger, more autonomous universities that focus on excellence, have modernised governance, and are highly productive" (Enserink 2009a and 2009b).

> We want the best universities in the world [...] How many universities do we have? 83? We're not going to divide the money by 83 (Nicolas Sarkozy, President, France, quoted in Enserink 2009b).

This strategy puts an end to the previous egalitarian tradition in French higher education, with the exception of the *grandes écoles*.

Germany

The results of the ARWU and THE-QS rankings, first published in 2003 and 2004, respectively, challenged the perceived wisdom that German universities were amongst the world's best. The Ministry of Education and Research put the situation in context:

> We have a lot of very good universities across the board in Germany, a high average standard, but what we lack are really top universities [...] The latest ranking table clearly shows why it is that Germany needs top universities (Dufner 2004).

A binary higher education system exists in Germany, with the main division between universities and *Fachhochschulen*. The former offer traditional academic or technological programmes of study while the latter, established in 1970, provide professionally-oriented programmes primarily at the ISCED 5 level (UNESCO 2011). Recently, in response to competitive pressures associated with the Bologna Process, many *Fachhochschulen* have adopted the nomenclature of University of Applied Sciences and offer both BA and MA qualifications.

In 2005, the German government launched the *Exzellenzinitiative* (Initiative for Excellence) in response to the fact that German universities did not appear among the top 20 or 50 in the university rankings (DFG n.d.). The aim of the initiative is to create a German Ivy League, focusing on internationally renowned publications/research activities, in an effort to reclaim Germany's historical leading position in research (Chambers 2007). In the first phase, €1.9 billion was earmarked for three initiatives: graduate schools (maximum €1 million annually), Excellence Clusters (maximum €6.5 million annually), and Institutional Strategic Development funds (maximum €13 million annually). The second phase of the *Exzellenzinitiative* was rolled out in 2012 with €2.7 billion to fund a total of 45 graduate schools, 43 clusters of excellence and 11 future development strategies in 44 universities by 2017.

In 2006, the government launched its *High Technology Strategy* to: (i) focus on climate/energy, health/nutrition, mobility, security and communication; (ii) pursue concrete scientific and technological developments targeting a period of 10 to 15 years; (iii) forge strong links with European research and innovation policy; (iv) improve the conditions for setting up a company and accessing venture capital; and (v) establish new platforms for dialogue on global and societal challenges (Federal Ministry 2006). This was renewed in 2010, with an emphasis on creating lead markets, deepening cooperation between science and business, and improving conditions for innovation.

At the same time, in 2007, the first phase of the *Higher Education Pact* was launched, running until 2010. €565 million of funds was released with the aim of creating larger numbers of highly qualified employees who could help improve the nation's R&D quality. That policy is also in its second phase, scheduled to go on until 2020, with a further €1.7 billion planned to be rolled out up to 2015.

Finally, the figures for 2010 showed that the proportion of expenditure on R&D in Germany was 2.8 percent of GDP – a new record. Nonetheless, the *Expertenkommission Forschung und Innovation* (EFI, or Commission of Expert Research and Development) called for the consistent development of science intensive industries in its 2012 annual report. In the face of increasing competition, including from developing countries, the EFO describes the target set by the government of 3 percent of GDP by 2015 for

R&D expenditure – equivalent to the Lisbon Strategy target – as "lacking ambition".

The initiatives described above mark a significant shift in German higher education policy, from a traditional emphasis on egalitarianism or "having good universities across Germany" towards competition and hierarchical stratification. Instead of the current binary system, the future system is likely to be hierarchically differentiated, with a small elite group, a larger middle group of "solid research universities [...] [with] a slight opportunity to move into the top group" and a larger group comprised of *Fachhochschulen* and some universities primarily providing undergraduate/BA qualifications and some amount of research in selected fields of expertise (Kehm 2006 and 2009, Hazelkorn 2011: 165-172).

United Kingdom

The United Kingdom has traditionally performed better in university rankings than France, Germany or any other European country (see Table 2). Because of this, the emergence of global university rankings was less of a shock although there is a keen desire to perform better, particularly in comparison to the United States.

> UK universities do well. To my surprise, Cambridge and Oxford are in the top 10 in the world. Partly that high ranking stems too much for comfort from data far in the past, so we should not be sanguine. Nevertheless, our nation has 11 universities in the top 100, which puts us second behind the United States (Oswald 2004).

Higher education in the United Kingdom (UK) was significantly reformed and restructured in 1992 by the *Further and Higher Education Act* which enabled polytechnics to become universities, thereby transforming the former binary system into a unified system. At the same time, changes in the governance and management of universities, frequently and pejoratively referred to as 'new public management' have introduced business-type management styles including quantitative performance indicators, consumerist approaches, and market discipline (Randle and Brady 1997, Deem and Brehony 2005).

> The broad philosophical and ideological thrust has been accepted - that the state should not – unless exceptionally – fund universities directly for providing teaching, but that the market, as manifested through student choice, should be the determining driver (Higher Education Policy Institute 2010).

The increasing influence of market thinking in UK higher education is observable in other ways, for example, in the way in which university-based research funding has been allocated under successive research allocation exercises (RAE). The RAE have supported curiosity-driven research and responsive research; this will continue to be the case under the Research Excellence Framework (2014), with increasing emphasis on the recognition of research excellence combined with rewards for the impact of past research. This competitive approach benefits those universities which effectively and strategically manage their research portfolio through targeted investment and recruitment over time.

Despite the highly competitive nature of the higher education system in the UK, there are concerns about maintaining the UK's position in the rankings, particularly in light of the recent gains made by Asian institutions (see Table 1). This disquiet is well illustrated by recent media reaction too, with headlines such as "Declining investment could trigger irreversible loss of British prestige" (Morgan 2012) or "Academic battle with the East looms for British universities" (Middleton 2012).

> We are slipping down the global league tables in terms of the quantity of higher level skills in the labour force and falling even faster on the measure of young people with higher level skills. The international competition will not let up – other countries will keep on capitalising on the benefits of higher education for their economies and citizens and raise the bar on participation and investment (Browne 2010).

The major policy change proposed by the report, *Securing a Sustainable Future for Higher Education* (Browne 2010), and accepted by the government, advocated that universities would no longer be funded directly

> except to a very limited extent – but that universities should instead be funded primarily through fees paid by students, with the Government providing loans to students in order to enable them to pay these fees (Thompson and Bekhradnia 2011: 1).

At the same time, the government has shifted core funding from arts, humanities and social sciences disciplines in favour of science, technology, engineering and mathematics (STEM). Universities are entitled to charge tuition fees up to a maximum of £9,000 per annum, depending upon what the market will bear, but the government will only provide core teaching support for STEM. The government has also introduced incentives for institutions catering to the widening participation students and for high achieving students (known as AAB students).

According to Barr (2012), the reforms

> include the good (a higher fees cap, a higher interest rate on student loans, better information and improved support for part-time study), the bad (abolishing most taxpayer support for teaching in the arts and humanities and the social sciences, and raising excessively the threshold at which loan repayments start) and the unspeakable (abolishing Education Maintenance Allowances and AimHigher).

The changes go further than previous policy decisions by using student-choice/demand to drive competition, transferring costs to students, and reinforcing "the social segregation between groups of institutions, as well as reducing the number of disadvantaged students at the most selective universities" (Thompson and Bekhradnia 2011: 11). This is likely to intensify the hierarchical stratification between institutions (Brown 2012).

Conclusion

This paper argues that the emergence of global university rankings was not only a challenge to the perceived wisdom about the status and reputation of European higher education, but has stimulated significant changes in European higher education policy. While increasing amounts of competitive pressure between countries would probably have led to a 'modernisation' agenda anyway, the onset of global rankings in 2003 accelerated and intensified the development of policy objectives to enhance the global competitiveness and performance of higher education institutions in Europe.

Further, given that the main responsibility for delivering reforms in European higher education rests with member states and education institutions themselves, it is important that policy developments are examined at the national (and EU) level. This paper has followed such an approach, reviewing policy developments in the three largest economies in the European Union: France, Germany and the United Kingdom.

One finding is that the impact of rankings on national-level policy is more apparent in France and Germany than in the UK. This may be attributed to the fact that the UK has always been the highest-ranking country in European comparisons of higher education performances (see Table 2). Therefore, France and Germany have been under relatively more pressure to improve their performance in global rankings; and needed to be more explicit in pursuing their modernisation agendas. Notably, reforms in France have occurred relatively more recently and were arguably more influenced by the global economic crisis (as well as university rankings) than the reforms in Germany.

Reforms in the UK over the last decade have been relatively more focused on issues relating to finance and access, reflecting not only a competitive advantage in university-based research but also the need to deal with higher levels of participation, compared to France and Germany. However, this is changing and recent reforms in the United Kingdom – inspired by the Browne report – are a direct response to concerns about global positioning, with an emphasis on those disciplines and students most likely to impact positively on performance.

At both the EU and national levels, there are many statements applauding the diversity of higher education missions; however, there is also mounting concern about mediocre universities being responsible for Europe's poor showing in global rankings. At a time of severe constraints on public budgets, and an accelerating global higher education 'arms race', national governments are making policy choices which are arguably driven by their current and desired position in university rankings. Across all the countries examined, and particularly in France and Germany, there is a strong emphasis on university reform and 'modernisation', and concentrating resources in a few 'elite' universities.

By stressing the importance of measuring performance and competitiveness, the EU and its member states are indicating that the future will be based upon demonstrated merit rather than assertion. Likely policy implications include greater system differentiation but also institutional stratification and targeted resource allocation, at both the national and European levels. Given the uneven distribution of capability and capacity across and within the EU's 32 member and candidate countries, it is not clear that the full implications for individual institutions and member states are understood. Overall, there is likely to be greater hierarchical differentiation, with an increasing concentration of resources in a handful of institutions and countries.

Finally, it is important to appreciate that new higher education policies do not make an immediate impact on institutional performance in rankings. There will be a lag between the introduction of new policies and any improvement in performance that can be attributed to those policies. Therefore, it is too soon to evaluate whether the recent national policy developments outlined in this paper have made the desired impact on the performance of European countries in the global university rankings. While this will be an interesting issue to investigate in the coming years, now is the time for debate on the apparent influence of global rankings on higher education policy in Europe.

References

Adelman, C. (2009). *The Bologna Process for U.S. Eyes: Re-learning Higher Education in the Age of Convergence.* Washington: IHEP.

Aghion, P., M. Dewatripont, C. Hoxby, A. Mas-Colell, A. Sapir (2007). "Why Reform Europe's Universities?" *Bruegel Policy Brief.* No. 4. September 2007. Brussels: Bruegel.

Anon (2008). "Under threat of change. Slowly but Surely, Universities in France – and Across All of Europe – Are Reforming". *The Economist.* 7 June 2008.

ATN – Australia Technology Network (n.d.). "The Bologna Process and Australia: Next Steps. Response from the Australian Technology Network". Available at http://www.atn.edu.au/docs/ATN%20submission%20to%20the%20Bologna%20Proce ss%20discussion%20paper.pdf (accessed 2 November 2012).

Barr, N. (2012). "The Higher Education White Paper: The Good, the Bad, the Unspeakable - and the Next White Paper". *Social Policy & Administration.* Vol. 46. No. 5. 483-508.

Brown, R. (2012). "Figures Reveal Deep Inequalities between Rich and Poor Universities". *The Guardian.* 24 September 2012.

Browne – Lord Browne of Madingley (2010). *Securing a Sustainable Future for Higher Education. An Independent Review of Higher Education Funding and Student Finance.* London: Department of Business, Innovation and Skills.

Butler, N. (2007). "Europe's Universities – Time for Reform". *Centrepiece* 10-11. Available at http://cep.lse.ac.uk/pubs/download/cp233.pdf (accessed 29 August 2011).

Chambers, M. (2007). "Germany Aims to Rebuild Research Strength". *International Herald Tribune.* November 22. Available at http://www.iht.com/articles/2007/11/22/business/ gbrain.php (accessed 19 April 2008).

Corbett, A. (2012). "Competing Leadership for Reform of Higher Education in Europe". Dubrovnik: Global Forum, STREW Project.

Dale, R. (2010). "Constructing Universities' Responses to Europe's Lisbon Agenda: The Roles of the European Commission in Creating the Europe of Knowledge". *Research paper 19.* Centre for Learning and Life Chances in Knowledge Economies and Societies, Institute of Education, London.

Davies, L. (2009). "Sarkozy Unveils €35bn 'Big Loan' Boost for French Universities and Museums". *The Guardian.* 14 December 2009. Available at http://www.guardian.co.uk/ world/2009/dec/14/spending-boost-for-french-universities (accessed 28 May 2010).

Deem, R., K. Brehony (2005). "Management as Ideology: The Case of 'New Managerialism'". *Oxford Review of Education.* Vol. 31. No. 2. 217-235.

Dempsey, N., Irish Minister for Education and Science (2004). Address at the Europe of Knowledge 2020 Conference, 24 April. Liege, Belgium: Europe of Knowledge 2020 Conference.

DFG – Deutsche Forschungsgeimschaft (n.d.). "Excellence Initiative". Available at http://www.dfg.de/en/research_funding/programmes/excellence_initiative/index.html (accessed 2 November 2012).

Dufner, B. (2004). "Educating the Elite". *Ministry of Education and Research, DW-World.* November 12, 2004. Available at http://www.dwworld.de/dw/article/ 0,,1393321,00.html (accessed 2 November 2012).

Enserink, M. (2009a). "Research Set to Win Big in France's Stimulus Plan". *Science Insider.* November 20, 2009. Available at http://news.sciencemag.org/scienceinsider/ 2009/11/research-set-to.html (accessed 2 November 2012).

Enserink, M. (2009b). "Sarkozy to French Universities: We're Going to Invest Massively". *Science Insider.* 9 December 2009. Available at http://news.sciencemag.org/ scienceinsider/2009/12/sarkozy-to-fren.html (accessed 2 November 2012).

EurActiv (2010). "Barroso Casts Europe as 'Innovation Union'". *EurActiv*, March 2. Available at http://www.euractiv.com/innovation-enterprise/barroso-casts-europe-innovation-news-299416 (accessed 2 November 2012).

European Commission (2001). *Communication from the Commission to the European Parliament and the Council on Strengthening Cooperation with Third Countries in the Field of Higher Education.* Brussels: European Commission.

European Commission (2003). *The Role of the Universities in the Europe of Knowledge. Communication to the Council and the European Parliament.* Brussels: European Commission.

European Commission (2006). *Delivering on the Modernisation Agenda for Universities: Education, Research and Innovation. Communication to the Council and the European Parliament.* Brussels: European Commission.

European Commission (2007). *Council Resolution on Modernising Universities for Europe's Competitiveness in a Global Knowledge Economy.* Brussels: European Commission.

European Commission (2010). *Europe 2020 Flagship Initiative. Innovation Union. Communication from the Commission to the European Parliament, the Council, the European Economic and Social Committee and the Committee of the Regions.* Brussels: European Commission.

European Commission (2011). *Supporting Growth and Jobs – an Agenda for the Modernisation of Europe's Higher Education Systems. Communication from the Commission to the European Parliament, The Council, The European Economic and Social Committee and the Committee of the Regions.* Brussels: European Commission.

Federal Ministry for Education and Research (2006). *The High-Tech Strategy for Germany.* Berlin: Bundesministerium für Bildung und Forschung/Federal Ministry of Education and Research (BMBF).

Gornitzka, Å. (2005). *Coordinating Policies for a 'Europe of Knowledge'. Emerging Practices of the 'Open Method of Coordination' in Education and Research.* Oslo: Centre for European Studies, University of Oslo, Norway.

Grabert, M. (2011). *Answering the Global Challenge – Experiences from European Excellence Initiatives.* Canberra, Australia: Group of Eight Universities.

Hazelkorn, E. (2011). *Rankings and the Reshaping of Higher Education: The Battle for World Class Excellence.* Basingstoke: Palgrave Macmillan.

Higher Education Development Association (2007). "French Government Grants Autonomy to Higher Education Institutions". Available at http://uv-net.uio.no/wpmu/hedda/2007/08/04/french-government-grants-autonomy-to-higher-education-institutions/ (accessed 2 November 2012).

Higher Education Policy Institute (2010). *HEPI Publishes Response to the Government's Proposals for Higher Education Funding.* Oxford: Higher Education Policy Institute.

Kehm, B. M. (2006). "The German Initiative for Excellence". *International Higher Education.* Vol. 44. Summer 2006. 20-22.

Kehm, B. M. (2009). "Germany: The Quest for World-Class Universities". *International Higher Education.* Vol. 57. Fall 2009. 18-21.

Lambert, R., N. Butler (2006) *Future of European Universities. Renaissance or Decay?* London: Centre for European Reform. Available at http://www.cer.org.uk/pdf/p_67x_universities_decay_3.pdf (accessed 2 November 2012).

Landry, C. (2010). "French Super-University Wants to be Among the Top 10". *Yahoo News.* May 4. Available at http://news.yahoo.com/s/afp/20100504/lf_afp/francepoliticseducation_20100504074528 (accessed 26 May 2010).

Lisbon European Council (2000). *Presidency Conclusions, March 23 and 24.* Brussels: European Commission.

Maassen, P., B. Stensaker (2011). "The Knowledge Triangle, European Higher Education Policy Logics and Policy Implications". *Higher Education.* Vol. 61. No. 6. 757-769.

Marshal, J. (2012). "More Funding for Higher Education, Priority for Students in Austerity Budget". *University World News.* 4 October 2012. Available at http://www.universityworldnews.com/article.php?story=20121004113619623 (accessed 26 October 2012).

Marshall, J. (2010). "How Sarkozy is Forcing Reform on a Reluctant Establishment". *The Independent.* July 1. Available at http://www.independent.co.uk/news/education/schools/how-sarkozy-is-forcing-reform-on-a-reluctantestablishment-2014821.html (accessed 1 July 2010).

Middleton, C. (2012). "Academic Battle with the East Looms for British Universities". *The Telegraph.* 16 October 2012.

Morgan, J. (2012). "Declining Investment Could Trigger Irreversible Loss of British Prestige". *Times Higher Education.* 18 October 2012.

Myklebust, J. P. (2012). "ERC Defends Concentration of Grants in Top Research Universities". *World University News.* Available at http://www.universityworldnews.com/article.php?story=20120308181711918 (accessed 1 July 2010).

NSF (2010). National Science Foundation (US): Science and Engineering Indicators. Available at http://www.nsf.gov/statistics/seind10/c4/c4h.htm (accessed 1 July 2010)

OECD (2012). *Science and Technology Indicators.* Paris: OECD.

Oswald, A. (2004). "How Should We React to World University League Tables?" *The Independent*. October 2004. Available at http://www2.warwick.ac.uk/fac/soc/economics/staff/academic/oswald/worldunis04.pdf (accessed 2 November 2012).

Prest, M. (2010). "A Technological Powerhouse to Rival MIT and Oxbridge; The French are Waking the Sleeping Giant". *The Independent*. 19 January 2010. Available at http://www.independent.co.uk/student/postgraduate/mbas-guide/a-technological-powerhouse-to-rival-mit-and-oxbridge-1880852.html (accessed 5 May 2010).

Randle, K., N. Brady (1997). "Further Education and the New Managerialism". *Journal of Further and Higher Education*. Vol. 21. No. 2. 229-239

Rauhvargers, A. (2011). *Global University Rankings and Their Impact*. Brussels: European University Association.

Ritzen, J. (2010). *A Chance for European Universities*. Amsterdam: Amsterdam University Press.

Thompson, J., B. Bekhradnia (2011). *Higher Education: Students at the Heart of the System – an Analysis of the Higher Education White Paper*. Oxford: Higher Education Policy Research Institute.

UNESCO (2011). *Revision of the International Standard Classification of Education* (ISCED). Paris: UNESCO.

Van Vught, F. A., ed. (2009). *Mapping the Higher Education Landscape. Towards a European Classification of Higher Education*. Dordrecht: Springer.

Van Vught, F. A., F. Kaiser, J.M. File, C. Gaethgens, R. Peter, D.F. Westerheijden (2010). *U-Map. The European Classification of Higher Education Institutions*. Enschede: Centre for Higher Education Policy Studies.

Van Vught, F. A., F. Ziegele, eds. (2012). *Multidimensional Ranking. The Design and Development of U-Multirank*. Dordrecht: Springer.

Diversification in Austrian Higher Education: A Result of European or National Policies?

Elsa Hackl

Abstract

The need to diversify European higher education has been a constant concern of European policy makers at the supranational and intergovernmental level. This chapter discusses the concepts of differentiation and diversification and relevant developments in European higher education. Regarding the case of Austria, it deals with the questions of whether and how policies on the European level have influenced its differentiation and diversification policies. Traditionally, in Austria higher education institutions have enjoyed the same status and their courses and degrees have been regarded as being equivalent. In the late 1980s/early 1990s this began to change and in the late 1990s/early 2000s further reforms in order to diversify higher education took place. Did policies at the European level cause or enhance the differentiation and diversification? Or was the start of differentiating and diversifying higher education in Austria and its accession to the European Union just a coincidence in time?

Key words: differentiation in higher education, diversity in higher education, Europeanisation, higher education reforms in Austria

Introduction

For more than a decade the need to diversify European higher education has been one of the persistent topics of European policy makers on the intergovernmental and supranational level (e.g. Prague Communiqué 2001, Commission of the European Communities 2006). This chapter deals with the questions of whether and how policies at European level influenced Austria's differentiation and diversification policies. Starting by discussing the concepts of differentiation and diversification and their effects on European higher education, it traces the transformation of the Austrian higher education system from a uniform system to a more diverse one: First, it looks at the period when a uniform higher education system was fully realised; subsequently, it concentrates on three distinct moves towards differentiation and diversification which took place in the late 1980s/early 1990s and the late 1990s/early 2000s. Finally, some conclusions on the impact of European policies on Austria's diversification measures are drawn.

The terms Europeanisation or European policies are generally used to indicate the impact on the national level of the European Union as well as that of the 'broader Europe', of supranational as well as well intergovernmental bodies. However, these terms will be specified when dealing with individual Austrian policy decisions.

Differentiation and diversification in higher education

Immanuel Kant was probably one of the first to address the issues of differentiation in the context of higher education. In his "Conflict of the faculties" published in 1798 and in essays written earlier, Kant informs us about the different and diverse faculties of the university in his time and previously. The "higher faculties" – theology, law and medicine – stood out due to the fact that their teaching and research (or scholarship) were in the immediate interest of the government. The "lower faculty" – philosophy – had no such close alliance to the government; on the contrary, it tended to challenge the existing order. Hence, its reduction to a mere auxiliary function for the "higher faculties" was in the interest of both the latter and the government.

Thereafter, many authors have addressed differentiation and diversification in higher education. Other dimensions have been discussed, e.g. levels of studies, types of institutions and individual institutions (Huisman 2009). Over the last 40 years, the focus has shifted to the differences between individual institutions. They are usually the basis for the league tables or rankings that are today flourishing. Occasionally, differentiation and diversification are used as interchangeable concepts. Some authors have engaged in a conceptual clarification by underlining that "differentiation denotes a dynamic process, diversity refers to a static situation" (Van Vught 2007; also see Bienefeld 2007); however, "diversification" denotes a process as well (UNESCO 2004). One might ask whether differentiation – a term first used when binary systems evolved, and diversification which is to lead to diversity – address different visions of or stages in higher education policy.

Differentiation became a major concern for higher education policy when higher education systems in most European countries massively expanded from the 1960s onwards. Comparative studies as well as studies on higher education in the United States (Trow 1979, Birnbaum 1983) suggest that differentiation or diversification were needed to reconcile elite and mass higher education (Scott 1995). As the OECD pointed out (1971, 1973 and 1991), notably European countries started to establish short study programmes and a second type of higher education institutions in addition to universities in order to facilitate the enrolment growth and to adapt to the needs of the employment system. While universities were expected to remain 'academic', i.e. relatively detached from real life, by contrast the new institutions (Polytechnics, "*Fachhochschulen*" etc.) were to provide vocationally-oriented programmes, in geographical proximity to the students, and at cheaper costs for governments (OECD 2005). As a rule, the new institutions were less prestigious than universities, even though they were claimed to be equivalent in some countries (e.g. in Germany: "gleichwertig, aber nicht gleichartig" – "on an equal footing but not of an equal kind"). Yet within quite a short period the distinction between the two types was challenged in two respects. On one hand, the non-university institutions tended to imitate universities – a process called "academic drift" (Burgess and Pratt 1974, Neave 1979). On the other hand, a "vocational drift" (Pratt 1997) emerged at universities wishing to serve economic rationales (see Meyer and Schofer 2007, Regini 2011, Bertrams 2007). Actually, the binary system was abolished in the UK in the 1990s but persisted in other European countries. Due to policies in favour of the "harmonisation of the architecture of the European higher education system" (Sorbonne Declaration 1998), the differences between the two sectors became smaller (de Lourdes Machado et al. 2008).

The erosion of sectoral differentiation was accompanied by policies of diversification. New Public Management (NPM) spread along with the neoliberal assumption that market regulation was preferable and that diverse institutional profiles and missions would serve well both the diversity of students and the demand of the economy. Concurrently, increased competition between institutions was expected to bring about greater efficiency in research. While governments tended to differentiate between institutional types, a diversification between individual institution and their stratification would be the typical results of market mechanisms.

This new discourse of diversity fit well with that of the European Higher Education Area where universities were to (inter)act without much interference by their national governments. On the intergovernmental level, in the course of the Bologna Process, a gradual shift in the meaning of "diversity" emerged. While traditionally "diversity in European higher education" was pointed out by European politicians with respect to the richness of diverse cultures, languages and education systems, the Prague Communiqué of 2001 suggested increasing the international attractiveness and competitiveness of higher education in Europe as a "Higher Education Area with institutions and programmes with different profiles". The European Commission pointed out that only "some 50 of the US research universities account for the lion's share of American academic research capacity", and noted a "trend towards greater differentiation" in Europe as well (Communication from Commission 2003: 6).

Kant already showed that differentiation in higher education – as in any other field of society – goes hand in hand with a hierarchical order. Governments may – and do so in some fields – take action in order to prevent or diminish discriminations that result from differences in society, but this has rarely been the case in higher education. At the height of the nation-states, disciplines that supported their formation and stability ranked on top; in times of globalisation globally competitive institutions excel as well as well as more or less universalist disciplines and abstract studies (Frank and Mayer 2007). While 'horizontal' (functional) differentiation was more strongly emphasised when a non-university sector was established in many European countries, the neoliberal belief in market regulation favours 'vertical' (hierarchical) differentiation in higher education (Teichler 2007, Brennan et al. 2009). This entails a vision of a hierarchy of institutions, reaching from "world-renowned research institutions" to "colleges which also provide shorter technical education" is also emphasised by the European Commission (2006).

Country studies on the impact of differentiation or diversification show that social selectivity persists in the wake of the expansion of higher education and that the higher tier sectors or institutions have remained socially selective (Higher Education 2011). This has raised concern in Europe: Will diversification exacerbate European disparities? Will higher education systems without highly ranked universities deteriorate, and will national cleavages grow? Will 'the richness of diverse cultures, languages and education systems' – the crucial value of European education – fade away? Will there also be in Europe a clear divide between top or globally competitive universities on one hand and institutions on the other hand that serve regional needs (Vincent-Lancrin 2004, OECD 2008)?

The following sections trace the development towards diversity in Austrian higher education in recent years. They address the characteristics of national and European policies in this respect and will examine the extent to which diversity is actually growing.

The case of Austria

Codifying and homogenising Austrian higher education

Traditionally, Austrian education has been marked by three characteristics. First, there was a clear divide between *"Bildung"* (education) and *"Ausbildung"* (vocational education and training). Secondly, pupils were divided according to educational tracks at the age of ten. Third, universities were expected to serve *"Bildung"* or at most to lay the foundations for professional training, while those taking over technical and middle-level management positions underwent vocational training lasting at most one year longer than schooling up to entry to universities.

At the beginning of the 1960s when demand for higher education grew and the role of highly skilled labour in economic development and innovation was emphasised, the higher education system in Austria responded by establishing new universities (Salzburg 1962, Linz 1966 and Klagenfurt 1970). In 1966, the new Act on University Studies aimed at broadening the range of study programmes, to safeguard quality, and to assure the similarity of the substance of courses within the same fields and levels of programmes. The Act listed new programmes, clearly differentiated between the level of *"Diplom"* and Magister on one hand and that of the Doctorate on the other hand. Subsequently, specifications were made regarding the content of programmes, the number of individual courses to be taken etc. Similarly, the Act on Studies at Art and Music Academies was to provide a new legal basis for the courses at these institutions.

About a decade later, in the University Organisation Act of 1975, the codification of the organisation of universities followed. It aimed at harmonising the organisation and management of universities and democratising decision-making in universities through co-determination. Through this legislation, the six specialised universities that were founded in the 19th century (Universities of Engineering and Technology in Vienna and Graz, University of Petrol Engineering and Mining in Leoben, University of Agriculture and Forestry in Vienna, University of Veterinary Medicine in Vienna, University of Economics in Vienna) were eventually put on an equal footing with the then six multi-disciplinary universities (Vienna, Graz, Innsbruck, Salzburg, Linz, Klagenfurt). Thus, all universities – with the exception of the academies/colleges of art and music –were subject to the same legal regulations, funding regime, and their employees enjoyed the same status. However, they remained federal institutions without a legal personality, their staff were civil servants or public employees, and funding remained item-based. Government remained strong, and university teachers enjoyed academic freedom guaranteed by constitutional legislation, while 'institutional autonomy' remained feeble.

The university legislation continued to be criticised notably by university professors as being characterised by over-regulation, red tape, and by curtailing legitimate self-determination. Junior staff and students voiced criticism that university funding fell short of the growth of enrolments, representatives of the economy argued that study programmes were long and did not meet the demands of the labour market, and the proportion of drop-outs was too high. By the end of the 1980s, the critique from inside academia that self-determination was lacking merged with advocacy of NPM, according to which deregulation would lead to greater efficiency. Both positions called for greater 'institutional autonomy'.

Steps towards diversification

A first step towards diversification was taken in the early 1990s. By the end of the 1980s, higher education reforms had reappeared more prominently on the political agenda. After the election of 1990, the coalition partners, i.e. the Social Democrats and Conservatives, issued a coalition agreement (Bundespressedienst 1990: 63 and 67) calling for various measures. As regards a new higher education sector: *"The adaptation of vocational education to European standards (making degrees conform with the EU) requires the establishment of 'Fachakademien' that supplement and relieve universities; 'Fachakademien' should serve as centres for training and continuing education in a variety of occupational fields. They should be open to graduates of upper secondary schools and graduates of the dual system (given the appropriate qualification)"*. As regards university reform: *"The establishment of a business-like university organisation which entails more quality, efficiency and cost transparency [...] the relocation of decision-making from the ministry to the universities [...] the setting of priorities in research and teaching* [...]. *The study reform is to modernise courses with the aim of* [...] *EC conformity"*.

At that time, Austria was preparing for accession to the European Union. Therefore, it is not surprising that the coalition parties referred to the EU also concerning their targets for education policy. But was there really an obligation to adapt Austria's higher education to the EU conformity, or was the EU accession simply used to legitimise certain national reform initiatives?

Proposals to *establish a second sector* beside the universities date back to 1970. Since the 1960s, various European countries, as already pointed out, have established a non-university sector in order to accommodate the growing number of students. Such plans were put forward in Austria as well, but did not gain the support of the major stakeholders. Actually, only a few fields – notably teacher training for compulsory schools, social work and paramedical professions – were transferred at that time to the post-secondary level yet without being formally integrated into the university sector and without similar degrees (Pechar 2004). In subsequent years, upper-secondary vocational schools expanded; industry underscored the strengths of these institutions not awarding higher education degrees. When Austria was to enter the European Union, the value of these certificates on the European labour market became an issue. Even though the value of the certificates in the Austrian labour market was viewed as being equal to that of the *"Fachhochschule"* degrees in the German labour market, it was evident that the Austrian certificates are not covered by Directive 89/48/EEC. This "Directive of 21 December 1988 on a general system for the recognition of higher-education diplomas awarded on completion of professional education and training of at least three years' duration" was at that time the most recent of a number of directives based on Articles 49, 57 (1) and 66 EEC for the mutual recognition of diplomas and certificates in order to enhance the movement of persons and establishment. Therefore, 'the adaption of vocational education to European standards' was announced in the coalition agreement, and a respective law was passed in 1993 by the Parliament. It provided for the establishment of *"Fachhochschulen"* (the name *"Fachakademien"* of the coalition agreement was dropped in favour of term already used in Germany); in 1994, the first courses of the new sector started.

The new sector abolished the monopoly of the federal state to establish and run higher education institutions by allowing private establishments as well. A special accreditation and evaluation agency was set up in order to guarantee standards and secure the quality of this sector. Fixed public subsidies per study place were made available. The governance and funding model of this sector reflected the NPM approach that spread at that time in Austrian public policy and was viewed as being compatible with the European Union's economic and monetary policy. Altogether, budget constraints were justified by the government at that time as necessary in order to conform to the 'Maastricht criteria' and to reduce national debt; as a consequence, public properties were sold and services outsourced.

Today, the establishment of the second sector of higher education that encompasses 21 institutions is predominantly viewed as a success. It accommodates about one-quarter of new entrants to higher education (academic year 2011/12, Bmwf, uni:data). Actually, a higher proportion of students at "*Fachhochschulen*" then at universities are from less privileged social strata and are beneficiaries of needs-based scholarships (Ungar 2009 and 2011). According to a recent expert report on the future development of higher education in Austria, the number of students at "*Fachhochschulen*" should increase significantly in the near future (Loprieno et al. 2011).

Over the years, the difference between the university and non-university sectors seems to be becoming less pronounced. Notably, as in other countries, there has been a "vocational drift" of universities. In the mid-1990s, universities were required by law to state an 'employment profile' of their graduates. Some years later, Austria changed its traditional study and degree structure in the wake of the Bologna Process, and "employability" became an imperative for initial degree courses. In 2011, organisational differences were reduced through the Bill on Quality Assessment in Higher Education (*Hochschul-Qualitätssicherungsgesetz* – HS-QSG), according to which a single agency is in charge of all higher education.

Measures for *university reform* were strongly inspired by the need to reduce costs and the assumption that efficiency gains could be achieved through business-like organisation and decentralisation. In fact, the changes envisaged in the 1993 Act on University Organisation were less salient than some of the actors had hoped. The new law strengthened the position of the rector and limited the role of the decision-making committees that represented all groups in a university. Universities remained federal state institutions with a limited legal capacity but got a greater say as regards the redeployment of posts and funds.

It is difficult to establish what the coalition partners of 1990 meant by *EC conformity* as one of the aims of an envisaged modernisation of university courses. Obviously, the Directive 89/48/EEC did not play a role because the official length of study programmes was not changed in the subsequent amendments of the Act on University Studies in Austria. Rather, the 'coalition agreement' and the subsequent 'coalition agreements' of 1994 and 1996 called for a reduction of the actual study duration which exceeded the required length substantially and they have therefore been a key issue in public debates on higher education already for a long time.

A second step was taken in the late 1990s. Based on the 'coalition agreement' of 1996, the Austrian government took further steps towards the liberalisation of higher education and provided room for setting up private and foreign universities in Austria. The respective bill was passed in 1999. Today, there are 13 private universities with a small range of disciplines and altogether only 7,000 students (Winter term 2011, BMWF: uni:data). Although the sector is small, it represents a further step towards diversification in terms of organisation, funding and course content. The institutions are private law entities. They do not receive federal funds, except for public funds from the "*Länder*" (provinces); the above mentioned expert report suggests transforming these institutions into "*Länder*" institutions in order to increase the transparency of funding streams (Loprieno et al. 2011). The private institutions charge tuition fees, while the issue of tuition fees at universities and "*Fachhochschulen*" is not legally regulated. Some study programmes at the private institutions are similar to those at public universities or "*Fachhochschulen*", while others are established in fields not offered by institutions (e.g. peace studies).

While introducing competition in higher education (one may, of course, muse about whether the underlying idea is indeed more governance by *divide et impera*) may have only been an implicit aim of policy makers in the 1990s who established "*Fachhochschulen*" and private universities, the government that came into power in 2000 explicitly declared in its programme the aim of reinforcing competition between universities (Bundeskanzleramt 2000: 64). The programme called for the transformation of universities into separate legal entities entering into performance contracts with the government. It also envisaged the establishment of courses at *Fachhochschulen* that were funded fully by tuition fees.

The Universitätsgesetz 2002 aimed at granting universities comprehensive 'institutional autonomy' – or, in the language of NPM, at outsourcing. The universities became legal entities of public law; they are now the employers of their personnel and they are to define their internal organisational structure within the framework of the Act. Managerial power rests with the rectorate (a rector and up to four vice-rectors), and the senate is responsible for academic affairs ('habilitation', the nomination of candidates for appointments as professors and as a rector as well as the approval of curricula). The Act provides for a university council composed of external members that are nominated by the government and the senate to function as a governing body and to elect the rector.

Performance contracts are the major means of government steering and funding. Since 2006, the rectors and the Federal Ministry for Science and Research have negotiated and entered into such contracts for a two-year period. Today, according to a recent autonomy scorecard (EUA 2011) Austrian universities rank among the 26 European countries included in the study as medium to highly autonomous institutions.

Through detachment from the federal administration and legal autonomy the universities ought to be provided sufficient scope of action and entrepreneurship. The stronger power of the central university management as compared to government on one hand and on the other compared to the departments should stimulate competition for funds, status and prestige among universities. The Universities Act 2002 envisaged the profiling of universities and them concentration on their strengths in order to reinforce their competitiveness on the international level in the years to come (Sebök 2002: 57). The then minister for higher education described the new law as a means to transform Austrian universities into world-class universities – an aim that today remains far from being realised according to international rankings. It seems doubtful whether the Universities Act can successfully reinforce competition among the Austrian universities because of the enormous heterogeneity in size: Vienna University has 87,668 students, almost one-third of all students, compared to the University of Arts in Linz with 1,258 students (Winter term 2010, BMWF: uni:data) and in subject areas (comprehensive and universities with limited ranges of areas) makes competition quite unlikely. Moreover, constraints on the federal budget seem to offer little room to strengthen institutions' competitiveness, even though tightened up support for research has increased the competition for research funds. However, this might contribute to institutional disintegration rather than to strategic competition.

The Universities Act 2002 also called for the realisation of the key action lines of the Bologna Process. By 2007, already more than 90 percent of all study programmes were in line with the new structural regime, i.e. notably bachelor and master programmes.

As a third step, measures were eventually discussed and taken to diversify the system in order to strengthen excellence within higher education. Doubts grew that strengthening entrepreneurship and competitiveness as such, as underscored by the Universities Act 2002, would be enough to enhance quality in higher education. In March 2001, the Federal Chancellor and the Minister of Finance invited a group of well-known scholars and scientists to discuss how best to promote elites. At this meeting, a prominent Austrian physicist (Anton Zeilinger, professor at the University of Technology Vienna) launched the idea of an elite university which he had already put forward a year before at the Alpach Technology Symposium. His idea of a "University of Excellence" was eventually taken up two years later by politicians, when the concept of research as a major promoter of innovation and economic growth spread both across Austria and Europe and when the Massachusetts Institute of Technology in Boston was widely viewed as a model. Many European governments announced the creation of so-called flagship institutes for research and doctoral or other initiatives to strengthen a sector of excellence such as, for example, the German "*Exzellenziniative*" (Bienefeld 2007, Huisman 2009). In 2005, the President of the European Commission proposed establishing a European Institute of Innovation and Technology (EIT) as a means of pursuing the Lisbon Strategy of enhancing the European Union's research and innovation capacity. In 2007, the creation of the EIT was approved by the Council of Ministers and a year later the Institute was established. Austria was among the bidders for the site of the EIT's headquarters which were ultimately established in Budapest.

In Austria, following controversies between federal and regional politicians as well as among scholars, the proposal to set up a 'University of Excellence' was eventually downscaled when the Austrian Parliament passed a related bill in 2006: Accordingly, the renamed "Institute of Science and Technology – Austria" (IST Austria) was established jointly by the Austrian federal government and the provincial government of Lower Austria in 2009. It is a doctorate-granting institution located in a small town close to Vienna. The Institute is dedicated to research in the natural and mathematical sciences. According to its first evaluation report (IST Austria

2011), it has succeeded in becoming a noteworthy institution for research at the interface of computer science, neurobiology, molecular and cellular biology and is "on the track to excellence", whereby continued government support is viewed as indispensable.

Conclusion: Has European policy promoted differentiation and diversification in Austrian higher education?

The first major step towards the differentiation of higher education in Austria might be called *differentiation for practice relevance*: the establishment of a second sector of higher education – *"Fachhochschulen"* – with a strong vocational emphasis. This step can be attributed to Directive 89/48 EEC and Austria's accession to the European Union. In contrast to various other European countries, Austria had not undertaken such an upgrading of education and training for technical and middle management positions in the late 1960s or early 1970s. Yet when Austria applied for EU accession representatives of graduates and staff from the respective institutions as well as industry feared competitive disadvantages. The government felt under pressure, but it could have opted for other solutions given the fact that Britain concurrently abolished its binary system and upgraded polytechnics to universities. But the option chosen in Austria reflected the critique on the long actual duration of study at universities and the universities' disregard of demands from industry and the economy. Austria's accession was taken as a window of opportunity for those who had pressed for reforms. Moreover, the government's concerns about the exploding costs of higher education were reinforced by the intention to meet the Maastricht criteria; in this way, European issues influenced the decisions in Austria as regards the governance and funding of the new sector of higher education.

The second major step might be called *diversification for competitiveness*. The 2002 university reforms, among other things, were inspired by the desire to ensure efficiency savings in the public sector. In addition, NPM – the idea that competition entails not only a reduction of costs but also an increase in quality – was linked to a changing understanding of what constitutes 'publicness' (Newman and Clarke 2009) and public responsibility (Hackl 2012). This can hardly be attributed to the influences of European Union policy, but to the widespread international discourse.

The third major step might be called *diversification for excellence*. Like with the second step, it is based on the assumption that internationally competitive universities are needed for economic success. But the conviction faded that competition among universities would be a sufficient driver for change. Instead, the establishment of the Institute of Science and Technology-Austria reflects a view that interventions in favour of excellent universities are needed. This change in the competition paradigm is also embodied in the decision within the framework of the Lisbon Strategy to establish the European Institute of Innovation and Technology and in various initiatives to foster excellence in other European Union member states. These initiatives were taken within a short period across European countries, and these ideas spread without much promulgation from the supranational level, e.g. initiatives of the EU.

In sum, the impact of the EU was visible about 20 years ago when Austria applied for EU membership. Later, ideas of university reforms were similar on the national and supranational level. The policies of individual countries and intergovernmental policies of the various European countries matched the opinions held by the European Commission without any clear influence from either side. Across Europe, the diversity of the higher education system characterised by autonomous institutions, competitiveness and flagship institutions became the target of higher education reforms, whereby much less was implemented than initially envisaged.

References

Bertrams, K. (2007). "From Managerial to Entrepreneurial: Universities and the Appropriation of Corporate-based Paradigms. An Historical Perspective from Europe and the United States". In: G. Krücken et al. (eds.), *Towards a Multiversity. Universities between Global Trends and National Traditions*. Bielefeld: Transcript Verlag. 179-200.

Bienefeld, St. (2007). "The Differentiation of German Higher Education and the Specific Impact of the 'Exzellenzinitative' – Preliminary Results and Possible Future Scenarios". Available at http://www.oecd.org/site/eduhe30/41886891.pdf (accessed 10 September 2012).

Birnbaum, R. (1983). *Maintaining Diversity in Higher Education*. San Francisco: Jossey Bass.

Brennan, J. et al. (2009). "Quality, Equity and the Social Dimension: The Shift from the National to the European Level". In: B. M. Kehm, J. Huisman, B. Stensaker (eds.),

The European Higher Education Area: Perspectives on a Moving Target. Rotterdam: Sense. 141-161.

Bmwf, uni:data. Available at http://eportal.bmbwk.gv.at/portal/page?_pageid=93,95229& _dad=portal&_schema=PORTAL& (accessed 10 September 2012).

Bundeskanzleramt (2000). *Zukunft im Herzen Europas: Österreich neu regieren* [Future in the heart of Europe: a new version of governing Austria]. Wien: Bundespressedienst.

Bundespressedienst (1990). Arbeitsübereinkommen zwischen der Sozialistischen Partei Österreichs und der Österreichischen Volkspartei über die Bildung einer gemeinsamen Bundesregierung für die Dauer der XVIII. Gesetzgebungsperiode des Nationalrates. [Working agreement of the Austrian Socialist Party and the Austrian People Party on the establishment of a coalition government for the XVIII. Legislative Period].

Burgess, T., J. Pratt (1974). *Polytechnics: A Report.* London: Pitman.

Commission of the European Communities (2003). "Communication from Commission. The Role of the Universities in the Europe of Knowledge". COM (2003) 58 final. Available at http://eur-lex.europa.eu/LexUriServ/LexUriServ.do?uri=COM:2003: 0058:FIN:en:pdf (accessed 10 September 2012).

Commission of the European Communities (2006). "Communication from the Commission to the Council and the European Parliament – Delivering on the Modernisation Agenda for Universities – Education, Research and Innovation". COM (2006) 0208 final. Available at http://eur-lex.europa.eu/LexUriServ/LexUriServ.do?uri=COM: 2006:0208:FIN:EN:PDF (accessed 10 September 2012).

De Lourdes Machado, M. et al. (2008). "Reframing the Non-University Sector in Europe: Convergence or Diversity?" In: J. S. Taylor, J. Brites Ferreira, M. de Lourdes Machado, R. Santiago (eds.), *Non-University Higher Education in Europe.* New York: Springer.

Directive 89/48/EEC. Available at http://eur-lex.europa.eu/LexUriServ/LexUriServ.do? uri=CELEX:31989L0048:EN:HTML (accessed 10 September 2012).

EUA (2011). *University Autonomy in Europe II.* Available athttp://www.eua.be/Libraries/ Publications/University_Autonomy_in_Europe_II_-_The_Scorecard.sflb.ashx (accessed 10 September 2012).

Frank, D. J., J. W. Mayer (2007). "Worldwide Expansion and Change in the University". In: G. Krücken et al. (eds.), *Towards a Multiversity. Universities between Global Trends and National Traditions.* Bielefeld: Transcript Verlag. 19-44.

Hochschul-Qualitätssicherungsgesetz – HS-QSG. Bundesgesetz über die externe Qualitätssicherung im Hochschulwesen und die Agentur für Qualitätssicherung und Akkreditierung Austria, BGBl.I Nr.74/2011 [Act on Quality Assessment in Higher Education]. Available at www.ris.bka.gv.at (accessed 10 September 2012).

Hackl, E. (2012). "Reconceptualizing Public Responsibility and Public Good in the European Higher Education Area". In: H. Schütze, G. Alvarez Mendiola (eds.), *State and Market in Higher Education Reforms.* Rotterdam: Sense. 115-127.

Higher Education (2011). Vol. 61. No. 3. DOI 10.1007/s10734-010-9373-z.

Huisman, J. (2009). "The Bologna Process towards 2020: Institutional Diversification or Convergence?" In: B. Kehm, J. Huisman, B. Stensaker (eds.), *The European Higher Education Area: Perspectives on a Moving Target.* Rotterdam: Sense, 2009. 245-262.

IST Austria (2011). Evaluation of the Institute of Science and Technology Austria. [IST Austria (2011)]. Report by the International Review Panel chaired by Professor David Baltimore, Caltech, March 2011. Available at http://ist.ac.at/fileadmin/user_upload/ pdfs/Evaluation_reports/110512_EvalReportEnFINALWeb.pdf (accessed 10 September 2012).

Kant, I. (1992, 2nd ed.). *Der Streit der Fakultäten* [The Conflict of the Faculties]. Leipzig: Reclam.

Loprieno, A. et al. (2011). "Zur Entwicklung und Dynamisierung der österreichischen Hochschullandschaft – eine Außensicht. Rahmenkonzept für einen Hochschulplan" [On the development and dynamic adjustment of the Austrian university landscape – a view from the outside. Frame concept for a university development plan]. Available at http://www.bmwf.gv.at/fileadmin/user_upload/aussendung/expertenbericht/Bericht_E xpertInnen_Final_110822.pdf (accessed 10 September 2012).

Meyer, J. W., E. Schofer (2007). "The University in Europe and the World: Twentieth Century Expansion". In: G. Krücken et al. (eds.), *Towards a Multiversity. Universities between Global Trends and National Traditions*. Bielefeld: Transcript Verlag. 45-61.

Neave, G. (1979). "Academic Drift: Some Views from Europe". *Studies in Higher Education*. Vol. 4. No. 2. 143-59.

Newman, J., J. Clarke (2009). *Publics, Politics and Power. Remaking the Public in Public Services*. London: Sage.

OECD (1971). *Towards New Structures of Post-Secondary Education: A Preliminary Statement of Issues*. Paris: OECD.

OECD (1973). *Short-Cycle Higher Education: A Search for Identity*. Paris: OECD.

OECD (1991). *Alternatives to Universities*. Paris: OECD.

OECD (2005). *Alternatives to Universities Revisited*. Paris: OECD.

OECD (2008). OECD/France International Conference: Higher Education to 2030: Four Future Scenarios for Higher Education. Available at http://www.oecd.org/site/eduhe30 /41809568.pdf (accessed 10 September 2012).

Pechar, H. (2004). "Should Austria Establish a Non-university Sector? 1969-1990". In: J. Pratt (ed.), *The 'Accreditation Model'. Policy Transfer in Higher Education in Austria and Britain*. Oxford: Symposium Books. 37-51.

Prague Communiqué 2001. Available at http://www.ond.vlaanderen.be/hogeronderwijs/ bologna/documents/MDC/PRAGUE_COMMUNIQUE.pdf (accessed 10 September 2012).

Pratt, J. (1997). *The Polytechnic Experiment 1965–1992*. Buckingham: SRHE and Open University Press.

Regini, M. (2011). *European Universities and the Challenge of the Market. A Comparative Analysis*. Cheltenham: Edward Elgar.

Scott, P. (1995). *The Meaning of Mass Higher Education*. Buckingham: SRHE and Open University Press.

Sebök, M., ed. (2002). *Universitätsgesetz 2002. Gesetzestext, Materialien, Erläuterungen und Anmerkungen* [University Act 2002. Text, Materials, Commentaries and Annotations]. Wien: WUV Universitätsverlag.

Sorbonne   Declaration   (1998).   Available   at   http://www.bologna-
    berlin2003.de/pdf/Sorbonne_declaration.pdf (accessed 10 September 2012).
Teichler, U. (2007). *Higher Education Systems: Conceptual Frameworks, Comparative
    Perspectives, Empirical Findings*. Rotterdam: Sense.
Trow, M. (1979). *Elite and Mass Higher Education: American Models and European
    Realities*. Stockholm: National Board of Universities.
UNESCO (2004). Diversification of Higher Education and the Changing Role of Knowledge
    and Research. Papers presented at the Second Scientific Committee Meeting for
    Europe and North America. Available at http://unesdoc.unesco.org/images/0014/
    001467/146736e.pdf (accessed 10 September 2012).
Unger, M. et al. (2009). *Studierenden- Sozialerhebung 2009. Bericht zur sozialen Lage der
    Studierenden.*   Available   at   http://ww2.sozialerhebung.at/Ergebnisse/PDF/
    sozialerhebung_2009_ueberarbeitete_version.pdf (accessed 10 September 2012).
Unger, M. et al. (2011). *Studierenden- Sozialerhebung 2011. Bericht zur sozialen Lage der
    Studierenden.*   Available   at   http://ww2.sozialerhebung.at/Ergebnisse/PDF/
    Studierenden_Sozialerhebung_2011_BAND_1_AnfaengerInnen.pdf;
    http://ww2.sozialerhebung.at/Ergebnisse/PDF/Studierenden_Sozialerhebung_2011_M
    aterialien.pdf (accessed 10 September 2012).
Universitätsgesetz 2002, BGBl.I Nr. 120/2002 i.d.F BGBl.I Nr. 74/2006 [Universities Act
    2002].   Available   at   http://www.bmwf.gv.at/fileadmin/user_upload/legislation/
    E_UG.pdf (accessed: 10 September 2012).
Van Vught, F. (2007). Diversity and Differentiation in Higher Education Systems. Key-note
    speech at the conference 'Higher Education in the 21st Century – Diversity of
    Missions'; Dublin, 26 June 2007. Available at http://docs.china-europa-
    forum.net/doc_759.pdf (accessed 10 September 2012).
Vincent-Lancrin, St. (2004). "Building Futures Scenarios for Universities and Higher
    Education: An International Approach". *Policy Futures in Education*. Vol. 2. No. 2.
    245-262.

The Effects of Europeanisation on Institutional Diversification in the Western Balkans

Manja Klemenčič

Abstract

A lack of diversity among higher education institutions is coming to be seen as one of the key weaknesses of European higher education. The European Commission [EC] suggests that a low degree of diversification – implying uniformity and egalitarianism among HE institutions – is an obstacle, indeed "a bottleneck", to achieving excellence and efficiency at the system level. The key question investigated in this article is to what extent national policy developments reflect the European recommendations on institutional diversification. In other words, to what extent can we speak about Europeanisation in the sense of policy adaptation and institutional change towards institutional diversity? This question is explored in the context of four Western Balkan countries: Albania, Croatia, Serbia and Slovenia. The article first reviews the European positions and recommendations on institutional diversity focusing on those formulated by the EC. The second section is devoted to an analysis of the key strategic and regulatory documents concerning institutional diversity within the last decade in these four Western Balkan countries. This section highlights the key dimensions of institutional diversity pursued by the respective governments, and how they are pursued. The article closes with a discussion of the key drivers for diversification within the national contexts, and how these play out with the impulses coming from the European context.

Key words: institutional diversity, institutional diversification, Europeanisation, diffusion, Western Balkans, higher education reforms

Introduction

A lack of diversity among higher education institutions is coming to be seen as one of the key weaknesses of European higher education. Diversity is defined here as "the existence of distinct forms of post-secondary education, of institutions and groups of institutions within a state or nation that have different and distinctive missions, educate and train for different lives and careers, have different styles of instruction, are organised and funded and operate under different laws and relationships to government" (Meek et al. 2000: 3). Institutional diversification within national higher education systems, as "a process by which a system becomes more varied or diverse in its orientation and operations" (Teichler 2008), is widely believed necessary to achieve two important goals: more equity in terms of access to a wider variety of students, and more excellence through institutional specialisation. The argument goes that a single European country, even a large one, cannot sustain several world-class universities that are similar in function and scope. Further, every country needs a variety of higher education institutions that address the needs of an expanding and increasingly diversified body of students, and the ever more precise expectations and demands of the knowledge society and economy.

Institutional diversity has several – interrelated – dimensions (Huisman 1995, Huisman et al. 2007). Such complexity poses a challenge for the researcher to select features that meaningfully depict both the similarities and differences within the system or systems (cf. Huisman et al. 2007). Drawing from existing literature on the topic (Huisman 1995, Meek et al. 1996, Meek and Wood 1998, Neave 2000, Huisman et al. 2007, Teichler 2008, Teixteira et al. 2012), and taking into consideration the prevailing characteristics of the Western Balkans region, this paper explores institutional diversity in terms of types of institutions according to: a) a binary divide (i.e. university versus other professional and vocational higher education institutions); and b) control found in the system (i.e. public versus private institutions). Indeed, these are the basic diversity indicators. In scholarly and policy documents of the last decade these have been supplemented by more advanced notions of diversity such as that of substantive profiles, i.e. relating to the focus of activities, mode of teaching, student and staff profiles, target communities etc. (Teichler 2008, Reichert 2009).

The national higher education systems vary not only in terms of the existing degrees and dimensions of institutional diversity, but also in terms of the diversification-promoting policies pursued by governments. In European countries with predominantly public sector higher education institutions, governments undoubtedly have a critical influence on systemic diversity (Codling and Meek 2006). The expectation that, given enough independence, autonomous institutions will automatically diversify when operating in a competitive market has largely been rejected (ibid.). The argument goes that in the absence of government intervention on this issue, institutions – in a homogeneous environment – will have a natural tendency to isomorphic behaviour ultimately resulting in increased institutional convergence. With various regulatory and funding mechanisms, governments can initiate and sustain differences between institutions and hence influence institutional diversity (ibid.).

There are basically three main types of interventions governments have available. The first type includes regulations of the formal diversity dimensions, namely the types of institutions and higher education structures, and levels of programmes and degree structures. For example, the existence of a binary system, at least in theory, guarantees that two distinct types of institution – professional and research-oriented – will exist within a higher education system. Similarly, provisions for private, extension and virtual-type universities add to the diversity of types (Guri-Rosenblit 2001). Second, funding is widely perceived as the most effective policy instrument to promote institutional diversification (Codling and Meek 2006). Codling and Meek (2006: 14) propose a funding scheme that is overtly directed at institutional diversification as a best strategy to achieve this goal: "The greater the financial incentives within a higher education system that do have explicit diversity objectives, the greater the potential for systemic diversity". They argue against uniform funding regimes on the grounds that institutions which are funded in exactly the same way for the same outputs will inevitably mimic the most successful among them in order to maximise their income (ibid.). Third, accreditation and quality assurance procedures are seen as important accompanying measures reinforcing the diversification policy. They are, however, unlikely to enforce diversification objectives on their own, i.e. in the absence of an appropriate funding regime (Guri-Rosenblit et al. 2007: 378).

But how do governments come to decide to apply these mechanisms, and which? The impulses certainly come from the conditions and developments of higher education, and the broader political, economic and social goals in national systems. Slovenia, Croatia, Serbia and Albania, the four Western Balkan countries considered in this article, all lie on the European 'periphery' and are relatively small in size in terms of their territory, economy and higher education systems. All of them underwent a transition from some type of a centrally planned economy to a more market-oriented one, within a democratic political framework. And in all of them, the higher education landscape is changing at a rapid pace. Substantial higher education reforms have been undertaken since the 1990s, prompted by political and economic reforms (and in the case of former Yugoslav republics also statehood-building) and the massification of student demand for educational services (Zgaga 2010 and 2012).

At the same time, impulses for domestic higher education reforms come from abroad. The environment which shapes what is valued by governments (and institutions) and influences their behaviour extends from the national to the international context. Indeed, the recommendations coming from the Bologna Process and EU initiatives such as the Lisbon Agenda (and its EU modernisation agenda for universities) resonate in national governments' decisions on what are viable and – indeed – desirable higher education institutional policies. The key question investigated in this article is to what extent national policy developments reflect the European recommendations on institutional diversification. In other words, to what extent can we speak about Europeanisation in the sense of policy adaptation and institutional change towards institutional diversity?

Conceptualising Europeanisation

In European studies, there is widespread Europeanisation research investigating the EU's impact on the domestic policies, institutions and political processes of member and prospective member states (Börzel and Risse 2012: 1; for an elaborate literature review see Vukasović 2012). The mechanisms of international influence on domestic institutional change span from direct mechanisms of influence, such as legislative coercion, positive and negative incentives, socialisation and persuasion to indirect mechanisms of emulation (Börzel and Risse 2012). The main difference between the direct and indirect mechanisms, as stipulated in the diffusion approach, lies in determining the active agent of diffusion. In direct mechanisms of influence, the EU (or other international actors) actively tries to diffuse their ideas in the national context. At the same time, the agents at the receiving end are not "simply passive recipients of EU policies and institutions" (ibid.: 8). Instead, the process of the adoption of and adaptation to international recommendations mostly involves active processes of "interpretation, incorporation […], and also resistance" (ibid.). In contrast, the indirect mechanism of emulation does not presuppose a necessarily active and direct involvement of an international actor. Emulation can happen because domestic agents are actively seeking solutions to solve particular domestic problems and find best practices that can be transferred to the domestic context (ibid.).

Socialisation through political dialogue and technical cooperation and persuasion through recommendations, country reports, and stocktaking reports are common mechanisms applied by the EU to diffuse its recommendations in the domestic context. In the domains of higher education policy, the EU cannot apply legislative coercion as member states have not transferred decision-making powers to the EU institutions. EU cooperation in education and training is conducted through the open method of coordination which is based on common objectives, reference tools and approaches, and draws on mutual (peer) learning and the exchange of good practices, periodic monitoring and reporting (European Council 2009, EC 2008c, Gornitzka 2005). The underlying expectation is that through communication, socialisation, social learning and peer pressure the non-coercive transposition of norms, ideas and collective understandings will take place across participating countries. This will result in convergence of policies and practices.

In addition, the EU routinely uses positive incentives in the form of technical and financial assistance towards capacity building. Capacity building provides targeted actors (governments and institutions) with resources to either begin certain reforms or to support the reforms that have already begun (cf. Börzel and Risse 2012). Over the last decade, higher education reforms have been supported through several funding lines: the Lifelong Learning Programme, the Tempus Programme and the EU's programme for worldwide academic cooperation: Erasmus Mundus, the 7th EU Framework Programme for Research, but also less well-known ones like the Instrument for Pre-accession Assistance (IPA), the European Neighbourhood and Partnership Instrument and the Development Cooperation Instrument (European Union 2010). Perhaps one of the most structured mechanisms of assistance is the Higher Education Reform Project funded by the EC which provides several trainings and thematic seminars for the National Teams of Bologna Experts and of the Higher Education Reform Experts in Tempus partner countries as well as other categories of persons involved in the modernisation of higher education.[1] The Western Balkan countries are all subject to intense EU intervention in terms of financial and expert support, albeit to varying degrees and through different mechanisms in different countries (Vukasović 2012). Slovenia and Croatia are respectively an EU member and a candidate member – with the latter expected to join in 2013 – and as such subject to EU regulations and eligible for all EU funding. Serbia as a candidate country since 2012 and Albania in the pre-accession stage both rely especially on TEMPUS, Erasmus Mundus

---

1   http://www.bolognaexperts.net (accessed 25 Oktober 2012).

and IPA funding. Since 2007 they have also participated in the 7th Framework Programme. For Serbia and Albania, funding from private and public donors, such as the World Bank in particular, is also characteristic.

The difficulty facing Europeanisation studies of change is establishing clear causal mechanisms since causes range from several international and domestic sources (Elken et al. 2011: 27). Acknowledging this difficulty, the analysis in this article is conducted on two levels. First, the article reviews the key European recommendations regarding institutional diversity. In the absence of concrete policy proposals from Bologna Ministerial Communiqués, it focuses on the policy recommendations coming from the EU, which are arguably the most elaborate amongst the members the Bologna Process. The key question here is what the EU's position on institutional diversity is and which policy instruments it advocates. Next, the analysis moves to the national level investigating national regulatory and strategic documents within the past decade and tracing evidence of European recommendations. The final section concludes with a discussion of the effects of Europeanisation on institutional diversity in the Western Balkans.

The data for this article were obtained through a content analysis of regulatory and strategic documents and interviews conducted in the project *Differentiation, Equity, Productivity: The Social and Economic Consequences of Expanded and Differentiated Higher Education Systems – Internationalisation Aspects* (DEP-08-EuroHESC-OP-016; 2010–2012) (CEPS 2012).

European policy recommendations on institutional diversification

The factors influencing governments' choices regarding higher education policy are no longer bound to the national context. Prior to the Bologna Process, national higher education policies were formulated using international cross-country comparisons as a tool for reflection (Huisman et al. 2001). After the initiation of the Bologna Process in 1999, a new forum evolved providing a space for various policy issues to emerge, develop and possibly diffuse into the national and institutional levels (Kehm et al. 2009). Indeed, the Bologna Process transformed higher education policy making "from an almost exclusively national affair with some international influences to one where national policy is systematically considered within a Europe-wide framework" (Westerheijden et al. 2010: 38). In the early stages of the Bologna Process, it was effectively the Bologna recommendations that 'captured' the higher education reform agenda across the EHEA (Gornitzka 2010: 11). Those recommendations have largely focused on structural convergence and convergence in terms of quality assurance systems in order to support mobility.

Within a couple of years, in the – subsumed – policy arena of the European Union, another powerful discourse has been launched that places higher education in the centre of economic competitiveness. The Lisbon Agenda, an influential action and development plan for the European economy, has paved the way for a more elaborate higher education policy to be proposed by the EC. From 2003, a series of influential policy documents and related financial instruments were developed under a general heading of the "higher education modernisation agenda" (EC 2003, 2005, 2006, 2008a and 2008b). Both Bologna and EU higher education reform discourses have become increasingly intertwined. Scholarly work suggests that the Bologna Process has been absorbed into the more general 'stream' of the Lisbon Agenda through the progressive convergence of documents (Capano and Piattoni 2011: 586). Specifically, the strategic role of higher education in promoting the competitiveness of the European economy set out in the Lisbon Agenda has held implications for certain emphasises within the Bologna documents and, more broadly, for the governance, funding reforms as well as institutional diversity within the EHEA.

Several notions of diversity feature within this overarching Bologna policy context. At the core of the Bologna Process lies, of course, structural convergence in terms of degree structures and mobility tools. With structural convergence increasing, other aspects of diversity in higher education systems are becoming accentuated, in particular the diversity of higher education institutions (Guri-Rosenblit et al. 2007: 380). The message from the Bologna Ministerial communiqués highlights that structural convergence should not diminish the inherent diversity of higher education institutions; but it does not go beyond this declarative statement. As Huisman and van Vught (2009: 22) observe, the Bologna Declaration and the following communiqués "highlight the importance of diversity of higher education systems, but in ambiguous terms", and without a clear indication of what aspect of diversity is worth pursuing beyond the general notions of linguistic and cultural diversity. It is only when we take a closer look at the policy documents issued especially by the EC in the framework of the 'Modernisation Agenda for Universities' that we find institutional diversity vocally promulgated as a policy goal.

In the chronological sequence of the Commission's communications we witness ever stronger and more precise statements in favour of institutional diversification accompanied by concrete policy recommendations. The Commission's initial promulgation of institutional diversity lies within a genuine concern regarding *"how to concentrate enough resources on excellence, and create the conditions within which universities can attain and develop excellence"* (EC 2003: 2). It notes the importance of the emergence *"of more specialised institutions concentrating on a core of specific competencies when it comes to research and teaching and/or on certain dimensions of their activities, e.g. their integration within a strategy of regional development through adult education/training"* (ibid.: 6). In line with this note, the Commission uses straightforward language regarding the desirability of institutional diversification (ibid.:18): *"A combination of the absolute need for excellence, the effects of the precariousness of resources and the pressure of competition, forces universities and Member States to make choices. They need to identify the areas in which different universities have attained, or can reasonably be expected to attain, the excellence [...] and to focus on them funds to support academic research [...], as no Member State is capable of achieving excellence in all areas"*. Such 'increased specialisation' of the universities, according to the Commission, does not preclude the natural link between research and teaching, but it is nevertheless *"not the same in all institutions, for all programmes or for all levels"* (ibid.). The stress in this initial communication is clearly on achieving excellence and institutional diversification as a means for achieving it.

The Commission's following communication (EC 2005: 3-4) strengthens the language of the desirability of institutional diversity even further. Importantly, it also accentuates the argument of improved access besides achieving excellence. The basic proposition is that a low degree of diversification – implying uniformity and egalitarianism among higher education institutions – is an obstacle ("a bottleneck") to achieving excellence and efficiency at the system level (ibid.): *"Most universities tend to offer the same monodisciplinary programmes and traditional methods geared towards the same group of academically best-qualified learners – which leads to the exclusion of those who do not conform to the standard model. Other consequences are that Europe has too few centres of world-class excellence".*

In the initial communications, the recommendation on how to achieve this diversification objective focuses on funding. The Commission unambiguously states that *"the concentration of research funding on a smaller number of areas and institutions should lead to increased specialisation of the universities, in line with the move currently observed towards a European university area which is more differentiated"* (EC 2003: 18; also see EC 2005: 5). This *"requires more competition-based funding in research and more output-related funding in education"* (EC 2005: 8). In other words, *"[u]niversities should be funded more for what they do than for what they are, by focusing funding on relevant outputs rather than on inputs, and by adapting funding to the diversity of institutional profiles"* (EC 2006: 7-8). It then further explicates the diversification of funding schemes as follows (ibid.: 8): *"Research-active universities should not be assessed and funded on the same basis as others weaker in research but stronger in integrating students from disadvantaged groups or in acting as driving forces for local industry and services. [...] Each country should therefore strike the right balance between core, competitive and outcome-based funding (underpinned by robust quality assurance) for higher education and university-based research. Competitive funding should be based on institutional evaluation systems and on diversified performance indicators with clearly defined targets and indicators supported by international benchmarking for both inputs and economic and societal outputs".*

From about 2008 on, another (complementary) recommendation on how to promote institutional diversification becomes highlighted. A new emphasis on the transparency of university missions and performances can be noted from the Commission's documents and – even more – from its project funding. Several pilot projects exploring ways to enhance the transparency and comparability of the missions and performance of higher education institutions, and indeed ways to rank the institutions, have obtained Commission funding (EC 2010: 10). These tools are seen as complementing the quality assurance reports, which according to the Commission (ibid.) *"contain a wealth of information, but they do not provide comparison".* The various transparency and performance measuring tools developed are intended not only to make institutional diversity in Europe more transparent, but also to help institutions *"to better position themselves, improve their development strategies and find the most suitable partner institutions"* (ibid.). The EC considers rankings as *"a useful tool for comparison and contrast between higher education institutions and their programmes"* (EC 2009: 9).

The question that now emerges is to what extent can we trace these policy recommendations in the strategic and regulatory documents of the four Western Balkan countries? All are members of the Bologna Process, and have – to different degrees and through different funding mechanisms – participated in the EU's education and research initiatives. Which policies regarding institutional diversification are being pursued in Albania, Croatia, Serbia and Slovenia?

A review of current national policy initiatives for institutional diversification

When comparing the countries' strategic and regulatory documents in terms of their institutional diversification strategy we can derive two main findings regarding the prevailing dimensions of diversity promoted, and the support measures in funding, accreditation and transparency tools.

First, all the countries have been working on consolidating a binary structure acknowledging that earlier efforts were not fully successful. For example, in Albania the Higher Education Strategy 2008–2013 recognises that "the current system is highly homogeneous and does not encourage higher education institutions to undertake any activities" (Albania 2008, point 7). In the preamble of the Croatian Draft Law on Universities released in 2011, it is stated that the binary structure has not been fully actualised. Professional studies continue to be performed also in universities where they are considered 'more demanding' than those performed in professional higher education institutions (Croatia 2011: 3). Accordingly, the Croatian Directions for the strategy for education, higher education and science and technology (Croatia 2012: 30) stipulate that "all colleges cannot and should not be in the same way [as universities] research-driven". In Serbia, the new higher education strategy is forthcoming in directing the academies of professional programmes, academics of professional schools and professional schools towards the development of professional education with an allusion to 'profiling' towards meeting the needs of the regions where they are located (Serbia 2012: 4). In addition, the strategy also aims to develop competency indicators for domestic higher education institutions and to boost a few universities to improve their standing in international university rankings (Serbia 2012). In Slovenia, the Higher Education Programme of 2011 identifies diversification as one of the four main policy priorities for the future reform of the system (Slovenia 2011). The idea is to remedy the situation "in which all higher education institutions attempt to be more or less equal and good in all areas and fulfil all goals or roles of higher education" (ibid.: 24). One of the measures suggested is a redefinition of the binary system via a clear separation of professional and university studies from the point of view of the content, implementation and organisation: "universities would no longer include professional colleges and would not perform professional study programmes" (ibid.: 9-10).

The more advanced level of institutional diversification, namely institutional profiling as advocated in European documents, only features unequivocally in the policy documents of Slovenia and Croatia, and only in the most recent documents. In the Slovenian strategy of 2011, the policy goal is to enable higher education institutions to profile – in terms of organisation, programme and operation: "higher education institutions will select their own profiles based on their fundamental mission, type and level of educational offer and achievement of excellence in selected areas" (ibid.: 31). In Croatian policy documents there are also indications of the intention to engage in institutional profiling: not in the stipulations regarding institutional development, but in the proposed funding arrangements (see below). In the Serbian and Albanian discourse, institutional profiling as such does not come forward. There is, however, ample mention of striving for research excellence. The Albanian strategy suggests merging the independent academies with universities to strengthen the research universities. The Serbian strategy expresses intentions of investing in a few research universities to climb the ranks of international university rankings.

While research excellence is a common denominator of all of the most recent policy documents, another relatively prevalent feature is the strengthening of professional and vocational education in regional centres. This objective does echo some of the Commission's early recommendations, but it is also clearly strongly domestically driven. Regional development is high on the political agenda in all countries and is one of the persistently salient political issues. Croatian and Albanian documents are especially detailed when it comes to promoting the polycentric development of higher education. The idea is to establish public and/or private institutions in regional centres, which would primarily have a vocational teaching profile, and possibly offer applied research and development to meet the needs of local communities (Albania 2012: 53).

Another dominant feature of policy documents (and discourse) in the four countries concerns private higher education providers. All the countries have made legislative changes providing for the emergence (and expansion) of private higher education. In those countries where private higher education institutions were present, the legislation enabled the equal legal treatment of private and public higher education institutions in terms of regulation and the recognition of degrees (Vukasović 2009: 72). In Albania, private higher education plays such a prominent role in the national HE strategy that a Department of Private Education Development (DZHAP) was created with the aim of encouraging the development of private education. The government website states that private education is considered "an important alternative in the provision of public services in the field of education, which improves the conditions under which the market operates, enhances competitiveness and encourages educational service quality". In all the countries except Slovenia there is a clear distinction between private and public in terms of their financing. In Slovenia, however, most private institutions qualify as government-dependent (Klemenčič 2012); they have private governance, but the private sector dominates in the contribution to their budget (Teixteira et al. 2011). Even though private higher education covers a relatively small share of the student population (i.e. less than 20 percent), it features prominently in the public and political discourse in all the countries (for details, see Klemenčič 2012).

Next, there is quite some diversity among the four countries in terms of the instruments to promote diversification. The funding mechanisms of Slovenia and Croatia are most closely aligned with the European recommendations. They include performance (output) based funding with an explicit diversification objective. Concretely in the Slovenian case, the novelty lies in rewarding performance on the basis of the agreed strategic goals and institutional profiles. A revised system of funding would allow the institutions to negotiate with the government for substantial additional funding for diversification. On top of the basic lump-sum, the institutions ought to be able to apply for funding for development and competitiveness, foreseen to amount to 20 percent of the basic funding (Slovenia 2011). Similarly, the Croatian proposed funding arrangements stipulate the financing of higher education institutions and research institutes through "programme contracts" (orig., *"programskih ugovora"*). These are based on a three-year institutional strategic framework which would be developed through negotiations between the Ministry and the institutions (Croatia 2011, Croatia 2012: 8). It is still unclear what the extent of the flexible development funding part will be and how exactly these parts will be negotiated, but the intention to reform the previous model is certainly present. The Serbian and Albanian policy documents display the continuity of a uniform funding regime in which – broadly speaking – the amount of funding is defined by taking the number of enrolled students into account. This money is typically allocated to universities and higher education institutions as a lump sum for the provision of basic educational activities. Typically, there are funds made available separately for development tasks and activities, for which institutions apply on a competitive basis. These include resources for infrastructure and equipment, but also for development, such as quality assurance, internationalisation or implementation of the Bologna recommendations (Vukasović 2009). In the absence of a coherent funding policy with a clear diversification objective, these funds cannot lead to major reforms towards institutional profiling.

Further, in the European recommendations, accreditation and quality assurance are stated as important mechanisms promoting institutional profiling. In this area, all the countries have followed the Bologna recommendations and are trying to align their standards to the European Standards and Guidelines for Quality Assurance. In fact, much of the EU funding through the Tempus Programme has been directed precisely to achieving this objective (Zgaga 2008). The starting point in basically all the countries was the initial absence of an independent quality assurance body. In 2012, only the Croatian Quality Assurance Agency (QAA) is included in the European QA Register for Higher Education (EQAR). Slovenia and Albania have independent QAAs, but they are not yet included in the EQAR. Serbia still operates with the Commission for Accreditation and Quality Assessment as the body legally responsible for organising and monitoring QA in all HE institutions. The importance of independent quality assurance features in policy documents in all the countries, but only the most recent Slovenian and Croatian policy documents freshly amplify the role of QAA also in promoting institutional profiling. Concretely, the Slovenian strategy stipulates that the output-based funding would also be distributed based on quality assessments, qualitative measures and international peer review. During cyclical reaccreditation, the Agency would be able – among other issues – to monitor how an institution has been following its diversification strategy. The existing accreditation mechanisms in the region are typically based on a set of uniform criteria and indicators for institutional and study programme evaluation, and institutions seek to reach the minimum indicators in order to obtain the accreditation. Such uniformity does not promote institutional diversity. In fact, as suggested by Codling and Meek (2006), it creates circumstances conducive to conformity, isomorphism and thus homogeneity among institutions.

Also, the transparency tools developed with support of the EC are not reflected in any of the reviewed policy documents. The countries typically disclose a list of all accredited public and private institutions on the website of the ministry responsible for higher education. National rankings of institutions have not been developed in any of the countries, except Albania. In 2011, the Albanian Ministry of Education and Science commissioned the Centre for Higher Education from Germany to conduct a pilot national ranking of higher education institutions in Albania (CHE 2011) with "the aim to increase transparency about the Albanian higher education system and to give information to (prospective) students so that they could to make an informed choice on their studies, as well as to inform policy makers and the broader public of the actual performance of Albanian higher education". The mention of capacity indicators in the Serbian strategy might be pointing to a similar direction. Our interviews with institutional leaders and our survey of academic opinions reveal that international university rankings are a relevant factor in defining institutional goals and strategies and that research excellence is a prevalent ambition in all the countries (CEPS 2012). In fact, in all the countries research policies include objectives of increasing research funding for excellent research, developing centres of excellence and the scientific profiling of universities (Croatia 2011, Slovenia 2011, Serbia 2012, Albania 2008). In other words, through research policy, research quality in universities is promoted and research quality is perhaps the single most important element of diversification. Hence, while traces of the European higher education policy recommendations appear somewhat patchily and unevenly across the four countries, the downloading of EU recommendations in terms of research excellence appears much more unequivocal.

There has been ample assistance from the EU to help the Western Balkan countries' integration into the European Research Area (ERA). In June 2006, the EC, together with the Austrian EU Presidency, launched the

Steering Platform on Research for the Western Balkans. Through the Framework Programme and support actions the EU funded several projects to support the exchange of information and national policy development. Most notable of these were: the FP6 Southern European Research Area project (SEE-ERA.NET), a networking project aimed at linking research activities within existing national, bilateral and regional programmes, and the FP7 WBC-INCO.NET, a project aimed at the co-coordination of research policies with the Western Balkans. Since 1 January 2009, all Western Balkan countries have been associated with the EU's Framework Programme 7; thus formally benefiting from the same research opportunities and being subject to the same obligations as entities established in the EU member states. In 2012, the EU and the World Bank signed an agreement to implement a technical assistance programme for the development of a Regional Research and Development Strategy for Innovation in the Western Balkans (not including Slovenia). The strategy aims in particular to increase the economic impact of R&D in the Western Balkans, and to develop a comprehensive approach to integrating the three axes of the knowledge triangle, namely education, research and innovation.

Finally, our research shows that European recommendations regarding institutional profiling have not diffused onto the institutional level (CEPS 2012). From our interviews conducted with institutional leaders at the biggest universities in the four countries, we may conclude that institutional profiling is not even considered (ibid.). One interviewee from a government body stated that the goal of institutional profiling was *"artificially introduced from the international context"* and that the *"national 'space' did not feel it like its own problem"* (Interview 43; 16/2/2012). While institutional profiling as recommended by the EC is largely absent from institutional strategies, our empirical data show that recommendations on other policy issues are perceived as diffused from the international context. The results from the interviews with academic personnel in the Western Balkan countries show that academics tend to see international organisations importantly influencing changes within their institutions (CEPS 2012). Bologna-related reforms, such as quality assurance, certainly fall in this category as indicated by the survey and also emerging from our interviews (ibid.). We asked academics in the region whether they agreed or disagreed with the following statement: "Reforms of the internal quality assurance procedures of my institution are imposed by various actors". International organisations specified such as the EU, OECD or Bologna Process were perceived to impose reforms even more than the national government (but less than institutional leadership) (Graph 1). Only in Albania did the academics evaluate the imposition of the government and international bodies on institutional reforms as having a similar value. The perceived influence by the 'internationals' was, however, perceived lower than that of governments when it came to the question of the reform of governance structures and financing (Graph 2).

Graph 1. Internal quality assurance procedures

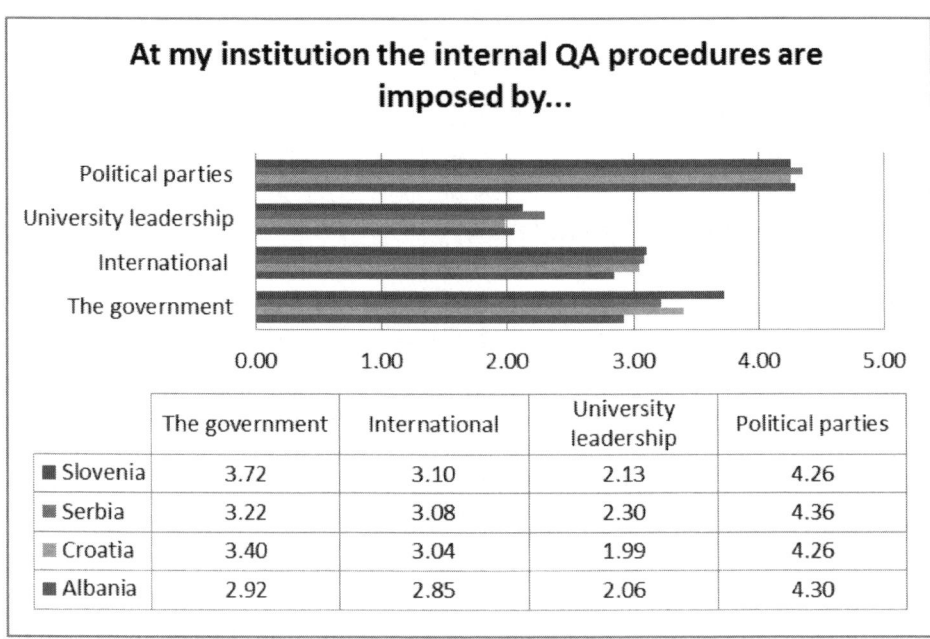

	The government	International	University leadership	Political parties
■ Slovenia	3.72	3.10	2.13	4.26
■ Serbia	3.22	3.08	2.30	4.36
■ Croatia	3.40	3.04	1.99	4.26
■ Albania	2.92	2.85	2.06	4.30

Note: 1 – strongly agree, 5 – strongly disagree

Graph 2. Reforms of the governance structure and financing

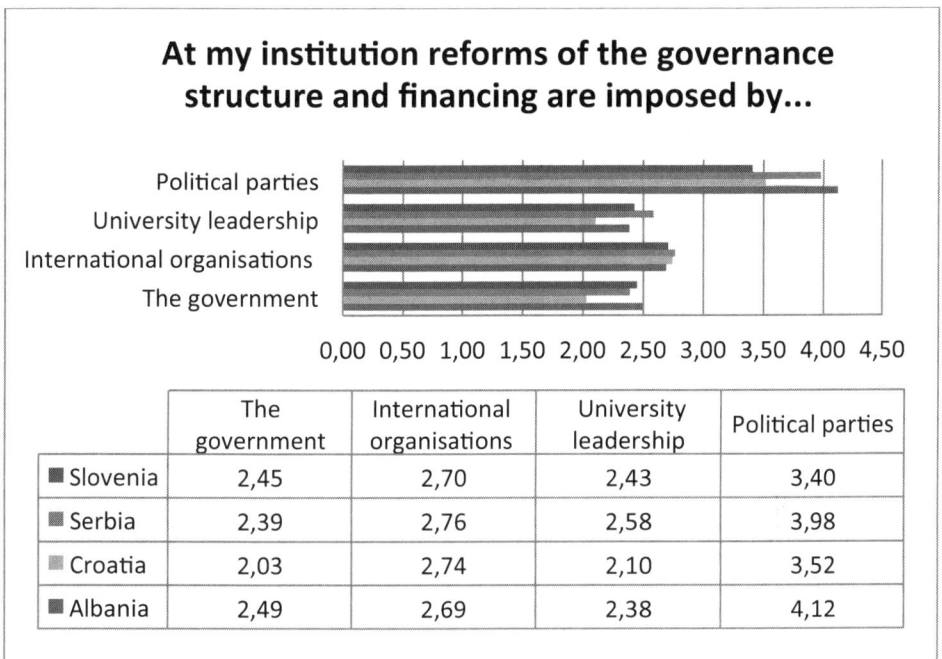

At my institution reforms of the governance structure and financing are imposed by...

	The government	International organisations	University leadership	Political parties
Slovenia	2,45	2,70	2,43	3,40
Serbia	2,39	2,76	2,58	3,98
Croatia	2,03	2,74	2,10	3,52
Albania	2,49	2,69	2,38	4,12

Note: 1 – strongly agree, 5 – strongly disagree

Conclusion

EU education policy is based on voluntary intergovernmental cooperation and does not fall within the legal accession conditionality. As pointed out by Börzel and Risse (2012: 195), Europeanisation still works through the harmonising of national legislation with the *acquis communautaire*, but on specific objectives of institutional profiling and systemic diversification, the persuasion- and incentive-based mechanisms of influence prevail. The various EU funding programmes earmarked for higher education reforms have so far not have a clear diversification objective. Hence, EU's influence comes predominantly through offering arenas for persuasion and socialisation. The empirical evidence in this article shows that the diversification objective features more clearly in Slovenian and Croatian policy documents confirming the typical Europeanisation proposition that EU's normative influence tends to be stronger in countries that are working under the "shadow of hierarchy" (Börzel and Risse 2012). By participating in the Council and Commission's working groups, Slovenia and Croatia are clearly more socialised into the EU policy processes and thus more susceptible to the persuasion effort of the EC.

Furthermore, the higher education systems in these two countries are more closely aligned to the average EU model for which the EC is drafting the recommendations. Both have below-average levels of investment in higher education, but not significantly lower. Both are coping with slowly but surely declining student numbers. And both see higher education as a key element of developing knowledge economy. In other words, their higher education systems are – broadly speaking – in the stage of development where they have the necessary capacity – if also the political will – to consider more advanced notions of diversity that is institutional profiling. By comparison, Serbia and Albania are in the situation where the political emphasis still lies in need to absorb the growing student demand. (The same concern could be found in Slovenia and Croatia in the earlier policy documents from the late 1990s and early 2000.) Accordingly, the salient policy issues for Serbian and Albanian policy makers are those allowing for new providers to absorb the demand, to ensure the quality when student numbers are increasing, and to reform funding systems to enable access. The domestic political agenda, hence, emphasises the higher education system diversification in terms of binary divide and public-private divide, but not yet institutional profiling.

Finally, the institutional profiling objective appears to be in all countries more unequivocally pursued through science and technology/research and innovation policies than education policies. In the area of research, the 'shadow of conditionality' applies much more clearly as research is one of those policy areas where EU institutions under the Community method enjoy decision-making powers and there are ample European directives. Also, there has been a significant 'deepening' of EU research policies in the aftermath of the Lisbon Agenda. All countries, including Serbia and Albania, participate in the 7th Framework Programme. This programme has strong impact on research capacity building, but also on policy alignment with the EU's policies in order to pave the way for these countries full integration into the European Research Area. The emphasis here is on developing appropriate regulatory and funding mechanisms that will help identify and develop centres or clusters of research excellence within individual countries or regions. Research-intensive universities are, naturally, one of the key actors within such policies. Hence, in the Western Balkans, as already seen in the rest of Europe, research excellence is on the way to becoming the single most powerful element of institutional diversification. This can, on one hand, usefully strengthen inter or intra-institutional diversity. Through competitive research funding, the few most successful universities will be able to further develop their areas of research excellence. On the other hand, there is a possibility that the already existing vertical differentiation will become even steeper. In absence of appropriate countervailing measures to acknowledge and reward other functions than research, there is a threat towards the imitation of the top-ranking universities and thus of weakening of functional diversity promulgated in the European recommendations.

Acknowledgments

The author gratefully acknowledges the support of the Slovenian National Agency for Research through its grant DEP-08-EuroHESC-OP-016.

References

Börzel, T. (2002). "Member State Responses to Europeanization". *Journal of Common Market Studies*. Vol. 40. No. 2. 193-214.

Börzel, T., T. Risse (2000). "When Europe Hits Home: Europeanization and Domestic Change". *European Integration Online Papers (EIOP)*. Vol. 4. No. 15.

Börzel, T., T. Risse (2003). "Conceptualising the Domestic Impact of Europe". In: K. Featherstone, C. Radaelli (eds.), *The Politics of Europeanization*. Oxford/New York: Oxford University Press.

Börzel, T., T. Risse (2012). "From Europeanisation to Diffusion: Introduction". *West European Politics*. Vol. 35. No. 1. 1-19.

Capano, G., S. Piattoni (2011). "From Bologna to Lisbon: The political uses of the Lisbon 'script' in European higher education policy". *Journal of European Public Policy*. Vol. 18. No. 4. 584-606.

CEPS (2012). Differentiation, Equity, Productivity: The Social and Economic Consequences of Expanded and Differentiated Higher Education Systems – Internationalisation Aspects (DEP-08-EuroHESC-OP-016). The Western Balkans Survey (January 2012 – June 2012). First results. Internal materials. Ljubljana: August 2012.

CHE (2011). *Development of a Ranking in Albania*. Final Report July 2011. Guetersloh: Centre for Higher Education.

Codling, A., L.V. Meek (2006). "Twelve Propositions on Diversity in Higher Education". *Higher Education Management and Policy*. Vol. 18. No. 3. 1-24.

Elken, M., Å. Gornitzka, P. Maassen, M. Vukasović (2011). *European Integration and the Transformation of Higher Education*. Oslo: Department of Educational Research, University of Oslo.

Gornitzka, Å. (2005). *Coordinating Policies for a 'Europe of knowledge'. Emerging Practices of the 'Open Method of Coordination' in Education and Research*. Working Paper. No. 16, March 2005. Oslo: ARENA, Centre for European Studies, University of Oslo.

Gornitzka, Å. (2010). "Bologna in Context: A Horizontal Perspective on the Dynamics of Governance Sites for a Europe of Knowledge". *European Journal of Education*. Vol. 45. No. 4. 535-548.

Guri-Rosenblit, S. (2001). "Virtual Universities: Current Models and Future Trends". *Higher Education in Europe*. Vol. 26. No. 4. 487-489.

Guru-Rosenblit, S., Sebkova, S., U. Teichler (2007). "Massification and Diversity of Higher Education Systems: Interplay of Complex Dimensions". *Higher Education Policy*. Vol. 20. No. 4. 373-389.

Huisman, J. (1995). *Differentiation, Diversity and Dependency in Higher Education: A Theoretical and Empirical Analysis*. Utrecht: Lemma.

Huisman, J., F. A. van Vught (2009). "Diversity in European Higher Education: Historical Trends and Current Polices". In: F. A. van Vught (ed.), *Mapping the Higher Education Landscape: Towards a European Classification of Higher Education*. Dordrecht: Springer.

Huisman, G., P. Maassen, G. Neave, eds. (2001). *Higher Education and the Nation State*. Oxford: Elsevier/ Pergamon.

Huisman, J., L. Meek, F. Wood (2007). "Institutional Diversity in Higher Education: A Cross-national and Longitudinal Analysis". *Higher Education Quarterly*. Vol. 61. No. 4. 563-577.

Kehm, B., J. Huisman, B. Stensaker (2009). *The European Higher Education Area: Perspectives on a Moving Target*. Rotterdam: Sense Publishers.

Klemenčič, M. (2012). "Higher Education Reforms in the Western Balkans – Exploring Institutional Differentiation, Diversification and Diversity". In: Panel presentation "Higher Education Reforms in the Western Balkans – an Internationalisation Perspective". The Consortium of Higher Education Researchers (CHER) Annual Conference. Belgrade, 10-12. September 2012. 25-47.

Meek, V. L., F.Q. Wood (1998). *Managing Higher Education Diversity in a Climate of Public Sector Reform*. Canberra: AGPS.

Meek, V. L., J. Huisman, L. Goedegebuure (2000). "Understanding Diversity and Differentiation in Higher Education: An Overview". *Higher Education Policy*. Vol. 13. No. 1. 1-6.

Meek, V. L., L. Goedegebuure, O. Kivinen, R. Rinne, eds. (1996). *The Mockers and Mocked: Comparative Perspectives on Diversity, Differentiation and Convergence in Higher Education*. Oxford: Pergamon.

Neave, G. (2000). "Diversity, Differentiation and the Market: The Debate We Never Had but Which We Ought to Have Done". *Higher Education Policy*. Vol. 13. No. 1. 7-21.

Reichert, S. (2009). *Institutional Diversity in Europe. Study on Institutional Diversity and Differentiation in Five National Systems of Higher Education in Europe (England, France, Norway, Slovakia, Switzerland).* Brussels: European University Association.

Teichler, U. (2008). "Diversification? Trends and Explanations of the Shape and Size of Higher Education". *Higher Education.* Vol. 56. No. 3. 349-379.

Teixeira, N. P., V. Rocha, R. Biscaia, M. Fonseca Cardoso (2011). "Public-Private Mix and Patterns of Program Diversification Across European Higher Education". The Consortium of Higher Education Researchers (CHER) Annual Conference. Reykjavík, Iceland, 23-25 June, 2011.

Teixeira, N. P., V. Rocha, R. Biscaia, M. Fonseca Cardoso (2012). "Competition and Diversity in Higher Education: An Empirical Approach to Specialization Patterns of Portuguese Institutions". *Higher Education.* Vol. 63. No. 3. 337-352.

Vukasović, M., ed. (2009). *Financing Higher education in SEE: Albania, Croatia, Montenegro, Serbia, Slovenia.* Belgrade: Centre for Education Policy.

Vukasović, M. (2012). European Integration in Higher Education in the Western Balkan Countries. A Review of Literature. EIHER-WBC Working paper Series. Working Paper. No. 1. October 2012.

Westerheijden, D. F., E. Beerkens, L. Cremonini, J. Huisman, B. Kehm, A. Kovač et al. (2010). *The First Decade of Working on the European Higher Education Area: The Bologna Process Independent Assessment. Vol. 1: Detailed Assessment Report.* Brussels: European Commission, DG Education and Culture.

Zgaga, P. (2008). *Review of Tempus Structural Measures (2003-2006).* Brussels: European Commission.

Zgaga, P. (2010). "The Role of Higher Education in National Development. South-Eastern Europe and Reconstruction of the Western Balkans". In: *The Europa World of Learning 2011.* London; New York: Routledge. 19-24. Available at http://bit.ly/rf4MpT (accessed 9 October 2012).

Zgaga, P. (2012). "Exploring Higher Education Reforms in the Western Balkans". In: Panel presentation "Higher Education Reforms in the Western Balkans – an Internationalisation Perspective". The Consortium of Higher Education Researchers (CHER) Annual Conference. Belgrade, 10-12. September 2012. 3-25.

Primary sources

Albania (2008). *National Strategy for Higher Education 2008-2013.* No. 1509, dated 30/7/2008.

Croatia (2003). Zakon o znanstvenoj djelatnosti i visokom obrazovanju [Law for research and higher education]. *Narodne novine,* no. 123/03, 198/03, 105/04, 174/04, 46/07.

Croatia (2005). *Plan razvoja sustava odgoja i obrazovanja 2005 - 2010.* [The Development Plan for Education 2005 to 2010]. Zagreb: Ministarstvo znanosti, obrazovanja i sporta.

Croatia (2007). *Science and Technology Policy of the Republic of Croatia 2006-2010.*

Croatia (2011). *Nacrt prijedloga zakona o sveučilištu* [Draft Law on Universities]. Zagreb, January 2011.

Croatia (2012). *Nacrt prijedloga zakona o izmjenama i dopunama Zakona o znanstvenoj dijelatnosti i visokom obrazovanju* [Draft Proposal for Amendments and Additions to the Law on Research and Higher Education]. Zagreb: Government of the Republic of Croatia, April 2012.

European Commission (2001). *Communication from the Commission to the European Parliament and the Council on Strengthening Cooperation with Third Countries in the Field of Higher Education*. Brussels: European Commission.

European Commission (2003). *Communication from the Commission. The Role of the Universities in the Europe of Knowledge*. Brussels: European Commission.

European Commission (2005). *Communication from the Commission. Mobilising the Brainpower of Europe: Enabling Universities to Make Their Full Contribution to the Lisbon Strategy*. Brussels: European Commission.

European Commission (2006). *Communication from the Commission to the Council and the European Parliament. Delivering on the Modernisation Agenda for Universities: Education, Research and Innovation*. Brussels: European Commission.

European Commission (2008a). *Report from the Commission to the Council on the Council Resolution of 23 November 2007 on Modernising Universities for Europe's Competitiveness in a Global Knowledge Economy*. Brussels: European Commission.

European Commission (2008b). *Commission Staff Working Paper Accompanying Document to the Report from the Commission to the Council on the Council Resolution of 23 November 2007 on Modernising Universities for Europe's Competitiveness in a Global Knowledge Economy*. Brussels: European Commission.

European Commission (2008c). *Progress Towards the Lisbon Objectives in Education and Training – Indicators and Benchmarks*. Commission Staff Working Document. Brussels: European Commission.

European Commission (2009). *Report from the Commission to the Council, the European Parliament, the European Economic and Social Committee and the Committee of the Regions: Report on progress in quality assurance in higher education*. Brussels: European Commission.

European Commission (2012). *Tempus Higher Education Reform Experts: Activity Report 2011*. April 2012. Brussels: EACEA – Education Audiovisual and Culture Executive Agency.

European Council (2009). *Council Conclusions on a Strategic Framework for European Cooperation in Education and Training (ET 2020)*. Brussels: European Council.

European Union (2010). *The EU Contribution to the European Higher Education Area*. Luxembourg: Publications Office of the European Union.

Serbia (2005). National Assembly of the Republic of Serbia. Law on Higher Education. *Official Gazette of the Republic of Serbia*. No. 76/2005.

Serbia (2012) *The National Education Strategy in Serbia until 2020*. Government of Republic of Serbia.

Slovenia (2002). *Republic of Slovenia Master Plan for Higher Education*. Ljubljana, 26 February 2002.

Slovenia (2011). *Bold Slovenia. Slovenia: Knowledge-Based Society. National Higher Education Programme 2011-2020*. Ljubljana, 8 September 2010.

Part 2

**Massified and Internationalised
Higher Education:
Equity, Values, Societal Issues**

The Monolithic Un-intentionality of Higher Education Policies: On the Continuing Importance of Karl Marx, Joseph Stalin and the Minor Classics Less Known

Voldemar Tomusk

Abstract

A simple truth, though often ignored, is that thinking makes us who we are and knowledge is the substance of thought. Recent higher education policies are not only ignoring this, but fighting it vigorously. While industries of higher education make increasingly unrealistic promises for social mobility and high income with the distinction between advertising tricks and statements of truth becoming blurred, knowledge is being rendered devoid of meaning and learning driven out of higher education. Far from being seen as a problem of a global magnitude, the trend is often being celebrated as a great success. Unless universities return to the educated individual as a knowing self and strong evaluator, this chapter argues that little purpose will have been left for them.

Key words: universities, cooling-out, massification, knowledge, knowing self

> Question to Radio Yerevan: How would you describe post-Communism in Georgia?
> Answer: It is the same Communism, except that now everybody has a post.
>
> From the Soviet folklore of the post-Soviet era

Access to higher education is most likely the single most important and widely discussed higher education policy issue since the end of World War II. Higher education has been seen as an institution capable of taking care of many concerns of contemporary societies. Universities have been instrumental in producing knowledge and technologies that have allowed the health, well-being and comfort of many to be lifted to levels unprecedented in human history. Universities have allowed sophisticated thinking to emerge on the nature of humans and the handing on of their culture from one generation to the next. The importance Western democracies in particular have attributed to knowledge has enabled universities and other institutions of post-secondary education to become some of the most significant producers of social and economic status. Higher education is seen as an instrument allowing talented individuals to reach the highest positions in societies independently of their social class, race or gender. With this, universities are seen as the most effective tools for altering the social and cultural capital gained by the mere chance of birth.

Widening access to higher education is therefore seen as a stone for hitting not merely one or two birds, but perhaps four or five at once. For several countries such as the United States, the United Kingdom and Australia, higher education also serves as a major export-oriented industry. Higher education institutions can also serve the purpose of "warehousing students during the years when they would otherwise face an elevated risk of unemployment and criminal behavior" (Arum and Roksa 2011: 55). In times when armies are professional and prisons crowded, higher education acts as an excellent storehouse of young people whose only alternative would be to roam the streets. It is an even more attractive public policy solution if the students and their families pay for this. However, considering that as a result of having been stored in such a manner for a few years young people move up the social ladder and gain access to rewarding jobs, little space is left for doubts about the power of education.

Yet doubts spread as more young people access higher education. A naïve person might ask here "what difference does it make if everybody is moving up simultaneously?". An elite to which most people belong has perhaps lost one of its most important characteristics – exclusivity. Higher education has, among others, served as an instrument for selecting exceptionally highly qualified and talented individuals to perform the most demanding tasks in modern complex societies. As Gellner has taught, societies with changing technologies can no longer rely on inherited status, but need to fill certain critical positions with individuals having substantive competence in particular areas (Gellner 1994). The democratisation of higher education puts increasing pressure on any such a selection mechanism. As Martin Trow argued in his seminal 1974 report to the OECD, at a certain stage of the expansion of higher education systems "a very significant shift from the principle of equality of opportunity for educational achievement, to a more radical principle of equality of educational achievement" is taking place (Trow 1974/2010: 110). Such a shift not only challenges the selection function of higher education, but also its knowledge functions since it is at least plausible to think that individuals claiming access to higher education qualifications as their right represent a wide variety of capacities to perform complex cognitive tasks in particular areas of expertise.

One should not be surprised if higher education systems are not able for much longer to demonstrate a satisfactory performance across the many tasks societies have assigned to them. The recent massive pressure for the vertical diversification of universities world-wide demonstrates a strong desire among certain stakeholders to separate elite institutions from the mass, with an obvious threat of impoverishing many higher education institutions that play important roles in their local or national settings. Despite the democratic rhetoric bordering with populism, higher education is becoming a cut-throat business where only a few are bound to survive. Reciting the usual statements regarding democracy and widening access no longer appears convincing. While talks from high offices spread less than simplified views on knowledge societies and knowledge economies, it has not been thought through as to what counts as knowledge beyond what could be patented and copyrighted and what the point of knowing any of it would be. Knowledge has been relativised to the extent that learning is disappearing from higher education. Perhaps it would make good sense to have a look behind the veil of political correctness and the interests of the higher education industry that seems to be driving much of the currently dominant rhetoric to gain a better understanding of the functions higher education could successfully perform in our societies. It may well be that in order for societies to continue benefitting from higher education, the connections between knowledge, societies and individuals would need to be revisited from a critical perspective.

From mass to universal higher education

The Western world has been moving towards the lofty goal of higher education for all since World War II. The 1944 G.I. Bill allowed over 2 million US war veterans to attend colleges and universities. By the 1970s, a radical transformation of the higher education sector was well on the way in the USA – moving from an elite to a mass to a universal system, as Martin Trow reported to the OECD in 1974.

In many of his writings, Trow looked at US higher education as it had been expanding from a highly elitist system where only some 5 percent of the age cohort group had access to it to a universal system, where 50 percent or more had access to post-secondary education, identifying a qualitative shift at the point of 15 percent access. At that point higher education is no longer seen as a privilege, but as a right; turning into an obligation at the next juncture of 50 percent access (Trow 1974/2010). Learned colleagues and highly learned policy activists propagating wider access to higher education seem to be assuming that throughout the widening process higher education institutions remain the same in the core – for their capacity to carry on knowledge work and as a result of this – to decorate those who have benefitted from that experience with degrees capable of boosting the holders' social and economic positions. Trow made it emphatically clear that this was not the case. The very nature of higher education and higher education experience was bound to change as a result of the widening of the sector, if for no other reason than the economic one:

> No society, no matter how rich, can afford a system of higher education for 20 or 30 percent of age grade at the cost levels of the elite higher education that it formerly provided for 5 percent of the population (Trow 1974/2010: 123).

The massification of higher education serves a democratic goal – "to achieve a social, class, ethnic, and racial distribution in higher education reflecting that of the population at large" (ibid.: 101). There is, however, a price to be paid for such democratisation of higher education, as the higher education experience was changing – the main instructional forms practised in the academic communities preparing the next generation of the elite – tutorials and seminars supported by a "personal relationship between student and teacher" is giving way to large lectures and seminars provided by teaching assistants (ibid.: 98). In effect, the very meaning of higher education was changing under the mass regime, involving a "softening of the boundaries between formal education and other forms of life experience" (ibid.: 97).

Trow thought there were limits to the extent to which higher education was to be used as an instrument for radically democratic social goals. He found it desirable to continue elite higher education within the mass systems:

> Indeed, elite forms of higher education continue to perform functions that cannot be performed as well by mass higher education – among them, the education, training, and socialization of very highly selected students for intellectual work at the highest standards of performance and creativity (ibid.: 102).

According to Trow, elite higher education carries an important mission beyond what mass higher education is in a position to offer, namely to prepare highly talented individuals who "make important discoveries, lead great institutions, influence their country's laws and government, and add substantially to knowledge", while mass higher education "is designed to prepare students for relatively modest roles in society" (Trow 1976/2010: 150).

While Trow acknowledged the importance of mass higher education and thought it had an important enlightening role to play in the modern world, he was particularly concerned that massification could possibly erode the elite sector and compromise societies' needs for exceptionally highly qualified individuals. He concluded, however, that while elite education was under pressure, there was a strong need for it to continue within the mass system. The most significant way Trow thought elite education was to continue within mass universities was via graduate training within academic departments, often constituting islands of elite education and socialisation:

> The assimilation by graduate students of a pattern of values, attitudes, and ways of thought and appreciation is the most important single function that a university department performs (ibid.: 164).

Yet Trow had noticed that there was another way for elite education to continue within mass universities – through small groups of students meeting with a particular faculty member for informal seminars. As he explained:

> Such extra work does not advance the students further toward the degree nor does it promise higher marks in the final examination. Under these conditions, there is a pronounced self-selection of students who are prepared to work harder in order to learn more (ibid.: 166).

Although informal, such education provides what has been essential for the elite higher education experience – "a personal relationship between student and teacher" similar to what the tutorial seminar had previously offered in elite institutions, unaffordable on a massive scale. Depending on the ideological position one may take here, this could be seen as an elite conspiracy to reproduce themselves in a particularly sinister manner – without any obvious immediate benefit in terms of marks and degrees. Although in the long run such informal educational experience may well be sufficient to distinguish the elite from the masses in the process of making selections for the most highly qualified and rewarded positions in society. Such hidden elitism is considerably harder to fight against than demanding that everybody is issued the same kind of degree or qualification.

The problem with massification of HE

This would require establishing a radically egalitarian regime, not only to the effect that everybody has access to the same education, but also that nobody should be allowed to achieve more than the rest. This would be the logical end of the radical egalitarianism pressing, as Trow put it, "for a greater substantive equality among all the members of society" (ibid.: 153). Demands for greater or perhaps even complete substantive equality have solid traditions particularly in European thought. The Soviet system did its utmost to institutionalise this as part of its "affirmative action empire" project (Martin 2001), ending up with one of the least economically efficient regimes ever invented – a negative value-added economy of an unprecedented magnitude. Michael Burawoy, the President of the International Sociological Association from the University of California, Berkeley sees the recent Bologna Process in Europe as a continuation of the same line of thought:

> The Soviet model has been exported to the European continent with the Bologna Process that homogenizes and dilutes higher education across countries, all in the name of the transferability of knowledge and the mobility of students, making the university a tool rather than a motor of the knowledge economy (Burawoy 2012: 8).

There seems to be widening awareness in Europe regarding the economic impact of the policies promoting substantive equality concerning educational outcomes, as the talent held back by such policies either fails to reach its full potential or chooses to vote with their feet. Either way, Europe is losing the talent it needs. Yet it appears highly likely that the policies to occupy its place are neither more sophisticated nor better thought through. International university rankings or, as a recent European euphemism expresses the same idea – "multidimensional transparency tools" – seem to have little connection to the ideas of elite education as positively understood.

The Cooling-Out Function in Higher Education

Back in the 1950s Burton Clark noticed that higher education carried a significant mission which those involved were not keen to address, although students of society, such as Pitirim Sorokin (Sorokin 1959), had certainly understood as to what was going on beneath the surface of the unprecedented expansion of higher learning. Well before Martin Trow became concerned about the future of elite higher education, Burton Clark had identified a major contradiction:

> A major problem of democratic society is inconsistency between encouragement to achieve and the realities of limited opportunity. Democracy asks individuals to act as if social mobility were universally possible; status is to be won by individual effort, and rewards are to accrue to those who try. But democratic societies also need selective training institutions, and hierarchical work organizations permit increasingly fewer persons to succeed at ascending levels (Clark 1960/2008: 18).

Studying junior colleges in California in the 1950s, Clark understood how slowly but surely the aspirations of many young people were systematically reduced and eventually buried under a terminal associate degree. He called this the cooling-out process:

> In a summary, the cooling out process in higher education is one whereby systematic discrepancy between aspiration and avenue is covered over and stress for the individual and the system is minimized (ibid.: 28).

But he also realised that:

> The cooling-out function – like democracy – is not very attractive until you consider alternatives (Clark 1980/2008: 31).

These were the early days of the expansion of American higher education and it was relatively simple to identify the one predominant method that allowed the Californian higher education to systematically bury the aspirations of many, without exposing the obvious – equal opportunity was a myth, or as Clark put it:

> "Everybody is equally entitled to credentials that have lost their value" (ibid.: 38).

By the 1970s American higher education had become massified, and over the next two decades many European countries were to follow suit. While many see widening access to higher education as a sign of the democratisation of societies, for Trow it was perhaps more like a price to be paid to allow elite education to survive, as massification is bound to change the very nature of higher education, levelling it downward: "those who are concerned with the survival of elite education should welcome the expansion of other paths of social ascent, and these include the institutions of mass higher education" (Trow 1976/2010: 161). Looking from Clark's perspective, mass – and universal higher education even more so – function predominantly as massive safety-valves releasing the social tension while maintaining peace.

People tend to think that, like a generation or two before, higher education qualification elevates one to some kind of an elite – social, economic, political. These days, however, different sections of higher education serve as stations where, slowly but surely, such expectations are being put to rest for good, increasingly as a service to an individual whose dreams are being killed while they pay for it. By the time the obvious emerges, the recipient of the service has other, more important things to take care of, such as repaying her student loan, than harbouring revolutionary thoughts. Meanwhile, the social meaning of higher education is changing. No longer is higher education, at least in the mass and universal sections of the system, sought in order to appear as a winner – to move up in some manner, but not to lose, not to lag behind all of those who already have tertiary education experience.

With the access to higher education widening, the social mobility providing capacity of university or college education is reaching that of having an automobile or washing machine, while participating in higher education is becoming an act of consumption:

> Giving one's children a higher education begins to resemble the acquisition of an automobile or washing machine, one of the symbols of increasing affluence- and there can be little doubt that the populations of advanced industrial societies have settled expectation of a rising standard of living (Trow 1974/2010: 127).

Once pretty much every family has a refrigerator, not having one looks odd indeed. So it seems to be increasingly the case with higher education qualifications – it is harder to impress somebody with not having one than having it. The cost of higher education in the United States, as Calhoun knowledgeably shares with us, is rising well beyond the rate of inflation. Its increase follows the price rises of other luxury goods, such as for example single malt whiskeys (Calhoun 2011: 31). It is not entirely obvious, however, whether the willingness to pay is still driven by the desire to progress socially and otherwise, or by the fear of taking a dive to the bottom by virtue of not having a higher education degree.

In his 1980 revisit to the cooling-out function, Clark makes it abundantly clear that higher education is bound to remain "a graveyard of hope" (Clark 1980/2008: 48):

> Only the naïve do not recognize that with hope there is disappointment, with success, failure. The settings that lead toward the cooling-out effort remain, all the more so as democracies open doors that were formerly closed. Any system of higher education that has to reconcile such conflicting values as equity,

competence, and individual choice – and the advanced democracies are so committed – has to effect compromise procedures that allow for some of each (ibid.: 48-49).

This is actually not that difficult to understand. A more interesting issue is that in a world with at least some degree of choice available, institutions known as graveyards of hope would not enjoy much popularity. For any college or university to function even in limited market conditions, hope should first be offered and then buried, after an agonising and often costly death. Eventually social learning will happen, students abandon the hope-killing institutions and new institutions take on the unfortunate mission at least initially hidden from the customers' sight. Clark made it abundantly clear, however, that eliminating two-year colleges would not eliminate the cooling-out function from higher education systems.

Recently further progress has been made. The idea of lifelong learning allows the keeping up of one's hopes from the birth till the deathbed, always looking forward to a new degree, qualification or credential that would finally allow the performing of the trick by Freiherr von Münchhausen – lifting oneself up (on the social ladder) by pulling one's own bootstraps. A question central to such higher education is whether it is indeed the best use of intellectual resources and human talent, both by the students as well as the teachers. Or, to put it differently – whether mere survival until getting caught by the biologically inevitable is indeed a satisfactory life project knowing what we collectively know about ourselves and our existence.

A degree of waste

If it is indeed the case that one of the main functions of higher education in democratic societies is securing social rest by cooling-out, slowly but certainly, the hopes and expectations of large segments of society, one may consider challenging some of the rhetoric by which these segments are being lured to participate in the cooling-out process in the capacity of the recipients of this somewhat unfortunate, even if socially and economically necessary, service. One such argument relates to the expanding knowledge economies and widening of knowledge societies. The argument being made, coming as no major surprise from the representatives of higher education industries themselves, is that investments in higher education drive economic growth. Therefore, the larger a policy maker proposes making the higher education budget, the smarter he appears! The somewhat self-serving nature of such conclusions of policy-related social science studies seems to have passed unnoticed.

Back in 1993, James Murphy took a different view on the matter by suggesting that it was not exactly obvious whether higher education was the horse or the cart of economic growth:

> instead of Britain needing, as this convention insists, more graduates to prosper, Britain needs first to prosper before it is likely to want, still less need, those graduates it currently produces (Murphy 1993: 19).

The higher education industry reacted painfully to the message that had intended to undermine its core interests right from within. As a result, Murphy never wrote another higher education paper, instead focusing on school improvement. Nevertheless, two decades later similar questions are still being asked and answers are not as one-sided as in the 1990s.

The horse or cart question and the chicken or egg problem; as we now know, higher education can serve as a significant engine of economic growth, at least in a country such as the United Kingdom where "the total net injection into the economy by international students in 2004-05 was around £3.74 billion", exceeding, for example, the export value of the cultural and media industries combined (Vickers and Bekhradnia 2007). This, however, is a role very different from what the knowledge economy argument has been suggesting. Although some recent arguments behind creating the European Higher Education Area have been directly motivated by the British success in turning higher education into a major export-oriented industry and replicating that success on the European scale, to the extent that all European higher education can be seen as a continent-wide higher education supermarket.

The university ranking fever and world-class university movement have undermined the European higher education supermarket strategy. The new idea is to create an explicitly elitist sub-sector – another fad that threatens to destroy entire higher education systems in some poorer countries which, in order to hire one or two world-class academics whose publications would boost the rankings of a chosen university, would need to drastically cut the budgets of the other institutions across the entire nation (see e.g. Burawoy 2012). Needless to say, little would such a "world-class university" resemble sites of elite education as, for example, Trow saw it. Discussing higher education marketing strategies in Europe and beyond would require a volume on its own. For our purposes, it suffices to say that the entire sector seems to be in a relatively desperate search for a strategy that would boost the confidence of the consumers of higher education services. The industry as such seems to have little interest in any further function of its outputs.

As an interesting turn, a recent EU report seems to corroborate Murphy's arguments. Surprisingly enough, the report (GHK 2011) was explicitly concerned with over-education along the lines of Murphy's argumentation. For example:

> Over education may be increasing during the economic recession and changing the behaviours of those most likely to be from lower income families who see greater risks in investing in tertiary education (ibid.: 38).

An increase in wage differences among people with higher education degrees has been offered as a sign of over-education. Yet it appears that this is not necessarily a short-term issue as those who at one stage land lowly paid jobs appear unlikely to increase their income later. In such a manner it may indeed well be the case that highly educated people are occupying jobs previously held by the less educated, pushing the latter further down the ladder so that increasingly higher educational levels are needed to have access to increasingly less well paid positions. However, the report seems to agree that while there is a "degree of waste" in higher education, there are also important benefits:

> While over-education has an impact on wage inequality [among the population of equally educated individuals V.T.], higher levels of education overall bring other benefits in relation to health and well-being (ibid.: 39).

On these grounds, or perhaps some other, higher education is still seen as superior to other forms of education, such as vocational training:

> While incentives to gain vocational qualifications should remain, this should not be at the expense of incentives to study for degrees. If it does, it will continue to draw young people from lower waged families into vocational qualifications (ibid.).

Who exactly benefits and how from the expansion of higher education at the expense of vocational training is not exactly obvious. It is simply ironic that the next step higher education is being asked to provide is job-relevant skills and competencies – that is vocational training (ibid.: 38). Obviously, the thinking behind this argument is that higher education qualifications, even if not leading to a higher income, would provide social mobility to representatives of groups previously excluded from higher education. As

Clark suggested, significant segments of higher education do not deliver much beyond cooling-out hopes and expectations. Expectations that diluted versions of higher education, both in terms of research and teaching (see e.g. Burawoy 2012, Calhoun 2011), would perform the trick are seriously misplaced.

Trapping "young people from lower waged families" in the cooling-out sections of higher education, and in the debt bondage to follow, serves the interests of the higher education industry and populist political goals, but is likely to leave young people worse off than vocational training. While the report wisely recognises that "increasing participation in tertiary education may not, by itself, provide for more equal access to high quality provision" (GHK 2011: 47), and only high quality education is in a position to deliver both in terms of knowledge and social mobility, in those terms mass higher education cannot be of high quality. High quality higher education, as Trow suggested, is too expensive to be provided on a mass scale and more importantly society, as Clark noticed already in the 1950s, needs mass higher education for exactly the opposite reason.

In their recent study, Arum and Roksa (2011) argue that while access was one of the main issues in late 20th century higher education policy discussions, respective policies have contributed little in terms of learning:

> Growing numbers of students are sent to college at increasingly higher costs, but for a large proportion of them the gains in critical thinking, complex reasoning and written communication are either exceedingly small or empirically non-existent (ibid.: 121).

The lack of such capacities relegates "U.S. college graduates to routine non-manual occupations within firms", while qualified personnel are being hired from among the graduate schools' graduates and sought from foreign countries (ibid.: 143).

The fact that almost half of college students do not make any significant progress acquiring the most critical capacities needed for both successful professional careers and participation in democratic societies is not, as Arum and Roksa notice, seen as a crisis. The problem is that apparently there is no problem at all and society is receiving exactly what it is asking for:

> No actors in the system are primarily interested in undergraduate student academic growth, although many are interested in student retention and persistence. Limited learning on college campuses is not a crisis because the institutional actors implicated in the system are receiving organizational

outcomes that they seek, and therefore neither the institutions nor the system as a whole is in any way challenged or threatened (Arum and Roksa 2011: 125).

Neither is that a problem for society at large. It is, indeed, a solution to many of its problems. As long as the required amount of high level skills is available from graduate schools or other sources, social rest and confident consumers are more important for societies' stability than capacities in critical literacy and complex reasoning. Students are assuming the position of consumers: "to the extent that undergraduate instruction matters at all in these institutions, it is assessed primarily in terms of students satisfaction on course evaluations" (ibid.: 134). Students are not at all seeing their college experience through the neo-liberal prism of social mobility and personal economic advantage (Clegg 2011: 40). Instead, they are interested in independent social experimenting, "while earning high marks in their courses with relatively little investment of effort" (Arum and Roksa 2011: 125). This is the kind of consumption that a significant part of student borrowing is financing. Needless to say – these are exactly the kind of consumers our societies need, particularly in times of an economic crisis, but not only then – young confident individuals who without the slightest hesitation charge the latest designer handbag or gadget to their credit cards at 20 percent interest.

The English novelist Sebastian Faulks thinks that this is not only an American problem. As a high school teacher in his novel explains, the English educational system started withholding knowledge from students in around 1975, initiating a downwards spiral:

> Then there came a time when they decided that because not every kid in the class could understand or remember those things, they wouldn't teach them any more because it was not fair for the less good ones. So they withheld knowledge. Then I suppose the next lot of teachers didn't have the knowledge to withhold (Faulks 2009: 305).

"It was," as Faulks explains, "a positive choice. We chose to know less" (ibid.: 306).

The same happens in large parts of higher education. While it has volunteered to take care of many of contemporary societies' problems, it is increasingly ignoring its core mission – "the professional production of knowledge" (Burawoy 2012: 19).

Why knowledge may still matter

Academics emphatically argue that for contemporary societies, perhaps even more than ever before, knowledge matters (see e.g. Rhoten and Calhoun 2011), while the messages higher education institutions receive from their stakeholders confirm exactly the opposite – in fact, knowledge does not matter.

Calhoun reminds us that "academic institutions have considerable ability to confer honor and legitimacy" (ibid.: 45) and that seems to be in the primary focus of the policy makers. Students would perhaps also value that part, if receiving it would not take too much of an effort. It is being ignored, quite conveniently one may think, that the source of that honour and legitimacy rests on the knowledge the university produces in its core. Without that knowledge, produced by "an aristocracy of trained intellect" (Searle 1975), the university loses its mystical powers.

Increasing numbers of young people participate in higher education and charge the cost of that experience against their future income. It seems to be the case that for many students it is more about taking time off before full adulthood arrives and experimenting with independent living than anything related to participating in the university knowledge production mission. This, as Arum and Roksa have confirmed, satisfies the academics as well as the students and meets society's economic as well as social needs. We also know that such participation in higher education does not reduce inequalities between various social groups, but tends to widen the gaps (Arum and Roksa 2011, Clegg 2011). Unless a student from an under-represented group gains access to an elite institution, his or her relative social position does not improve (Clegg 2011).

Highly respected practically-minded readers may now question the very purpose of this essay. After all, why should anybody take a critical stance against higher education when everybody seems to be satisfied with what it produces and societies receive what they are asking for? One answer would suggest that the current balance comes at a high ethical price – the role of higher education in contemporary societies appears to be being systematically misrepresented by the industry itself as well as politicians at many levels. Social learning may take a long time, but eventually the emptiness of many of the promises made to students and taxpayers will be revealed. Higher education functioning as a pyramid investment scheme will sooner or later collapse. Another way of looking at the current situation suggests there could be better uses for the intellectual resources available in higher education that could be put to good use in building better informed, more just democratic societies. As Clegg argues:

> The systematic mis-description of the goods of higher education in terms of personal economic advantage is problematic for its actors and practitioners, not just because it obscures some unpalatable truths about inequality, but also because it blocks the articulation of alternative visions of what the benefits of higher education might be in terms of the broader value for students and their futures (Clegg 2011: 40).

I would argue that the issue extends further than students and their futures. What hinges on what higher education delivers or conveniently does not deliver is the future of societies and the quality of democracies. It is convenient indeed to declare students as being the customers of higher education services, luring them to invest their future income in social experiments and then slowly killing off their hopes and expectations. The industry flourishes and political leaders with a populist bend declare their priorities: "education, education, education", as comrade Lenin once did. What we seem to be losing out here is the educated citizenry and highly educated public capable of taking informed positions on important public issues globally. Instead, what is being promoted is hedonism, intellectual ignorance and economic irresponsibility. In that sense at least, the social rest provided by the cooling-out higher education and resources it mobilises from the students and taxpayers alike are borrowed against the stability and welfare of future generations. Not only are we likely to hand over to the next generation an institution critically devoid of moral responsibility, but we are also missing an opportunity to prepare responsible citizens able to participate in the democratic political process on grounds other than a narrow-minded ideology or immediate consumption.

While the university is and is to remain an institution primarily concerned with professional knowledge production, for the future of higher education and societies the nature of knowledge should be reconsidered:

> Knowledge [...] is socially produced, temporarily bounded, and fallible; but [it is also] knowledge of something, and [with this] there is an ontological, not just epistemological, dimension to knowing (ibid.: 101).

Knowledge, as Bernstein argued, no longer resembles money. Like money, it is expected to circulate separately from the personal commitments of the knower, generating more knowledge and ... money:

> This new concept [of knowledge; V.T.] is a truly secular concept. Knowledge
> should flow like money to wherever it can create advantage and profit. Indeed,
> knowledge is not like money, it is money. Knowledge is divorced from persons,
> their commitments, their personal dedications. These become impediments,
> restrictions on the flow of knowledge, and introduce deformations in the
> working of the symbolic market. Moving knowledge about, even creating it,
> should not be more difficult than moving and regulating money. Knowledge,
> after nearly a thousand years, is divorced from inwardness and literally
> dehumanized (Bernstein 1996: 87).

This is a problem central to the universities of our times. What is needed, as
Michael Young suggested, is to bring knowledge back in (Young 2007).

It appears highly likely, at least to this author, that without establishing
a connection between knowledge and the knower we will not be able to
attribute a meaning to undergraduate education, and much of university
knowledge production alike. Unless knowledge takes on an ontological
dimension, as Clegg has argued, the fact of knowing makes little difference
for the knower so that cheating at tests is not an issue worth mentioning and
minimising one's effort in studying is an entirely rational approach. For a
personally uncommitted knowledge producer, the issue is not who is she/he
as a knowing person. All that matters is the metrics of the knowledge being
produced – the productivity of personally uncommitted labour. If there is
one issue the knowledge economy rhetoric is paying no attention to, it is
knowledge itself. Michael Young (2012) argues:

> the category of 'knowledge' appears to be used in an almost entirely rhetorical
> way; the meaning of knowledge is at best implicit and at worst virtually empty
> of content. One consequence is that such policies deny or disregard the idea that
> access to knowledge in the strong sense that involves its claims to reliability is
> central to the purpose of education.

He continues:

> If I have accurately identified this trend and it continues, it is a highly
> problematic heritage that we leave to future generations – namely that there is no
> explicit knowledge that is important enough to be 'transmitted' to the next
> generation. It is a heritage that has none of the visibility of the environmental or
> sustainability crises, although arguably, addressing it is fundamental to whether
> we are able to deal with either (ibid.: 139).

On the pretext of rapid growth in knowledge, understanding is being
smuggled in that nothing is worth knowing any longer and that managing
the flows of knowledge – a process of production where money is being
ceaselessly made – is possible without understanding any of it. Taking

knowledge away from humans, even if higher education consultants succeed in demonstrating this as progress, is an act against humanity as such. Ben Okri has offered a different vision for higher education:

> The academies of the future will do one thing we do not do today. They will teach the art of self-discovery. There is nothing more fundamental in education. We turn out students from our universities who know how to give answers, but not how to ask questions. The wisdom centres in our culture do not reach our students. They leave universities with skills for the workplace, but no knowledge of how to live, or what living is for. They are not taught how to see. They are not taught how to listen. They are not taught the great art of obedience, and how it precedes self-mastery. They are not taught the true art of reading (Okri 2008: 8).

So far, we have unfortunately not seen this happening. If anything, over the decade since Ben Okri spoke these words during an after-dinner talk at the British Embassy in Paris in September 2002, the world has been moving in exactly the opposite direction. Increasingly, students even do not have the skills for the workplace, while societies find it difficult to establish a connection between policies and the long-term future of societies.

When thinking about the future of higher education, particularly mass undergraduate education, it seems to be justified at this stage to call for a deep re-thinking of the very purpose of that education, returning to the student as a knowing self (Clegg 2011), and to ask fundamental questions regarding the knowledge a young person should be able to have to decide who they want to be in the context of human history and culture. As Clegg argues, discussions on future desirable selves of the students have been reduced to the level of the labour market and the student's financial contribution (ibid.: 104). This falls short of what students as knowing selves need and what is needed for the future of democratic societies. Charles Taylor finds that "we are not beings whose only authentic evaluations are non-qualitative as the utilitarian tradition suggests" (Taylor 1985: 23).

What we would need, following Taylor's language and thinking, is higher education that allows young people to become "strong evaluators":

> for the strong evaluator reflection also examines the different possible modes of being of the agent. Motivations or desires do not only count in virtue of the attraction of the consummations but also in virtue of the kind of life and kind of subject that these desires properly belong to (Taylor 1985: 25).

Fundamental to any such programme is, as Clegg (2011) rightfully notices, the issue of curriculum, which fundamentally is a question about knowledge worth knowing and ourselves as knowers shaped by that very knowledge. As

Lauder and colleagues correctly argue – despite the high sounding rhetoric regarding the increasing importance of knowledge even thinking, at least in the workplace, is being kept as a privilege for a select few (Lauder et al. 2012). It is perhaps quite likely that in this sense higher education institutions as places of work follow the climate in the rest of societies. The role higher education has assumed is not particularly encouraging. It is indeed hard to see how this could be reversed without individuals becoming interested in knowledge beyond the limits of the obvious neo-liberal agenda. It is perhaps not only that the answer has been withheld so far, but even the question.

It is intriguing to notice that modest related conversations seem to be taking off in UK higher education, not because there has been any particularly positive policy shift recently, but because student identity is becoming a significant issue in the context of the large number of overseas students that UK universities have a vital interest in (see e.g. Wang 2012).

Conclusion: The monolithic unintentionality of higher education policies

Higher education policies often resemble monolithic intentionality as described by Glaeser (2010), intended to function as a form of self-fulfilling prophecy. As Glaeser argues, it was widely believed in the former German Democratic Republic that, as long as the citizenry monolithically believed in the vision of building communism, communism was to emerge as a result of the joint efforts. Apparently what happened was that the monolithic sharing of a strong vision prevented the citizenry and their leaders adequately perceiving their daily realities, until the situation moved beyond the point of a possible correction.

The state of higher education policies in many countries is similar to this to the extent that citizens are expected to trust monolithically in these policies. What seems to be missing, however, is the intentionality part. Beyond the overly simplistic rhetoric to the effect of building knowledge societies and the many benefits to follow, which may actually appear even less sophisticated than the East German socialism, very little by way of a convincing idea of what kind of future societies we are building is being offered. Unless a connection is established between knowledge and responsible humane agency, one should remain cautious about this ending in a way better than what happened in the German Democratic Republic.

References:

Arum, R., J. Roksa (2011). *Academically Adrift: Limited Learning on College Campuses.* Chicago: Chicago University Press.

Bernstein, B. (1996). *Pedagogy, Symbolic Control, and Identity.* London: Rowman & Littlefield Publishers, Inc.

Burawoy, M. (2012). The Public University – A Battleground for Real Utopias. Work in progress.

Calhoun, C. (2011). "Libyan Money, Academic Missions, and Public Social Science". *Public Culture.* Vol. 24. No. 1. 9-45.

Clark, B. R. (1960/2008). "The 'Cooling-Out' Function in Higher Education". In: *On Higher Education: Selected Writings 1956-2006.* 18-30.

Clark, B. R. (1980/2008). "The 'Cooling-Out' Function Revisited". In: *On Higher Education: Selected Writings 1956-2006.* 31-49.

Clegg, C. (2011). "Cultural Capital and Agency: Connecting Critique and Curriculum in Higher Education". *British Journal of Sociology of Education.* Vol. 31. No. 1. 95-110.

Faulks, S. (2009). *A Week in December.* London: Hutchinson.

Gellner, E. (1994). *Conditions of Liberty: Civil Society and Its Rivals.* London: Viking/Allen Lane.

Glaeser, A. (2010). *Political Epistemics: The Secret Police, the Opposition, and the End of East German Socialism.* Chicago and London: Chicago University Press.

GHK (2011). *Education, Inequality and Social Exclusion: Policy Lessons from EU-supported Research Projects.* London: GHK Consulting Ltd.

Lauder, H., M. Young, H. Daniels, M. Balarin, J. Lowe (2012). "Introduction: Educating for the Knowledge Economy? Critical perspectives". In: H. Lauder, M. Young, H. Daniels, M. Balarin, J. Lowe (eds.), *Educating for the Knowledge Economy? Critical Perspectives.* London: Routledge. 1-24.

Martin, T. (2001). *The Affirmative Action Empire: Nations and Nationalism in the Soviet Union, 1923-1939.* Ithaca, New York: Cornell University Press.

Murphy, J. (1993). "A Degree of Waste: the economic benefits of educational expansion". *Oxford Review of Education.* Vol. 19. No. 1. 9-31.

Okri, B. (2008). "What are Universities for?" In: P. Flather (ed.), *The Future of European Universities. An International Investigation into How European Universities Can – and Must – Operate at the Forefront of the Knowledge Revolution in the 21st Century.* Oxford: Euroepeaevm.

Rhoten, D., C. Calhoun, eds. (2011). *Knowledge Matters: The Public Mission of the Research University.* New York: Columbia University Press.

Searle, J. R. (1975). "Two Concepts of Academic Freedom". In: E. L. Pincoffs (ed.), *The Concept of Academic Freedom.* Austin: The University of Texas Press.

Sorokin, P. (1959). *Social and Cultural Mobility.* New York: Free Press.

Taylor, C. (1985). *Human Agency and Language. Philosophical Papers 1.* Cambridge: Cambridge University Press.

Trow, M. (1974/2010). "Problems in the Transition from Elite to Mass Higher Education". In: *Twentieth Century Higher Education: Elite to Mass to Universal.* Baltimore: The Johns Hopkins University Press. 88-142.

160   Voldemar Tomusk

Trow, M. (1976/2010). "Elite Higher Education: An Endangered Species". In: *Twentieth Century Higher Education: Elite to Mass to Universal.* Baltimore: The Johns Hopkins University Press. 145-172.

Vickers, P., B. Bekhradnia (2007). "The Economic Costs and Benefits of International Students". *HEPI Report Summary* 32. Oxford: Higher Education Policy Institute.

Walker, M. (2008). "Widening Participation; Widening Capability". *London Review of Education.* Vol. 6. No. 3. 267-279.

Wang, Y. (2012). "Transformations of Chinese International Students Understood through a Sense of Wholeness". *Teaching in Higher Education.* Vol. 17. No. 4. 359-37.

Young, M. (2012). "Education, Globalisation, and the 'Voice of Knowledge'". In: H. Lauder, M. Young, H. Daniels, M. Balarin, J. Lowe (eds.), *Educating for the Knowledge Economy? Critical Perspectives*. London: Routledge. 139-151.

Young, M. (2007). *Bringing Knowledge Back In: From Social Constructivism to Social Realism in the Sociology of Education.* London: Routledge.

"Hullabaloo in the Groves of Academe": The Politics of 'Instituting' a Market in English Higher Education

Susan L. Robertson — finds holes in all gov. HE policy & justifications. for it see from Py 172

Abstract

This chapter examines the complexities of the development of a competitive higher education market open to for-profit providers. It does this through a case study of Higher Education policies in England. A core argument is that markets do not emerge as a result of policy fiat; rather, markets must be instituted. Creating a competitive higher education market, however, directly challenges existing institutionalised interests including its rules, routines and values. To develop my case, I draw upon the work of Karl Polanyi (1992) who points out that instituting a market is a highly political process involving competing values, the exercise of authority, claims to what is legitimate, and the possibility of failure. I reflect on these developments for higher education policymaking in England, on what these developments might mean for the sector, and their implications for higher education across Europe.

Key words: higher education, universities, private for-profit actors, England, privatisation, governance, education financing

Introduction

Over the past decade, the growth of private provision in higher education has become an important topic of discussion, largely because these developments challenge existing conceptions of what a university is for, of how best to think about concepts such as 'public' and 'private', and what we mean when we talk about concepts such as marketisation, privatisation or indeed commodification. Yet private providers have existed in higher education for as long as the sector has existed (Levy 1979 and 1986), raising questions about quite what the fuss is about, and indeed what it is that is at stake. For observers of contemporary developments (cf. Maldonado-Maldonado et al. 2004, Kinser 2006, Carpentier 2012), something new is afoot here. They argue that it is not so much that there is a growth in private actors *per se*, but that we are currently witnessing a rapid expansion of for-profit private providers within the sector in areas that might be regarded as core business. Their growing presence is supported by neo-liberal arguments that the expansion of higher education cannot be supported by the public purse, that students should bear a bigger proportion of the cost of their higher education, that students should be given a choice regarding the nature of their higher education experience, and that institutions would be more efficient in their operations if they operated in a competitive higher education market.

In this chapter I examine the complexities of these developments through a case study of Higher Education policies in England. My focus will be on the UK Coalition Government's policies aimed at putting into place a regulatory framework to create a competitive market that is also open to for-profit providers. A core argument of this chapter will be that markets do not emerge as a result of policy fiat. Rather, markets must be instituted. Creating a competitive higher education market, however, directly challenges existing institutionalised interests including its rules, routines and values. As a result, and to paraphrase the title of Kieran Desai's (1998) wonderful book – *Hullabaloo in the Guava Orchard* describing a major disturbance in village life – higher education policymakers are likely to set into motion a major disturbance, and commotion, within the sector. To develop my case, I draw upon the work of Karl Polanyi (1992) who points out that instituting a market is a highly political process involving competing values, the exercise of authority, claims to what is legitimate, and the possibility of failure. I reflect on what these developments mean for higher education policymaking in England, on what these developments might mean for the sector, and their implications for higher education across Europe.

On strategy, selectivity and the 'institutedness' of markets

As Slater and Tonkiss (2001: 104) note, whilst Polanyi's work on the economy as embedded in social relations has become a central idea in economic anthropology and sociology, this has tended to displace the equally valuable concept of economic 'institutedness'. By institutedness, Polanyi (1992: 33) means that markets are made, or produced, through social institutions and legal and political strategies and processes. In arguing this, Polanyi is rejecting the classical liberal assumption that market society arises organically out of humankind's natural preference for market exchanges and private property rights.

To produce rational economic behaviour (Peck 2010), policy projects must therefore imagine 'a market', whilst state policies must be aimed at how to strategically advance and materially institute this imagined market in a range of hard and/or soft law, for instance as forms of ownership rights, as new kinds of governance structures, and in rules of exchange and changed conceptions of control (Fligstein 1996). Hard law secures market relations through legal contract. Soft law encourages agents, or subjects, to perform or materialise the market, guided by disciplinary techniques such as audit, quality assurance, benchmarking, and key performance indicators (Hood 1991, Rhodes 1997). Gill (2003: 131-132) described the two mechanisms deployed for the purposes of market-making as "the constitutionalisation of neoliberalism" (hard law), and "disciplinary neoliberalism" (soft law).

However, markets are not instituted from a blank slate or neutral terrain of institutional practices. Rather, as I have argued above, making a market must contend with already existing institutionalised interests. Breaking this path-shaping activity is important in order to bring into being a new regulatory system with very different logics, values, and modes of being. Successfully making a market will be dependent upon strategies, the capacity to mobilise interests, and new forms of selectivity, which capture, materialise and institute new interests, structures, social relations and subjectivities, in turn transforming the existing landscape.

Here Jessop's (2005) Strategic Relational Approach (SRA), with its innovative approach to structure and agency as selectively and strategically formed, is useful for highlighting the dialectical and evolving relationship between structures and agents:

> structures are thereby treated analytically as strategically selective in their form, content and operation; and actions are likewise treated as structurally constrained, more or less context sensitive, and structuring. To treat structures as *strategically selective* involves examining how a given structure may privilege some actors, some identities, some strategies, some spatial and temporal horizons, some actions over others. Likewise, to treat actions as *structurally constrained* requires exploring the ways, if any, in which actors (individual and/or collective) take account of this different privileging through strategic context analysis when undertaking a course of action [...] In short, the SRA is concerned with the relations between structurally inscribed strategic selectivities and (differentially reflexive) structurally-oriented strategic calculation (Jessop 2005: 48).

Jessop's (ibid.) Strategic Relational Approach is used therefore to help us see higher education in England at any particular juncture as the outcome of the specific patterning of strategically-selected social relations constituted through economic and political imaginaries, with actors having differential capacities to selectively engage in, and reorganise, structures and strategies over different spatio-temporal horizons. Projects and processes aimed at transforming the strategic selectivities of the higher education sector can be described as a process of "resectoralising" (Robertson 2011); that is the rules around the sector itself, including who can operate within as opposed to being located outside, are being contested and reworked.

Instituting a market in the groves of English academe

We can get a sense of the complexities and dilemmas facing the current Coalition Government in imagining and instituting a competitive 'free' higher education market open to for profit providers by examining the 2012 press release from Pearson, a FTSE 100 company with pre-tax profits in 2011 of £1.2 billion (Matthews 2012: 1),[1] announcing it would open a degree-awarding education college. A small cohort of "pioneers" were to be recruited by September 2012 into a Pearson Business and Enterprise degree course (BSc Hons), especially designed by organisations that included British Telecom (BT), Cisco[2], the Peter Jones Foundation[3], and Atos[4]. Students enrolling in this degree could choose to study following either: (i) a conventional pattern of 3 years; (ii) accelerate progress and complete within 2 years; or (iii) complete over 4 years whilst mixing work and study. The cost of the degree would be £6,500 per year. Whilst such a fee level across Europe is likely to be viewed as excessive, it is nevertheless well under the ceiling of £9000 that has now been implemented in England with the beginning of the 2012/13 academic year (BIS 2011a and 2011b). The new fee ceiling, it should be pointed out, is triple that set in 2006 (£3,000), making it one of the most expensive undergraduate systems in Europe.

---

1   Pearson owns the Financial Times, the qualifications company Edexcel, and has major interests in publishing learning and testing and assessment materials. It also recently branched out to invest in low-fee schools in Africa.
2   Cisco Systems is a global technology firm specialising in the development of platforms for system integration. It also has a large education and learning portfolio.
3   The Peter Jones Foundation aims to provide support to children in many different stages and circumstances of their lives. The Peter Jones Enterprise Academy educates young people in the UK, encouraging a confident 'can do' attitude amongst them.
4   Atos is an international information technology services company with annual 2011 revenues of EUR 8.5 billion and 74,000 employees in 48 countries.

Yet Pearson's new course was to be validated by Royal Holloway, University of London, rather than Pearson having its own degree-awarding powers as hoped for by the Minister for Higher Education for the start of the 2012/13 academic year.   Pearson's announcement therefore signalled business as usual within the sector. In other words, like in a range of other countries across Europe, North America and Latin America, a range of private higher education providers has been operating in England for some time. For instance, the University of Buckingham was established in 1973 as the first private provider in an otherwise public system of higher education.[5] Buckingham also pioneered a different delivery model – some of which has been taken up by Pearson: high cost; students can complete a 3-year degree in two years; and it services an international student population willing to pay full fees.

However, the conditions for entry, the nature of operations and mechanisms of governance of the new alternative providers (including transnational higher education conglomerates such as Laureate and Kaplan) into UK higher education (including access to degree awarding powers, state funding, and recognition as a university – all crucial to marketing and profitability) are different than for universities *within* the sector. This is what the new for-profit providers want to change. For Pearson, the gap between the government's policy ambitions and its capacity to navigate the political space sufficient to realise a new regulatory framework favourable to new for-profit providers is particularly irksome.

Yet, over the past decade there has been growing pressure on government to rethink its position. This has paralleled the steady expansion of private providers in the UK higher education sector (Fielden and Middlehurst 2010, Middlehurst and Fielden 2011), though the scale and scope of their activity has not been officially monitored. Many are branch campuses of foreign universities whose degrees are awarded by their home institution. Others are firms, such as INTO[6], which specialise in joint ventures with existing public higher education providers, largely in the area of foundation and language courses for international students in preparation for entry to university programmes. Many of these firms have intentions of

---

5   The University of Buckingham, a chartered university, was established in 1973 as a not-for-profit company.

6   INTO has a wide range of 'products' that include organised student exchanges, and joint ventures with universities to provide preparation courses for universities (see http://www.into-corporate.com/en-gb/about-into.aspx - accessed 20 August 2012).

expanding, and it is possible to detect a degree of mission creep as these for-profit education providers learn how to work with, and around, the existing regulations.

From the early 1990s onward, there has also been interest by international agencies, such as the Organisation for Economic Cooperation and Development (OECD), some governments and education service firms in viewing higher education as a services sector with education internationally traded, and regulated globally (Larsen and Vincent Lancrin 2002, Kelsey 2008). The launch of the World Trade Organisation's (WTO) General Agreement on Trade in Services (GATS) in 1995, with its intention to progressively liberalise sectors such as education, was an ambitious project aimed at market making through multilateral agreements. Liberalisation in effect meant opening up public higher education to foreign direct investment, increased international student and academic mobility, and commercial operators. This meant 'levelling the playing field' so that commercial operators could access similar conditions (such as subsidies, student loans, degree awarding powers, nomenclature) (Robertson et al. 2002, Verger and Robertson 2012). Yet this project became dogged by considerable organised resistance, particularly around arguments that education was a public good and should not be opened to commercial interests. By 2003, the WTO's GATS negotiations had largely stalled.

One outcome of the difficulties facing the GATS negotiations is that new providers wanting to enter the English higher education sector have turned to making their claims for entrance and recognition to national regulatory bodies on a case-by-case basis. This has slowed the new providers' entry to the sector as well as confronted them with a regulatory environment that differs from the existing providers. Up until the beginning of 2012, only five organisations had acquired Degree Awarding Powers (DAPs) in England. Amongst the five is BPP Ltd, a high profile, for-profit, provider (of undergraduate and graduate law, accounting and health studies) acquired in 2009 by the private equity firm, Apollo Global, a subsidiary of the Apollo Group based in the USA. In April 2012, Montagu Private Equity acquired the College of Law for £200 million in April 2012 and, in doing so, acquired the DAPs from the Privy Council in 2006.

The situation in England can be contrasted with the United States where, until recently, there had been remarkable year-on-year growth over the past decade amongst for-profit providers (cf. Kinser 2006, Breneman, Pusser, and Turner 2006, Hentschke, Lechuga, and Tierney 2010). However, these providers have been confronted with more demanding regulations by the US Department of Education. Seeking economies of scale and scope through transnational expansion, these for-profit providers have also looked to enter new markets, including England. This has meant pressuring governments to 'level the playing field' to enable their entry.

The Conservative Party in the UK has been ideologically open to these kinds of arguments. Since coming to power in May 2010, the Coalition Government, formed out of a contentious alliance between the Conservative and Liberal Democrat Parties (with the Conservatives well-disposed to a Hayekian version of neo-classical economics), have pressed ahead with promises and policies aimed at creating a 'more competitive higher education' system open to for-profit providers which, it is argued, will expand the number of student places at a lower cost than current providers. In the words of the Coalition Minister for Higher Education, David Willetts (2010: 1), for-profit providers are: "unencumbered by the weight of history... They offer a salutary challenge and new approaches to delivering higher education efficiently – and, in turn, cheaply for students". However, the Government's main political challenge has been *how* to institute this imagined higher education market.

Beginning in October 2010, a series of Government policies were released laying out the basis for a radical restructuring of the English higher education sector. Yet, by August 2012, the legislation necessary to realise the intent of the White Paper (BIS 2011a), and the Technical Consultation to establish a new Regulatory Framework (BIS 2011b) to legally and politically create a market, continued to be seriously delayed. Advancing legislation was, and continues to be, viewed as politically difficult and likely to seriously compromise the governing Coalition. This also explains why Pearson's entry to the sector, for the moment at least, continues to be dependent upon the existing regulatory framework which in turn limits Pearson's capacity to operate under the same conditions as the existing providers. There is little doubt Pearson will continue to pressure the Government for ongoing changes.

From 'skills, global competition, quality' to 'making a free market'

I have argued already that strategies for making a market must contend with institutionalised interests, projects and politics. Yet, in the case of the Coalition Government, they could count upon a range of market-oriented activity that already reshaped the sector beginning in the late 1980s (Hood 1991, Deem 1998). The higher education sector had also faced major pressures for reform in order to engage more directly with the government's knowledge-economy agenda. The election of New Labour in 1997 intensified this agenda. Flagship policies included *Our Competitive Future: Building the Knowledge Driven Economy* (DTI 1998); the creation of English Regional Development Agencies (RDAs) to link universities to their regional economies (DTI 1998: 7); the Lambert *Review of Business-University Collaboration* (Lambert 2003) to foster university-business collaborations; *Race to the Top* (Sainsbury 2007) aimed at fostering more innovation and commercialisation in universities; and *Higher Ambitions* (BIS 2009) intended to promote high value-added human capital for the creation of a knowledge-based economy. Labour's approach to higher education favoured skill development through human capital formation, along with innovation policies and commercialisation projects (Brown 2011). Labour's policies, however, stopped short of viewing higher education as an unfettered marketplace open to new for-profit providers.

Yet, by 2009 an urgent policy question facing the Labour Government was how to "widen access and sustain and improve standards of university excellence in an increasingly pressured international context and in a more constrained public spending environment" (BIS 2009: 3). It was this question – of how to open up more places in higher education without increasing the longer-term financial burden on government – that set the terms of reference for the *Independent Review of Higher Education Funding and Student Finance* (the "Browne Review" led by John Browne, formerly Chief Executive of the oil and gas multinational, BP). The arrangements at this point meant that the Higher Education Funding Council for England (HEFCE) partially funded each student place. However, it limited its annual outlay by imposing a total recruitment cap on student numbers for each institution.

However, before the Browne Review could report the Labour Government was heavily defeated in the May 2010 general election. The

Conservative Party, unable to form a majority on its own, after weeks of fraught politicking, managed to negotiate a political deal with the Liberal Democrats to form a Coalition Government. Yet on higher education policy more generally, and the question of increased student fees in particular, the two parties in the Coalition held fundamentally opposite views. Indeed, the Liberal Democrats had campaigned on a ticket that promised to abolish student fees. *May 2010 elections*.

What might this change of government in England, and the opposed ideological positions within the Coalition Government, mean for the Browne Review which would report in October 2010, and the Coalition Government's approach to higher education policy? To begin, it was widely agreed that the Browne Review was forewarned of the new Coalition government's decision to slash the HEFCE's budget as part of the *key* Comprehensive Spending Review (to report in November 2010), which took the form of a block grant to universities for their teaching programmes (McGettigan 2011a). The Browne Review (Browne 2011) therefore built into its recommendations the withdrawal of the block grant to the social sciences, humanities and arts (with sciences and technology areas, and vulnerable subjects like languages protected). It also recommended lifting the ceiling on student fees to enable universities to recover their lost block funding via significantly increased student fees. Fee increases were justified with the following observation; that in 2006, the ceiling of the Graduate Student Contribution had been raised to £3,000 and that, far from discouraging students from seeking places, demand had instead increased (ibid.: 20). The Review also proposed a readjustment of the student loan system, which now placed the burden of the costs of an undergraduate degree on the student. However, students have to repay their loan following graduation over a 30-year period when incomes have reached £21,000. Monies not paid back after this period would be written off by the state.

The justification for the increased burden on students was that having a degree generated a significant increase in salary for graduates. However, reporting an average in this way makes invisible the fact some professions (medicine, law, dentistry and business studies) generate significant returns which distort the average. Yet working class males enrolled in the arts, for instance, may never earn sufficient to cover the initial investment (Robertson 2010). *Flaws*

Browne also promised the creation of a Higher Education Council that would be at arms-length from government to ensure the public interest. The

Review, however, contains only one reference to "new providers" (Brown 2011: 46) where it states: "new providers will be able to apply for targeted Higher Education Council investment if they offer priority programmes – and they will be subject to the same quality requirements as other providers". The Review, therefore, moved in the direction of a model of funding aimed at privatising the cost of higher education. Students rather than the state were now expected to shoulder the burden of the cost of undergraduate higher education. However, it stopped short of encouraging the entry of new providers into the mainstream activity of the sector.

"Ignoring Browne's request; that his recommendations be treated as a whole, the Coalition Government rejected the removal of an upper limit to what universities could charge. In December 2011 a 'snap' parliamentary vote – with no draft legislation in sight – was called to set a new maximum of £9,000 to come into effect from 2012/13" (McGettigan 2011a: 2). This move circumvented the possibility of any organised opposition to beginning the process of making a higher education market. However, the effect of setting an upper limit meant most universities in the sector, irrespective of their mission, status or social class intake, expected to charge students at or close to the ceiling of £9,000 and not the recommended £6,000. This has generated a significant problem for the government; it has escalated the cost to the state of underwriting the student loan system.

Whilst the Coalition Government promised a comprehensive response to the Browne Review early in 2011, the Government's response only materialised in June 2011 in the form of a White Paper presented by the Secretary of State for Higher Education, David Willetts (BIS), to Parliament. Paradoxically, the Report was entitled, *Students at the Heart of the System* (BIS 2011a). The publishing of a 'Technical Consultation' paper – *A New Fit-for-Purpose Regulatory Framework for the Higher Education Sector* followed in August 2011 (BIS 2011b).

Taken together, the two documents build upon, but depart from, the Browne Review in important ways. Whilst accepting the bulk of Browne's proposals, it outlines a more explicit agenda for creating a competitive higher education market that now included: (i) to promote student choice; (ii) to reduce direct government subsidies for places (except in the STEM areas and some languages); (iii) open to new providers – including for-profit providers with DAPs and the opportunity to claim the title of a university based on a significantly smaller student intake; (iv) remove the cap on the number of students a provider can take if a student's grades are two A's and one B (AAB); (v) a light-touch approach to the regulation for quality providers; (vi) the use of 'risk' as the mechanism for governing; (vii) to sell off some, or all, of the student loan book to a commercial provider of student finances; and (viii) a strengthened role for the HEFCE as a champion and protector of student choice, as well as the first point of call for claiming degree-awarding powers (and not the Privy Council – which in this new model can only make recommendations and not the final decision). As the regulator, the HEFCE would be more responsive to ministerial fiat. Yet more than 12 months after the release of the White Paper and Technical Consultation, the Coalition Government has failed to present draft legislation that would help materialise the new policies. Observers argue that the Coalition Government is concerned about how best to manage the political fallout that would accompany any legislation. This has left for-profit providers, like Pearson Education, dependent on the existing institutional arrangements.

Legitimating strategies and recognition shortfalls

A proposal this radical requires legitimation if it is to be successfully instituted. And as Habermas (1997: 178) reminds us: "Legitimacy means that there are good arguments for a political order's claims to be recognised as right and just: a legitimate order deserves recognition. *Legitimacy means a political order's worthiness to be recognised* [italics in original]".

Habermas' understanding of legitimation highlights two things that are important for my argument: that the state's legitimacy is dependent upon contestable validity claims; and that the stability of a political order and its right to rule depends upon recognition by its citizens. How 'right' and 'just' are the claims made in the Coalition Government's policies for its fit-for-purpose regulatory framework in higher education? Do the claims made for this imagined market offer sufficient incentive, or opportunity, for some of the actors within the sector (as opposed to those who are outside) to strategise their own path, in turn generating support for this market-making project? To answer these questions we can now examine the legitimatory discourses in the White Paper, of "saving", "sustainability", "efficiency", "levelling the playing field" and "enhanced social mobility", and circulating counter-evidence, to get a sense of the "recognition shortfalls" the Government faces in strategising the instituting of a higher education market.

172 Susan L. Robertson

Legitimation claim 1: Savings

[handwritten: in the name of AUSTERITY NARRATIVE]

The claim that the new framework will generate "savings" taps into the wider austerity narrative the Coalition Government has mobilised to cut back on public sector expenditures across the board. This kind of discourse has some traction in that the Coalition Government argues that it is not the creator of the financial disaster – the previous Labour Government is. The two Reports (BIS 2011a and 2011b) point to significant savings of around £3 billion per year by the government by 2015/16, which it argues will reduce the budget deficit. It also points to an expectation that all public sectors need to "pull their weight" by making a commitment to austerity. Yet as McGettigan (2012a) shows, the savings are nothing more than an accounting trick. In moving the funding of higher education from an institutional subsidy to a Student Loan Book underwritten by government, the government is using off-balance accounting techniques. Now the money does not show up on the government's books as a deficit, but is a government asset to be repaid by students over a 30-year period.

[handwritten margin note:) facts]

But it is who pays, and when, that is also revealing regarding the long-term consequences of the proposed new regulatory system in English higher education. As it currently stands, the student loans scheme is reasonably generous compared to what it might have been: the outcome of a combination of factors including the difficult negotiations within the Coalition Government; major student demonstrations; and the need to sell the new market model to a concerned public. So, at one level, the twin objectives – of reducing the deficit and generous support to students – have been achieved. However, some students will never pay this loan off as a result of factors that include intermittent access to the labour market, low salaries, or time out of the labour market. At this point, the debt is the government's responsibility (and *ipso facto,* the public's).

Yet it has become apparent that Government officials have seriously under-estimated the amount of likely unpaid loans. That is, all three Reports (Browne 2010, BIS 2011a and 2011b) view the shortfall as being around 30 percent, or 30 p in every £1. However, experts[7] offer a different estimate. They state the figure will be much closer to 40% – significantly increasing the cost of borrowing to underwrite the Student Loan Company and the overall long-term debt. Indeed, it is argued that government borrowing for

---

7   Hepi suggests 35%; the London Economic Consultancy says 37%; the Million+ lobby group says 38%.

[handwritten: Does not add up]

student loans will account for a substantial portion of the UK national debt into the future – with some pundits worried about an equivalent to the sub-prime mortgage disaster that sparked off the 2008 financial crisis. McGettigan (2012a) notes the Office for Budget Responsibility has stated the total student loan repayment would peak at 6.1% of GDP (£91 billion) around 2030, and then fall to 4.4% (£67 billion) by 2061–62. However, at least £67 billion would continue as a government debt 50 years afterward. In short, the government will pay significantly more than it might have had it remained with the previous system of funding. *This does not add up!* *Ridiculously arguey/jumey*

The key issue facing government is the size of the shortfall between the total value of the student loan book and what students will ultimately repay. These are all currently unknown. The student loan repayment rate is also very sensitive to levels of income for graduates. If wages stagnate, then the government risks facing a higher debt via the Student Loan Book, unless of course the conditions of repayment are altered. However, for the moment, changing the conditions of repayment would create a major political crisis within the Coalition and because graduate students are also voters. Yet advisors like Nicholas Barr argue that Government should remove the cap on fees, and minimise number controls so as to create conditions enabling a wider range of prices and thus the basis for a competitive higher education market (Barr 2011). The other would be to press for other forms of efficiency, such as 2-year accelerated courses, allowing in low-cost providers, and promoting more 2- rather than 3-year study/living packages. The government could also try to sell the Student Loan Book to minimise it losses. Currently, however, the private sector is not keen on taking on the whole of the Student Loan Book as it is not sufficiently profitable.

Legitimation claim 2: A more sustainable system

A second legitimation claim is built on the promise that even in the short term a competitive higher education market will bring more money into the system and thus create the basis for a sustainable higher education system. In this regard, the Minister for Higher Education, David Willetts (2012) claims:

> Funding for university teaching is expected to grow by 10 per cent over this Parliament. Although the central HEFCE grant is falling, more money will reach institutions as resources follow the decisions made by students. We want a student-focused higher education sector, more choice over where to study and a renewed

> focus on the quality of the student experience. That's why we are freeing up
> centralised number controls, improving the information for prospective students
> and driving a new focus on the academic experience (ibid.: 1).

Whilst at face value there is more funding coming into the system, this is
because students are taking out higher levels of loans but also assuming a
greater level of the responsibility for the financial burden of higher
education as opposed to government. Will for-profit providers bring more
money into the system? Not likely. This is because the for-profits see either
the student (full-fee/student loan), or the state (teaching subsidy to the
provider), as generating the financial basis for them to profitably enter into
the sector. In all, this model is not a sustainable system. Rather, like all
markets it will be prone to tendencies of monopoly control, crises and
instability.   *Another ridiculous claim by gov,*

Legitimation claim 3: More efficient

The Reports (BIS 2011a and 2011b) argue a market model is more *efficient*
because there is a single set of rules for all players based on competition,
student choice, diverse providers, and light-touch regulation of quality
providers. The idea of competition leading to greater efficiencies is a trope
common amongst those promoting education markets (Barrera-Osorio,
Guaqeta, and Patrinos 2012: 207). Such claims are built upon a series of
premises: that, students accept that their learning is a form of consumption,
as consumers they are responsible for their choices, there is widely available
information, there exists a perfect relationship between preferences and
education products, and finally and a range of diverse providers in the sector
are able to respond to student demands for different kinds of 'education'
experiences.

Aside from assumptions about human behaviour (as *homo-
economicus*), we can also challenge the premises of choice (demand) driving
competition (supply). For instance, not all students are able to realise their
choice, not simply for economic but also for social and cultural reasons
related to the supplier. Not all students are able to realise their choice to
attend an elite institution (assuming better grades than their potential
competitor choosers) because they do not have the social and cultural capital
that is also part of the rules of the game of choice and competition.
Sociologists have long since also pointed out that social classes exploit the
idea of choice in that it conceals (as individual freedom) those rules of the

game which reproduce social class relations and therefore the conditions of their own advantage.

Consumer-driven systems are also dependent on larger amounts of the overall budget being allocated to marketing and recruiting, so that the balance between allocations to teaching courses versus marketing tends to shift in the direction of marketing departments. This in turn encourages providers to look more closely at economies of scale (large classes, on-line learning etc.), at different ways in which they can lower labour costs (hourly paid tutors), and pare back costs such as research as it is indirectly associated with the costs of teaching. Many of the for-profit providers in the United States have recently been criticised for this approach to learners (Bennett, Luccesi, and Vedder 2010).

Poo poo. Does not make sense as a ger. claim

Legitimation claim 4: 'Levelling the playing field'

The metaphor – 'levelling the playing field' – is used to legitimate the entry of for-profit providers to the sector. The metaphor suggests all current and potential providers are similar kinds of actors, with similar levels of resources, and similar kinds of commitments. This is far from the case. Pearson Education, for example, is a vast global conglomerate able to access resources far in excess of most universities. Similarly, within the current higher education sector, institutions are differently positioned and resourced, dependent on their history either as part of the putative Russell Group (elite providers to largely privately educated students) or as a former poly-technical provider of higher education. In reality, for the new for-profit providers to move in, levelling the playing field means removing those barriers which currently prevent them from acquiring the 'currency' of the existing sector (status, marketing, recruitment) whilst minimising the costs of compliance (validation, regular quality assurance); removing both should enhance the predictability of the environment, and most importantly potential levels of profit. Already new openings have emerged for the new providers as a result of government using the existing legislation; students enrolled with the new private providers (including for profits) are now able to access student loans so that numbers doubled in a year (from 4,300 in 2009/10 to 9,360 in 2010/11) (Morgan 2012).

One mechanism, however, has continued to prove elusive and would likely need changes via the parliamentary system to alter regulations around the right to claim the title "university". Currently the size of the student

Definition of a University 9

body, the range of what is taught, the link between teaching and research, and the nature of the faculty, are all used to define who is and who is not able to use the title of "university". Clearly universities in the sector have held onto this definition as it also protects their own status and interests.

Finally, the 'levelling the playing field' discourse disguises the new disadvantages built into the new regulatory environment. For instance, the Secretary of State for Education can alter the conditions of the student loan without consultation and without a parliamentary vote (in the 2012/13 Student Loans – A Guide to terms and Conditions, p. 8 it notes that students will: "Pay loans as due, *and as amended...*"). Students do not have the right to consumer protection or appeal under the Consumer Protection Act. Further, given that the new funding regime is likely to move most English universities outside EU procurement rules on public institutions since the majority of revenue streams will now be private and not public, this in turn means the academy will be exempt from these regulations (McGettigan 2012b). The long-term consequences of this for students and for the sector remain unchartered territory. *of concern.*

Legitimation claim 5: Improved social mobility through fairer access

A fifth legitimation claim is that the policies must promote social mobility. The Report notes that currently fewer than 1 in 5 young people from the most disadvantaged areas enter higher education compared to more than 1 in 2 for the most advantaged areas (BIS 2011a: 54). So what are the solutions that are proposed that would realise this claim that a higher education market would create greater social mobility through fair access?

One is the development of a career service to provide advice to prospective students. This kind of approach understands the causes of social immobility as individual, and about knowledge and choices as opposed to an outcome of social class relations and their reproduction. Will this market framework challenge the role of higher education, and specific providers as carriers of elite status, in social class reproduction? Early evidence suggests that in the 2012/13 intake there is a slight increase in the numbers of working class students applying for places, and a slight drop in the overall number of the middle class in comparison to previous years although it is unclear where these middle-class students are going – whether into other parts of the higher education sector (such as further education/ apprenticeships) or abroad (such as Europe) in search of lower fees.

In relation to working class students, it may be that they recognise the relatively generous conditions for working class students in the current student loan offer (now payments beginning after earnings of £21,000, and a more generous living away from home grant). An Independent Commission on Fees (chaired by the left-leaning public intellectual Will Hutton) has been established to generate three reports over three years to assess the impact of fees on low- and middle-income backgrounds (Independent Commission on Fees 2012). All universities charging above the ceiling will have had to develop an Access Agreement with the Office for Fair Access (Offa). This means universities have had to make proposals regarding fair access and widening participation with appropriate measures and targets in place. However, as Attwood (2011) reported, Offa says that it will only use the penalties available to it if a university commits a serious and wilful breach of its access agreement. Failure to meet targets is not one of them.

Politics, selectivity, and the future of the sector in Europe

Taken together, we can begin to see that there are significant legitimation deficits, political unknowns and economic risks associated with the new proposed regulatory framework to institute a market in English higher education that now includes an expanding private sector component. Far from being an easy outcome of policies, this paper reveals that such attempts are shaped by the nature of political alliances, wider political pressures over the deficit, accounting trickery, the promise of opportunities for expansion for high status providers, and major challenges and bungles in getting the formulas right. To date, no legislation has been proposed to Parliament – largely as that would make it the object of particularly fraught parliamentary politics.

Yet, there are now significant pressures to stay on course from a number of quarters. After all, there will be winners and losers in those parts of the new framework that the government has managed to launch. The winners have already been strategically selected into the project of instituting a market. For one, many of the elite universities (known as the Russell Group) are now able to take as many high achieving (referred to as

AAB) applicants as they wish, and view the current system very favourably. They are also likely to see the new private providers as not generating any major threat to their capacity to operate competitively in the sector. Yet the activities of the for-profit providers, and their new conditions of operation, are likely to exaggerate the social inequalities in the system both directly and as a result of their efforts to enter the sector.

Second, the new (for-profit) providers will want to ensure that promises made around their ease of entry into an HE market are realised. For the moment, they are stalled on questions of recognition as a university, and degree-awarding powers. But the critical component is already in place to enable the market to work in their favour; access to student loans. Their ongoing struggle will be to pressure the state around ensuring light-touch regulation, and a lifting of the fee ceilings, to enable it to strategise its market-making activity. Large firms like Pearson have deep pockets when it comes to courting political favours and they have been visible in their presence on platforms discussing the future of higher education.

But much will depend on how the legitimation burden is managed by the state in the short term, and whether it can defer the legitimation shortfalls into the longer term sufficient for it to secure recognition and buy-in. This will require close scrutiny of the mechanisms and how they work, and a high level of financial literacy amongst observers. The danger, of course, for academics researching the academy is that their findings may well be regarded as compromising the commercial interests of their own institution. After all, where would critical HE research fit in a market-driven system?

The losers, of course, will be a mixture of students, academics and the old academy, whom will be selectively disadvantaged in the "restructuring" and "relevelling" (Robertson 2011) within the sector. For students, by being positioned as a 'consumer' of credentials rather than a 'producer' of knowledge, they are now offered a diminished set of possibilities for critically understanding our social and natural worlds, for interrogating 'truth' and for how to re-imagine our futures. Unless the state pursues a social equity agenda concerned with the social outcomes of choice (jobs/income) and not just inputs (e.g. information/loans), then some students will also be part of a sector that is characterised by widening social inequalities. To be sure, the loans system as it stands looks relatively more favourably toward working class students, but that assumes low levels of social mobility in terms of occupational salaries and a willing state and public able to pick up the financial burden.

Academics will be selectively advantaged, depending on where in the groves of academe they find themselves, or how prominent consumer satisfaction is, as a disciplinary logic within the institution in which they are working. Already academics in social sciences, arts and humanities are differently situated in relation to their STEM colleagues regarding the nature of their annual funding. That is, social sciences, arts and humanities departments will now be thrust into the new higher education market with all of its repercussions. In relation to which part of the sector academics find themselves in (high or low status), the conditions of work for academics will be highly dependent upon status, student fees and potential profits. In relation to consumer satisfaction as a disciplinary logic, what does it mean for a student to be satisfied as a consumer? What does this look like from the point of view of an academic? Taken together, these new logics will transform the old academy. This is not to assert an over-romantic view of the old academy as equitable, as outside capitalist logics, and so on. But it does make the obvious point that a higher education market, like all markets, will be driven by a logic that has little time for truth, curiosity, critique and reflection.

Yet it is the loss of a proportion of middle-class students (Boffey 2012) and where they have gone and why which is particularly critical to understanding the potentially wider effects of English higher education policies on European higher education more generally. European universities share a common regulatory framework – the Bologna Process – that mandates a common degree architecture of a 3-year Undergraduate, 2-year Masters and 3-year doctoral programme. Students are also encouraged to be mobile across the European higher education sector. If English middle-class students leave England and its higher education institutions in search of cheaper degrees in European countries, what will be the likely impact of this on the country in question? Will there be pressure to develop a differential fee structure for home versus EU students? Will there be pressure to change the language of instruction? Where does the burden for funding an increased number of students from elsewhere fall, and what might be the implications for England when it loses its students to other countries in relation to its knowledge-economy strategies? Will English students feel the pull of China and be attracted to the more generous funding for international students that is currently on offer from the Chinese government? As we can see from these questions, the creation of a competitive market in English higher education has important relational consequences for other countries and their own higher education policies and programmes.

Finally, I began this chapter by arguing it is important we look more closely at discourses such as privatisation and marketisation, and the need to theorise these as processes that must be strategised and instituted if they are to secure the basis of their ongoing re/production. But I also pointed out that this is a highly contested and political set of processes, with tendential though not inevitable outcomes. That politics matters, is the key message here. And it matters in multiple ways; in seeing that we can, and must, contest these ideologically-mistaken policies; that we can, and must, think beyond what is good for 'my' situation, or 'my' institution and think of the sector and its higher purpose; and that we can, and must, think about how to re-imagine a new kind of academy that boots into the long grass this current, divisive, effort to institute a market. In short, we must continue to create a hullabaloo in the groves of academe.

Acknowledgement

The author would like to acknowledge the support of the ESRC-funded Research Centre, Learning and Lifechances in Knowledge Economies and Societies (LLAKES) [RES-594-28-0001] which enabled her to undertake the work on UK higher education and the global marketplace.

References

Attwood, R. (2011). "No penalties for missed targets". *InsideHigherEd*. 11 March 2011. 1.

Ball, S. (2007). *Education plc*. London: Routledge

Barr, N. (2011). *Assessing the White Paper on Higher Education, Supplementary Submission to the Business, Innovation and Skills Committee. The Future of Higher Education*. London: UK Parliament.

Barrera-Osorio, F., J. Guaqeta, H. Patrinos (2012). "The Role and Impact of Public Private Partnerships in Education". In: S. Robertson, K. Mundy. A. Verger, F. Menashy (eds.), *Public Private Partnerships in Education*. Cheltenham: Edward Elgar

Bennett, D., A. Lucchesi, R. Vedder (2010). *For-Profit Higher Education: Growth, Innovation and Regulation*. Washington: Centre for College Affordability and Productivity.

BIS (2009). *Higher Ambitions: the Future of Universities in a Knowledge Economy.* London: BIS.

Boffey, D. (2012). "Middle-class Pupils Shun Universities as Fees Rise". *Guardian.* 11 November 2012. Available at http://www.guardian.co.uk/education/2012/nov/11 /middle-classes-shun-university (accessed 11 November 2012).

Browne, J. (2010). *Securing a Sustainable Future for Higher Education: An Independent Review of Higher Education Funding and Student Finance.* London: BIS

Breneman, D., B. Pusser, S. Turner (2006). *Earnings from Learning: The Rise of For-Profit Universities.* New York: SUNY.

Brown, R. (2011). The New English Quality Assurance Regime. *Quality in Higher Education.* Vol. 17. No. 2. 213-229.

Business, Innovation and Skills (2011a). *Students at the Heart of the System.* London: HMSO.

Business, Innovation and Skills (2011b). *A New Fit-for-Purpose Regulatory Framework for the Higher Education Sector - 'Technical Consultation'.* London: HMSO.

Carpentier, V. (2012). "Public-private Substitution in Higher Education: Has Costs Sharing Gone Too Far?" *Higher Education Quarterly.* Vol. 66. No. 4. 363-390.

Cox, R. (1996). *Approaches to World Order.* Cambridge: Cambridge University Press.

Deem, R. (1998). "New Managerialism and Higher Education: the Management of Performances and Cultures in Universities in the United Kingdom". *International Studies in Sociology of Education.* Vol. 8. No. 1. 47-70.

Desai, K. (1998). *Hullabaloo in the Guava Orchard.* New York: Grove Atlantic.

DTI (1998). *Our Competitive Future: Building the Knowledge-Driven Economy.* London: HMSO.

DTI (1999). *Our Competitive Future: UK Competitiveness Indicators, 1999.* London: HMSO.

Fielden, J., R. Middlehurst (2010). *The Growth of Private and For Profit Higher Education Providers in the UK.* London: Universities UK.

Fligstein, N. (1996). "Markets as Politics: A Political Cultural Approach to Market Institutions". *American Sociological Review.* Vol. 61. No. 4. 656-673.

Gill, S. (2003). *Power and Resistance in the New World Order.* London and New Work: Palgrave Macmillan.

Habermas, J. (1976). *Communication and the Evolution of Society.* Boston: Beacon Press.

Harvey, D. (1996). *Justice, Nature and the Geography of Difference.* Oxford: Blackwell.

Hentschke, G., V. Lechuga, W. Tierney (2010). *For Profit Colleges and Universities.* Virginia: Stylus.

Hood, C. (1991). "A Public Management for All Seasons?" *Public Administration.* Vol. 69. No. 1. 3-19.

Independent Commission on Fees (2012). Home. Available at http://www.independentcommissiononfees.org.uk (accessed 20 August 2012).

Jessop, B. (2005). "Critical Realism and the Strategic Relational Approach". *New Formations.* Vol. 56. 40-53.

Kelsey, J. (2008). *Serving Whose Interests.* New York: Routledge Cavendish.

Kinser, K. (2006). *From Main Street to Wall Street.* San Francisco: ASHE Higher Education.

Lambert, R. (2003). *Lambert Review of Business-University Collaboration*. London: HMSO.

Larsen, K., S. Vincent-Lancrin (2002). "International Trade in Educational Services: Good or Bad?" *Higher Education Management and Policy*. Vol. 14. No. 3. 9-45.

Levy, D. (1979). *The Private-public Question in Higher Education: Distinction or Extinction?* New Haven: Yale University Press.

Levy, D. (1986). *Private Education: Studies in Choice and Public Policy. Yale studies in Non-Profit organisations*. Oxford: Oxford University Press.

Maldonaldo- Maldonaldo, A. et al. (2004). Private Higher Education: An International Bibliography. PROPHE, University of Albany, New York.

McGettigan, A. (2011a). "Meanings of Private and Privatisation". Critical Education Blog. Available at http://andrewmcgettigan.org/2011/09/10/meanings-of-private-and-privatisation/ (accessed 13 January 2013).

McGettigan, A. (2011b). "New Providers: The Creation of a Market in Higher Education, Radical Philosophy". Available at http://www.radicalphilosophy.com/ commentary/%E2%80%98new-providers%E2%80%99-the-creation-of-a-market-in-higher-education (accessed 12 August 2012).

McGettigan, A. (2012a). *False Accounting: Why the government's Higher Education reforms don't add up*. London: Intergenerational Foundation.

McGettigan, A. (2012b). "Update on student loans: Four points". Critical Education Blog. Available at http://andrewmcgettigan.org/2012/07/21/update-on-student-loans-four-points/ (accessed 13 January 2013).

Middlehurst, R., J. Fielden (2011). *Private Providers in UK Higher Education: Some Policy Options*. London: UniversitiesUK.

Morgan, J. (2012). "Oversight to Private Providers Is Introduced as State Funded Loans Soar". *Times Higher Education*. 10 May 2012.

Peck, J. (2010). *Constructions of Neoliberal Reason*. Oxford: Oxford University Press.

Polanyi, K. (1992). "The Economy as an Instituted Process". In: M. Granovetter, R. Swedberg (eds.), *The Sociology of Economic Life*. Boulder, CO.: Westview Press.

Rhodes, R. A. W. (1997). *Understanding Governance: Policy Networks, Governance and Reflexivity*. Maidenhead, UK: Open University Press.

Robertson, S., X. Bonal, R. Dale (2002). "GATS and the Education Service Industry: The Politics of Scale and Global Reterritorialisation". *Comparative Education Review*. Vol. 46. No. 4. 472-496.

Robertson, S. (2011). "The New Spatial Politics of (Re)Bordering and (Re)Ordering the State-Education-Citizen Relation". *International Review of Education*. Vol. 57. 277-297.

Sainsbury, L (2008). *The Race to the Top, Review of Government's Science and Innovation Policies*. London: DIUS.

Shore, C., Wright, S. (2011). "Conceptualising Policy: Technologies of Governance and the Politics of Visibility". In: C. Shore, D. Pero, S. Wright (eds.), *Policy Worlds: Anthropology and the Analysis of Contemporary Power*. New York: Berghahn Books.

Scott, P., ed. (2000). *Higher Education Reformed*. London: Falmer.

Slater, D., F. Tonkiss (2001). *Market Society*. Cambridge: Polity.

Willetts, D. (2010). "The Future of Higher Education". Available at http://www.bis.gov.uk /news/topstories/2010/Sep/Willetts-UUK-Speech (accessed 12 September 2010).

Willetts, D. (2012). "BIS Press Release 28 March". Available at http://news.bis.gov.uk/content/Detail.aspx?ReleaseID=423901&NewsAreaID=2 (accessed 20 August 2012).

Verger, A., S. Robertson (2012). "The GATS-game-changer: International Trade Regulation and the Constitution of a Global Education Marketplace". In: S. Robertson, K. Mundy, A. Verger, F. Menashy (eds.), *Public Private Partnerships in Education.* Cheltenham: Edward Elgar.

Higher Education Differentiation and the Myth of Meritocracy: The Case of the UK

John Brennan

Abstract

The UK possesses one of the most unequal societies in the developed world together with one of the most stratified higher education systems. The chapter explores the relationships between these two features of modern British society. It draws on the concept of 'meritocracy' to explore the ways in which a massified and differentiated higher education system is able to contribute simultaneously to both social reproduction and social change. It also considers the implications for the experiences of students, both academic and social.

Key words: higher education, universities, meritocracy, inequality, differentiation, social change, elite reproduction, social mobility

In common with most other developed countries, higher education has expanded massively in the UK in recent decades. This has involved the creation of new institutions and the upgrading and expansion of others. It has drawn in growing numbers of students, many from families which had no previous experience of higher education. The expansion has been driven largely by economic imperatives accompanied by considerations of social equity and meritocracy. Higher education is perceived to be the necessary and legitimate route to wealth and social privilege, reflecting the central features and democratic credentials of modern knowledge societies.

The aim of this chapter is to consider the contributions higher education is making to social equity in one society, the United Kingdom, although the conclusions to be reached may well be applicable elsewhere. However, some particularly relevant features of the UK are the high and growing levels of inequality in society and the highly stratified higher education system. The extent to which the latter reflects, reproduces and legitimises the former will be a prime consideration of the chapter.

A concept central to the argument to be developed here is that of 'meritocracy' as coined by the British sociologist, Michael Young, in 1958 in a subsequently much misquoted book, The Rise of the Meritocracy, 1870 to 2033 (Young 1958). What Young had intended as a political satire on contemporary society has often been referenced as representing support and advocacy for a new 'meritocratic' kind of society. The central idea of meritocracy was that wealth and privilege within society were increasingly a function of 'merit', of ability and hard work and therefore deserved support and reward. The education system, consequently, had a key role to play in ensuring the continued economic success and social stability of society. Young's actual thoughts on the matter are presented with some humour and some cynicism as the following quotation indicates:

> The superior classes took for granted that their children should enjoy higher education; the difficulty was not to get the able to stay at school, but to get the stupid to leave and put up with the manual jobs for which their intelligence fitted them. In the lower classes the situation was reversed (Young 1958: 23).

In other words, Young was referring to the ideological functions performed by the education system and the role which they played in legitimising social inequalities rather than in removing them.

At the time Young wrote the meritocracy book, higher education in the UK was a small system to which only around 6% of the population could aspire. It was, in Trow's terms, an "elite" system, "shaping mind and character of ruling classes; preparation for elite roles" (Trow 2010: 556), whereas today with a participation rate of well over 40% it is closer to Trow's notion of a "mass" system, providing the "transmission of skills; preparation for a broader range of technical and economic elite roles" (ibid.: 556) and is in the process of transforming into a "universal" system, with responsibilities for the "adaptation of the 'whole population' to rapid social and technological change" (ibid.: 557). While Trow's model is often used to indicate the changing central features of higher education systems as they expand, he also acknowledged that expanded systems would need to contain characteristics of all three models, with elite parts nested within the mass and universal systems. Part of the way in which this has been achieved is through the differentiation of higher education institutions, with a small number of prestigious places pretty much focused on the elite functions, leaving the mass and universal functions to a wide range of other institutional types. Several authors, e.g., Clark (1983) and Teichler (2006), have drawn a distinction between "vertical" differentiation – where difference is seen to lie principally in a status hierarchy of institutions – and "horizontal" differentiation –where institutional differentiation rather reflects functional and educational differences. A central question to be posed, however, is the relationship between the differentiation of higher education institutions and the differentiation of the larger societies of which they are part. It is to these two forms of differentiation and the relationships between them in contemporary UK society that we now turn.

A stratified society

On all kinds of indicators, the UK is one of the most unequal of modern developed societies and it has been becoming more unequal over the last 30 years. The following statistics are taken from a report from the Institute of Fiscal Studies (2008). In the UK:

– the bottom 10% receive 2.6% of the national income and the top 10% receive 27.3% of the national income (and the top 1% receive 13% of all income);
– looking at personal wealth, the top 10% possess 54% of it;
– 20 years ago, the average chief executive of a large company received 17% more than the average worker, while in 2009 the figure was 75.5% more; and
– between 1999 and 2009, money earned by the poorest tenth fell by 12% while money earned by the richest tenth rose by 37%.

In a recent study, Toynbee and Walker conclude that "Birth is now destiny, and the predictive power of family background stronger than at any time since the 39-45 war". And they continue, "our background predicts who will run the investment banks and who will clean the floors" (Toynbee and Walker 2008).

Thus, not only are inequalities getting steeper but opportunities for upward mobility are getting fewer. A British Social Attitudes survey showed that 76% of respondents believed that the gap between the top and bottom was too high (British Social Attitudes 2005).

A recent report from the Institute for Fiscal Studies and the Institute for Employment Research[1] predicts that these levels of inequality will not be changed by economic growth, implying that they are not the result of economic decline but are reflective of broader features of the social structure. They predict an increasingly polarised society with a poorer half whose incomes are set to fall and a top half whose living standards will continue to rise. In part, this is a polarisation resulting from a changing

---

1   *Who gains for growth?* (2012), a report for the Resolution Foundation by the Institute for Fiscal Studies and the Institute for Employment Research.

labour market with growth in the numbers of jobs at both the 'top' and 'bottom' ends but with a decline in the numbers of jobs in the 'middle'. In looking at how these positions are filled, and hence in reproducing (and legitimising) these differences in opportunity and equality, we find a central role being performed by the education system, and in particular by higher education.

A stratified higher education system

If, as is often claimed, higher education plays a key part in providing a route for social mobility and a more equal and meritocratic society, is the opposite then also true? Namely, how far is the UK's higher education system responsible for the inequalities in today's Britain? And how far are these social inequalities responsible for the characteristics of Britain's higher education system? In other words, we have a question of the direction of causality. But we also have some tensions between the different functions of higher education and these may be reflected in its differentiated institutional forms. Thus, higher education – at least in some of its forms – undoubtedly does provide a route for upwardly mobility. At the same time, we shall argue that it continues to provide the means for the social reproduction of existing patterns of inequality.

Higher education in the UK consists of around 140 separate universities, with more being created almost daily as government relaxes the criteria for the award of university status. Size, degree-awarding powers, range of subjects and research functions are among the conditions being relaxed in the process. And at the time of writing, further relaxations are being lined up in order to support the entry of private providers into the system.

A crude way of distinguishing institutions in the UK system is to refer to pre-92 and post-92 universities. This refers to a distinction made between the universities and the polytechnics which existed in the so-called binary system between the late 1960s and the early 1990s. As with other binary systems in Europe, this could be regarded as a 'horizontal' form of differentiation. But this is somewhat misleading in the UK case. The polytechnics covered the whole subject range of courses, with the one exception of medicine, and to all academic levels, including doctorates. Their degrees were awarded by a national quality assurance agency, the

Council for National Academic Awards, which was charged by statute to ensure that the degrees from the polytechnics were the equivalent in standard to those awarded by the universities. It was misleading to refer to the polytechnics as technological and vocational institutions. Most of the things that went on in them also went on in universities, and vice versa. For those reasons, it was quite easy to give them all university titles in 1992. But one of the consequences was that what had been portrayed, rather misleadingly, as a functional (or 'horizontal') difference became more explicitly a status (or 'vertical') difference as a result of the replacement of the binary with a unitary system in the 1990s.

While there have always been reputational differences between universities in the UK, the substantial increase in their numbers with the conversion of the polytechnics meant that reputational differences became steeper and equivalence claims more difficult to make.

There are many features of the UK higher education system that support and reflect its stratification and vertical differentiation. One longstanding one is the practice of students to leave their home region when they go to university. In countries where students tend to attend the local university, there is less potential for hierarchy, for a public conception that a few universities are the 'best' ones. Whereas many universities in the UK are today increasingly recruiting large numbers of their students from within their own regions, the so-called 'best' universities in the UK continue to draw on students from across the entire country. This makes admission highly competitive which itself enhances reputation. In other words, one of the reasons a university can claim to be one of the 'best' is that it can plausibly claim to be admitting only the 'best' students.

The more informal status differentiation of UK higher education has been around for a very long time. In recent years, vertical differentiation has been strengthened by the introduction of national (and international) assessment systems leading to published rankings and league tables of institutions. The most prominent ones are based on research performance although there is also a regular National Student Survey (NSS) based on student evaluations. The rankings largely reflect and reinforce the existing reputational hierarchies, though it is interesting to note that those which do not (e.g. those based on widening participation measures) receive little publicity.

One of the reasons for actual rather than just reputational differences between institutions lies in different levels of funding. In a set of data published recently by the Guardian newspaper, in a scoring system of funding per student which saw Oxford University scoring 10 and Cambridge University scoring 9.76, London Metropolitan University and West of Scotland University (the bottom two) scored only 3.57 and 3.23, respectively. Staff-student ratios reveal similar massive differences. It would be unsurprising, therefore, if funding differences of this magnitude were not related to differences in the quality of the experience provided although, as we shall see, there is some evidence that these are typically overstated or even the reverse of realities.

One of the perhaps inevitable consequences of the steep reputational hierarchy of institutions is that for graduates entering the labour market, 'where' you study can often be more important than 'what' you study. Comparative studies of graduate employment across Europe show that institutional reputation rather than subject studied is more important to achieving labour market success in the UK than it is elsewhere in Europe (Brennan 2008, Schomburg and Teichler 2006). Indeed, many leading employers pride themselves with claims that they recruit only from 'top universities', claims which inevitably reinforce the 'top university' claims of those same institutions.

The data on graduate employment reveal something of the social functions of higher education. Compared with many other countries, the labour market is quite lightly regulated in the UK. Instead of named qualifications being required for particular jobs, UK employers have much greater flexibility over their recruitment practices. And for jobs in more prestigious employment fields, it matters little what you studied in higher education providing that you attended one of the 'right' institutions. In a study conducted some years ago, it was noted that while engineering graduates from 'mass' institutions were mostly to be found in engineering jobs a few years after graduation, quite a high proportion of the engineering graduates from 'elite' institutions were in jobs that were quite unconnected with engineering, for example, the civil service or the banking and finance sectors of the economy (Brennan et al. 1993).

Differentiation and meritocracy

The relationship between higher education differentiation and social equity in the UK is therefore reasonably clear. Students from upper socio-economic backgrounds are more likely to get into the elite universities, partly because they are motivated to do so and partly because they attend well-resourced private schools that are focused on providing routes into elite higher education institutions. It may be that these students are also more able and hard-working, conditions which are central to the meritocratic case. But the evidence is unclear on this point.

We have noted above that recruitment of graduates into 'top' and 'influential' jobs in the UK is not strongly related to the subject-matter of their courses in higher education. This implies that higher education is providing a 'selection' rather than a 'preparation' function for entry into the labour market. There is also evidence that the graduates from 'top universities' are well-networked and socially confident and ambitious when they emerge from higher education, features which may bring value to their employers as well as to the graduates themselves.

There are also differences in the way higher education is experienced by students and these reflect both social backgrounds and the kinds of institutions attended. Students from working-class origins are much more likely to have part-time jobs and other external commitments alongside their studies. They are more likely to study vocational subjects, more likely to live at home, and consequently have less time for the social aspects of university life. And at those institutions which recruit high proportions of such students, there is likely to be relatively little 'social life' at the university. Thus, the broader social and networking aspects of the higher education student experience – which appear to be particularly valued in the UK labour market – may tend to be absent at many of the institutions at the 'mass' end of the system.

This is supported by research evidence which shows that students from lower socio-economic backgrounds are likely to be more interested in 'getting a qualification' and 'getting a job' and simply do not have the time or social awareness to value the social networking and identity forming/confirming processes characteristic of the university experience at the elite end of the system (Brennan et al. 2010).

The following quotes[2] from students at different UK universities illustrate something of the diversity of student experiences and of the things that students most value from them.

---

2   These data are drawn from a recent study of students from across 15 different UK universities (Brennan et al. 2010, Brennan and Patel 2011).

A bioscience student attending a 'top 10' university reflected on his reasons for choosing it:

> I decided that I'd rather go to (this university) than anywhere else in the country. Probably because of the prestige of (this university). And with (this university) having a better status I thought it would be the best for my degree.

A sociology student at a 'top 20' university reflected on its social attractions:

> I'm just, you find yourself, just going out a lot because there's nothing like hanging around, talking in people's rooms and stuff, going to base and just filling time really. It's just surprising the amount of time you can waste. Just sit and talk because I think you have to make decisions when you came here, because like at the end of the day you're only going to do sociology for like 6-10 hours a week.

In contrast to the attractions of institutional status and the social life, students attending less prestigious institutions tended to give more attention to the academic experience and the qualifications to be gained from it. They also often had concerns about finances so they were more likely to attend a university close to home and more likely to take some part-time work alongside their studies. Here is a sociology student attending a lowly-ranked institution and reflecting on her experiences:

> Using my mind academically, writing essays, discussing academic subjects. I have never done that before, and I find myself happy doing it. I am a more confident person as a result of it. It has been a very positive experience for me.

Another student from the same institution expressed it in these terms:

> You learn the skill of er, you know, not to take things on face value. It teaches you to look from every angle. You know, way of consider that point that you wouldn't have done before, consider that. Especially with my degree it's about community and people. [...] It just teaches you to look deeply and think a little bit more as to why things happen as they do.

Thus, students at the low status institutions tended to emphasise the academic while those at the high status institutions were more likely to value the social.

The lifestyles of students while they attended university reflected both the status of the institution and the social background of the student. Thus, at the more prestigious universities, 69% of first-year students were living in university halls of residence compared with only 25% of students at lower status institutions. The latter were more likely to be living at home with family or friends (54% compared with only 24% of students at the 'top' universities).

The student experience in British higher education has become an increasingly differentiated one. But it is a differentiation which reflects lifestyle contexts which are themselves a function of social backgrounds. These factors of themselves do not necessarily reflect differences in achievement or 'merit' from attending different institutions even if they appear to be interpreted that way by employers and (most) politicians.

Some implications

We can see from the UK case a number of elements which indicate a complex and in some ways a contradictory relationship between higher education and social equity.

First, we see a relationship – and possibly a tension – between academic and social elitism in the most prestigious universities. Recent research has indicated a high valuation among students at these institutions of factors such as the university 'brand', the social life at university and the networking opportunities available there (Brennan and Patel 2011). As we have already indicated, at other universities it tends to be the qualification and the courses that are most frequently mentioned. The exceptions at the 'elite' end tend to occur in particular subject fields where the university has a strong reputation as a 'world leader' as this serves as a stimulus for students to apply for places because of subject content and not just because of institutional 'brand'.

There are also differences between students at these institutions. The large numbers who come from elite fee-paying private schools arrive with a confidence and 'nothing to prove' in contrast to their peers from the public education system who often report feeling they are outsiders, less comfortable with the social and less confident with the academic, all characteristics which imply a somewhat different relationship to the university and a different experience as a student. It is worth observing that data from the study mentioned above showed that while 88% of students attending the more prestigious institutions wanted to remain associated with their university in some way after they graduated, the comparable figure at the lower status institutions was only 28% (Brennan et al. 2010).

Second, and central to the argument of this paper, is the way in which the differentiation of higher education in the UK allows the performance of an elite reproduction role within a mass system. Recent policy statements by government ministers indicate that the differentiation of institutions in terms of the functions performed appears to be getting more explicit with policy distinctions distinguishing 'world class excellence' for the few and 'good employment skills and competencies' for the many. And in so doing, it would appear that higher education continues to provide meritocratic legitimisation of existing social inequalities. We will return shortly to the question of whether the claims of meritocracy can be justified by the evidence.

However, thirdly, it is important to acknowledge that whatever its function of ensuring elite reproduction in UK society, higher education also plays an important role in providing opportunities for social mobility. For a few, this may entail access to elite positions and privileges, often routed through attendance at one of the elite universities, but also it can provide more modest opportunities for advance and improvement compared with the occupational and income levels of the student's parents, or "giant leaps for the few" contrasting with "small steps for the many" (van der Graff et al. 2009). Whether such opportunities will continue to exist in a changing labour market and economic conditions where there will be less 'room at the top' than existed for the post-war generation remains to be seen (Brown and Lauder 2001).

Fourthly, it does seem that the steep vertical differentiation of UK higher education plays an important role in maintaining and legitimising existing social differentiation or, using Martin Trow's terminology, performing "elite" functions within a "mass" system. Whether there are also dysfunctions in terms of employability and professional effectiveness and, perhaps most importantly of all, the maintenance of social order and cohesion, remains a key research question.

In the remainder of this paper, we will return to the issue of meritocracy and the usefulness of the concept in exploring the social impacts of higher education.

On meritocracy

While the focus of this chapter is upon higher education and society in the UK, the issues raised are much more widely applicable. Thus, referring to his own experiences as a student at the elite end of the French higher education system, Pierre Bourdieu wrote that

> the keystone of the whole edifice encouraged a self-confidence often verging on the unself-consciousness of triumphant ignorance (Bourdieu 2008)

and he went on to argue that

> It is indeed this socially constructed feeling of being of a 'superior essence' which, together with the solidarities of interest and affinities of habitus, does most to engender and support what must be called an 'esprit de corps' among the social elite (ibid.).

However, there are differences in the processes that Bourdieu describes in France compared with the UK situation. In France, it is not just a matter of institutional differentiation which is important for elite reproduction, what you have studied also matters and for the French elite this means philosophy. Sociology (Bourdieu's own discipline) is described in contrast as "a plebeian and vulgarly materialistic science of ordinary things" and is seen as "given to coarse analyses of the most vulgar, common and collective dimensions of human existence" (ibid.).

The central argument of meritocracy is that wealth, power and privilege are 'deserved' and based on the merits of the individual. Those with the ability and motivation to achieve these merits are rewarded and society as a whole benefits by having the most able people filling the most important positions in society. Young's 1958 book indicated the consequences when this failed to happen or, more exactly, when significant numbers in society refused to believe that it had happened, i.e. refused to accept that their lower status and wealth were 'deserved' because of their lack of merit. The book ends with the prediction of a major breakdown in public order.

Coming back to the role played by a differentiated higher education system in supporting a meritocratic society, we have to ask whether the graduates emerging from the elite institutions and obtaining 'top jobs' in society are indeed 'better' than their counterparts at less prestigious universities and, if so, in what ways. In the words of Toynbee and Walker, the coincidence between social origin and educational and professional achievement could mean that "these are really special and able people on whose brains and talent the prosperity of the nation depends" and this would be the meritocratic argument. Or it could be "the result of luck and circumstance rather than merit", although this 'luck and circumstance' could be a contrived and socially constructed phenomenon, reflecting existing power and status relationships within society.

While it is not possible to choose between these different interpretations definitively, some indications can be found in recent research. We have already noted the different balance in emphasis between the social and the academic sides of the student experience in different institutions and between students from different social backgrounds. We now turn to a recent study which attempted to compare explicitly the quality and standards achieved by students attending institutions of different reputation and status.

The project, entitled "Pedagogic Quality and Inequality"[3] was a study of undergraduate social science courses at four contrasting universities with a focus on the experiences and achievements of students. The four universities have been anonymised in the project's publications where they are referred to as "Prestige", "Selective", "Community" and "Diversity", with the names indicating the status and reputational positions of the universities so called. As part of the research, courses at the four institutions were located on six scales reflecting both quality processes and quality outcomes. The former were "engagement with academic knowledge" and "good teaching" and the latter were "enhanced academic skills", "enhanced employability skills", "increased social confidence" and "changing self and society".

In a recent report (Ashwin et al. 2012), the four institutions are ranked according to their performance on each of the six scales. Rather than supporting the reputational hierarchy of institutions, the rankings show the *Prestige* University coming *bottom* on three of the six scales, including the two scales on enhanced academic and enhanced employability skills. There was just one of the scales where the *Prestige* University came top and that was "increased social confidence". This does not completely undermine the meritocracy argument but it would imply that 'confidence' rather than 'competence' is what matters and is what is rewarded in British society. It also accords with the earlier evidence we referred to which indicates a relatively weak relationship between the academic content of studies and the

---

3   The project was funded by the Economic and Social Research Council and led by Paul
     Ashwin, Monica McLean and Andrea Abbas.

subsequent employment of graduates in the higher status areas of employment within British society.

At the very least, this research poses questions for our understanding of the nature of meritocracy, if not for its very existence. It may indeed be the case that, for many positions in society, it is social confidence and one's personal networks which are the keys to success. If these are present, the knowledge and skills required to do the job can probably be acquired 'on the job' although whether they allow the job to be done 'excellently', 'adequately' or 'hopelessly' are questions which require further research. The social and political implications of such research will be profound!

Conclusions

A recent report for the European Science Foundation stressed the importance of the linkage between social equity and higher education's increasing differentiation. It notes that

> the idea that a single narrative or 'idea' can any longer capture the complex and often contradictory nature of higher education and its relationship with other parts of society has to be dispensed with (Brennan and Naidoo 2010).

Different things are happening in the different parts of different national systems. Opportunities are being created for some people while opportunities for other people are being blocked by higher education. Moore (2004) contrasted "liberal re-allocative" and "elite reproduction" approaches. The former place attention on meeting the human capital requirements of a high skill economy efficiently and fairly through a meritocratic selection/allocation system involving high levels of social mobility. The latter put the emphasis upon the reproduction and legitimisation of existing social relations and the inequalities they represent. In a way, this takes us back to Trow's elite and mass/universal functions of higher education with the reminder that *both* can be features of the relationships between higher education and its host societies.

However, the balance and tensions between the two are important and have major implications for societies, not just in economic but also in social and cultural terms.

There is evidence to suggest that in the UK the differences between institutions on purely academic terms are often overstated and, moreover, that quality differences which do exist may contradict the differences in reputation and status. Yet these latter differences are, if anything, tending to increase significantly and are entering the political discourse. Where a person studies may be crucial for future life chances whereas 'what' one studies and learns may not matter all that much.

The differentiation of higher education institutions cannot be separated from the differentiation of the societies of which they are part. The futures of those societies may be profoundly affected by how this relationship is worked out.

References

Ashwin, P., M. McLean, A. Abbas (2012). *Quality and Inequality in Undergraduate Courses.* Nottingham: Universities of Nottingham, Lancaster and Teesside.

Bourdieu, P. (2008). *Sketch for a Self-Analysis.* Chicago: University of Chicago Press.

Brennan, J., S. Lyon, P. McGeevor, K. Murray (1993). *Students, Courses and Jobs: The relationship between higher education and employment.* London: Jessica Kingsley Publishers.

Brennan, J. (2008). "It's not always what you know – why graduates get jobs". In: B. Kehm (ed.), *Hochschule im Wandel. Die Universität als Forschungsgegenstan (Festschrift für Ulrich Teichler).* Frankfurt: Campus Publisher.

Brennan, J., R. Naidoo (2010). "Higher education and the achievement (or prevention) of equity and social justice". In: *Higher Education Looking Forward.* Strasbourg: European Science Foundation.

Brennan, J., R. Edmunds, M. Houston, D. Jary, Y. Lebeau, M. Osborne, J. T. E Richardson (2010). *Improving what is learned at university.* London: Routledge.

Brennan, J., K. Patel (2011). "'Up-market' or 'down-market': Shopping for higher education in the UK". In: P. N. Texeira, D. D. Dill (eds.), *Public Vices, Private Virtues: assessing the effects of marketisation in higher education.* Rotterdam: Sense Publishers.

British Social Attitudes (2005). *The 27th report.* London: Sage publications.

Brown, P., H. Lauder (2001). *Capitalism and Social Progress, the Future of Society in a Global Economy.* London: Palgrave Macmillan.

Clark, B. (1983). *The Higher Education System in Cross-National Perspective.* Berkeley: University of California Press.

Institute for Fiscal Studies (2008). *Racing Away? Income Inequality and the Evolution of High Incomes.* Briefing notes, BN 76.

Moore, R. (2004). *Education and Society: Issues and Explanations in the Sociology of Education.* Cambridge: Cambridge University Press.

Schomberg, H., U. Teichler (2006). *Higher Education and Graduate Employment in Europe: Results from Graduate Surveys from Twelve Countries.* Dortrecht: Springer.

Teichler, U. (2007). *Higher Education Systems: Conceptual Frameworks, Comparative Perspectives, Empirical Findings.* Rotterdam: Sense Publishers.

Toynbee, P., D. Walker (2008). *Unjust Rewards: Exposing Greed and Inequality in Britain Today.* London: Granta Books.

Trow, M. (2010). "Reflections on the Transition from Elite to Mass to Universal Access: Forms and Phases of Higher Education in Modern Societies since World War II". (Originally published 2006) In: M. Burrage (ed.), *Martin Trow: Twentieth Century Higher Education – Elite to Mass to Universal.* Baltimore: The John Hopkins University Press.

Van der Graaf, P., T. Chapman, E. Bailey, C. Iles (2009). *Small Steps or Giant Leaps: An Evaluation of UK Youth's Youth Achievement Award.* Social Futures Institute, University of Teesside.

Young, M. (1958). *The Rise of the Meritocracy: 1870 to 2033.* London: Penguin Books.

The Recognition of Prior Learning and Dutch Higher Education – At cross-purposes?

Leon Cremonini

Abstract

Education (and higher education in particular) is said to empower upward social mobility for people from lower social strata who cannot inherit privilege. However, sociological studies on stratification and mobility emphasise that education can also contribute to persistent inequality in educational opportunities (IEO) between generations because of its unequal distribution across strata (Shavit et al. 2008). Many countries have initiated policies to recognise prior and experiential learning to credit experiences acquired outside the classroom and enable otherwise ineligible individuals to access and complete higher education. Though strongly advocated in European circles, many question RPL's ability to uphold the quality of the skills it purports to recognise and reward. By examining how a system – the Netherlands – where students are channelled into curricular pathways very early in life manages RPL, the chapter considers how 'recognising experience' can contribute to reducing inequality in higher education while upholding its quality and benefits.

Key words: recognition of prior learning (RPL), access, inequality in educational opportunities (IEO), tracking, pathways to higher education, lifelong learning (LLL)

Introduction: A theoretical background

This volume focuses on access and equity in higher education at a time when universities worldwide are battling for their place amongst the top notch of global excellence (as evidenced, for example, by today's obsession with global rankings). "Access", "equity" and "excellence" are praiseworthy goals yet carry with them risks and may not necessarily yield the expected benefits. The preoccupation with league tables and excellence may lead to a state of *bellum omnium contra omnes* that is detrimental rather than beneficial to higher education systems and societies; boosting participation without ensuring success (i.e. completion and subsequent employability) might simply exacerbate existing injustices.

Inherent in the latter point is the belief that although (higher) education may empower equity of opportunity and upward social mobility for people from lower social strata who cannot inherit privilege – as functionalist theorists such as Parsons (1959) have long argued – as massification produces internal stratification, it remains a mechanism for perpetuating inequalities in society – as contended by conflict theorists (such as Bourdieu 1979, 1990 [1970] and 1996 [1989], Shavit et al. 2008). Bourdieu (1990 [1970]) explained social inequality as resulting from the possession of different forms of capital, including economic (material wealth), social (networks of social relationships) and cultural (accumulated knowledge, competencies, skills etc.). Equity in (higher) education opportunity is thus correlated to the possession of one or more of these forms of capital.

In general, it is widely recognised that deciding to participate in tertiary education is influenced by antecedent circumstances such as socioeconomic or ethnic background, prior educational attainment etc., which can either discourage or ease access. Therefore, initiatives to promote participation are as globally widespread as diverse –depending on priorities and contexts.

Many policies make a direct link between access and success in higher education and a student's financial situation. In England and Wales, the 2004 *Higher Education Act* introduced means-tested financial aid to help poorer students access higher education, and established the Office for Fair Access with which universities must make agreements to invest some of their additional income from fees to attract applications from students from low income groups. As of 2012–2013, the Higher Education Funding Council of England has a budget of £140.4m for widening participation – including investments in teaching for improving retention rates (Cremonini et al. 2011: 56 ff). Australian universities have traditionally received special funds for enrolling students from lower socio-economic groups and remote areas and to pay study grants for these students. In addition, the performance monitoring by the Commonwealth government takes into account the proportion of students from disadvantaged backgrounds (Beerkens-Soo and Vossensteyn 2009: 10). Other initiatives (notably in the USA where many programmes are also initiated by private foundations) focus on ethnic background. [1] Age has also been (and increasingly is) a matter of consideration in stimulating equitable participation opportunities. In Sweden, for instance, since the 1970s the focus has been on increasing educational opportunities for the generations of students who had not been able to profit from the expansion of the upper secondary school system. The

---

1   See, for example: http://www.ihep.org/Research/access-success.cfm for a compendium about this issue in the USA.

so-called '25/4 rule' fixed a percentage of study places for adult applicants (Cremonini et al. 2011: 103 ff).

All educational systems involve some form of track placement (i.e. a 'pathway') to enable participation in higher education. Some systems are selective at entry (for example in the USA and Japan); other systems have an 'open entry policy' whereby applicants with the necessary secondary exit diploma can enrol in tertiary-level education (e.g. in most of Europe). Systems which allow greater selection are often considered closer to the 'world-class' ideal.[2] However, critics argue that current pathways to higher education cannot ensure equity in participation and access 'with success' because of inequalities in the possession of capital at the outset.[3] In the Netherlands (a country with open access) students are channelled into curricular pathways early in life. Hence, certain students may not qualify for university education because they have not followed the necessary propaedeutic education (i.e. the *Voorbereidend Wetenschappelijk Onderwijs* (VWO) [Preparatory Scientific Education]). But such curricular pathways are determined by students' prior achievements which are often correlated with their family and social background. Consequently, access to university is more likely for students who possess (more of) some form of capital (in the Bourdieuan sense).

The Recognition of Prior Learning (RPL) is a strategy to address the problems of inequality in educational opportunities. We argue that, since RPL credits competencies, skills and knowledge regardless of how they are acquired, it aims at reducing gaps in cultural capital possession. Hence, RPL policies are rooted in a conflict approach to the sociology of education and focus on one of its constituent elements, namely cultural capital, to reduce inequality. This suggests that the fundamental ratio behind an RPL policy is the expectation that tackling the cultural gap will *ipso facto* affect economic and social capital, thus initiating a virtuous process leading to exponentially

---

2   Evidence of this is, for example, the importance attached to student selection in institutional rankings and in worldwide endeavours to build "world-class universities" (see, for instance, Altbach and Salmi 2011).

3   For instance, a number of studies from the USA show that parents of lower socioeconomic extraction are less likely to make plans to pay for their children's college (see the 2009 paper by Deborah M. Warnock, *Inequalities at the Outset: Identifying Factors that Affect Parents' Perception of Paying for College*, which includes a compendium of literature on the topic, at: http://inpathways.net/ Inequalities_at_the_Outset.pdf, accessed 1 August 2012).

fairer educational opportunities. For example, since higher education is known to yield individual economic benefits[4] such as higher salaries, once the cultural capital gap is reduced and access is widened, economic capital gaps will also narrow.

This chapter contributes to a critical academic and policy debate about equity and access in higher education and their relationship to excellence and quality. It starts by setting out a framework by which current arguments in favour and against RPL can be understood (in the policy and academic fields), and against which claims by advocates or detractors may be tested (by necessity, such a framework begins with clarifying key definitions). Then, to test the framework we explore the example of the Netherlands where one would expect RPL's benefits to be clearest in virtue of this country's early tracking mechanism in education. One can argue that early tracking intensifies existing cultural capital gaps because it prevents certain students from progressing, by design. Indeed, the Dutch early track placement is often blamed for imbalanced participation rates between different groups in society. This is notably the case of an often-cited divide in Dutch society between *Allochtoon* and *Autochtoon* (literally 'non-native' and 'native') (OCW 2009, OECD 2007a, Van Elk et al. 2009).[5] The chapter takes this relatively narrow perspective to understand to what extent RPL addresses this divide while maintaining the quality of Dutch higher education and the country's ambitions for excellence.

But RPL is also relevant for the Netherlands because there appears to be a clash between two conflicting trends. On one hand, data suggest that there is an attainment gap between 'native' and 'non-native' Dutch (see the next sections), but on the other hand, earlier Organisation for Economic Co-operation and Development (OECD) (2007b) data show that, when controlled by socioeconomic status, pupils aged 15 of immigrant origin are significantly more likely to expect to complete tertiary education than their 'native' counterparts. That the existing track placement system might thwart their aspirations could be a good argument in favour of implementing RPL.

---

4 Several studies on the public and private benefits have been undertaken. A useful synthesis is, for example, IHEP 2005.

5 We are aware of the critiques raised against the persistent use of racially loaded terminology (such as "native", "non-native", "non-western background") in government research (also see: Institute of Race Relations 2010: 50). However, for the purposes of this chapter we adopt this wording since we use nationally available statistics (which to date embrace this taxonomy).

Finally, that RPL retains its salience is demonstrated for instance by the increase in applications (e.g. +42% in the Netherlands between 2008 and 2011[6]), or the European Commission's (EC) and the European Centre for the Development of Vocational Training's (CEDEFOP) efforts to produce an inventory of validation of non-formal and informal learning in 2007, and the 2009 publication of the *European guidelines on the validation of non-formal and informal learning* (European Commission Website).

Although, as mentioned, RPL is implemented to different extents and with varying degrees of success across Europe, at the heart of the matter lie three fundamental issues:

- Purposes and boundaries: should RPL encompass the whole array of tertiary qualifications or should it be further limited (e.g. to secondary professional qualifications)? What purpose should prevail (certificate/diploma attainment, individual employability, enabling career mobility within a firm or enterprise, etc.)? (Also see Thomas et al. 2000.)
- Quality: can RPL uphold the quality of the skills it purports to recognise rather than leading to 'degree inflation'?
- Reduction of inequality: could RPL simply re-route IEO to more élite tracks if, as Lucas (2001) has argued, the saturation of a certain level of education has been reached?

A framework to make sense of the RPL debate

At this point it is necessary to call attention to the possible friction relating to the role of RPL in the higher education system more generally. On one hand, calls – for example by government – to recognise individuals' prior and/or experiential learning are justified on the grounds that opportunities for participation should be more equitable and, therefore, that the system's output of recognised (i.e. formal) qualifications should increase and better represent the social make-up. At the same time, this argument is grounded (whether consciously or not) in a transformative notion which rejects the conventional divide between the formality and informality of learning in favour of a position where attributes of both are blended in all learning situations (Duvekot and Konrad 2006). In fact, RPL qualifies 'non-learners'

---

6   Despite a dip in 2010. See http://www.evcnederland.nl/evc-nieuws and http://www.kenniscentrumevc.nl/index.php/nieuwswerkgever2/163-nieuws-56.

as 'learners' and is seen as a way to formalise "individual discourse from everyday language registers to more formal (even academic) registers" (Whittaker et al. 2006, quoted in Duvekot and Konrad 2006). It is this problem that this chapter explores, namely the alignment of claims that informal learning can legitimately produce formal qualifications (and the learning outcomes that accompany them) with the value bestowed by systems and societies to the qualifications thus attained. To confront this question, we start by adopting the policy framework proposed by Duvekot (2008 and 2009), which requires categorising the different practices of "recognition" and clarifies key definitions in the field.

Terminology matters

So far, this chapter has used the generic term "RPL" to define policies that wish to take stock of *all* prior learning modes (classroom-based learning, informal learning, work experience etc.). The Dutch term used to describe the process of recognizing competences is *Erkenning van verworven competenties* ("recognition of acquired competences") (EVC)[7]. A policy framework to evaluate the impact of prior learning on equity and success in tertiary education is, by necessity, situated within the greater context of lifelong learning (LLL), and requires taxonomising different types of 'recognition'. The Council of the European Union (2009) appreciates the vital role of education and training in sustaining the continent's knowledge society and economy. The Council particularly stresses the importance of LLL in its *Strategic Framework for European Cooperation in Education and Training* (known as "ET 2020"):

> European cooperation in education and training for the period up to 2020 should be established in the context of a strategic framework spanning education and training systems as a whole in a lifelong learning perspective. Indeed, lifelong learning should be regarded as a fundamental principle underpinning the entire framework, which is designed to cover learning in all contexts – whether formal, non-formal or informal – and at all levels [...].

---

7   Henceforth, this chapter will adopt the original Dutch term "EVC" (Erkenning van verworven competenties [recognition of acquired competencies]). The English versions of the Dutch acronym EVC are always translated into APL in all official publications.

Among the European Union's actions to foster LLL (e.g. study exchange programmes at different education levels [8] and projects to develop technology and language skills), recognising beyond-the-classroom learning retains a special place (European Commission, Directorate General Education and Training 2012a):

> Countries around Europe are increasingly emphasising the need to take account of the full range of an individual's knowledge, skills and competences – not only those acquired at schools, universities or other formal education and training institutions. Recognising all forms of learning is therefore a priority of EU action in education and training.

However, "recognizing all forms of learning" can take a number of forms, including (Duvekot 2008):

1. *Accreditation* of Prior Learning (APL), a practice that focuses on the summative effects of accepting experience directly and solely relevant to the achievement of a specific standard. APL is thus a top-down institution-steered process where personal competencies are not relevant if they do not match the standard sought.
2. *Recognition* of Prior Learning (RPL), which emphasises the formative connotation – that is, a bottom-up individual-steered process where applicants gather all their personal learning experiences and decide what sort of validation/accreditation best suits their ambitions.
3. *Valuation* of Prior Learning (VPL), which lies at the crossroads of APL and RPL, has both summative and formative paths and can satisfy all actors (citizens, providers and organisations) in how they formulate their lifelong learning strategies (ibid.).

Duvekot distinguishes between two main approaches to EVC ("summative" and "formative") depending on its intended effects, and two main frames of reference ("national standards" or "sectoral standards") depending on the context or benchmark that is applied. A summative approach aims to provide candidates with a certificate or a diploma (it is strictly *recognition* of achievements), whereas a formative path includes practical learning and/or competence development (it is career-development-oriented (Duvekot 2008: 7) and is thus better labelled *valuation*). Moreover, the functions of

---

8   Including: (a) Comenius for all levels of school education, from pre-school to secondary school; (b) ERASMUS for higher education; (c) Leonardo da Vinci for vocational education and training; and (d) Grundtvig for adult and "alternative" education (see http://ec.europa.eu/education/lifelong-learning-programme/index_en.htm).

EVC are also affected by the context, which may be the national higher/vocational education sectors or other providers such as sectoral training institutes, company schools and voluntary organisations that validate competencies according to their own standards (Duvekot 2009: 15 ff).

This framework leads to a typology of EVC models which captures the expected returns for the individual, namely (ibid.):

1. a "qualification model", i.e. a bridge between vocational or higher education and the labour market,
2. an "empowerment model", enabling the acquisition of initial qualifications,
3. an "employability model", which upgrades competencies within any structured context,
4. lifelong learning.

Chart 1 below shows how these different models fit with the roles of EVC in the Netherlands as agreed in the 2012 National Covenant (see later).

Chart 1.   EVC in the Netherlands (Source: Knowledge Centre APL 2012)

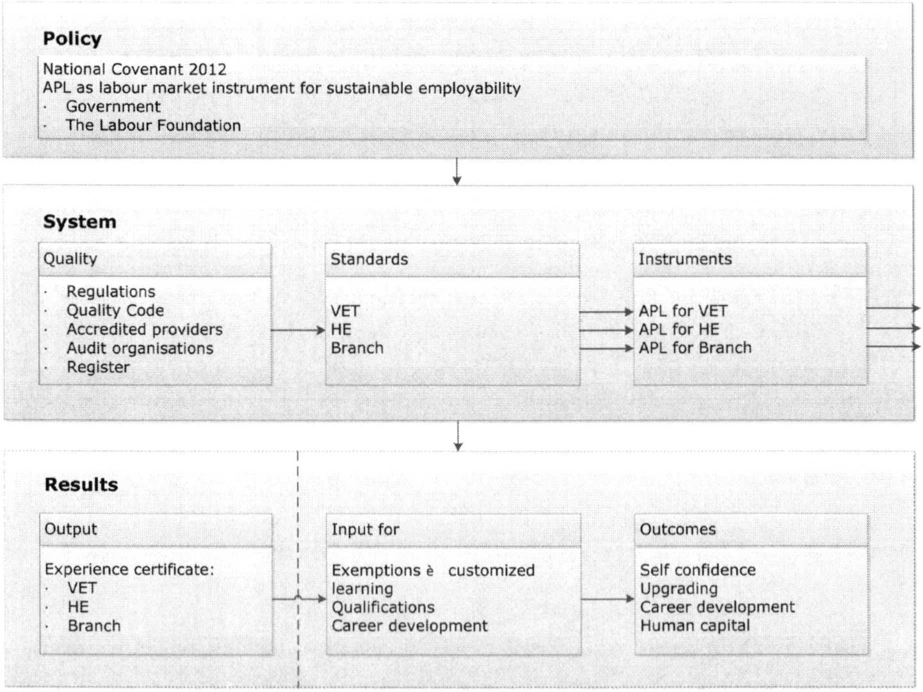

APL in the Netherlands (Knowledge Centre APL, 2012)

But at the aggregate level (i.e. higher education system and social levels), two sorts of outcomes might be produced – although they do not necessarily supplement each other. The first is that the education system, including but not limited to the higher education sector, may produce more formally credentialed individuals ("qualification" and "empowerment" models apply). Such a development may improve cohesion in the system and reduce inequality in educational attainment, for instance between different socioeconomic or ethnic groups. Secondly, EVC-induced career development may improve a country's social and economic performance regardless of increases in the number of credentials.

Both outcomes fit into the Commission's LLL policy framework to enable individuals to achieve learning outcomes that make them employable throughout their lives, and they take respectively a summative vs. a formative view as to how policies should be enacted (see Chart 2 below). It is important to consider whether: (a) these two outcomes benefit or damage the perceived quality and reputation of the higher education system as a whole; and (b) whether they cause shifts within the system (e.g. in student demand and success at the different qualification levels).

Chart 2.   EVC and LLL (source: Duvekot 2009: 15 [2008: 15], modified by author)

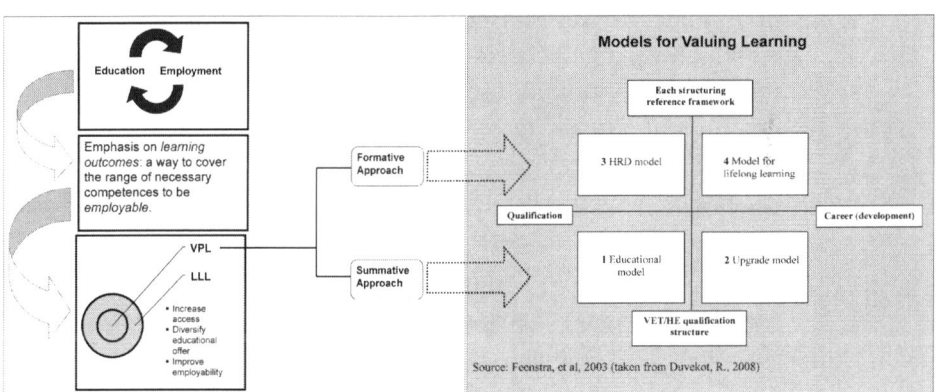

Higher education and EVC in the Netherlands

Thus far, this chapter has stressed the potential role of EVC in equity and access in higher education and proposed adopting a framework wherein to position the EVC discourse vis-à-vis LLL. The next sections will describe

EVC practices in the Netherlands and their relevance (or not) for Dutch higher education and for the higher education discourse more generally. First, this section will briefly describe the history and practices of EVC in the Netherlands. Next, we outline some of the key problem areas in Dutch higher education, which some might argue are good reason for a wide-scale use of EVC. Finally, conclusions will be drawn on the role and (potential) impact of EVC in Dutch higher education more generally.

EVC in the Netherlands: A brief history and description

In the Netherlands, the first form of EVC was conceived in the 1990s, a time when the concept of a guaranteed lifelong occupation with a single employer was increasingly coming into question. But the early version of EVC was limited to individual company-led initiatives to recognise prior *qualifications* (i.e. formal proofs of certification) for career progression.[9] There was no clear vision, regulation, nor central steering (van den Dungen 2009). It was a decade later that the Dutch government and its social partners embarked on the 'EVC path', which regards the *learning experience itself* (whether formal or not) as a stimulus for *lifelong employability*. With EVC now firmly on the agenda, two key developments ensued (ibid.):

–   the creation in 2001 of a *Kenniscentrum EVC* ("Knowledge Center APL"), which collects and shares EVC knowledge and good practices and stimulates its adoption in education and the labour market; and

–   the development by the *Kenniscentrum EVC* of a "Quality Code" including five standards ("codes") and several criteria ("details of implementation"), which providers must meet to qualify as "registered EVC providers" (it is in fact a set of accreditation standards).[10]

The EVC process is relatively straightforward.[11] The stated goal is to compare the applicant's competencies against learning outcomes of a formal qualification. It is thus the candidate's responsibility to build up a "portfolio" wherein he or she demonstrates that the acquired competencies match the

---

9   This early version was called *Erkenning van Verworven Kwalificaties* (Recognition of Prior Qualifications).

10   The APL Quality Code is available (in Dutch) at http://www.hbo-raad.nl/component/content/article/28/243.

11   This information is taken from http://www.kenniscentrumevc.nl/. There is a section in English with a summary of the procedure.

learning outcomes at the level of the qualification sought. If successful, the candidate receives a "certificate of proved experience" (*ervaringscertificaat*) that can be used for new job opportunities or to accelerate – or enable entry into – formal learning. Nevertheless, an *ervaringscertificaat* does not guarantee access since programme examination committees (e.g. at Vocational Education and Training Colleges or Universities of Applied Sciences) decide if the certified experience satisfies the level applied for, and whether knowledge beyond "on-the-job skills" such as literacy and numeracy, is sufficient (interview data, 29 June 2012).

Every three years, Dutch "Review and Assessment Boards" (*Visiterende en Beoordelende Instanties*) conduct external quality control of aspirant Registered Providers. EVC procedures are assessed against the national Quality Code. Providers must fulfil the standards set in the Code, which include: (i) goals; (ii) individual entitlements; (iii) research (reliability of procedures and instruments); (iv) quality of assessors; and (v) quality control of the EVC procedure (Kenniscentrumevc 2012)[12]. If the evaluation is positive, providers are formally listed in the "Register of Recognised EVC providers" (*Register van Erkende EVC aanbieders*) and may offer their customers benefits such as tax breaks. However, audits represent an out-of-pocket expense for organisations, which can only afford them if the number of EVC applicants is sufficient to cover the costs. This is alleged to be an important reason for businesses opting for in-company training (aimed at supporting staff development) rather than EVC registration which, in principle, has broader aims (interview data, 29 June 2012).

The Quality Code is the core of the first EVC Covenant (*Het convenant: een kwaliteitscode voor EVC* ["The Covenant: A Quality Code for EVC"]) signed on 14 November 2006 in Rotterdam by several parties including the Secretary State for Education, Culture and Science, the Dutch Association of Universities of Applied Sciences (*HBO-raad*) and the Dutch Association of VET Colleges (*MBO-Raad*). The new Covenant signed in Utrecht on 12 June 2012 maintains the existing Quality Code but re-emphasises that the ultimate *raison d'être* of Dutch EVC is to support the labour market, as the title (*Convenant ter stimulering van het arbeidsmarktinstrument EVC als onderdeel van een Leven Lang Leren* ["Covenant to stimulate the labour market instrument EVC as part of Lifelong Learning"]) clearly states.

---

12 See http://www.kenniscentrumevc.nl/index.php/mt-kcevc-kwaliteitscode (accessed 1 June 2012).

Higher education in the Netherlands: About access, hope and success

How EVC can contribute to improving opportunities for participation in higher education relates to its place in the system and the system's challenges. Dutch higher education has often been praised for its quality (for example by citing the numerous national universities' listed in global rankings) but an inclusive assessment of educational opportunities must reflect on how access is governed and how it relates to students' preceding expectations as well as their ensuing success.

Participation in Dutch higher education depends on a tracking system by which pupils are granted access only if they have followed a certain pathway during their secondary schooling.[13] Further, because the Dutch higher education system is binary, including universities (*Wetenschappelijk Onderwijs* (WO) [Scientific Education]) and universities of applied science (*Hoger beroepsonderwijs* (HBO) [Higher Vocational Education]), different secondary education choices pave the way to different tertiary education options (which means that other options are denied).

Primary schooling starts at age five.[14] After seven years, (i.e. at age 12) students choose their secondary education path which will have significant implications for their tertiary studies later on in life. There are various forms and different levels of secondary education but only two of them grant direct admission to higher education, namely:

- the *Hoger Algemeen Voortgezet Onderwijs* (HAVO) (Higher General Secondary Education), which lasts five years and allows entry to the HBO sector; and
- the *Voorbereidend Wetenschappelijk Onderwijs* (VWO) (Preparatory Scientific Education) lasting six years and enabling admission to WO programmes.

Other secondary education includes the four-year *Voorbereidend middelbaar beroepsonderwijs* (VMBO) (Preparatory Secondary Vocational Education) leading to the *Middelbaar beroepsonderwijs* (MBO) (vocational

---

13   There are innumerable descriptions of the Dutch higher education system which are fairly simple to find on-line. This very short compendium is necessary to set the stage for the chapter's EVC discussion. It is based on the description offered by Nuffic to its international applicants (see http://www.nuffic.nl/international-students/dutch-education/education-system).

14   Children are allowed to begin school at four but are not legally required to do so.

education and training (VET) Colleges).[15] The MBO can last up to four years and only its highest level ("MBO-4") grants access to HBO programmes (but not to WO). The first and second year of secondary education, called *algemeen leerjaar* (general learning year), can incorporate several course combinations, some of which are part of the education path enabling access to higher education, while others are not. For example, the Gymnasium, Lyceum and Athenaeum (all leading to WO), the HAVO and the combination of HAVO/VWO allow higher education access. Other combinations, with mostly different VMBO elements lead to MBO education, although they may have different levels of theory vs. practice in their curricula.[16] The Chart in Annex 2, taken from Nuffic, shows the Dutch educational system and its pathways to different levels of education.

The success of the streaming system just outlined is mainly reliant on providing students and parents with good advice concerning their secondary education choices because it is largely at this juncture that their higher education future is determined. Data show that differences across groups in society still persist, despite encouraging[17] changes over time.

The latest data released by *Statistics Netherlands*[18] *(Centraal Bureau voor de Statistiek* (CBS) [Central Bureau of Statistics])[19] show that in the 2010–2011 academic year there were over 656,000 tertiary education enrolments, of which 64% (416,900) were at HBOs and about 37% in WOs. Participation by "non-western *Allochtonen*"[20] was 14% overall (15% in HBO and 13% in WO). First-year enrolments followed a roughly similar

---

15 MBO is post-secondary vocational education which leads to lower qualifications than tertiary education.

16 There are four levels in the pathways, namely: (i) theoretical programme; (ii) combined programme; (iii) management vocational programme; and (iv) basic vocational programme.

17 The term "encouraging" is intentionally value-loaded. This chapter assumes that improving participation for under-represented socioeconomic and ethnic groups is positive.

18 "Statistics Netherlands" is the official English CBS denomination although the literal translation of *Centraal Bureau voor de Statistiek* is "Central Bureau of Statistics".

19 The CBS website also provides data for 2011–2012. However, they are not used here since at the time of writing they are still classified as "provisional".

20 This excludes so-called "westerse allochtonen" and those classified as unknown.

214 Leon Cremonini

pattern – 69% "*Autochtoon*" and 15% "non-western *Allochtoon*" (with a similar distribution across HBO and WO).[21]

This information can be mapped against enrolments in secondary and MBO education. About half of the 950,000 pupils in secondary education in 2011–2012 may become eligible for some form of higher education once they graduate successfully. At MBO level, the figure is slightly higher with 57% of students enrolled at Level IV, which grants access to HBO (2010–2011).[22]

However, the figures uncover divergences between groups with different ethnic backgrounds – particularly the "*Autochtonen*" vs. the "non-western *Allochtonen*"[23] (see Charts 3 and 4). Of all "native Dutch" enrolled in secondary education after the *algemeen leerjaar* (i.e. excluding all "*Allochtonen*" who are also enrolled), over 50% are in courses which will enable them to access higher education; for "non-western non-native" students the figure is 35% (i.e. of all "non-western *Allochtoon*" students currently in years 3 and above of secondary schooling, the majority is placed in a track that will not enable their participation in higher education later on in their life). A similar pattern appears in the *algemeen leerjaar*, where 27% of all "non-western *Allochtonen*" are enrolled in a track that will give them the possibility to pursue higher education while for "*Autochtoon*" Dutch this figure is 44%. The trend is similar at the MBO-4 (which qualifies for HBO education), with 46% of all "native" Dutch enrolled at MBO at level 4 against 37% of "non-western *Allochtoon*".

21 See   http://statline.cbs.nl/StatWeb/publication/?DM=SLNL&PA=70943ned&D1=0 &D2=a&D3=0&D4=0-1,42,88,149,181,217,233,273,300&D5=0&D6=0&D7=20 &HDR=G5,G4,T,G2,G6,G1&STB=G3&VW=T for the 2010–2011 data.
22 See Centraal Bureau voor de Statistiek (CBS) Database 2012, and Centraal Bureau voor de Statistiek 2011: 85 ff).
23 Data for the so-called "westerse allochtonen" are similar to the figures for the "natives".

Chart 3. Participation in general years of secondary education ("algemeen leerjaar") by their enabling tertiary access, by "native" vs. "non-native" background (source: CBS database 2012)

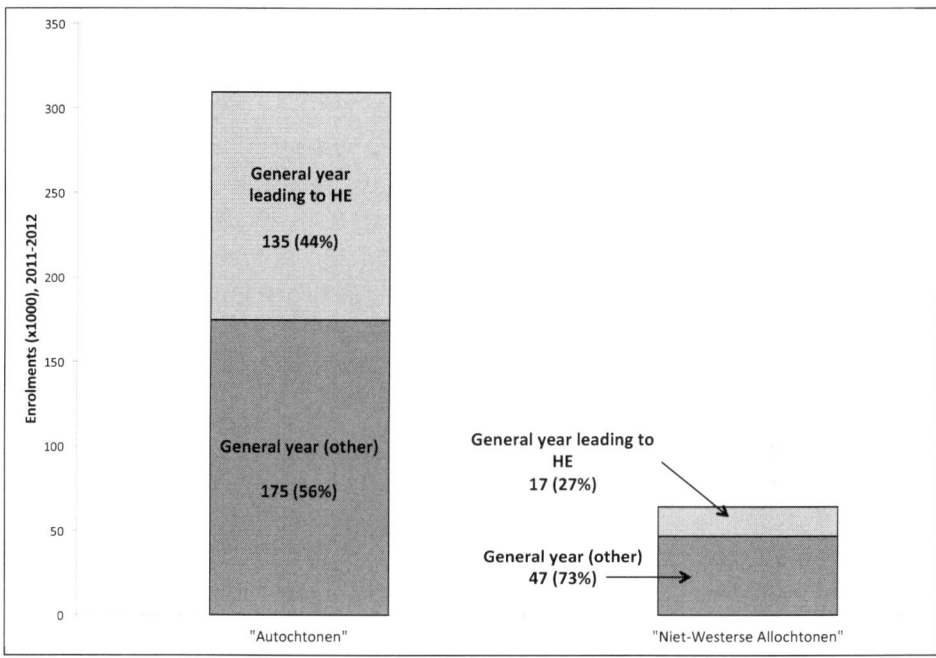

Chart 4. Participation in "post-general years" of secondary education tracks ("post-algemeen leerjaar") by their enabling tertiary access, by "native" vs. "non-native" background (source: CBS database 2012)

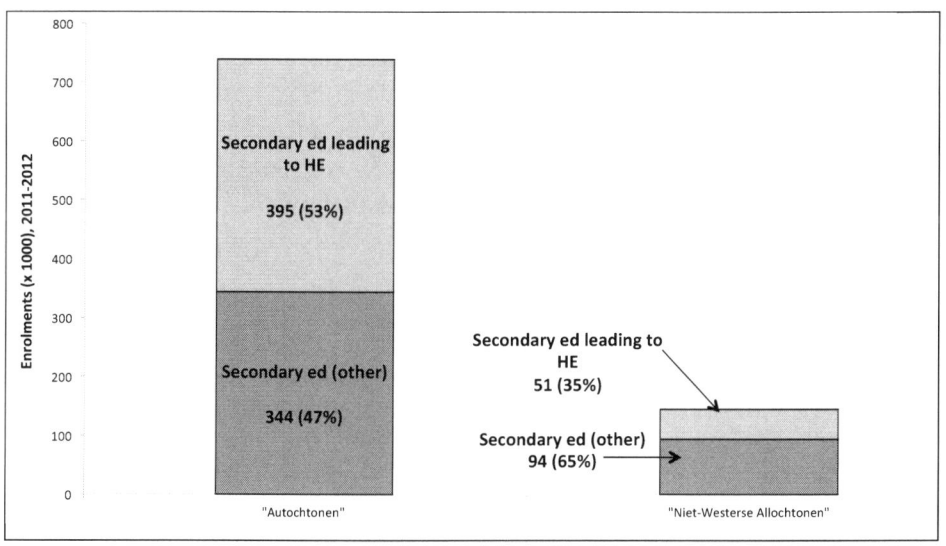

These data suggest that pupils with a non-western immigrant background have fewer chances to access higher education because of their prior schooling. In other words, even relative to their numbers in the secondary education system they are predominantly placed on paths that will not grant future access to higher education.

Also other factors, notably family income, have an effect on the type of (secondary) education followed and the achievement of the qualifications sought. The Ministry's publication on key statistics (Ministerie van Onderwijs, Cultuur and Wetenschap 2012: 110) shows that pupils from families with higher incomes are more likely to complete a HAVO or a VWO. In 2011, about 15% of pupils in secondary education achieved a VWO and 21% a HAVO diploma. However, while over 25% of children from families earning four times or more the minimum national salary[24] left with a VWO diploma and about 30% with a HAVO, the figures are closer to 10% for children coming from families earning less the twice the minimum salary. Conversely, drop-outs in secondary school are lower for high-income families than for low-income families (>10% and >20%, respectively). But it is also known that the average income of "Native Dutch" is higher than that of "non-Western Allochtonen"[25] (the relationship between "immigrant background" and economic capital possession remains thus intertwined).

Hope and success

At higher education levels, two points are particularly relevant to the EVC discourse, namely differences in attainment and differences in expectations. First, the main problem of Dutch higher education is not only (and not so much) the under-representation of minorities in enrolment, but differences in their attainment. CBS demographic data shows that, of all 18–30 year-olds in the country in 2011, 17% were "non-western *Allochtonen*" and 73% "*Autochtonen*" (which does not conflict radically with a 14% vs. 74%

---

24   The minimum salary is set by the government and corrected every six months (January and July). As of July 2012 it amounted to €1,456.20 before tax per month (see http://www.rijksoverheid.nl/onderwerpen/minimumloon).

25   See the CBS data at http://statline.cbs.nl/StatWeb/publication/?DM= SLNL&PA=70843ned&D1=0,4&D2=0&D3=0,17,26-28&D4=l&HDR=G1,G2,G3 &STB=T&VW=T.

enrolment rate)[26]. Also, the distribution of these different groups across the WO and HBO sectors is similar (in 2011, 37% of "non-western *Allochtonen*" and 37% of "*Autochtoon*" first-year enrolments were in the WO sector; 76% and 79%, respectively, were in HBO). But a divide is apparent when looking at students' performance according to their (immigrant) background[27]. Chart 5 shows the proportions of full-time "*Autochtonen*" and "non-western *Allochtonen*" students who graduated, dropped out or are still in education (without a degree) after six years – at both HBO and WO levels.

Chart 5. *Study progress in 6 years, by "native" vs. "non-native" background, WO and HBO 2005 cohort, full-time students (source: CBS database 2012)*

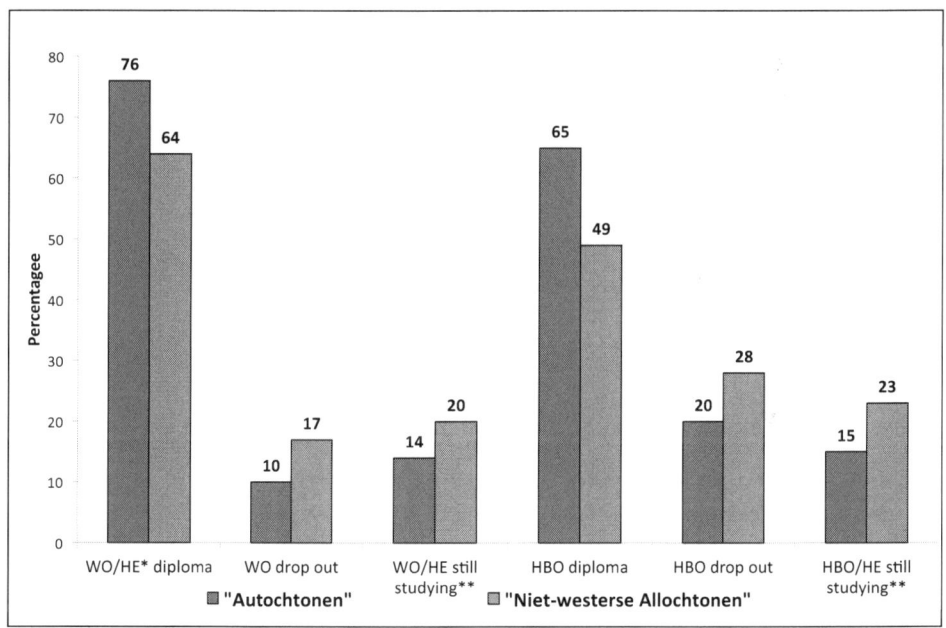

*   Includes students who began WO and might have graduated with another higher education diploma (e.g. HBO)
** Includes students who are still studying in higher education but may have changed course (e.g. transferred to HBO or WO)

---

26   See http://statline.cbs.nl/StatWeb/selection/default.aspx?DM=SLNL&PA=37325&VW=T.
27   See http://statline.cbs.nl/StatWeb/selection/?DM=SLNL&PA=71037NED&VW=T.

Second, earlier data from OECD (2007b) drawn from the Programme for International Student Assessment (PISA) 2003,[28] which compares several countries, indicate that secondary students of immigrant background aged 15 are often more likely to expect to complete tertiary education (International Standard Classification of Education (ISCED) 5A/6) than "natives". When controlled by socio-economic status (SES) and mathematics performance, the relationship between immigrant status and expectation for higher education is stronger. In the Netherlands, 15-year-old "*autochtonen*" and "*allochtonen*" appear to have similar expectations (i.e. the odds ratio[29] is very near 1, indicating no difference) but significant divergences emerge after controlling by SES and mathematics performance when "*allochtonen*" (both first and second generation) are over five times more likely to expect to complete higher education than "*autochtonen*". This figure is significant in two ways in that: (a) it is high (amongst the countries surveyed, only Denmark scores higher on this indicator for both first- and second-generation pupils, and Sweden scores higher for first-generation ones only); and (b) of all countries surveyed, it is the most apart from the general figure (i.e. before controlling by SES and mathematics performance). The latter point may indicate a strong hope not always matched by reality. The same OECD study reveals that teenagers of higher SES are about twice as likely to expect to complete higher education (i.e. the odds ratios that students expect to complete higher education by socio-economic status in the Netherlands is 2.2 – which is similar to the other countries surveyed).

---

28   PISA is an international study which began in the year 2000. It aims to evaluate education systems worldwide by testing the skills and knowledge of 15-year-old students in participating countries/economies. Since 2000 over 70 countries and economies have participated in PISA. The 2003 round was the only one that explicitly covered the issue of 15-year-olds' expectations to complete tertiary education (ISCED 5A and 6). Although this information is not as recent as other information provided in this chapter it can be used as an indication of the effects of socioeconomic status on expectations.

29   An odds ratio compares the probability (expressed as odds) of an event occurring for two different groups. The odds ratio takes values between zero (0) and infinity. One (1) is the neutral value and means there is no difference between the groups compared; close to zero or infinity means a large difference. An odds ratio larger than one means that group one has larger odds than group two (i.e. the event is more likely to occur for group one than for group two) – if the opposite is true, the odds ratio will be smaller than one (see OECD 2007b: 81).

Chart 6. *Odds ratio that 15-year-olds expect to complete tertiary education in the Netherlands, by immigrant background (source: OECD 2007b: 87 ff. tables A4.4 and A4.5)*

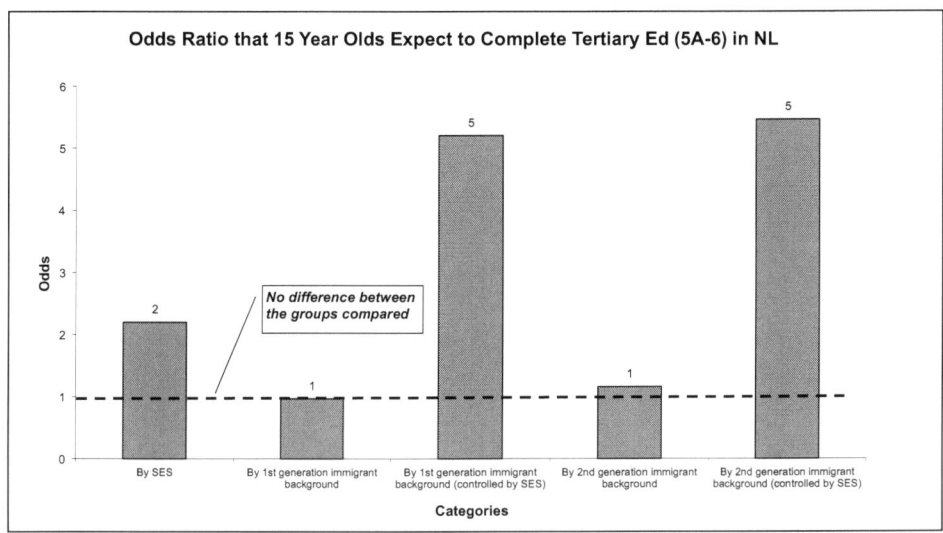

The information presented in Sections 3.2.1 and 3.2.2 brings to the surface some key overarching issues and questions related to equity and access for different groups in Dutch higher education. Most students with an immigrant background (so-called "niet-westers *Allochtonen*"):

– are channelled into secondary school paths that will not enable them to access higher education (while the reverse is true for "native" secondary level students);
– at the same time, at age 15 they have stronger expectations of tertiary completion than their "native" peers;
– however, relative to the size of the immigrant population aged 18–30, their enrolment numbers appear in line with the rest of society;
– but, they remain more likely to drop out and less likely to graduate[30]...
– ...although year-on-year improvements (for example in graduation rates) appear stronger than for the "native" student population.

Yet, the EVC tool appears to remain primarily employment-driven. At the recent EVC National Conference (where the new Covenant was signed) it was said on more than one occasion that EVC is a labour market instrument and that organisations offering EVC trajectories are not concerned with

---

30   Which might be an argument for EVC.

education but with improving employees' on-the-job competencies as an investment for the business and the worker. Moreover, that EVC is more MBO- than HBO-related was attributed (*inter alia*) to the fact that the MBO qualifications framework applies consistently nationwide but the same does not hold true for the HBO sector (HBO qualification descriptors are more general than those at MBO level so there are differences in how they are implemented in different programmes, which in turn leads to less comparability also for EVC procedures).[31]

A survey commissioned in 2012 by the Dutch Ministry of Education Culture and Science to ECORYS, a Rotterdam-based consulting firm, measured several aspects of Dutch EVC, which appear to corroborate an understanding of EVC as an employment enhancement tool, and also for this reason utilised mostly at MBO level. As of 2011 there were 83 registered EVC providers, of which 33 were MBOs, 11 were HBOs, and the other 39 were non-education institutes including individual organisations and knowledge centres (ECORYS 2012, Table 1.1). In the same year, the number of completed EVC procedures totalled 17,700. While this was a drop of over 2,000 units from 2010, it represents a 79% increase over a five-year period (ECORYS 2012, Table 2.3).

Some key information that emerges from the ECORYS report includes (but is not limited to) the following:[32]

- over 50% of EVC procedures are undertaken at MBO and "branch-specific" level. EVC at HBO level accounts for approximately 11% (Chart 2.2);
- almost 70% of EVC providers are non-government-funded institutions (i.e. not MBO or HBO institutions, nor "Centres for Vocational Education and Industry" (*kenniscentrum voor beroepsonderwijs en bedrijfsleven* (*KBB*)) (Chart 2.3);
- the number of EVC procedures is expected to increase over the coming two years. However, 70% of the HBO providers anticipate no change (30%) or a strong decrease (40%) (Table 3.3);

---

31   The conference report is online at: http://www.kenniscentrumevc.nl/index.php/ nieuws?id=171.

32   For the full report (the charts and tables in brackets refer to the chart/table numbering in the original ECORYS report), see http://www.kenniscentrumevc.nl/ attachments/article/163/Ecorys-onderzoek%20EVC%20gemeten%20-%20actualisatie% 202010-2011.pdf.

- providers expect an increase of EVCs at "branch-specific" level training (+64%) and at MBO-3 level (+62%), while 36% expect an increase of EVCs at HBO level (and 64% think HBO-level EVCs will remain stable (23%) or contract (41%)) (Table 3.6);
- according to the providers surveyed, EVC participants are motivated equally by continuing education and diploma attainment (44%), and by labour market goals (47%) (9% are "unknown/other") (Table 4.1, N=81);
- providers also state that of their EVC participants who have received the *ervaringscertificaat*, 34% are directly eligible for a formal qualification (6% HBO, 44% KBB, 37% general, and 39% MBO) (Table 4.3, N=63);
- at the same time, according to "Training and Development Funds" (*Opleidings- en Ontwikkelingsfondsen*), which support in-company development, EVC contributes predominantly to developing insight into one's acquired skills and to personal development. Continuing education, diploma attainment and intra-organisational career steps rank lowest (Table 4.2, N=13); and
- 54% of surveyed providers who discontinued their EVC procedures did so because of the influence of the EVC Quality Code. The same proportion stated that EVC was not usable as a marketing tool for their organisation (Table 4.9, N=24).[33]

But the achievement of credits and diplomas remains crucial. New research on the benefits of *ervaringscertificaten* produced by the *Kenniscentrum EVC* stresses that EVC is individually and societally advantageous because *verzilvering* (literally "redemption") is a means for career transition, employability and ultimately labour market development (see Chart 7 below, taken from van den Dungen et al. 2012: 42). In the Netherlands, efforts to boost the educational value of EVC as independent from its on-the-job value – especially at tertiary level, e.g. through government support, the HBO sector's and the Open University's involvement – have not met

---

33   As mentioned above, this is related to the fact that formalised external quality control must be matched by a sufficient intake of EVC applicants to cover the audit costs. However, this finding also reinforces the point that in essence EVC is not believed to be an education tool but only a labour market tool. Institutions of higher learning (HBOs, WOs) are also liable for the costs of NVAO accreditation (which *de jure* is voluntary but *de facto* obligatory because of the consequences of non-accreditation) but see it by and large accepted as part of being an educational provider.

with success. The goal of EVC is individual employability and educational attainment is a means to that end. Yet the fact that over 40% of candidates see EVC as a way to move forward in their education and attaining a diploma may indicate they intend it to be an educational endeavour – which in the long term might bring the relationship between the demand and supply of EVC into question.

Chart 7.   Possible EVC route from the perspective of a fictional participant (taken from Van den Dungen et al. 2012; translation of terms by author and listed alphabetically)

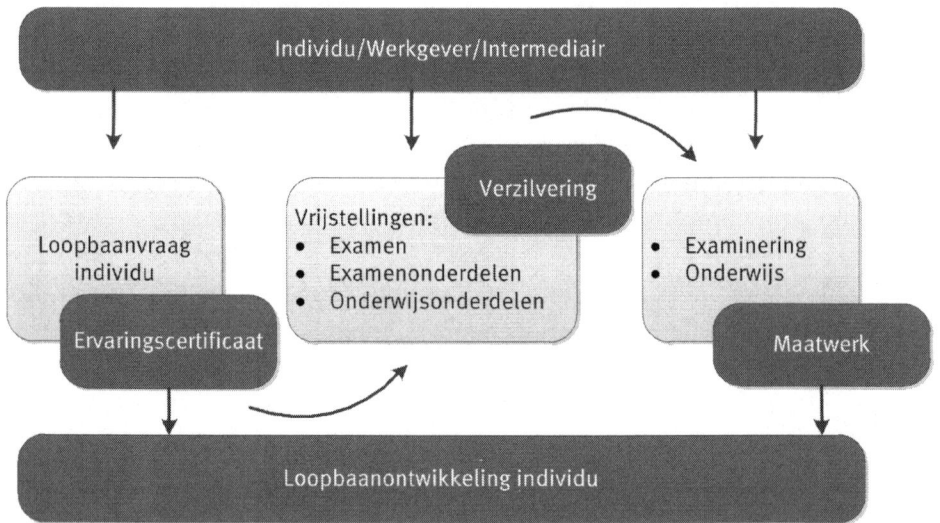

Ervaringscertificaat: certificate of proved experience
Examen: examinations
Examenonderdelen: examination components
Examinering: examination
Individu: Individual
Intermediair: Intermediary*
Loopbaanvraag individu: individual career request
Loopbaanontwikkeling individu: individual career development
Maatwerk: customisation
Onderwijs: education
Onderwijsonderdelen: education components
Verzilvering: redemption
Vrijstellingen: Exemptions
Werkgever: Employer

* For example (public) employment agencies

EVC and its contribution to Dutch higher education

The previous sections described EVC as an increasingly accepted way to acknowledge and reward individual experiences which, though not always acquired in formal settings, nonetheless improve personal skills and knowledge. The chapter posited that EVC has the potential to bridge participation divides in higher education and looked at the case of the Netherlands as illustrative because its educational system places students in pathways enabling or precluding access at an early age. This section draws conclusions from the materials presented thus far on the contribution of EVC to reducing inequality in tertiary education participation. In a closing discursive table, we provide preliminary answers to the three questions raised at the chapter's outset, namely "what are the boundaries of EVC?", "Does EVC affect the quality and reputation of higher education?", and "Does EVC in fact reduce inequality in tertiary education participation?".

The evidence shown thus far suggests that from its inception EVC in the Netherlands was a tool for empowerment in employment rather than for dealing with disparities in higher education participation. Analyses of LLL in the Netherlands have suggested that EVC has much to offer to higher education but at the price of a mind shift from supply-driven to demand-driven education and a less "school-centred" approach to teaching and learning (van den Dungen 2009). However, EVC can also be a gateway to new forms of higher education provision, such as Associate Degrees (ibid.) These short-cycle programmes are relatively new in the Dutch landscape and considered a potential way to address the access and diversity of students (Beerkens-Soo and Vossensteyn 2009).

The findings point to two aspects. First, because EVC is seen as an employment tool, when applying the EVC framework presented earlier in the chapter, the qualification and empowerment models are not so central. The "EVC community" (providers, the Covenant signatories etc.) seems to endorse this conclusion. For instance, that the Quality Code requirement should have led 50+% of providers to cease their EVC projects can be construed as a clue that in essence such providers do not deem EVC as part of education and thus do not believe it should be subjected to quality control mechanisms that are the norm for institutions delivering educational programmes.[34] Moreover, formalised external quality control should be matched by sufficient student demand (i.e. EVC candidates) to cover its costs but applicants whose object is to achieve a HBO degree might have simpler and cheaper options (e.g. intake assessments and other forms of exemptions) at their disposal, inducing providers to limit or cease their EVC trajectories. Often institutions also choose to favour initial learning over LLL for adults.

Second, the EVC discourse and practice in the Netherlands is deep-rooted in the country's binary education system, not only as far as the "formal" vocational vs. academic divide goes but also in the long-held beliefs of Dutch society. Over the years WOs have staunchly refused to partake in any EVC agreement because of its intrinsically vocational nature.[35] Hence, the case indicates that *EVC is aligned with the value attached by the system and society to the qualifications it confers* because it is related predominantly to vocational and on-the-job training, scarcely (and decreasingly) to professional tertiary education and, as yet, not at all to university education.

These conclusions question the role of EVC, as implemented in the Netherlands, in expanding access to higher education. Other intake instruments, such as interviews or exemptions, often inhibit the use of EVC (albeit often applying its principles). Whether and to what extent imbalances in participation in the Dutch system can be addressed by an inherently vocationally and career-oriented mechanism remains an open problem.

Drawing from the case of the Netherlands, Table 1 addresses the three key EVC issues presented in opening the chapter, namely: (a) its boundaries – what array of qualifications should it encompass?; (b) its contribution (or not) to promoting access to tertiary education; and (c) its effect on the quality and excellence of higher education. The concluding section draws on Table 1.

---

34   This does not mean that in-company training is "bad" but that the control of its quality
      does not necessarily reflect standards and criteria like in formal education. Rather, it is
      geared to assuring employees become more successful on the work floor.

35   With the exception of the Open University, which until recently was an EVC provider
      with its EVC centre – a choice that can be explained by the mostly mature make-up of
      this university's student population. However, even the Open University has of late
      opted out (interview data, 29 June 2012).

Table 1.   EVC and its Place in (Dutch) Higher Education

Boundaries	EVC in the Netherlands is *in principle* applicable to all levels of education because it is a regulated tool to recognise all forms of learning and its quality is controlled through a Quality Code and external audit mechanisms. There are no obstacles for institutions at any level to assess and accept (or reject) experiential certificates (also see van den Dungen et al. 2012: 35 ff). However, in practice when it relates to higher education EVC in the Netherlands is limited to professional higher education (HBO) and that, too, is increasingly uncommon and mainly at Level 5 of the European Qualifications Framework (Associate Degree). It thus seems that in this national context the boundaries of EVC are *shifting to VET and branch qualifications* – a trend that is consistent with a strong binary divide and the nature and history of Dutch EVC. Yet, it may be at odds with the Bologna Process goal of making Bachelor degrees *for both Universities of Applied Sciences and Research Universities* fully employable rather than a *de facto* inevitable avenue leading toward the second cycle of formal education (which is, today, the case of Dutch WOs).
Impact on access	EVC in the Netherlands has *the potential* to enable access for under-represented groups and those who generally did not acquire the requisites through 'standard pathways', but to date *this is incidental* rather than the norm. Also returning drop-outs occur but very seldom (interview data, 29 June 2012). At the higher education level, the direct impact of EVC on access and equity in the Netherlands remains limited (mainly because of its vocational/employment functions described throughout this chapter). However, what is of interest is the aforementioned contrast between the intentions of many EVC applicants – who wish to obtain credit exemptions or degrees through their experiences – and institutions offering EVC projects primarily as an investment in their own employees. Hence, the friction between the hopes and opportunities of disenfranchised 15-year-olds regarding their future participation in higher education that emerged from the PISA study (see section 3.2.2) might persist in later life as experiential/non-formal/informal learning rarely results in access, or the attainment of a formal tertiary education qualification.
Impact on quality	The Dutch government is very focused on quality, excellence, "world class" etc. – ever more so at a time when global rankings have almost become a global hysteria. There is no evidence that EVC challenges these aims. First, the Quality Code is confirmation that there is interest in ensuring that recognised learning, whatever form it takes, is good and that the public is protected against 'rogue EVC providers' just as it is against 'rogue universities'. But, in addition, all over the globe the excellence and prestige discourse is focused on research. It is the latter – not professional education – that is seen as the measure of a system's distinction.[36] Moreover, where

---

36   Whether this is an appropriate measure of excellence is beyond the scope of this chapter and is an on-going debate.

education is concerned, rankings often see selection – not increased access – as a sign of institutional status. The fact that research universities have unfalteringly refused to partake in EVC together with the decline in HBOs' interest are signs that an extension of EVC in the higher education system (not its application 'as is') is considered potentially threatening to ambitions of world-class provision. Yet again, to date EVC is fundamentally not an educational tool but an employment tool. The case cannot conclusively determine whether widespread EVC would have an effect on the quality of higher education in the Netherlands. There are other systems in the world where EVC is recognised as an educational pathway in its own right and there is no evidence that it has lowered the worldwide perception of those higher education systems.

Discussion and the need for future exploration of the issue

The case of the Netherlands shows that EVC has the *potential* to address inequality in higher education in a streamlined education system such as the Dutch one. No threat to educational quality has emerged, provided that an appropriate set of standards and a quality control is put in place – as is the case in the Netherlands. But the case suggests that the benefits of EVC by way of reducing inequality in (higher) education opportunities can only be truly realised if EVC itself is rooted in a more general reform agenda which must consider: (a) where disadvantage is actually present in the educational process; (b) how experience and other non-traditional forms of learning *fit in academic education;* and hence (c) whether and how such forms of learning can contribute to 'excellence' as it is currently understood.[37]

A second issue relates to EVC's contribution to reducing different forms of gaps (to use the conflict theory approach). In the Netherlands, the strong vocational/professional development nature of EVC suggests that it is used predominantly to address economic gaps in society. An avenue of study to pursue, which is beyond the scope of this chapter, might look into inter-generational trends of EVC's contribution to participation in higher education in relation to socioeconomic improvement. It is known that

---

37 For example, in his well-known characterisation Salmi (2009) states that to be a "world-class university" the alignment of three determinants is necessary, i.e. a critical mass of top students and faculty, an abundance of resources, and good governance. The question is how recognising and rewarding experience and other non-traditional forms of learning contributes to these elements –particularly top talent (to date there is no evidence either way, but there is strong anecdotal evidence of fears that doing so would be deleterious).

socioeconomic background (e.g. measured by parental income and/or educational level) plays a role in tertiary participation and Dutch EVC is particularly focused on supporting socioeconomic improvement through progression on the job. However, 'educational stagnation' appears to be looming in several countries. For example, the Goethe Institute's portal on migration and integration, which provides information on this topic from various complementary perspectives, mentions that since the mid-1990s immigrant groups in Germany have faced "educational stagnation" – or even deterioration – despite earlier advances in scholastic levels[38]. This raises questions about EVC's *long-term sustainability* as a tool to ensure that future generations have fair chances to become highly educated as opposed to its short-term visibility in promoting access *nunc pro tunc*.

References

Altbach, P. G., J. Salmi, eds. (2011). *The Road to Academic Excellence. The Making of World-Class Research Universities*. Washington DC: The International Bank for Reconstruction and Development/The World Bank.

Beerkens-Soo, M., H. Vossensteyn (2009). *Higher Education Issues and Trends from an International Perspective. Rapport tbv Commissie Veerman*. Enschede: CHEPS. Available at http://www.utwente.nl/mb/cheps/publications/publications%202010/ veerman%20committee/cheps%201%20international%20trends%20and%20issues%2 0report.pdf (accessed 4 January 2013).

Bourdieu, P. (1979). *Distinction: A Social Critique of the Judgement of Taste*. Harvard: Routeledge & Kegan, Harvard University Press.

Bourdieu, P. (1996 [1989]). *The State Nobility: Elite Schools in the Field of Power*. Cambridge: Polity Press.

Bourdieu, P., Passeron, J. (1990 [1970]). *Reproduction in Education, Society and Culture*. London, New Delhi: Sage Publications, Thousand Oaks. Available at http://www.revalvaatio.org/wp/wp-content/uploads/bourdieau-reproduction_in_ education_ society.pdf (accessed 4 January 2013).

Centraal Bureau voor de Statistiek (2011). "Jaarboek onderwijs in cijfers—2011". Available at http://www.cbs.nl/NR/rdonlyres/FC6D3388-0F9E-4129-8F2B-53022BA3F774/0/ 2011fl62pub.pdf (accessed 4 January 2013).

Council of the European Union (2009). "Strategic Framework for European Cooperation in Education and Training". Available at http://eur-lex.europa.eu/LexUriServ/ LexUriServ.do?uri=OJ:C:2009:119:0002:0010:EN:PDF (accessed 4 January 2013).

Cremonini, L., L. Leisyte, E. Weyer, H. Vossensteyn (2011). "Selection and Matching in Higher Education". An International Comparative Study. Report for the Ministry of Education Culture and Science of the Netherlands (Ministerie van Onderwijs, Cultuur

---

38   See http://www.goethe.de/lhr/prj/daz/mag/igd/en3146846.htm.

and Wetenschap). Enschede: CHEPS. Available at http://www.utwente.nl/mb/cheps/ publications/Publications%202011/C10HV101%20selection_final_report_2011.pdf (accessed 4 January 2013).

Duvekot, R. (2008). "Dutch EVC at a glance 2008. The development of APL, RPL & EVC in the Netherlands". National report European Commission's Life Long Learning Programme, OBSERVAL Project. Available at http://www.valuenetwork.org.uk/ Documents%20for%20Website/Subgroup%20B/Background%20papers/Dutch%20VP L%20at%20a%20glance%202008-def.pdf (accessed 4 January 2013).

Duvekot, R. (2009). "The Individual Learner as Change Agent in the Learning Society. From European to National Guidelines in Promoting Valuation of Prior Learning". Paper presented at NVR konference Realkompetencevurdering – en udfordring i teori, praksis og politik 5 marts 2009 Odense Danmark. Available at http://www.viauc.dk/ projekter/NVR/Documents/Udgivelser/EVC-DK%2005-03-2009.pdf (accessed 4 January 2013).

Duvekot, R., Konrad, J. (2006). "Towards a Transnational Concept of Valuing Lifelong Learning: Some Practical Reflections on Developing Theory". Available at http://www.leeds.ac.uk/educol/documents/166725.htm (accessed 4 January 2013).

Institute for Higher Education Policy (IHEP) (2005). *The Investment Payoff. A 50-State Analysis of the Public and Private Benefits of Higher Education.* Washington, D.C. Available at http://www.ihep.org/assets/files/publications/g-l/InvestmentPayoff.pdf (accessed 4 January 2013).

Institute of Race Relations (2010). *Alternative Voices on Integration in Austria, France, Germany, the Netherlands and the UK.* London: UK. Available at http://www.irr. org.uk/pdf2/AlternativeVoicesOnIntegration.pdf (accessed 4 January 2013).

Lucas, S. R. (2001). "Effectively Maintained Inequality: Education Transitions, Track Mobility, and Social Background Effects". *American Journal of Sociology.* Vol. 106. No. 6. 1642-1690.

Ministerie van Onderwijs, Cultuur and Wetenschap [Ministry of Education Culture and Science of the Netherlands] (2009). *Kennis in Kaart* [Knowledge in Paper]. The Hague : OCW.

Ministerie van Onderwijs, Cultuur and Wetenschap [Ministry of Education Culture and Science of the Netherlands] (2012). *Kerncijfers 2007-2011* [Key Figures]. The Hague: OCW.

Organization of Economic Cooperation and Development (OECD) (2007a). *Thematic Review of Tertiary Education – The Netherlands, Country Note.* Paris: OECD.

Organization of Economic Cooperation and Development (OECD) (2007b). *Education at a Glance 2007.* Paris: OECD.

Parsons, T. (1959). "The School as a Social System". *Harvard Education Review.* Vol. 29. 297-318.

Salmi, J. (2009). *The Challenge of Establishing World-Class Universities.* Washington DC: The International Bank for Reconstruction and Development/The World Bank.

Shavit, Y., M. Yaish, E. Bar-Haim (2008). "The Persistence of Persistent Inequality". Available at http://www.ccsr.ac.uk/qmss/seminars/2008-crossnat/documents/shavit_ new.pdf (accessed 4 January 2013).

Thomas, E., S. van Broekhoven, J. Frietman (2000). *EVC aan de poorten van het hoger onderwijs, handreiking voor de implementatie van EVC in hogescholen en universiteit.* Nijmegen: ITS, Radboud Universiteit.

van den Dungen, M. (2009). "Lifelong Learning within HE in the Netherlands". *European Journal of Education.* Vol. 44. No. 3 (Part I). 339-350.

van den Dungen, M., P. Heuts, A. Venema (2012). *Onderzoek naar verzilvering van ervaringscertificaten. Belemmeringen, oplossingen en aanbevelingen. [Research on Redemption of Certificates of Proved Experience. Barriers, Solutions and Recommendations].* Utrecht: Kenniscentrum EVC. Available at http://www.kenniscentrumevc.nl/attachments/article/164/Verzilvering%20van%20erv aringscertificaten_v02.pdf (accessed 4 January 2013).

van Elk, R., M. van der Steeg, D. Webbink (2009). *The Effect of Early Tracking on Participation in Higher Education.* The Hague: Centraal Planbureau. Available at http://www.cpb.nl/en/publication/effect-early-tracking-participation-higher-education (accessed 4 January 2013).

Whittaker, S., R. Whittaker, P. Cleary (2006). "Understanding the transformative dimension of RPL". In: P. Anderson, J. Harris, eds., *Re-theorising the Recognition of Prior Learning.* Leicester: NIACE. 301-319.

Websites Consulted

CBS Database 2012:
http://www.cbs.nl/nl-NL/menu/themas/onderwijs/cijfers/default.htm (accessed 4 January 2013)

European Commission:
– http://ec.europa.eu/education/lifelong-learning-policy/doc52_en.htm
– http://ec.europa.eu/education/lifelong-learning-policy/informal_en.htm
– http://ec.europa.eu/education/lifelong-learning-policy/framework_en.htm
– http://ec.europa.eu/education/lifelong-learning-policy/mobility_en.htm (all accessed 15 May 2012)

Kenniscentrumevc (2012): http://www.kenniscentrumevc.nl/attachments/article/19/Information_ APL_in_the_Netherlands_2009.pdf (accessed 4 January 2013)

NUFFIC (2012):
http://www.nuffic.nl/international-students/docs/Diagram-DES.pdf (accessed 4 January 2013)

Annex 1: List of Abbreviations

Acronym	Original Extended Version	English Translation
APL	Accreditation of Prior Learning	---
CBS	Centraal Bureau voor de Statistiek	*Statistics Netherlands*
EVC	Erkenning van verworven competenties	*Recognition of acquired competences*
HAVO	Hoger Algemeen Voortgezet Onderwijs	*Higher general secondary education*
HBO	Hoger beroepsonderwijs	*Higher vocational education*
ISCED	International Standard Classification of Education	---
KBB	Kenniscentrum voor beroepsonderwijs en bedrijfsleven	*Center for vocational education and industry*
MBO	Middelbaar beroepsonderwijs	*Secondary vocational education*
OECD	Organisation for Economic Co-operation and Development	---
PISA	Programme for International Student Assessment	---
RPL	Recognition of Prior Learning	---
SES	Socioeconomic Status	---
VMBO	Voorbereidend middelbaar beroepsonderwijs	*Preparatory secondary vocational education*
VWO	Voorbereidend wetenschappelijk onderwijs	*Preparatory scientific education*
WO	Wetenschappelijk onderwijs	*Scientific education*

Annex 2: The Dutch Higher Education System (Source: NUFFIC 2012)

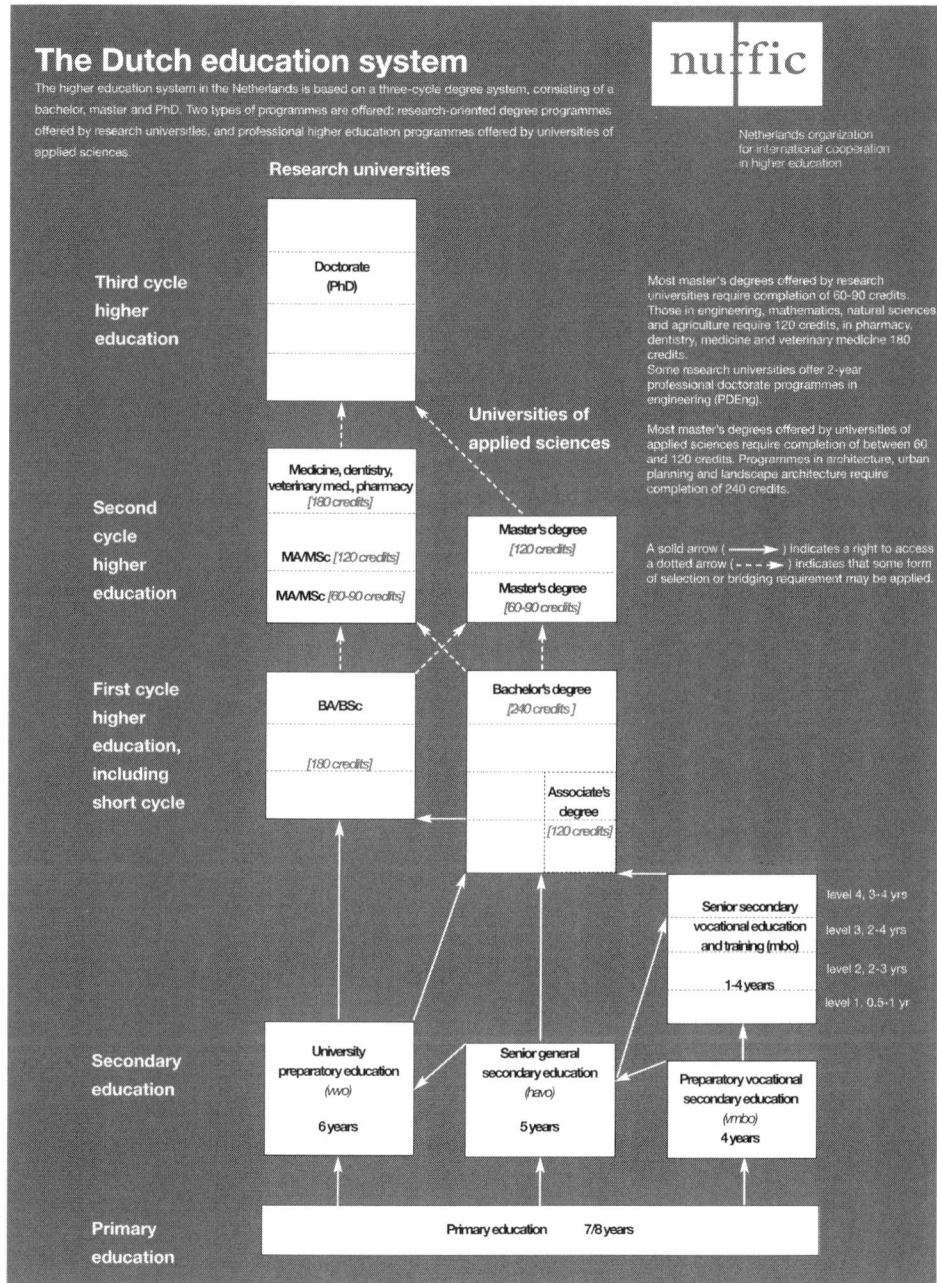

From System Expansion to System Contraction. Access to Higher Education in Poland

Marek Kwiek

Abstract

The chapter explores access to higher education in Poland when demand-driven educational expansion is changing into educational contraction driven by demographic factors. It combines a theoretical framework with substantial original data analysis. The empirical evidence comes from educational statistics and statistical demographic projections. Educational expansion in Poland in 1995–2010 is related to four major dimensions: age, gender, sector (public/private) and status (full- and part-time). In addition, a section about access related to the intergenerational social mobility in Poland is based on microdata analysis of the EU SILC dataset (European Union Survey on Income and Living Conditions) – to explore the relative mobility of Polish society in Europe (in terms of educational attainment levels and occupational groups). The chapter contributes to academic discussions in four areas: global comparative research on private higher education (and related public/private dynamics), research on inter-sectoral and intra-sectoral differentiation of higher education, international comparative research on post-communist European higher education systems, and international comparative research on social stratification. The chapter refers to Poland and several post-communist European higher education systems which combine two features: a vast expansion following the fall of communism after 1989 and sharply falling demographics in the next two decades.

Key words: higher education contraction, demographics, equity and access, selectivity, Polish universities

Introduction

The chapter explores access to higher education in Poland at a specific moment when demand-driven educational expansion following the collapse of communism in 1989 is changing into educational contraction driven by demographic factors. The pairs of expansion/contraction and growth/decline in European higher education, related to demographic trends, have not been discussed in research literature so far and the chapter is intended to contribute to themes expected to be highly relevant to most European post-communist countries.

The chapter is divided into six sections: a brief "Introduction"; "System expansion and its major parameters"; "System expansion and selectivity in higher education"; "Inequality in access to higher education: Poland in a European comparative perspective"; "The demographic decline and the universal fees options"; and "Conclusions". The chapter combines a theoretical framework with substantial original data analysis. The empirical evidence of the chapter comes from both Polish national educational statistics and Polish national statistical demographic projections. Two sections in particular provide detailed analyses of original empirical data: the second section presents analyses of educational expansion in Poland in 1995–2010 based on four major dimensions: age, gender, sector (public/private) and status (full- and part-time). The fourth section about access related to intergenerational social mobility in Poland is based on a microdata analysis of the EU SILC dataset (*European Union Survey on Income and Living Conditions*) that explores the relative mobility of Polish society in Europe (in terms of educational attainment levels and occupational groups). The chapter refers and contributes to several lines of theoretical thinking in global higher education research. In particular, it contributes to academic discussions in four areas: global comparative research on private higher education (and related public/private dynamics), research on the inter-sectoral and intra-sectoral differentiation of higher education, international comparative research on post-communist European higher education systems, and international comparative research on social stratification. The chapter refers not only to Poland but also to several post-communist European higher education systems which combine two features: a vast expansion following the fall of communism after 1989 and sharply falling demographics in the next two decades.

Two national contexts are relevant to the present chapter. The first is that Polish higher education shows complicated inter-sectoral public-private dynamics and one of the highest degrees of marketisation of the system in Europe (in 2010, it had the biggest share of enrolments and enrolment numbers in the private sector in Europe, 31.5% and 0.56 million, and a high share of fee-paying students, 51.6%, GUS 2011: 55). Studies in the public sector are either tuition-free (full-time) or fee-based (part-time); studies in the private sector are fee-based in both full-time and part-time modes. The second context is that radical demographic changes have been projected for the next three decades. The population of the 19–24 age group is projected to be decreasing in the 2007–2025 period by 43% (GUS 2009: 171) and the number of students is projected to be decreasing from 1.82 million (in 2010) to 1.33 million (in 2020) to 1.17 million (in 2025; see Instytut Sokratesa

2011: 10-14, IBE 2011: 110-111, Vincent-Lancrin 2008: 45).[1] The decline in student numbers in the coming decade is a relatively disregarded parameter in national higher education strategies (see Ernst and Young 2010: 20-21) in international country reports (by both the OECD and the World Bank) or in academic discussions of mass higher education in Poland (Bialecki and Dabrowa-Szefler 2009: 185-186 and 194). The chapter links access to higher education in Poland to the exploration of different past roads of expansion of the system and to the implications of the system's contraction.

It is generally assumed in both higher education scholarly and policy literature that, generally, major higher education systems in both the European Union (EU) and the OECD area will be further expanding in the next decade (Altbach et al. 2010, King 2004, Attewell and Newman 2010, Santiago et al. 2008, OECD 2008, EC 2011). Expanding systems generally contribute to social inclusion because, as recently concluded in a large-scale comparative study on stratification in higher education, the expanding pie "extends a valued good to a broader spectrum of the population" (Arum et al. 2007: 29). In the knowledge economy, the expansion of higher education systems is key and higher enrolment rates and increasing student numbers in the EU have been viewed as a major policy goal by the European Commission throughout the last decade (EC 2011: 3, Kwiek 2006, Kwiek and Kurkiewicz 2012). Questions of admission, selection criteria and funding mechanisms in the last two decades in Poland were until recently asked in a rapidly expanding system, with ever growing numbers of both students and institutions (Duczmal and Jongbloed 2007, Dobbins 2011: 155-162, Bialecki and Dabrowa-Szefler 2009). Yet they may need to be reformulated for the coming decade of the system's contraction. The dramatically changing demographics introduce new dilemmas related to public funding and admission criteria.

The present chapter explores specific Polish responses to questions about who is admitted and publicly funded and who should be admitted and publicly funded, changing over time, viewed as highly relevant to other countries in Europe with similar admission patterns (with public/private

---

1   In a less pessimistic enrolments scenario, the decrease is expected to be from 1.82 million in 2010 to 1.48 million in 2020 to 1.34 million in 2025 (Vincent-Lancrin 2008: 47). A report from a Polish think tank, the Socrates Institute, predicts a decline in the number of students from 1.82 million in 2010 to 1.52 in 2015 to 1.25 million in 2010 (Instytut Sokratesa 2011: 14).

dynamics) and similar demographic trends for the future (such as Bulgaria, Romania, Estonia, Lithuania, Latvia and Slovakia as well as, to a smaller degree, the Czech Republic, Hungary and Slovenia). Research into the two decades of expansion is combined with a brief exploration of the possible implications for access of the contraction of the higher education system in the next decade.

System expansion and its major parameters

Access to higher education, the credentials arising from it, and employability are closely linked (Schomburg and Teichler 2011, Knight 2009). In general, throughout the 1990–2010 period in Poland, there was a clear divide between credentials from traditional metropolitan, elite public universities (in the tuition-free, full-time mode of studies) and credentials from all other types of institutions and modes of studies (with the part-time fee-paying mode of studies in the Polish context being much less academically demanding than the tuition-free full-time mode). The hierarchy of institutions and programmes was clear: "most highly valued were non-paying regular courses in trendy and attractive fields of study at several renowned state universities" (Bialecki and Dabrowa-Szefler 2009: 194-195). Selection criteria are demanding in the former case only. They are often merely formal (meeting minimum formal requirements) in all other (public and private) higher education institutions and in both (full-time and part-time) modes of studies. Consequently, educational outcomes, the quality of diplomas and the life chances of graduates tend to vary increasingly, leading to the diversification and segmentation of Poland's higher education system.

Generally, strict meritocratic criteria are only used for deciding on institutional admissions in two cases: in highly competitive elite metropolitan and in less competitive non-elite regional public universities – but only in their tax-based or tuition-free places. In all other cases, and whenever fees are charged, in both public and private sectors higher education has for two decades been open to all those who could afford it and meet the basic formal criterion: the possession of a secondary school matriculation certificate. Higher education in all those other cases became affordable because of the "quasi-market" competition pressures (Le Grande and Bartlett 1933: 13-34) between the ever increasing numbers of private higher education institutions

(334 in 2010) and the growing engagement of all public institutions (131 in 2010) in providing additional, part-time, fee-based studies. The large-scale competition for fee-paying students led to open-access policies for fee-paying students in both sectors (Kwiek 2008 and 2010).

In the first decade of the expansion (in the 1990s), following the collapse of communism, the difference between graduating from elite metropolitan public universities and graduating from all other types of institutions was not an issue of public concern. The differences in the life chances of graduates were not clearly visible. Families with high socio-economic capital, usually from the former class of intelligentsia then turning gradually into the new middle class of professionals, were sending their children to full-time, tuition-free places in elite metropolitan public universities, as they had always done in the whole post-war period. The social structure in Poland shows not only a very high level of inheriting levels of education and occupations across generations, as discussed in more detail in section 4, but also a very high level of inheriting institutional types of higher education: first-generation students are far more likely to choose academically less demanding higher education: the fee-based, part-time mode in both sectors.

Tuition-free places in elite metropolitan public universities were scarce and available on rigid meritocratic selection criteria, although increasing throughout the 1990s. These universities were trying to retain their high quality teaching in times of ever increasing student numbers by channelling the newcomers, mostly from lower socio-economic classes, into their paid study offers, especially bachelor degree studies of considerably lower academic quality. This is consistent with the results of a recent large-scale empirical study of education and labour markets in Central Europe, where Poland was included in the case studies (Kogan et al. 2011: 337).

The expansion took different routes, as discussed in detail below; to a large extent, these routes determine the routes of the future contraction and the major policy strategies to combat it. The expansion is broken down here into four components: expansion by age, by gender, by sector (public/private), and by student status (full-time/part-time). The data below show disaggregated enrolments in 1995 and 2010, and the disaggregated enrolment increase in the 1995–2010 period. Overall, student numbers rose from about 790,000 to about 1,841,000 (or by 133%). Bialecki and Dabrowa-Szefler (2009: 185) recently summarised the drivers of the expansion in enrolments as being "on the one hand, the society's growing educational aspirations and, on the other, a significant broadening of the tertiary-level education on offer".

Analysing the age structure of students in 1995 and in 2010, the increase in enrolments was most marked in the traditional student age group (the percentage of the distribution of the increase was 70% for those aged 19–24 and about 30% for those aged 25 and more). While the enrolment increase in the former age group was about 955,000, in the latter it was about 405,000 (GUS 1996: 192-193, GUS 2011: 138-142). The expansion was also heavily gendered: about 40% of the increase involved male students, and about 60% female students. Consequently, the feminisation of studies, already present in 1995, became even more marked in 2010: while the rise in the number of male students in the period was about 412,000, for female students it was more than 50% more, or about 640,000 (GUS 1996: 2, GUS 2011: 55). From a public-private sectoral perspective, despite the emergence and massive growth of the private sector in the period, the private sector accounted for less than half of the total growth (about 47%, or about half a million students; ibid.). Finally, the expansion was fuelled slightly more by fee-based part-time studies in both sectors than by full-timers. The number of part-timers went up from about 340,000 in 1995 to about 900,000 in 2010. As a consequence of the 163% increase in numbers of part-timers, the distribution of the 1995–2010 rise was about 48% for full-time students and about 52% for part-time students (ibid.). To sum up, the distribution of the expansion in the period studied was the following: new students were mostly of a traditional age (70%), female (60%), studying slightly more often in a part-time mode (52%) and slightly more often in the public (54%) than in the private sector.

What is important in the context of the changing access to higher education is the fact that the past distribution of the increase in enrolments (by age, gender, sector and status) in the period of educational expansion is highly relevant to the possible future distribution of the decrease in enrolments in the contraction period, as well as for national policies in the conditions of educational contraction. The patterns of expansion may determine the patterns of contraction. For instance, one evident way to combat the contraction is to increase the participation rate of male students in both the traditional 19–24 age bracket and older. Other traditional tools for increasing student numbers may fail: these include lowering the rate of early school-leavers, increasing the transition rate from secondary to tertiary education, raising the graduation rate from higher education, and increasing enrolment rates. As a recent *Youth in Europe* report shows, Poland already has the second lowest rate of early school-leavers in the European Union (after Slovenia, with only 5%, EC 2009: 94); Poland also ranks first in entry rates at the tertiary education level (with 85% in 2009, OECD 2011: 316), and ranks second in graduation rates at tertiary level (after Slovakia, with 50.2%, OECD 2011: 68). Finally, enrolment rates are already higher than the average for both EU and OECD countries (reaching 53.8% in 2010, GUS 2011: 26). Any research into future educational contraction must take the above limitations into account.

As discussed above, the expansion was accompanied by the hierarchical differentiation of the system (see Huisman and van Vught 2009, Meek et al. 1996, and Goedegebuure et al. 1996): much of the growth was absorbed by public and private second-tier institutions and by first-tier public institutions in their academically less demanding and less selective part-time study mode. The expansion also took place in specific fields of study, in particular such as social sciences, economics and law (in 2000, the share of enrolments in this field of study was 37% in the public sector and 72% in the private sector, and a decade later in 2010 it was still 32.8% and 52.6%, respectively, GUS 2011: 58). When, as in the Polish case, quantitative equality is reached at the level of higher education, qualitative differentiation becomes increasingly important: "qualitative differentiation enables education systems to reduce inequalities along the quantitative dimension because qualitative differences replace quantitative ones as the basis for educational selection" (Shavit et al. 2007: 44). Qualitative differentiation means different types of institutions and different types of study programmes. As Shavit et al. argue, "expansion can be implemented in different ways. It is reasonable to assume that the effect of the expansion of higher education on inequality in enrolments depends on the characteristics of the new institutions" (ibid.). The new institutions in the Polish case were both new public regional universities, new private institutions as well as metropolitan elite public universities in their fee-based part-time, academically much less demanding, mode of studies. The access of older students to second-tier institutions is considerably higher in the private sector and marginal in the first-tier institutions (GUS 2011: 138-142).

While communist period higher education between 1970 and 1990 in Poland could be described as unified, following Meek, Goedegebuure, Kivinen and Rinne (Meek et al. 1996: 206-236) and Shavit, Arum, and Gamoran (Shavit et al. 2007: 5-6), the last two decades of its expansion reveal a transformation from a unified to a diversified system. Unified systems, as under communism in Poland, "are controlled by professional elites who are not inclined to encourage expansion, either of their own universities or through the formation of new ones" (ibid.: 5). Higher education in Poland was also predominantly "a political force and a political institution. It has been given precise political tasks" (Szczepanski 1974: 7). It was also highly research-focused, in a Humboldtian manner. The number of students in the two decades of 1970–1990 was strictly controlled and, in general, was not increasing (but fluctuating between 300,000 and 470,000), and the strict *numerus clausus* policy was the rule in all Central European countries. While Western European systems were already experiencing massification processes in the 1980s, higher education in Central Europe was as elitist in 1990 as it was in decades past (for Western Europe, see especially Scott 1995 and Palfreyman and Tapper 2009). One of the major reasons of the phenomenal growth of private higher education following the collapse of communism in 1989 in (some) Central European countries, and in Poland in particular, was the heavily restricted access to public higher education under communism combined with newly opened private sector employment. Increasing salaries in the emerging private sector gradually pushed young people into higher education. Consistently with Geiger's findings (1986: 107), the private sector in Poland was forced to operate "around the periphery of the state system of higher education".

System expansion and selectivity in higher education

The newcomers to the education sector after 1989, especially from the lower socio-economic classes, were going *en masse* to new regional public universities and to fee-based tracks in elite metropolitan public universities, as well as to the emergent fee-based private sector. The expansion of the system between 1990 and 2005 increased the number of students from about 0.4 million to almost 2 million. In the first decade of expansion, the difference between graduating from various types of institutions seemed largely irrelevant, especially to first-generation students and their families. After 1989, "the 'entrepreneurial spirit' and 'possessive individualism' – which had been blocked under communism by administrative obstacles – found an outlet" (Domanski 2000: 29). Higher education credentials from any academic field, any institutional type and any mode of studies were viewed by the newcomers as a ticket to a good life and rewarding jobs.

The most valuable vacancies – those in elite metropolitan public universities in full-time mode of studies – were scarce and competitive. They were socially valuable not only because they were tuition-free but because they were academically demanding. All other vacancies, much less socially valuable from a larger perspective, and conceived as much less socially valuable by the intelligentsia-turned-middle classes – were offered to all, in fee-based modes, over the two decades. During the expansion period, higher education was both accessible and affordable (Duczmal and Jongbloed 2007, see the definitions in Knight 2009) and the recognition of its differentiation by type of institution and by mode of studies was low. The undifferentiation of the educational arena, paradoxically, seemed useful to all stakeholders: students and their parents, public and private institutions, and the state. The state was boasting ever rising enrolment rates and increasing education of the workforce; public institutions were offering part-time studies for fees and this non-core non-state income played a powerful role in maintaining the morale of academics by increasing their university incomes; and private institutions were showing all elements of a traditional institutional drift – they were emulating the public institutions. The gradual stratification of the system increasingly became common knowledge and governed most student choices only in the second decade of the expansion when the labour market was saturated with new graduates (totalling about 2 million in 1990–2003).

During the times of expansion, questions about equitable access (Knight 2009) and fair selection criteria were not asked and issues of social justice (Furlong and Cartmel 2009) were not publicly raised, either in official policy documents (including several national strategies for higher education and official rationales for new draft laws on higher education, see Ernst and Young 2010), or in the scholarly discourse. Expansion was viewed as a public good in itself, and its details related to fairness and inclusion were generally both under-researched in academia and under-debated in the public domain. Official higher education statistics and labour force statistics were showing a highly positive picture of the emerging well-educated society with an increasing share of the workforce with higher education credentials. The national and regional statistics did not differentiate between the types of institutions attended and modes of studies. But the system's expansion stopped in about 2005 and enrolments contracted from about 2 million to about 1.8 million in 2010. This contraction continues today and is expected to go on at least until 2025.

    The expansion in Poland in both public and private sectors was demand-driven: students and their families demanded more access to higher education following the collapse of communism, and their demand was being increasingly met (Bialecki and Dabrowa-Szefler 2009, Duczmal and Jongbloed 2007, Kwiek 2008). Higher education was no longer strictly rationed by the state, and the processes of massification were fuelled by both sectors and both modes of studies. External shocks related to the "post-communist transition" in the economy and the financial austerity prevalent throughout the 1990s were driving the dynamics of institutional change. Universities were driven by expansion-related phenomena and academic institutions (and academics themselves) were responding in the way the resource dependence perspective used in organisational studies would expect them to: seeking how to manage to survive, in the mutual processes of interaction between organisations and their environments (Pfeffer and Salancik 2003: 258-262, also see van Vught 2009), at both the micro-level of individuals and meso-level of institutions. Specifically, "the key to organisational survival is the ability to acquire and maintain resources" (Pfeffer and Salancik 2003: 2): In the Polish context of the 1990s, maintaining resources meant additional private expenditures borne by students (in both public and private sectors) and additional per-student public funding from the state (public sector only; on the consequences for the university research mission, see Kwiek 2012a and Kwiek and Maassen 2012).

    Following Arum et al. (2007: 8ff), we can use the distinction between "client-seeker" (with low admissions criteria) and "status-seeker" (with "fewer clients than could otherwise be admitted") institutions. Both public and private sectors were strongly "client-seeking" in the times of the expansion; the question is to what extent "client-seeking" behaviors may be even more pronounced in these times of contraction, with far-reaching consequences for admissions criteria and selectivity throughout the system. "We expect to find greater enrolment rates and more institutional differentiation in market systems than in state-funded systems" (Arum et al. 2007: 8).

    The Polish system is more market-like than most state-funded European systems but also much more state-funded than most global market-funded systems, as in the United States, Korea or Japan. The increasing stratification of higher education institutions along the client-seeking and prestige-seeking lines was a discernible process in the times of system expansion. What will happen to the process in the times of the system's contraction? All institutions, public (elite and regional) and private (both semi-elite and demand-absorbing, see Levy 2011: 388-389) might be forced to become increasingly client-seeking (with perhaps no significant difference as to whether the clients will be tuition-free students funded by the state or self-funded fee-based students, and no matter whether universal fees in the public sector are finally introduced in the coming decade or not). The public sector may find it necessary to become aggressively client-seeking, as the private sector was throughout the last two decades.

It can be assumed that in contracting systems the selectivity of all institutions, both elite and regional, semi-elite and demand-absorbing, in both public and private sectors can be expected to decrease over time. Admissions criteria can be expected to be less stringent, and access for candidates from lower socio-economic classes may be increasingly less based on meritocratic criteria in institutions which are highly selective today. The metropolitan elite public universities may be expected to become more accessible to all social strata if their current capacities (human resources and infrastructure) are to be maintained. To continue their current levels of selectivity, they would have to decrease their capacities as the contraction processes impact in the next 15 years.

Consistently with findings in global private higher education literature, in Polish private higher education the largest growth occurred through the non-elite, mostly demand-absorbing, types of institutions (Levy 2009, Levy 2011, Geiger 1986). As elsewhere in rapidly expanding systems, most students were "not choosing their institutions over other institutions as much as choosing them over nothing" (Levy 2009: 18). Like in other countries, a demand-absorbing private subsector tended to be both the largest private subsector and the fastest growing one. Now this is the most vulnerable subsector in the setting of declining demographics. The growth of private higher education did not necessarily mean 'better' services, or 'different' services: it meant most of all 'more' higher education (Geiger 1986: 10, Enders and Jongbloed 2007: 20). Consistently with Geiger's findings about "peripheral private sectors" in higher education (as opposed to "parallel public and private sectors", 1986: 107ff), the university component of higher education was monopolised by a public institution and non-university, postsecondary component by private institutions. "Market segmentation" rather than open competition with the dominant public sector, operating in "special niches" (Geiger 1986: 158), was the general characteristic throughout the last two decades.

Recent policy proposals about the public subsidising of the private sector and the introduction of universal fees in the public sector (2011) seem to indicate a possible change in policy patterns in financing higher education. Following Levy's typology of public/private mixes in higher education systems (Levy 1986), recent changes might indicate a policy move towards the homogenisation of the two sectors. Private-public blends involve a number of important questions: a single sector or a dual one, if a single sector – statist or public-autonomous, if dual sectors, homogenised or distinctive, if distinctive, minority private or majority private (ibid., 198)? The move, in this typology, would be from the fourth pattern (dual, distinctive higher education sectors: smaller private sector funded privately, larger public sector funded publicly) to the third pattern (dual, homogenised higher education sectors: minority private sector, similar funding for each sector; Levy's first and second patterns refer to single systems, with no private sectors). The policy debates about private-public financing emergent in Poland today are not historically or geographically unique. Levy identified three major policy debates in his fourth pattern of financing: the first concerns the very growth of private institutions; the second concerns whether new private sectors should receive public funds; and the third policy debate concerns tuition in the public sector. While in the expansion period of the 1990s the debate about growth dominated in Poland, the contraction period of the 2010s can be expected to be dominated by fees and public subsidy debates.

The question of inequality in access to higher education, usually asked in the context of educational expansion, could also be asked in the context of educational contraction: "the key question about educational expansion is whether it reduces inequality by providing more opportunities for persons from disadvantaged strata, or magnifies inequality, by expanding opportunities disproportionately for those who are already privileged" (Arum et al. 2007, 1). In the Polish case, the question can refer to the (past) expansion and the (expected) contraction of the system. Contraction seems unexpected in the context of the knowledge-economy policy discourse which refers to the ever increasing need for a better educated workforce (see e.g. Santiago et al. 2008, EC 2011 and education attainment benchmarks in the EU *Europe 2020* strategy for growth and jobs). This policy discourse in Europe largely ignores the sharply falling demographics in major post-communist European countries, with Poland in the forefront.

Inequality in access to higher education: Poland in a European comparative perspective

The decade and a half of continuous educational expansion in Poland is expected to reduce social inequality and enable faster upward social mobility. Traditionally, higher education is the main channel of upward social intergenerational mobility (that is, it enables individuals to cross class boundaries between generations, see DeShano da Silva et al. 2007, Holsinger and Jacob 2008). Intergenerational social mobility reflects equality of opportunities. Class origins in more mobile societies determine labour market trajectories to a higher degree than in less mobile societies (Archer et al. 2003, Bowles et al. 2005, Furlong and Cartmel 2009). Younger generations 'inherit' education and 'inherit' occupations from their parents to a greater extent in less mobile societies. Young European's educational futures and occupational futures look different in more and in less mobile European societies.

Our brief comparative analysis of social mobility is based on microdata from the European Union Survey on Income and Living Conditions (EU-SILC).[2] For research on intergenerational educational and occupational mobility in Poland, the most useful is the EU-SILC 2005 module on "The intergenerational transmission of poverty". The module provides data on the attributes of respondents' parents during their childhood (age 14–16) and reports the educational attainment level and the occupational status of each respondent's father and mother. In almost all European OECD countries there is "a statistically significant probability premium of achieving tertiary education associated with coming from a higher-educated family, while there is a probability penalty associated with growing up in a lower-educated family" (Causa and Johansson 2009b: 18). Fairness in access to higher education in Poland is linked here to the issue of the intergenerational transmission of educational attainment levels and occupational statuses of parents from a European comparative perspective. If Polish society is less mobile than other European countries, then the need for more equitable access is greater. While

---

2   The survey collects microdata on income, poverty and social exclusion at the level of households and collects information about individuals' labour market statuses and health. The database includes both cross-sectional data (in a given period of time) and longitudinal data (which can be followed periodically). For most countries in the pool of 26, the most recent data available come from 2007 and 2008.

absolute numbers can speak for themselves, we are assuming here that the numbers will tell us more in the comparative context set out below.

What we present here is a brief assessment of the relative 'risk ratio' (which shows how a given attribute of one's parents makes it more likely that the offspring will show the same attribute, see Causa and Johansson 2009b: 51 and 2009a) of 'inheriting' levels of educational attainment and 'inheriting' occupations in transitions from one generation to another generation in Poland from a cross-national perspective.

Poland is a European country with one of the highest relative risk ratios (over 10) for persons with a tertiary education having their father with a tertiary education. There are only four European systems (Poland, Portugal, Italy and Ireland; plus the two tiny systems of Luxemburg and Cyprus) which markedly stand out in variations across countries: in all of them, the probability of a person whose father's education is 'tertiary' having a tertiary education is about ten times higher than someone whose father's education is lower than tertiary. The probability of 'inheriting' tertiary education in Poland is on average almost two times higher than in other European countries (the average for 26 countries being 6.06, and the average for eight post-communist countries being 5.97). The details are given below in Figure 1.

Figure 1.   Relative risk ratio for a person with a tertiary education relative to their father's tertiary education

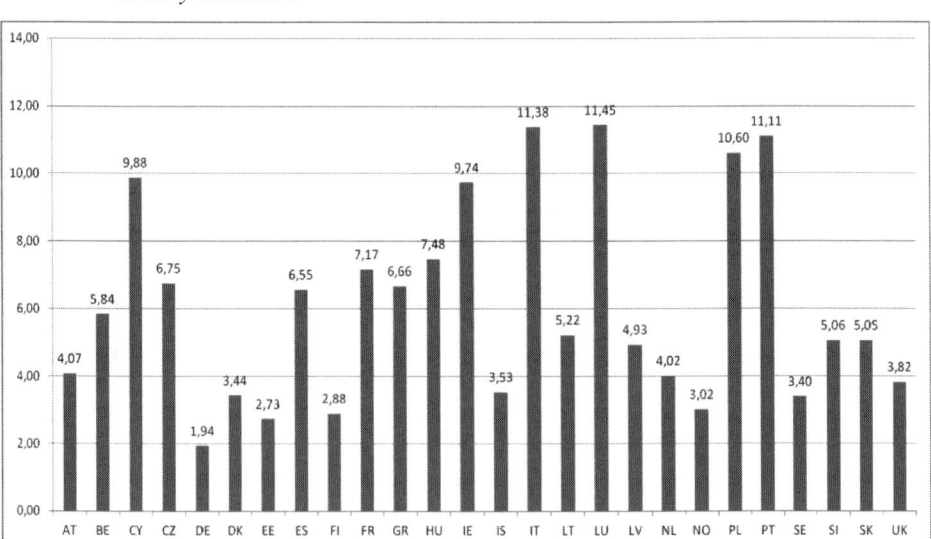

Source: own study based on the EU-SILC 2005 module on "The intergenerational transmission of poverty"

On the basis of the EU-SILC data, we can follow the transmission of education and the transmission of occupations across generations: how parental educational and occupational backgrounds are reflected in children's educational and occupational backgrounds. Educational status and occupational status are strong attributes carried across generations (Archer et al. 2003, Breen 2004: 1-17, Goldthorpe 1987: 121-146, Kogan et al. 2011: 337-345).

Figure 2 below shows the probability of a respondent achieving a tertiary education given that his/her parental level of education is only primary. In more mobile societies, the probability will be higher; in societies in which intergenerational mobility is lower, the probability will be lower. There is a major divide between a cluster of countries which include Poland (and several other former communist countries, as well as Italy) in which the upward mobility is low, and the probability is in the range of 4–6%, and Nordic countries, Belgium Germany, Estonia, Spain and the UK in which the mobility is 3–4 times higher, and the probability of a 'generational leap' between generations is 3–4 times higher, in the range of 17–23%). Other countries are in the middle. The probability of upward intergenerational mobility through higher education is, from a comparative perspective, clearly very low in Poland.

Figure 2. Transition from parents' primary education to respondents' tertiary education

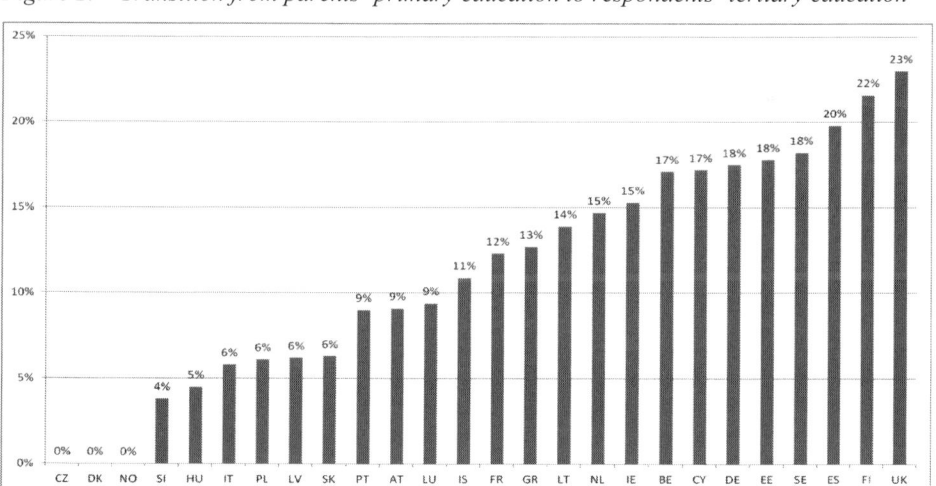

Source: own study based on the EU-SILC 2005 module on "The intergenerational transmission of poverty" (0% for CZ, DK, and NO results from a too low number of respondents in these countries).

248   Marek Kwiek

Figure 3 below explores social mobility in Poland from a different perspective: the rigidity of educational backgrounds across generations, or the inheritance of tertiary education across generations. Overall, in all 26 European countries studied (except for Slovenia), the chance of a respondent whose parents have a tertiary education attainment level having a tertiary education attainment level is more than 50%. The lowest range (50–60%) dominates in several post-communist countries, as well as in Denmark, Austria, Norway, Germany and Sweden). The highest range (70–79%) is shown only for Spain, Ireland and Belgium, as well as the two small systems of Luxembourg and Cyprus. Poland (67%) lies in the upper-middle range of 65–70%, and eighth from the top.

Figure 3.   Transition from parents' tertiary education to respondents' tertiary education

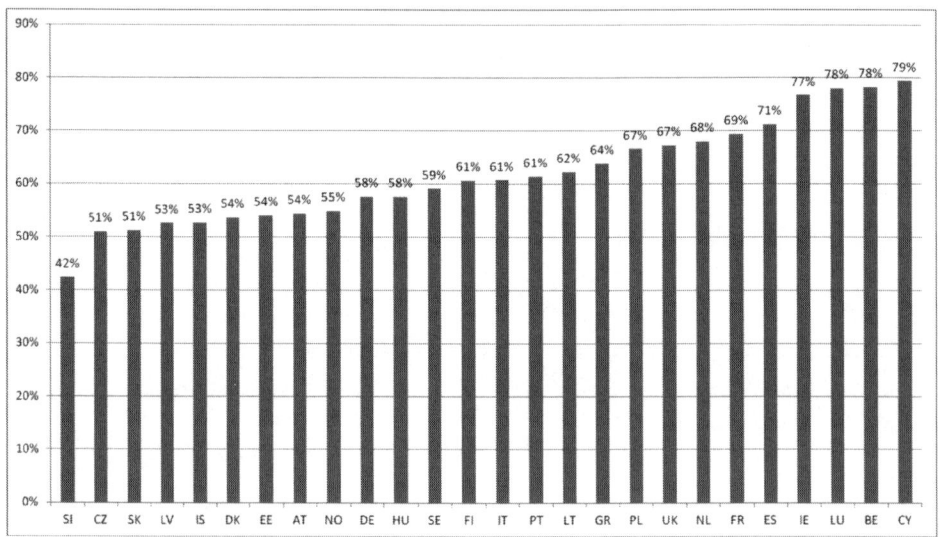

Source: own study based on the EU-SILC 2005 module on "The intergenerational transmission of poverty"

Analyses performed with reference to ISCO-88 (International Standard Classification of Occupations) Group 1 occupations (translated into "highly skilled white collar") in relation to parents' occupation show that while, overall in Europe, the 'inheritance' of highly skilled white-collar occupations is high, and is generally in the 50–70% range, in Poland it is very high and reaches 67% (fifth from the top).

Thus, to sum up the above comparative section: upward educational social mobility in Poland (despite the 1990–2005 expansion period) is still limited, and the level of inheritance of both educational status and occupational status across generations is quite high, compared with other European countries. The changes in mobility between social strata are long-term, and the recent expansion period in higher education is still short enough to change the basic social structure in Poland. Both the highest educational attainment levels and the most socially rewarded occupations ("highly-skilled white-collar") are inherited in Poland to a stronger degree than in most European countries, except for most post-communist countries. Poland seems to differ more from more mobile Western European systems and less from most immobile post-communist systems in its educational social mobility than traditionally assumed in the research literature (e.g. Domanski 2000). Polish society in general is less mobile compared with most Western European systems because the links between parents' and children's social status as adults (in both educational and occupational terms) are closer. "In a relatively immobile society an individual's wage, education or occupation tends to be strongly related to those of his/her parents" (OECD 2010: 184; see Kwiek 2013). While the expansion period substantially increased equitable access to higher education in Poland, upward social mobility viewed from a long-term perspective of changes between generations is still limited. Consequently, from a European comparative perspective there is a much greater need for fair access to higher education than commonly assumed in educational research.

The demographic decline and the universal fees option

The continuance or reversal of the trend of reducing inequality in access to higher education in Poland depends on a number of factors: gross enrolment rate; wage premium for higher education; the number of tuition-free vacancies and fee-based vacancies available in the public sector; national higher education funding policies (including cost-sharing mechanisms in the public sector, state subsidising of the private sector, public investments in education and research infrastructure); the internationalisation of studies; and enrolments of students in non-traditional ages.

Some factors may redefine public-private dynamics in the system without actually changing the trend of inequality reduction (the system may move gradually from a "dual and distinctive" ideal typical model to a "dual and homogenised" ideal typical model according to Levy's typology of public/private mixes in funding regimes: both sectors may be funded in the next decade through fees and direct public subsidies, see Levy 1986). Further inequality reduction from this perspective may thus be sector-blind. (In the present chapter, we are focusing more on the intersectoral public/private differentiation rather than on intrasectoral differentiation in any of the two sectors; on various notions of differentiation in higher education, see Rhoades 1990: 191, Geiger 1986: 75-106, van Vught 2009: 7-11, Goedegebuure et al. 2007: 11-13, and on explorations of how social change in general can be seen as a process of differentiation, see Alexander 1990: 1-15).

Demographic shifts are expected to powerfully affect new admission patterns in both sectors and may increase the access of lower socio-economic classes to higher education throughout the system. The number of 19-year-olds was increasing throughout the 1990s and until 2002. Since then, already for a decade, the number has been decreasing and, according to national demographic projections, it will be dropping for more than a decade. In 2020, there will be about 360,000 19-year-olds compared with about 612,000 in 2005 and 534,000 in 2010 (GUS 2009: 171). Moreover, the pool of potential students (traditionally in the 19–24 age bracket in Poland) will be steadily decreasing every year until 2020, from about 3.4 million in 2010 to about 2.3 million in 2020, in both urban and rural areas (a decrease of 31% within a decade). The fall in the size of the population in the 19–24 age bracket will continue until 2025 and in 2035 the population will be only 64.15% of the 2007 population (ibid.: 170).

The future of equitable access to higher education, inequality reduction and changing admission patterns are linked to demography much more strongly in post-communist European countries (Poland in particular) than in Western European countries (although, as reminded by Preston, Heuveline, and Guillot (2001: 135), "the accuracy of population forecasts can only be assessed after the fact"; in this particular case, population forecasts are more accurate because, for the period up to 2025 studied here, "after all, the people have already been born and almost all of them will survive" (Frances 1989: 143). Just as there were several parallel routes via which the educational expansion occurred in Poland (as shown in section 2 above), there are possible several parallel routes leading to the educational contraction.

Overall, an increase in rates of access or a change in the length of studies may offset decreases in the cohort size. Studies may last longer and access rates depend on the eligibility rate and the proportion of those eligible who indeed enrol (different aspirations, incentives, but also different numbers of vacancies): "the actual proportion of entrants also depends, among other things, on the cost of higher education, the financial pressures confronting those otherwise eligible, pecuniary (and non-pecuniary) advantages that they hope to gain from higher education and the length of their studies from an opportunity cost perspective". Student enrolment levels lag behind changes in the size of younger age cohorts, and the demographic shift takes several years to become noticeable (Vincent-Lancrin 2008: 44).

The fall in enrolment levels in Poland is projected to be one of the highest in Europe, and comparable only with other post-communist countries: Bulgaria, Romania, Slovakia, Estonia, Lithuania and Latvia. According to several consistent enrolment scenarios based on national statistical data (such as e.g. Vincent-Lancrin 2008: 45, Instytut Sokratesa 2011: 10-14, IBE 2011: 110-11, Ernst and Young 2010: 20) enrolments in Poland in 2025 are expected to drop to 55–65% % of the 2005 levels. In Western Europe, only Spain and Germany can expect numerical decreases of more than 200,000 students by 2025 (Vincent-Lancrin 2008: 49-51). Certainly, as Easterlin (1989: 138) confirmed in the US context, there is an "inverse association between college enrolment rates and the size of the college-age population" (and what Frances terms "the cohort effect", Frances 1989: 143): "enrollment rates, in fact, partly depend on the size of the college-age population – other things remaining constant, at the aggregate level a larger college-age population makes for lower enrollment rates, while a smaller college-age population makes for higher rates" (Easterlin 1989: 137). Demographic factors need to be combined with social, economic and public-policy related factors in any meaningful projections for the future.

Higher education systems in the OECD area in general are expected to continue to expand (Altbach et al. 2010); as Attewell in his global study of educational inequality around the world put it, "so far, the growth in demand for more years of education seems to have no limit. ... Each new generation exceeds its parents in terms of average years of schooling completed" (Attewell 2010: 1). Therefore, the implications of an educational contraction for equitable access, institutional selectivity and admissions criteria in Polish higher education (as well as higher education in such post-communist

European countries as Bulgaria, Romania, Estonia, Lithuania, Latvia and Slovakia) are important research areas. The institutional will to survive the demographic decline is overwhelming, but the logics governing access to publicly-funded vacancies in the past expansion era may differ from the logics governing them in the expected contraction era.

Access to higher education in Poland has been powerfully related to the public-private dynamics in higher education (Duczmal and Jongbled 2007, Kwiek 2008, 2011a and 2012b). The biggest private higher education system in Europe ("independent private" in OECD terms, fee-based in practical terms) may be heavily dependent in its future survival on a change in higher education financing – namely, the introduction of universal fees (that is, for both full-time and part-time students) in its competing public sector. Within the current funding architecture (with no fees in the growing full-time segment in the public sector), namely, if universal fees are not introduced, the private sector may be heavily reduced in size until 2025. Maintaining the tax-based public sector amid declining demographics might threaten the very existence of the private sector as there have been divergent trends of decreasing numbers of students and increasing numbers of tuition-free vacancies in the public sector, combined with substantial public investments in public university infrastructure in the last five years. Mergers between public and private institutions, envisaged in the new law of March 2011, might be a possible survival strategy for the sector.

The decline of private higher education is a rare theme in scholarly literature, as it is a rare phenomenon from a global perspective. As Levy stresses, "the most vulnerable private higher education is the demand-absorbing type, which underscores that all parts of the sector do not face constant vulnerability" (Levy 2010: 11-12). Poland (together with several other post-communist European countries) is exceptional from a global perspective: both private shares in enrolments and also absolute enrolments in the private sector were decreasing in the 2007–2010 period. The private higher education sector may expect to have fewer students every year and, for a system in which there are 325 private institutions, this poses an enormous challenge. In post-communist Europe short-term declines have already occurred (Slantcheva-Durst 2010: 13). The expected demographic shift creates a major institutional challenge to all public institutions; but for private institutions it may be a life or death challenge, as lamented by the Polish conferences of private sector rectors (KRUN, and since 2005, KRZaSP). As a recent study by the national Institute for Educational

Research (IBE 2011: 110) points out, "it has to be assumed that a part of newly created private institutions, of relatively poor educational offer, opened to meet the demand from the generation from the 1980s … will not be able to survive" (ibid.). The single survival strategy suggested by the Institute is to change the offer from higher education to adult education. These findings are consistent with Levy's global conclusions about private higher education (ibid.: 5): "Much PHE [private higher education] has not had to offer very much, other than access and the prospect or hope of a degree. Logically, then, it is the demand-absorbing subsector of PHE that is most vulnerable when demands slows". But the trend will affect each institution separately, and it is important to recognise that each university can determine its own future.

But, finally, 'fair' access to higher education and reducing social inequality in access to higher education is actually sector-blind. From the perspective of equitable access to higher education, the intersectoral differences (that is, future sector-related differentiation or de-differentiation (de-differentiation being the 'natural' trend in higher education, Rhoades 1990: 191) seem largely irrelevant. The expansion of the tuition-free public sector (from 0.85 million in 2010 to, say, 1 million students in 2020) amid declining demographics, accompanied by the contraction of the fee-based private sector and the contraction of the whole system, may contribute significantly to widening access to higher education. From a sector-blind perspective, regardless of the future of the private sector institutions, the expansion of tuition-free vacancies in the public sector in tough financial times may contribute more to social justice (see Furlong and Cartmel 2009) than the emergence of fee-based vacancies in both sectors with mechanisms of cost-sharing introduced universally across the two sectors.

Conclusions

The dramatically changing demographics in Poland are creating new dilemmas related to public funding and admissions criteria in both public and private sectors. Public policy for higher education in times of expansion can be expected to be fundamentally different from public policy in times of contraction. The chapter explored the question of inequality in access to higher education with reference to the past two decades of expansion and to the expected upcoming two decades of contraction of the system. The era of contraction seems unexpected in the knowledge-economy policy discourse which generally ignores the possibility of sharply falling demographics that is relevant to higher education systems in only several European countries and only a few OECD economies, Poland included. Educational contraction in Poland's highly diversified and strongly market-oriented system may continue the inequality reduction trend if national policies adequately respond to the changing demographics combined with new social and economic determinants. There are several countries in the European Union – all post-communist new member states – in which similar demographic shifts are leading to shrinking student populations to a comparable degree. Poland has the biggest higher education system and provides an inspiring case study, relevant to those countries in which the changing public/private dynamics are combined with falling demographics. Powerful demographic shifts may change the structure of the system, and the options of the remonopolisation of the system by the public sector and the gradual (spread over the next decade) decline of the private sector cannot be excluded (but the market-driven private sector has also been highly resilient and easily adaptable to changing environments in its history). The processes of the inter-sectoral differentiation of the expansion era may be replaced with the processes of the inter-sectoral de-differentiation (or homogenisation) of the contraction era.[3]

Acknowledgments

The author gratefully acknowledges the support of the National Research Council (NCN) through its grant DEC-2011/02/A/HS6/00183.

References:
Alexander J. C., P. Colomy, eds. (1990). *Differentiation Theory and Social Change. Comparative and Historical Perspectives.* New York: Columbia University Press.
Altbach, P. G., L. Reisberg, L. E. Rumbley (2010). *Trends in Global Higher Education. Tracking an Academic Revolution.* Rotterdam/Boston/Taipei: Sense.
Archer, L., M. Hutchings, A. Ross (2003). *Higher Education and Social Class. Issues of Exclusion and Inclusion.* London: RoutledgeFalmer.

---

3   An expanded version of this chapter is forthcoming in *Comparative Education Review* (2013). Vol. 57. No. 1.

Arum, R., A. Gamoran, Y. Shavit (2007). "More Inclusion than Diversion, and Market Structure in Higher Education". In: Y. Shavit, R. Arum, A. Gamoran (eds.), *Stratification in Higher Education: A Comparative Study*. Stanford: Stanford University Press. 1-35.

Attewell, P., K. S. Newman, eds. (2010). *Growing Gaps. Educational Inequality Around the World*. Oxford: Oxford University Press.

Bialecki, I., M. Dabrawa-Szefler (2009). "Polish Higher Education in Transition. Between Policy Making and Autonomy". In: D. Palfreyman, D. T. Tapper (eds.), *Structuring Mass Higher Education. The Role of Elite Institutions*. London: Routledge. 183-199.

Bowles, S., H. Gintis, M.O. Groves, eds. (2005). *Unequal Chances. Family Background and Economic Success*. Princeton: Princeton University Press.

Breen, R. (2004). "The Comparative Study of Social Mobility". In: R. Breen (ed.), *Social Mobility in Europe*. New York: Oxford University Press. 1-16.

Breen, R., ed. (2004). *Social Mobility in Europe*. New York: Oxford University Press.

Brown, P., H. Lauder, D. Ashton (2011). *The Global Auction. The Broken Promises of Education, Jobs, and Incomes*. Oxford: Oxford UP.

Causa, O., A. Johansson (2009a). "Intergenerational Social Mobility". In: *Economics Department Working Papers No. 707*. Paris: OECD.

Causa, O., A. Johansson (2009b). "Intergenerational Social Mobility in European OECD countries". In: *Economics Department Working Papers No. 709*. Paris: OECD.

DeShano da Silva, C., J.P. Huguley, Z. Kakli, R. Rao, eds. (2007). *The Opportunity Gap. Achievement and Inequality in Education*. Cambridge: Harvard Education Review.

Dobbins, M. (2011). *Higher Education Policies in Central and Eastern Europe: Convergence towards a Common Model?* London: Palgrave Macmillan.

Domanski, H. (2000). *On the Verge of Convergence. Social Stratification in Eastern Europe*. Budapest: CEU Press.

Duczmal, W., B. Jongbloed (2007). "Private Higher Education in Poland: A Case of Public-Private Dynamics". In: J. Enders, B. Jongbloed (eds.), *Public-Private Dynamics in Higher Education. Expectations, Developments and Outcomes*. Bielefeld: transcript Verlag. 415-442.

Easterlin, R. A. (1989). "Demography Is Not Destiny in Higher Education". In: Levine, A., Associates (eds.), *Shaping Higher Education Future: Demographic Realities and Opportunities, 1990-2000*. San Francisco: Jossey-Bass Publishers. 135-141.

EC (2009). *Youth in Europe*. Brussels: the European Commission.

EC (2011). "Supporting Growth and Jobs – an Agenda for the Modernisation of Europe's Higher Education Systems". Communication form the European Commission. Brussels. COM(2011) 567/2.

Enders, J., B. Jongbloed, eds. (2007). *Public-Private Dynamics in Higher Education. Expectations, Developments and Outcomes*. Bielefeld: transcript Verlag.

Ernst and Young (2010). *Strategia rozwoju szkolnictwa wyzszego w Polsce do 2020 roku*. Warsaw: Ernst and Young.

Frances, C. (1989). "Uses and Misuses of Demographic Projections: Lessons for the 1990s". In: A. Levine et al. (eds.), *Shaping Higher Education Future: Demographic Realities and Opportunities, 1990-2000*. San Francisco: Jossey-Bass Publishers. 142-160.

Furlong, A., F. Cartmel (2009). *Higher Education and Social Justice*. Maidenhead: Open University Press.

Geiger, R. L. (1986). *Private Sectors in Higher Education. Structure, Function, and Change in Eight Countries*. Ann Arbor: The University of Michigan Press.

Goldhorpe, J. H. (1980). *Social Mobility and Class Structure in Modern Britain. Second Edition.* Oxford: Clarendon Press.

GUS (1996). *Higher Education Institutions and Their Finances in 1995*. Warsaw: GUS (Central Statistical Office).

GUS (2009). *Population Projection for Poland 2008-2035*. Warsaw: GUS (Central Statistical Office).

GUS (2011). *Higher Education Institutions and Their Finances in 2010*. Warsaw: GUS (Central Statistical Office).

Holsinger, D. B., J. Jacob, eds. (2008). *Inequality in Education. Comparative and International Perspectives.* Hong King: CERC.

IBE (2011). *Spoleczenstwo w drodze do wiedzy. Raport o stanie edukacji 2010*. Warsaw: Instytut Badan Edukacyjnych.

Instytut Sokratesa (2011). *Demokratyczne tsunami. Raport Instytutu Sokratesa na temat wpływu zmian demograficznych na szkolnictwo wyższe do 2020 roku*. Warsaw: Instytut Sokratesa.

Jablecka, J., B. Lepori (2009). "Between historical heritage and policy learning: the reform of public research funding systems in Poland, 1989-2007". *Science and Public Policy*. Vol. 36. No. 9. 697-708.

King, R. (2004). *The University in the Global Age*. New York: Palgrave.

Knight, J., ed. (2009). *Financing Access and Equity in Higher Education*. Rotterdam: Sense.

Kogan, I., C. Noelke, M. Gebel, eds. (2011b). *Making the Transition: Education and Labor Market Entry in Central and Eastern Europe*. Stanford: Stanford University Press.

Kwiek, M.(2006). *The University and the State. A Study into Global Transformations*. Frankfurt and New York: Peter Lang.

Kwiek, M. (2008). "Accessibility and Equity, Market Forces and Entrepreneurship: Developments in Higher Education in Central and Eastern Europe". *Higher Education Management and Policy*. Vol. 20, No. 1.

Kwiek, M. (2009). "The Two Decades of Privatization in Polish Higher Education. Cost-Sharing, Equity and Access". In: J. Knight (ed.), *Financing Access and Equity in Higher Education*. Rotterdam/Boston/Taipei: Sense. 149-168.

Kwiek, M. (2010). "Creeping Marketization: Where Polish Private and Public Higher Education Sectors Meet". In: R. Brown (ed.), *Higher Education and the Market*. New York: Routledge. 135-146.

Kwiek, M. (2011a). "The Public/Private Dynamics in Polish Higher Education: Demand-absorbing Private Growth and its Implications". *Higher Education Forum*. Vol. 8. March.

Kwiek, M. (2011b). "Universities and Knowledge Production in Central Europe". In: P. Temple (ed.), *Universities in the Knowledge Economy. Higher Education Organisation and Global Change*. New York: Routledge.

Kwiek, M. (2012a). "Changing Higher Education Policies: From the Deinstitutionalization to the Reinstitutionalization of the Research Mission in Polish Universities". *Science and Public Policy*. Vol. 39. No. 5. 641-654.

Kwiek, M. (2012b). "Public-Private Intersectoral Competition: Fees and Declining Demographics". *Compare: A Journal of Comparative and International Education*. Vol. 42. No. 1. 153-157.

Kwiek, M. (2012c). "Universities, Regional Development and Economic Competitiveness: the Polish Case". In: R. Pinheiro, P. Benneworth, G. A. Jones (eds.), *Universities and Regional Development. A Critical Assessment of Tensions and Contradictions*. New York: Routledge. 69-85.

Kwiek, M. (2013). *Knowledge Production in European Universities. States, Markets, and Academic Entrepreneurialism*. Frankfurt and New York: Peter Lang.

Kwiek, M., A. Kurkiewicz, eds. (2012). *The Modernisation of European Universities. Cross-National Academic Perspectives*. Frankfurt and New York: Peter Lang.

Kwiek, M., P. Maassen, eds. (2012). *National Higher Education Reforms in a European Context: Comparative Reflections on Poland and Norway*. Frankfurt and New York: Peter Lang.

Le Grand, J., W. Bartlett, eds. (1993). *Quasi-Markets and Social Policy*. Basingstoke: The Macmillan Press.

Levy, D. C. (1986). "'Private' and 'Public': Analysis Amid Ambiguity in Higher Education". In: D. C. Levy (ed.), *Private Education. Studies in Choice and Public Policy*. Oxford: Oxford University Press.

Levy, D. C. (2009). "Growth and Typology". In: S. Bjarnason et al., *A New Dynamic: Private Higher Education*. Paris: UNESCO.

Levy, D. C. (2010). "An International Exploration of Decline in Private Higher Education". *International Higher Education*. No. 61. Fall.

Levy, D. C (2011). "Public Policy for Private Higher Education: A Global Analysis". *Journal of Comparative Policy Analysis*. Vol. 13. No. 4. 383-396.

Meek, V. L., L. Goedegebuure, O. Kivinen, R. Rinne, eds. (1996). *The Mockers and Mocked: Comparative Perspectives on Differentiation, Convergence and Diversity in Higher Education*. Oxford: Pergamon/IAU Press.

OECD (2008). *Higher Education to 2030. Volume 1. Demography*. Paris: OECD.

OECD (2010). *Going for Growth. Economic Policy Reforms*. Paris: OECD.

OECD (2011). *Education at a Glance 2011. OECD Indicators*. Paris: OECD.

Palfreyman, D., Tapper, T., eds. (2009). *Structuring Mass Higher Education. The Role of Elite Institutions*. London: Routledge.

Pfeffer, J., G. R. Salancik (1978). *The External Control of Organizations. A Resource Dependence Perspective*. Stanford: Stanford University Press.

Preston, S. H., P. Heuveline, M. Guillot (2001). *Demography: Measuring and Modeling Population Processes*. Oxford: Blackwell Publishers.

Rhodes, G. (1990). "Political Competition and Differentiation in Higher Education". In: J. C. Alexander, P. Colomy (eds.), *Differentiation Theory and Social Change. Comparative and Historical Perspectives*. New York: Columbia University Press. 187-221.

Santiago, P., K. Tremblay, E. Basri, E. Arnal (2008). *Tertiary Education for the Knowledge Society. Volume 1. Special Features: Governance, Funding, Quality*. Paris: OECD.

Schomburg, H., U. Teichler, eds. (2011). *Employability and Mobility of Bachelor Graduates in Europe: Key Results of the Bologna Process*. Rotterdam: Sense Publishers.

Scott, P. (1995). *The Meanings of Mass Higher Education*. Buckingham: Open University Press.

Shavit, Y., R. Arum, A. Gamoran, eds. (2007). *Stratification in Higher Education: A Comparative Study*. Stanford: Stanford University Press.

Slantcheva-Durst, S. (2010). "Ups and Downs in Central and Eastern Europe". *International Higher Education*. No. 61. Fall.

Szczepanski, J. (1974). *Higher Education in Eastern Europe*. New York: International Council for Educational Development.

Vincent-Lancrin, S. (2008). "What is the Impact of Demography on Higher Education Systems? A Forward-looking Approach for OECD Countries". In: *Higher Education to 2030. Volume 1. Demography*. Paris: OECD.

Part 3

**Higher Education
in Eastern and South-east Europe:
New Trends, New Challenges**

Higher Education Policy Dynamics in a Multi-level Governance Context: A Comparative Study of Four Post-communist Countries

Martina Vukasović and Mari Elken

Abstract

The last 10–15 years in European higher education have often been labelled as times of unprecedented change, mostly in relation to the Bologna Process as "possibly the deepest and most far reaching higher education reform process since World War II". Often falling into the trap of concept stretching, a number of studies employ the label 'Europeanisation' to describe these changes and focus on patterns of convergence and divergence, rarely discussing these patterns in relation to the concepts and mechanisms of policy transfer and Europeanisation. This chapter provides: (1) a conceptual clarification of Europeanisation and policy transfer; (2) a systematisation of theorised mechanisms of these processes; and (3) the application of these concepts and mechanisms to the analysis of national policy dynamics in four European countries. Croatia, Estonia, Serbia and Slovenia were chosen due to the unique mix of similarities and differences deemed useful for exploring the differences between policy transfer and Europeanisation. The analysis is based on qualitative analysis of various policy documents, interviews with key actors, and secondary sources.

Key words: policy transfer, policy changes, Europeanisation, policy convergence, Croatia, Estonia, Serbia, Slovenia, post-Communism

Introduction

The last 10–15 years in European higher education have often been labelled as times of unprecedented change, mostly in relation to the Bologna Process as "possibly the deepest and most far reaching higher education reform process since World War II" (Kehm 2010: 530). Coupled with a strengthening of the EU's interest in higher education (Gornitzka 2007), this 'unprecedented change' has been the focus of much scholarly attention.

Often falling into the trap of concept stretching, a number of studies employ the label 'Europeanisation' to describe these changes, without necessarily accounting for the different uses of the term (Olsen 2002) and without reflecting on the understanding of the concept and mechanisms of Europeanisation developed in the more general European studies literature (Börzel 2003, Börzel and Risse 2003, Featherstone and Radaelli 2003, Vink and Graziano 2007). The volume by Amaral et al. (2009) and in particular the chapters by Musselin and Maassen are notable exceptions.

Other studies conclude that both convergence and divergence can be identified (Westerheijden et al. 2010), with the nature of European initiatives and the specificities of domestic policy context accounting for the identified patterns of convergence and divergence (Dobbins and Knill 2009, Heinze and Knill 2008, Voegtle, Knill, and Dobbins 2011, Witte 2008). Although a distinction between horizontal convergence (towards each other) and vertical convergence (towards a particular model) is employed in some of these studies (Heinze and Knill 2008), this distinction is rarely discussed in relation to the concepts and mechanisms of policy transfer and Europeanisation. Therefore, there is a need for a conceptual clarification of Europeanisation and policy transfer and the systematisation of theorised mechanisms of these processes. This will be one of the aims of this chapter.

The other aim of this chapter is to employ the concepts of Europeanisation and policy transfer to four European countries – Croatia, Estonia, Serbia and Slovenia, all often labelled post-communist countries, presumed to exhibit similar characteristics, and so far somewhat neglected by higher education research. The overall political and economic transition of these four countries has been heavily marked by the "return to Europe" idea (Héritier 2005), though the actual dynamic of these processes differs from country to country. Three countries have similar starting positions: Croatia, Serbia and Slovenia were part of the Socialist Federal Republic of Yugoslavia (SFRY), whereas Estonia was part of the Soviet Union. Given the specific combination of similarities and differences, the patterns of policy changes in the four countries will be used to critically assess the robustness of the theorised mechanisms of Europeanisation and policy transfer.

The chapter is guided by the following research questions:

– Which patterns in higher education policy changes can be identified in these four countries in the last 15–20 years?
– How are these policy changes related to the European initiatives in higher education, most notably the Bologna Process?
– What are the areas of higher education policy in which horizontal and vertical convergence can be identified and how can this be accounted for theoretically?

Policy changes are understood here as changes in policy outputs: policy problems, aims, and policy instruments. Thus, this chapter does not focus on the implementation of policies and, accordingly, not on policy outcomes.

The chapter is structured as follows: the second section introduces the four countries, followed by a discussion of the theoretical perspectives on policy transfer, Europeanisation and policy convergence in the third section. The fourth section includes both a within- and cross-case analysis of policy changes and the extent to which they follow European initiatives in higher education. The conclusion reflects back on the research questions, provides an assessment of the usefulness of the conceptualisations and operationalisation of the key concepts, and gives some suggestions for future studies.

Introducing the cases

Croatia, Serbia and Slovenia have many commonalities with respect to higher education. While predecessors of the flagship universities of Slovenia, Croatia and Serbia (Ljubljana, Zagreb and Belgrade) can be traced back at least to the mid-19th century (Belgrade) or even as early as the end of the 16th century (Ljubljana) (Šoljan 1991), other higher education institutions began to emerge only after WWII. The student population has been steadily increasing, in particular during the 1990s and early 2000s. Having been part of the SFRY, these countries have a common communist legacy, though much different than Estonia given the relatively limited influence the Soviet Union had on former Yugoslavia. One of the elements of this legacy was the reform of secondary education introduced in the 1980s, focused on the narrow specialisation of programmes and qualifications which, due to access restrictions, also had a notable impact on higher education. In higher education terms, the SFRY legacy primarily includes: (a) the significant fragmentation of universities with faculties as legal entities divided along traditional disciplinary lines; (b) the separation of teaching and research (though not as strong as in Estonia); and (c) a relatively limited and later developed private sector. While having similar starting points in the early 1990s, the three countries, primarily for general political reasons, differ in terms of the dynamics of their political and economic transitions (with Slovenia arguably having had the most stable transition and Serbia the most turbulent one), which is also reflected in the different dynamics and outcomes (at the moment) of European accession processes.

Table 1.   *Key characteristics of the higher education systems*

	Students (approx.)	GER[**]	HEIs	Public/ Private univ.	Non-univ. HEIs	Type of system[***]	Participation in Bologna	EU status
Croatia	160,000	50%	51	7/0	44	Binary	2001	Member in July 2013
Estonia	67,600	63%	33	6/3	24	Binary, elements of the dual	1999	Member 2004; Euro 2011
Serbia	202,000	49%	89	7/10	72	Stratified	2003	Candidate since early 2012
Slovenia	97,500	67%	36	3/1	32	Towards unified	1999	Member 2004; Euro 2007

Sources: national statistical offices, national ministries responsible for higher education and World Bank database[*]

[*]   All data related to 2011, except for GER which are for 2009
[**]   Gross-enrolment ratio: the ratio between the total number of students regardless of their age and the number of people belonging to the higher education relevant age cohort (usually 18–25 years of age)
[***] According to Kyvik (2004)

In Estonia, the oldest institution is the University of Tartu, established in 1632, for a long time being the only higher education institution in the country. By 1940 there was one large university (Tartu) and a number of other professionally oriented higher education institutions (e.g. Tallinn Technical University). A significant aspect of the Soviet heritage was the clear separation of research and teaching sectors, leading to a large-scale reform initiative in the mid-1980s in the whole of the Soviet Union (Avis 1990). After re-independence in 1991, teaching and research were again brought together. The general political and economic liberalisation was also reflected in higher education, leading to considerable growth in both the number of institutions and number of students, the latter growing most during the 1995–2005 period. Nevertheless, the private sector in Estonia is quite small, covering 1/6 of the student population. The enrolment rates in higher education have shown a slight decrease in recent years, but the change is small and can also be linked to a demographic decline in recent years. In the next ten years the system is likely to face a number of challenges related to this.

On one hand, all the countries have some form of communist legacy. However, three countries (Croatia, Serbia and Slovenia) operated under a federal framework and were not under Soviet influence, while Estonia was part of the USSR. Two countries have been EU members since 2004 and Bologna Process signatories since 1999 (Estonia and Slovenia), while Croatia and Serbia are lagging behind on both accounts. Therefore, the four countries exhibit a unique mix of similarities and differences useful for exploring national policy dynamics and the extent to which changes of higher education policy are driven by domestic or external concerns.

Policy transfer, Europeanisation and policy convergence: Theoretical perspectives

This section provides the analytical framework necessary for an analysis of policy changes in the four countries. It first presents key characteristics of the Bologna Process and the Lisbon Strategy, and the emerging multi-level governance arrangement, followed by a discussion of the concepts of policy transfer, Europeanisation and policy convergence, and a number of propositions.

Multi-level governance of higher education in Europe

The beginnings of the multi-level governance arrangements in higher education in Europe can be traced back to 1999 and the launching of the Bologna Declaration and 2000 and the emergence of the EU's Lisbon Strategy (Heinze and Knill 2008, Witte 2008). These two initiatives are often seen as the two main pillars of European integration in higher education (Maassen and Musselin 2009) which have, for different reasons and not necessarily intentionally, resulted in increasing the importance of the European level for national higher education policy dynamics, i.e. the emergence of an additional governance level.

Though having a long history (Corbett 2005), the EU activities in the area of higher education have intensified since the introduction of the Lisbon Strategy. Historically, this has been a supranational process focused on developing various policy instruments, ranging from legally binding directives in the areas of recognition of qualifications in regulated professions (Beerkens 2008), through recommendations (e.g. in the area of qualification frameworks), to allocating funding to a number of cooperation programmes such as the Lifelong Learning programme. This increase in activities since the Lisbon Strategy has largely been enabled by the use of open method of coordination (OMC) that removes dependence on formal legally binding instruments as a basis for European involvement (Gornitzka 2007). Although EU competencies have been steadily increasing in the area of education (Pollack 2000), the principle of subsidiarity is still formally in force.

The Bologna Process has an intergovernmental character, with almost no administrative capacity and no own funding to facilitate the implementation. Its voluntary nature implied that it was the national ministries responsible for higher education which were steering the process through the Bologna Follow-Up Group (BFUG). The European Commission is the only supranational organisation that is a full member of the BFUG, with all other relevant organisations (EUA, ESU, EURASHE, EI, Business Europe and Council of Europe) having an observer status. This has established a link to the Commission's administrative capacity and financial resources, enabling the Commission to gain an increasingly prominent role (Gornitzka 2007), and arguably leading to the convergence of the policy goals (Beerkens 2008).

From the Commission's point of view, the Bologna Process is not a separate process but has become an important part of its policy objectives. Further, its characterisation as strictly voluntary may be misleading given that many countries found it necessary to commit themselves to the Bologna goals (Ravinet 2008). However, the Bologna Process is to an extent similar to the EU's Lisbon Strategy in terms of its reliance on OMC-like mechanisms, including regular assessment of the progress of Bologna through the Stocktaking reports and similar exercises. The Bologna Process is also marked by significant ambiguity, seen as necessary for any agreement to take place amongst such a diverse group of countries (ibid.). However, such ambiguity can also lead to significant diversity in terms of implementation outcomes (Westerheijden et al. 2010) as well as an opportunity for national policy makers to use the Bologna Process to promote their own policy preferences under the Bologna umbrella (Gornitzka 2006, Musselin 2009). In sum, these two initiatives have institutionalised an additional governance layer which essentially challenges the subsidiarity principle of the EU and the intergovernmental character of the Bologna Process. The common objectives developed in these initiatives through the Open Method of Coordination (OMC) or OMC-like mechanisms may be (and are) seen in the domestic contexts as more binding than they actually are and therefore have a stronger and deeper impact.

The additional governance layer can be seen as a "transnational communication platform" (Voegtle et al. 2011: 83) that is not a source of new policy preferences but only facilitates policy transfer, potentially leading to horizontal policy convergence, i.e. the convergence of higher education policies towards each other. Following this understanding, none of the Bologna action lines or priorities of the Lisbon Strategy are completely original (most of them can be traced to domestic arrangements of particular countries). However, the discourse through which they are promoted (extensive use of "European" in labelling initiatives in quality assurance, mobility, recognition etc.) and their perception as being European in domestic arenas, in particular in post-communist countries, provides a justification to see this additional layer also as an arena that promotes particular European rules, both formal and informal. Therefore, institutionalisation of these rules in the domestic higher education context may lead to vertical policy convergence, i.e. convergence towards a particular (European) model.

Policy transfer vs. Europeanisation: Horizontal vs. vertical policy convergence

There seems to be no strong agreement within the literature on the definitions of and delineations between the concepts of policy transfer, Europeanisation and policy convergence. For example, when it comes to Europeanisation, Olsen (2002) maps five dimensions of Europeanisation, although others would see some of the dimensions as policy transfer or policy borrowing (Stone 2001), with relatively few studies discussing the two concepts one against the other (Bomberg and Peterson 2000). Reacting to such concept stretching, Radaelli (2003) makes a strong argument in favour of disentangling Europeanisation from harmonisation, EU policy formation, political integration and policy convergence. When it comes to the latter, though it is a concept much used in higher education research (Garben 2010, Huisman 2009, Karseth and Solbrekke 2010, Trondal 2002), relatively few contributions have explicitly attempted to disentangle the different types of convergence and explore the underlying mechanisms (one exception being Heinze and Knill 2008). For the purposes of the present analysis, both Europeanisation and policy transfer are seen as processes and not outcomes, while vertical and horizontal policy convergence are seen as possible, but not necessary outcomes.

Within this chapter, policy transfer is understood as "a process whereby knowledge about policies, administrative arrangement, institutions, ideas and so on are used across time and/or space in the development of policies, institutions, and so on elsewhere" (Bomberg and Peterson 2000: 10). Policy transfer does not necessitate a formal structure to facilitate it, since it relies primarily on intentional activities of various policy actors who may or may not be part of domestic governmental structures and who, for different reasons, promote the use of foreign solutions to (perceived) domestic problems. Thus, the term policy transfer will in this chapter be reserved for processes in which 'policies, administrative arrangements, ideas and so on' from another country and not from a higher governance level are used in domestic policy development. Policy transfer can go from: (a) the direct copying of policy instruments, through (b) emulation in terms of accepting particular solutions as the best practice but formulating in own words, (c) synthesis and hybridisation which involves combining solutions from several different countries to develop a solution deemed to be best suited for domestic needs, to (d) using policy developments in other countries as a source of inspiration for domestic developments (Dolowitz and Marsh 1996). In terms of the objects of policy transfer, these can include: (1) policy goals, structure and content; (2) policy instruments and administrative techniques; (3) institutions; (4) ideology; (5) ideas, attitudes and concepts; and (6) negative lessons (ibid.). Policy transfer in higher education therefore may lead to horizontal policy convergence in cases in which there is a similarity of languages, a similarity of university cultures, a prior similarity of higher education policies, a similarity of governmental policy preferences, a similarity of problem pressures and a similarity of socio-economic structures (Heinze and Knill 2008).

Following the top-down perspective on European integration processes, expressed both in comparative politics and international relations literature (Börzel and Risse 2003, Radaelli 2003) and in higher education literature (Musselin 2009, Pabian 2009), the Europeanisation of higher education is understood here to be "the [process of] institutionalisation of formal and informal rules developed in a process that involves a supranational or an intergovernmental body (such as the European Union – EU, the Council of Europe – CoE or the Bologna Follow Up Group – BFUG)" (Vukasović

2012: 213). This definition requires that formal and informal rules being institutionalised in the domestic context are developed within a European policy arena and are promoted as European rules. Since this implies the existence of a European model (even if only for specific elements of higher education, e.g. the 3+2 vs. 4+1 degree structure), Europeanisation may lead to a higher level of vertical policy convergence in cases where there is: more clarity of demand, stronger conditionality of rewards, a lower density of veto players, a balance between power and information asymmetry, stronger administrative capacity, weaker institutional legacies, higher legitimacy of demand or processes through which demand was defined, higher resonance between European and domestic rules, more identification with European rules, more participation in epistemic communities or issue networks, and higher internationalisation of the domestic policy arena (Börzel and Risse 2003, Sedelmeier 2011). The literature usually groups these mediating factors into two 'models': (1) external incentives model; and (2) social learning model (Sedelmeier 2011), following the distinction between the rationalist and sociological institutionalism, or between the logic of consequence and the logic of appropriateness.

Table 2 presents a comparative overview of the two theoretical perspectives. The elements of the European model(s) for higher education were developed on the basis of the official Bologna Process and EU documents (EC communications and funding criteria in the Lifelong learning and Tempus programmes).

Here it should be noted that, depending on the presence (or absence) of mediating factors, both the process of policy transfer and the process of Europeanisation allow for piecemeal convergence, i.e. less than wholesale incorporation of rules from abroad or European rules in the domestic context. Similar to the situation in which policy developments from other countries can be used as a source of inspiration for domestic developments (policy transfer), so can European rules, particularly if they suffer from ambiguity, be used to legitimise particular national policy preferences (Europeanisation). Thus, in both process, the re-nationalisation of foreign or European policy preferences can take place, thereby providing room for a variety of unintended effects, as is anyway common in any policy implementation process (Gornitzka 2006, Musselin 2009).

Table 2.   Comparative overview of policy transfer and Europeanisation perspectives

	Policy transfer	Europeanisation
Definition	Use of policy preferences from abroad in the domestic context	Institutionalisation of European rules in the domestic context
European model(s) for higher education systems	None	- Degree structure (3+2, 4+1) - Use of ECTS and learning outcomes in curriculum development - European Standards and Guidelines for Quality Assurance (ESG) - Emergence of national qualification frameworks in line with EQF and EHEA QF - Recognition procedures in line with the Lisbon Recognition Convention (LRC)
Role of the European level of higher education governance	Transnational communication platform	Source of particular policy preferences
Mediating factors	Similarity of: - languages - university cultures - of previous higher education policies - governmental policy preferences - problem pressures - socio-economic structures	- Greater clarity of the model - Bigger rewards for adopting the model - Lower density of veto players - More power asymmetry in favour of Europe than information asymmetry in favour of country - Stronger domestic administrative capacity - Weaker domestic institutional legacies - Greater legitimacy of the model - Stronger resonance between the European model and domestic context - More identification with the European model - Higher domestic participation in European epistemic communities or issue networks - Higher internationalisation of the domestic policy arena
Outcome (if mediating factors favourable)	Horizontal policy convergence – increasing similarity between countries	Vertical policy convergence – increasing similarity with the European model

Based on this distinction and in light of the characteristics of the four countries under study, the following propositions are put forward to guide the analysis in the next section:

Proposition 1: After the start of the Bologna Process and the introduction of the Lisbon Strategy, national policy changes are more characterised by Europeanisation than by policy transfer.

Proposition 2: In cases where there are controversial national policy reforms, there will be attempts to introduce these reforms as part of the Bologna umbrella.

Proposition 3: More horizontal policy convergence is expected between Slovenia, Croatia and Serbia than between Estonia and the other three countries.

Comparing national policy dynamics in Croatia, Estonia, Serbia and Slovenia

This section provides a comparative overview of national policy dynamics in each of the four countries in the last 15–20 years. The overview is based on a qualitative analysis of various policy documents, such as white papers, legislation, other types of regulation (e.g. funding mechanisms), quality assurance standards and procedures (if existing), and secondary sources etc. In Croatia, Serbia and Slovenia the analysis also relies on interviews with system- and university-level actors who were active in the period under study. The section starts with a within-case analysis of each of the four countries, with a cross-case analysis following in the second part of the section.

General political developments

Croatia, Serbia and Slovenia were part of the SFRY until the early 1990s. After the first multi-party elections, which brought nationalist forces to power in Croatia and Serbia and a more liberally oriented coalition in Slovenia, Croatia and Slovenia declared independence from SFRY in 1991[1]

---

1   In Slovenia and Croatia, independence was declared in June 1991. To the south of the SFRY, Macedonia also declared independence in September 1991. An independence referendum in Bosnia and Herzegovina was held between 29 February and 1 March 1992; it led straight to a war.

and were recognised in 1992 as independent states, while Serbia remained in the Federal Republic of Yugoslavia with Montenegro. While Croatia and Serbia were either busy fighting each other (until 1995) or focusing on internal concerns, Slovenia, given that it had quite a stable liberal-democratic government from 1992 onwards, applied for EU membership already in 1997. The year 1999 was marked by the climax of the conflicts over Kosovo between the Serbian military, policy and paramilitary forces and the Kosovo Liberation Army which led to NATO's bombing of Serbia.

The 2000s began for Croatia and Serbia with regime changes, the end of international isolation, wide and deep political, economic and societal reforms gaining new momentum and the process of accession to the EU speeding up. In both countries, the new democratic governments did not manage to be in the driver's seat for the full term and a change of government happened in 2003/2004. In Croatia, the CDU that led Croatia during the 1990s came back to power in 2003 (until 2011), but continued to follow up Croatia's EU accession commitments, culminating with a date of accession set for 1 July 2013. The situation in Serbia was more turbulent, shifting from (1) a conservative coalition government in the 2004–2008 period (which tried and in some aspects succeeded to redress a number of reforms introduced from early 2001 until late 2003) to (2) a more European oriented coalition government that came to power in mid-2008 and filed a formal application for EU membership in 2009. After some toing and froing, Serbia obtained candidate status in early 2012. Compared to the 1990s, the period after 2000 in Slovenia has been a little more turbulent with two instances of conservative right-wing governments: from 2004 to 2008 and from early 2012 onwards. Slovenia became a NATO and EU member in 2004, joining the Schengen and Euro zones in 2007.

The developments in Estonia have been marked with fewer controversies than the Balkan cases. Soon after gaining independence in 1991, Estonia signed an association agreement with the EU and applied for membership in 1995. Its general political development has been relatively stable, with high levels of economic freedom and growth throughout the period (almost doubling its GDP per capita between 1996 and 2007) and foreign policy (the relationship with Russia) as one of the key concerns in the public debate. However, the economic crisis had a severe impact, especially in the period between 2008 and 2010. Estonia became both a NATO and EU member in 2004, part of Schengen in 2007 and introduced the euro in 2011. In general, 'all things European' are seen as positive, and the EU has enjoyed relatively high public acclaim. In terms of the process of joining the EU, compared to the three Balkan cases, Estonia is most comparable to the case of Slovenia.

Croatia: Higher education developments

With regard to higher education developments, the 1990s were relatively quiet for Croatia (in particular compared to the 2000s). The draft Law on Higher Education was discussed already in 1990, but the new legislation was only formally adopted in 1994. The new legislation introduced new buffer structures (National Council for Higher Education – NCHE and the Higher Education Funding Council), as well as provisions for quality assurance (foreseeing evaluations of higher education institutions taking place every five years) and a reference to a credit system, although not explicitly referring to the ECTS. However, due to the lack of capacity of the NCHE, no evaluations took place (Orosz 2008).

Croatia joined the Bologna Process in 2001 and the Lisbon Recognition Convention came into force in 2002. In the same year, a debate on the new draft Law on Higher Education which was planned to correspond to the Bologna Process started, but the proposal did not make it to parliament in 2002 since the proposed changes were supposedly too profound (ZG-meso-3 interview). A more moderate proposal was adopted by parliament in 2003, bringing the education and research function of the universities in Croatia under one legislative umbrella. The main changes brought about were: (a) the new degree structure (with both 3+2 and 4+1 allowed) and a requirement to use ECTS in developing study programmes; (b) a demand that the quality assurance of both study programmes and institutions should be completed by June 2005; (c) the introduction of new buffer structures (two national councils for HE and research each, one agency for HE and research and one HE and research funding council); and (d) an internally important provision related to the internal structure of universities, foreseeing the legal and functional integration of universities as well as a move towards lump-sum funding. In 2004, the official content of the Croatian Diploma Supplement was introduced as well as new legislation concerning the recognition of foreign qualifications in line with the Lisbon Recognition Convention. In the 2005/06 academic year, the first 'Bologna' generation started studying, which meant that higher education institutions had only two years to respond to the Bologna requirements and push their programmes and themselves through the accreditation process.

In 2006, lump-sum funding was introduced and while funding now comes to the university level and is then distributed to the constituent faculties, the outcome of the process does not seem to be very different from the previous situation in which constituent faculties were receiving their funding directly from the Ministry (ZG-macro-2 and ZG-meso-1 interviews). The year 2009 saw the adoption of new legislation focusing on quality assurance in higher education and research, which is in line with the European Standards and Guidelines for Quality Assurance in the European Higher Education Area (ESG), with the previously introduced Agency for Higher Education and Research as the main actor in the quality assurance processes. The agency is a full member of ENQA[2] and is registered in the European Quality Assurance Register for Higher Education (EQAR). In late 2010 the Croatian government developed three proposals for legislation in the area of higher education, but these proposals were not very welcomed by the academic community and, also because of a change in government, did not reach the parliament.

In summary, and similar to Serbia and to a somewhat lesser extent to Slovenia (as will be demonstrated later), national policy changes in Croatia are predominantly introduced as changes in legislation. These changes became much more intense after the regime change in late 1999/early 2000 and with Croatia joining the Bologna Process. However, it should be noted that some changes were part of the legislation introduced already in the 1990s, driven by internal concerns related to the massification of higher education. However, during the 1990s the changes did not go further than legislative changes, given the lack of capacity of the established buffer structures. The first wave of Bologna-related reforms took place relatively quickly (essentially within two years), which raises concerns about the actual depth of implementation (Orosz 2008). It also seems to have led to a somewhat negative attitude to the Bologna reforms in part of the student and academic staff population, though the negative attitude might be not towards Bologna as such but towards the Croatian re-nationalisation of Bologna (ZG-macro-1, ZG-macro-3 and ZG-meso-1 interviews). The new provisions related to the internal structure of universities (the so-called functional integration) were introduced as part of the Bologna package, and even

---

2   Until today, it is the only full member among the countries of the region.

though actors supporting such developments recognise that Bologna as such does not include any explicit provisions with regard to institutional governance, the claim is that Bologna cannot be implemented properly without such changes in institutional governance (ZG-meso-4 interview).

Estonia: Higher education developments

Estonia first introduced a general Education Act structuring the overall education system in 1992, and later on adopted a particular University Act (1995). The second half of the 1990s was marked by the introduction of the Estonian Higher Education Accreditation Centre and the Estonian Higher Education Quality Assessment Council, primarily motivated by the significant expansion of the higher education system, as well as new legislation focusing on research and development, professional higher education and private education (including higher education), and the introduction of common assessment practices. The Lisbon Recognition Convention was ratified in 1998 and came into force in 1999. When the Bologna Declaration was signed in 1999, Estonia was in the middle of negotiations with the EU, and thus joining the Bologna Process was seen as an additional means to demonstrate it was European (Lukas 2008). In 2001 the Estonian Higher Education Accreditation Centre became a member of the Central and Eastern European Network for QA agencies in HE and, one year later, it also become a member of ENQA.

2002 can be labelled 'the Bologna year' in Estonia, given that the so-called Standard of Higher Education, regulation related to the Bologna degree structure, was introduced. The following years were marked by legislative activity in the areas of student grants and loans, programme accreditation, use of the Diploma Supplement, recognition of old Soviet and foreign degrees, the latter with a clear reference to the Lisbon Recognition Convention. The Higher Education Strategy for 2006–2015 was adopted in 2006, followed up in 2007 by a particular implementation plan focusing on the 2008–2010 period.

The year 2008 saw further extensive Bologna-related reforms, with the adoption of the new Standard of Higher Education, defining staff requirements, degrees, the recognition of previous studies and formulating a national qualifications framework (NQF) using a learning outcomes approach, in line with the requirements of the Bologna Process. The NQF in Estonia is now linked to both European frameworks – the EQF and QF-

EHEA – corresponding both to the requirements of the Bologna Process and the EQF recommendation of the EU Parliament. During this time, significant amendments to the law focusing on institutional accreditation, quality assurance and rights to issue diplomas were introduced as well as provisions allowing for the introduction of joint degrees. From 2009 onwards, ECTS is officially the only credit system in Estonia (replacing a previous system with a similar philosophy) and a complete transfer towards a learning outcomes approach was made (Udam 2008). In 2009, the Quality Assessment Council and the Accreditation Centre were merged into the Estonian Higher Education Quality Agency (EKKA), which is now independent in its operations and a candidate member of ENQA. This also marked a turn towards institutional accreditation and the new procedures explicitly refer to the ESG. Use of learning outcomes in curriculum development has also been required from 2009 onwards.

Through the last 15–20 years there have been minimal changes in funding arrangements. Recently, a decision was made that an option whereby institutions could take in a number of students who pay a tuition fee will now be removed and a principle of general free higher education will be introduced for full-time students with normal progression. Potentially as a response to the Soviet era and communist legacy, universities in Estonia have been quite autonomous throughout the whole period, and in the recent EUA study (Estermann, Nokkala, and Steinel 2011) were evaluated as being amongst the most autonomous in the EU. In sum, a number of changes that were in the core of Bologna, such as the study point system based on workload, accreditation with external experts, institutional autonomy and the inclusion of students in governance procedures, were already introduced in the 1995 University Act. Therefore, in the eyes of the public, the introduction of 3+2 was "the Bologna" structure (Lukas 2008), receiving as such a number of criticisms, in particular related to the transfer from the previous 4+2 to the Bologna 3+2 degree structure, that raised questions about the quality of education, especially amongst academic staff (Aru 2008). These criticisms also led to the relatively superficial implementation of the new bachelor programmes, thus further undermining the process (Tina 2008). The idea of "returning to Europe" (Héritier 2005) was quite prominent in the Estonian case and, though Estonia has not been very active in the shaping of the process, it has generally been quite a rapid reformer if one examines the various scorecards (cf. Stocktaking reports).

Serbia: Higher education developments

In 1990 Serbia adopted new legislation defining the basic characteristics of the university system as well as introducing students as participants in governance. The years 1991 and 1992 were marked by student protests against the Milošević regime, resulting in amendments to the law in 1992 which, while explicitly introducing the principles of institutional autonomy and academic freedom, took away provisions guaranteeing student participation in governance. In 1995 a new funding mechanism, input-based and leaving faculties with little room to manoeuvre, was introduced.

The 1996/97 academic year was a turning point for the university/regime relationship. After the regime committed fraud at the local elections in November 1996, opposition parties as well as students took to the streets. After three months, the regime recognised the actual election results and the Rector of the University of Belgrade resigned (in line with the students' demands). The Milošević regime pushed through a new Law on University in 1998 by which all governing bodies at all levels are appointed directly by the government. The adoption of this legislation was again preceded by student and academic staff protests, and followed by the expulsion of a number of students and professors who were most vocal in their opposition. While it was claimed by the government that the law was essentially a policy transfer from France, it had a perverse (though supposedly intended by the government) effect of abolishing university autonomy. This view was shared by the international academic community: the CRE (European University Association predecessor) suspended Serbian universities' membership until 2000.

Following the regime change in October 2000, the first discussions on changes in higher education took place as early as 2001, with the Bologna Process taken as guidelines for discussions, even though Serbia would not join the process until September 2003 (and the Lisbon Recognition Convention would be ratified in 2004). While there were intentions to introduce Bologna-related reforms in 2002, due to the fact that there was no agreed proposal for a more comprehensive legislative change, the Serbian Parliament adopted legislation with the sole purpose to redress the negative consequences of the 1998 Law (the text of the 2002 Law was very similar to the one from 1992).

In early 2003 a national working group was established to work on the so-called Bologna legislation. Their proposal, apart from the provisions related to degrees, ECTS, quality assurance and student participation, intended to bring the university and non-university sector under one legislative umbrella and to increase the organisational integration of universities. The latter was justified as necessity to facilitate the introduction of the Bologna reforms (BG-macro-2, BG-meso-4 interviews). The proposal was opposed by some universities, with the University of Belgrade being the most vocal (Branković 2010) and it did not reach the Parliament because of premature elections at the end of 2003. The minister responsible for higher education in the new government gave the mandate to the University of Belgrade to complete the draft proposal (ibid.).

Eventually, in the summer of 2005 the 'Bologna Law' was adopted, introducing a 3+2 (or 4+1) degree structure, quality assurance procedures and both programme and institutional accreditation, explicit references to the Diploma Supplement and the ECTS, student participation in all governing structures, and provisions for non-university higher education. However, the legislation had relatively weak provisions concerning the integration of universities and allowed faculties to remain separate legal entities. The law also introduced two buffer structures: the National Council for Higher Education and the Commission for Accreditation and Quality Assurance, the latter being in charge of developing the standards and procedures for the quality assurance of programmes and institutions and conducting the process of accreditation. The Commission is a candidate member of ENQA.

The next three to four years were marked by programme and institutional accreditation based on the standards and procedures for quality assurance in line with most of the ESG, but without provisions for student or international participation. The accreditation process pushed the institutions to reform their study programmes; the bulk of the changes had to take place within a year or so. In 2008, the first round of amendments related to student progress as well as provisions related to the relationship between old and new degrees were adopted, essentially postponing full implementation of the legislation for some years and creating an impression that the Bologna Declaration was not properly implemented. Up until this point, there has been no change in the funding regulation.

In sum, the policy changes in Serbia were more concerned with general political issues during the 1990s and clearly linked to the Bologna Process from 2000 onwards. Despite several attempts, the Bologna label proved to be insufficient to push through more controversial reforms related to internal governance structures.

Slovenia: Higher education developments

Partly due to the relative political and economic stability during the 1990s, Slovenia has had the opportunity to introduce significant changes in higher education policy well before the start of the Bologna Process.

The first higher education legislation in the independent Slovenia was adopted in 1993, introducing: (a) possibilities for both professional and academic programmes within universities; (b) private higher education (although the expansion of the private sector essentially happened only in the second half of the 2000s); (c) the legal basis for accreditation and evaluation; and (d) the introduction of two buffer bodies: the Council for Higher Education and the Quality Assessment Commission, although it took respectively one and three years to establish them. In addition, the 1993 law also included provisions related to institutional status, governance and autonomy, foreseeing that only the university level can have legal capacity. The latter caused a stir in the higher education policy arena and a total of six appeals to the Constitutional Court were filed after the law was adopted (Zgaga and Miklavič 2011), demanding an assessment of whether the legislation was constitutional or not, i.e. whether it breached the principle of institutional autonomy. The majority of these appeals was filed by the University of Ljubljana and some of its faculties (LJ-macro-1, LJ-macro-3 interviews). The first court decision came in 1995, allowing for dual legal capacity, i.e. for both faculties and universities. Other appeals were resolved in 1998 with an interpretation that the principle of institutional autonomy is related to the university and not its constituent units, as well as that the university, being part of a social system, cannot and should not be absolutely autonomous (Zgaga and Miklavič 2011).

In 1998 Slovenia ratified the Lisbon Recognition Convention and, as the only country of the ex-SFRY, it was included amongst the original signatories of the Bologna Declaration. Similar to Estonia, Slovenia was at that time in the midst of EU negotiations and the key actors felt it was necessary to signal their commitment to European integration by joining the Bologna Process (LJ-macro-3 interview). The 1999 amendments to the legislation were only narrowly related to the Bologna Process (the Diploma Supplement was introduced), and were more a reflection of the decision of the Constitutional Court as well as a response to the earlier demands for the inclusion of students, academic and other staff regardless of rank in decision-making processes. The amendments also included provisions for EU citizens to study in Slovenia on the same conditions as Slovenians once

Slovenia became a full member of the EU. In addition, clarifications concerning access to higher education from secondary vocational schools and lump-sum funding of the university as a whole based on input and output criteria were introduced.

It took until 2004 for Slovenia to adopt its 'Bologna amendments', following the adoption of the National Master Plan for Higher Education in 2002 and appointment of a national Working Group in 2003. Though the academic community, in particular the University of Ljubljana, were somewhat sceptical about the reform (LJ-macro-1, LJ-macro-3, LJ-meso-1 interviews), they did not oppose it and the working group was able to prepare the proposal. The amendments introduced a new degree structure (allowing for both 3+2 and 4+1), made the use of ECTS obligatory and introduced provisions for an independent quality assurance agency.

After almost 15 years of liberal-democratic coalitions in power, in 2004 a conservative coalition won the elections. It quickly proposed various reforms of the public sector, introducing the principle of quality assurance through competition and market steering into higher education (Zgaga and Miklavič 2011). In 2006, with significant opposition from various stakeholders and quite a tight majority (LJ-macro-5 interview), it pushed through the Parliament new legislative changes diminishing the independence of the quality assurance agency. The changes also gave the pre-Bologna first degrees equal status in terms of labour market recognition as the Bologna second-cycle degrees, a move that was seen as directly undermining the essence of the Bologna reforms (Zgaga and Miklavic 2011). The counter move came again in 2009: after the government changed back to a centre-left liberal orientation, the quality assurance agency became independent again and became fully operational in 2010. It is currently in the process of joining ENQA and EQAR.[3]

In sum, national policy dynamics in Slovenia are marked by significant changes introduced in higher education in both the 1990s and 2000s. While in the 1990s the changes were focused on more internal policy concerns (some of which were controversial), in the 2000s there was a clear link to European initiatives in higher education. Though it was a front runner with regard to joining the Bologna Process, Slovenia took some time in developing its legislation fully in line with Bologna. The developments with

---

3   Recently (autumn 2012), the newly elected conservative government proposed new
      changes to the Higher Education Law which seem to present another counter move.

regard to quality assurance in the second half of the 2000s also demonstrate the vulnerability of higher education policy to government turnovers.

Cross-case analysis

As was demonstrated and expected, given the conceptual clarification between policy transfer and Europeanisation, national policy changes prior to the Bologna Process are characterised more by policy transfer and particular internal (national) policy concerns than by Europeanisation. Further cross-case analysis will refer to the propositions formulated in section three of this chapter, by comparing the policy changes identified in the four case studies presented above.

Proposition 1: After the start of the Bologna Process, national policy changes have been characterised more by Europeanisation than by policy transfer.

All four countries have, since the beginning of the Bologna Process, shaped their national policies clearly in line with the Bologna preferences. This is most notable in the introduction of the 3+2 and/or 4+1 degree structure, the use of ECTS and introduction of quality assurance procedures. All four countries (although in Slovenia this is less visible given the relative delay in legislative changes), adapted their legislation and introduced Bologna study programmes relatively quickly. That does not mean, however, that Europeanisation processes account for the entirety of the national policy dynamics, given that in all four countries idiosyncratic policy concerns were also addressed. In Croatia and Serbia these concerns were connected to the integration of universities, Croatia and Slovenia focused on developing new funding mechanisms, the Slovenian quality assurance system went through a back-and-forth stage due to other domestic concerns (private higher education) and Estonia addressed the recognition of old Soviet degrees during these times.

Proposition 2: In cases where there are controversial national policy reforms, there will be attempts to introduce these reforms as part of the Bologna umbrella.

This is most clearly the case with regard to the 'integrated universities and faculties as legal entities' issue in Croatia and Serbia. Quite clearly, in both of these countries these changes were (and still are) framed as part of the Bologna package. However, such a framing proves not to be a completely successful strategy given that in both of the countries (and in Slovenia for that matter), it is still possible for constituent units (faculties) to have legal capacity. This also points attention to the power of certain actors in the national policy arena, most notably the flagship universities, to block particular changes despite the European framing and the overall 'return to Europe' atmosphere.

Proposition 3: More horizontal policy convergence is expected amongst Slovenia, Croatia and Serbia than between all of the four countries together.

Given the similarities in previous higher education policy, cultural (and language) similarities, as well as similarities in problem pressures and socio-economic characteristics, indeed more horizontal convergence can be identified in the case of the three former Yugoslav countries than if all four countries are analysed together. Horizontal convergence is evident in the treatment of the issue of the integration of universities, both in terms of identifying this as a policy problem as well as in terms of identifying the solutions. While in Croatia and Serbia the solution is labelled 'functional integration', in Slovenia the use of the term is not as widespread but the changes introduced do largely amount to functional integration. However, it is also evident that the internal political developments play a role and as such the speed of reforms varies among these three countries.

Conclusion

As presented in the previous section, the changes before the start of the Bologna Process were predominantly addressing national policy concerns. Even though some of the changes related to particular national policy concerns might have been embedded in the wider process of "returning to Europe" (Héritier 2005), this should not be labelled Europeanisation given there was no clear European policy preference to adapt to. Following the developments of Bologna action lines from the Bologna Declaration and through subsequent communiqués, higher education policies in all four countries clearly correspond to the Bologna agenda. Therefore, vertical policy convergence with the degree structure, quality assurance procedures, use of ECTS and to a lesser extent student participation was identified in all four countries. In addition, and in accordance with the policy transfer literature, horizontal policy convergence was identified between Croatia, Serbia and Slovenia.

The distinction between the processes of policy transfer and Europeanisation, and consequently between their outcomes (horizontal and vertical policy convergence), proved useful for providing a fuller account of policy dynamics and disentangling the underlying mechanisms of particular policy changes. The limited influence these countries have had on the shaping of European preferences as well as the aforementioned embeddedness of national policy dynamics in the European context means that in these countries the European initiatives are taken more on face value than might be the case in some Western or Northern European countries: they are taken as European, despite the fact they may in essence result from uploading particular policy preferences by European countries which have a stronger influence on European level policy developments. Therefore, one issue worth research attention in the future would be to examine policy transfer and Europeanisation in Western and Northern European countries and to explore their scope conditions, in particular with regard to the possibility and capacity of the country to upload its policy preferences to the European level. Another question arising from this analysis is how post-conflict societies deal with policy transfer and the construction of higher education systems and to what extent current theoretical models can take the particularities of transition countries into account.

The analysis in this chapter was limited to an analysis of policy outputs (changes in policy instruments) and not an analysis of policy outcomes (results of implementation). Therefore, further enquiry should also focus on the changes that have taken hold on the grass-roots level, i.e. the relationship between the convergence of outputs and the convergence of outcomes. This would imply a process tracing these changes back to their (potential) origins in particular policy changes, keeping the explanatory toolbox open for both policy transfer and Europeanisation, in addition to including the notions of layering, incremental change and translation.

References

Amaral, A., G. Neave, C. Musselin, P. Maassen, eds. (2009). *European Integration and the Governance of Higher Education and Research*. Dordrecht: Springer.

Aru, H. (2008). "Sissejuhatus". In: A. Valk (ed.), *Bologna Eestis 2004-2008*. Tallinn: SA Archimedes. 5-8.

Avis, G. (1990). "The Soviet Higher Education Reform: Proposals and Reactions". *Comparative Education.* Vol. 26. No. 1. 5-12.

Beerkens, E. (2008). "The Emergence and Institutionalisation of the European Higher Education and Research Area". *European Journal of Education.* Vol. 43. No. 4. 407-425.

Bomberg, E., J. Peterson (2000). "Policy Transfer and Europeanisation: Passing the Heineken test". *Queen's Papers on Europeanisation* 2000. No. 2.

Börzel, T. A. (2003). "Shaping and Taking EU Policies: Member State Responses to Europeanisation". *Queen's Papers on Europeanisation* 2003. No. 2.

Börzel, T. A., T. Risse (2003). "Conceptualizing the domestic impact of Europe". In: K. Featherstone, C. M. Radaelli (eds.), *The Politics of Europeanisation.* Oxford: Oxford University Press. 57-80.

Branković, J. (2010). Decision making on decision making: deciding governance in higher education in Serbia 2002-2005. Master thesis. Department of Educational Research, University of Oslo. Oslo: University of Oslo.

Corbett, A. (2005). *Universities and the Europe of Knowledge: Ideas, Institutions and Policy Entrepreneurship in European Union Higher Education Policy, 1955–2005.* Basingstoke: Palgrave MacMillan.

Dobbins, M., C. Knill (2009). "Higher Education Policies in Central and Eastern Europe: Convergence toward a Common Model?" *Governance.* Vol. 22. No. 3. 397-430.

Dolowitz, D., D. Marsh (1996). "Who Learns What from Whom: A Review of the Policy Transfer Literature". *Political Studies.* Vol. 44. No. 2. 343-357.

Estermann, T., T. Nokkala, M. Steinel (2011). *University Autonomy in Europe II: The Scorecard.* Brussels: European University Association.

Featherstone, K., C. M. Radaelli, eds. (2003). *The Politics of Europeanisation.* Oxford: Oxford University Press.

Garben, S. (2010). "The Bologna Process: From a European Law Perspective". *European Law Journal.* Vol. 16. No. 2. 186-210.

Gornitzka, Å. (2006). "What Is the Use of Bologna in National Reform? The Case of Norwegian Quality Reform in Higher Education". In: V. Tomusk (ed.), *Creating the European Higher Education Area: Voices from the Periphery.* Dordrecht: Springer. 19-41.

Gornitzka, Å. (2007). "The Lisbon Process: A Supranational Policy Perspective". In: P. Maassen, J. P. Olsen (eds.), *University Dynamics and European Integration.* Dordrecht: Springer. 155-178.

Heinze, T., C. Knill (2008). "Analysing the Differential Impact of the Bologna Process: Theoretical Considerations on National Conditions for International Policy Convergence". *Higher education.* Vol. 56. No. 4. 493-510.

Héritier, A. (2005). "Europeanization Research East and West: A Comparative Assessment". In: F. Schimmelfennig, U. Sedelmeier (eds.), *The Europeanization of Central and Eastern Europe.* Ithaca: Cornell University Press. 199-209.

Huisman, J. (2009). "Institutional Diversification or Convergence?" In: B. Kehm, J. Huisman, B. Stensaker (eds.), *The European Higher Education Area: Perspectives on a Moving Target.* Rotterdam: Sense Publishers. 245-262.

Karseth, B., T. D. Solbrekke (2010). "Qualifications Frameworks: The Avenue Towards the Convergence of European Higher Education?" *European Journal of Education*. Vol. 45. No. 4. 563-576.

Kehm, B. (2010). "Editorial". *European Journal of Education*. Vol. 45. No. 4. 529-534.

Kyvik, S. (2004). "Structural changes in higher education systems in Western Europe". *Higher Education in Europe*. Vol. 29. No. 3. 393–409.

Lukas, T. (2008). "Eesti Euroopa kõrgharidusruumis". In: A. Valk (ed.), *Bologna Eestis 2004-2008*. Tallinn: SA Archimedes. 3-4.

Maassen, P., C. Musselin (2009). "European Integration and the Europeanisation of Higher Education". In: A. Amaral, G. Neave, C. Musselin, P. Maassen (eds.), *European Integration and the Governance of Higher Education and Research*. Dordrecht: Springer. 3-14.

Musselin, C. (2009). "The Side Effects of the Bologna Process on National Institutional Settings: The Case of France". In: A. Amaral, G. Neave, C. Musselin, P. Maassen (eds.), *European Integration and the Governance of Higher Education and Research*. Dordrecht: Springer. 181-205.

Olsen, J. P. (2002). "The Many Faces of Europeanization". *Journal of Common Market Studies*. Vol. 50. No. 5. 921-952.

Orosz, A. (2008). "The Bologna Process in Croatia". *European Education*. Vol. 40. No. 2. 66-84.

Pabian, P. (2009). "Europeanisation of Higher Education Governance in the Post-Communist Context: The Case of the Czech Republic". In: A. Amaral, G. Neave, C. Musselin, P. Maassen (eds.), *European Integration and the Governance of Higher Education and Research*. Dordrecht: Springer. 257-278.

Pollack, M. A. (2000). "The End of Creeping Competence? EU Policy-Making Since Maastricht". *Journal of Common Market Studies*. Vol. 38. No. 3. 519-538.

Radaelli, C. M. (2003). "The Europeanisation of Public Policy". In: K. Featherstone, C. M. Radaelli (eds.), *The Politics of Europeanisation*. Oxford: Oxford University Press. 27-56.

Ravinet, P. (2008). "From Voluntary Participation to Monitored Coordination: Why European Countries Feel Increasingly Bound by Their Commitment to the Bologna Process". *European Journal of Education*. Vol. 43. No. 3. 353-367.

Sedelmeier, U. (2011). "Europeanisation in New Member and Candidate States". *Living Reviews in European Governance*. Vol. 6. No. 1.

Šoljan, N. N. (1991). "The Saga of Higher Education in Yugoslavia: Beyond the Myths of a Self-Management Socialist Society". *Comparative Education Review*. Vol. 35. No. 1. 131-153.

Stone, D. (2001). Learning lessons, policy transfer and the international diffusion of policy ideas. CSGR Working paper. University of Warwick 2001 (69).

Tina, A. (2008). "Kahetsükliline kõrgharidus ehk 3+2 süsteem". In: A. Valk (ed.), *Bologna Eestis 2004-2008*. Tallinn: SA Archimedes. 13-17.

Trondal, J. (2002). "The Europeanisation of Research and Higher Educational Policies: Some Reflections". *Scandinavian Political Studies*. Vol. 25. No. 4. 333-355.

Udam, M. (2008). "Ainepunktide süsteemi loomine". In: A. Valk (ed.), *Bologna Eestis 2004-2008*. Tallinn: SA Archimedes. 19-21.

Vink, M. P., P. Graziano (2007). *Europeanization: New Research Agendas*. Houndmills: Palgrave Macmillan.

Voegtle, E., C. Knill, M. Dobbins (2011). "To What Extent Does Transnational Communication Drive Cross-national Policy Convergence? The Impact of the Bologna Process on Domestic Higher Education Policies". *Higher education*. Vol. 66. No. 1. 77-94.

Vukasović, M. (2012). "Europeanisation of the Education Function of Universities: Preliminary Comparison of Norway and Poland". In: M. Kwiek, P. Maassen (eds.), *National Higher Education Reforms in a European Context: Comparative Reflections on Norway and Poland*. Berlin: Peter Lang. 209-226.

Westerheijden, D., E. Beerkens, L. Cremonini, J. Huisman, B. Kehm, A. Kovač, Y. Yagci (2010). *The First Decade of Working on the European Higher Education Area: Executive Summary, Overview and Conclusions*. Enschede: CHEPS.

Witte, J. (2008). "Aspired Convergence, Cherished Diversity: Dealing with the Contradictions of Bologna". *Tertiary Education and Management*. Vol. 14. No. 2. 81-93.

Zgaga, P., K. Miklavič (2011). "Reforming Higher Education in 'Transition': Between National and International Reform Initiatives: The Case of Slovenia". *European Education*. Vol. 43. No. 3. 13-25.

What Kind of University for What Kind of Society? Nation-States, Post-National Constellations, and Higher Education in the Post-Yugoslav Space

Jana Baćević

Abstract

The text investigates the transformation of higher education following the dissolution of Yugoslavia from the perspective of the changing concept of political communities that universities 'belong' to. It argues that, besides the development of 'post-national constellations' mediated through processes of European integration in higher education, we need to acknowledge the effects of the parallel process of 'fragmentation' along ethnic, political and religious lines on higher education in the region. Utilising examples from Bosnia, Kosovo, Macedonia and Sandžak, the text points to the relevance of understanding the interplay within the broader political dynamics, and the role of universities in politics and policies of identity, in an effort to explain the change processes in higher education in Europe and beyond.

Key words: higher education, ethnicity and education, post-conflict education, politics of education, identity and difference, post-national constellations, former Yugoslavia

Introduction: Higher education – where, by whom, for whom?

Authors writing about higher education – including those featured in this volume – seem to agree on one thing: higher education has fundamentally changed. These changes have been manifested in diverse, more or less evident forms. Some authors writing in critical, predominantly Marxist, traditions have grouped these transformations under the umbrella term "neo-liberalisation", denoting the growing treatment of education as a (public or private) commodity to be exchanged in international (global) markets, the rise of "knowledge economies" and related changes in the modes of knowledge production, including the precarisation of the academic workforce (Krause 2009, Lynch 2006, Olssen and Peters 2005, Reading 1996). Others have focused on the policy implications of these changes, including the transformation of the modes of governance and financing, the changing role of international and supranational actors in defining policy goals and objectives, and the processes of target-setting, "benchmarking", quality control and quality assurance (e.g. Amaral et al. 2009, Maassen and Olsen 2007, Tomusk 2007).

Regardless of the similarities and differences in approaches to the issue of change in higher education, it has triggered a bigger and much more significant question: that of the *role* of higher education in a society (cf. Brennan 2002). This problematique is not to be mistaken with the much narrower and politicised concept of 'universities' responsibilities to society', which is frequently used to provide ideological justification for mechanisms of accountability (cf. Neave 2000); rather, it entails a prior discussion of what, exactly, *is* a society. Of course, this does not refer to the ontological and epistemological question that has been extensively discussed throughout the history of the social sciences, but to a more practical issue: what kind of society do we talk about when we talk about higher education's role or function in 'the society'? The question is not purely sophist. On the contrary, it concerns the *structure* and *nature* of the *political communities* that are involved in the making and contestation of discourses related to higher education. In other words, who is higher education for? Who should have a say in higher education? Which criteria are used to define the members of communities involved in higher education? How are these communities delineated, and what are their boundaries (cf. Britez and Peters 2010)?

Fundamentally, these questions boil down to one: what is higher education *for*? Possible answers include the transmission of specific professional skills, usually connected to economic development and growth, the transmission of democratic values and norms, and social integration and participation (Delanty 2001). Rather than being a "random" assembly or "natural" reaction to environmental constraints, however, the ordering and prioritisation of these responses provide important clues to the ideological orientations and political agendas that shape education policies (ibid.; cf. Zgaga 2009). In other words, the way that different institutions construct their missions is part of the broader societal dynamics, and thus cannot be understood outside of the immediate political context. At the same time, given the paramount role of higher education in social reproduction, the approach of different institutions to these questions is also bound to shape the future social dynamics of the societies in question.

This text applies this perspective to some recent developments in higher education in the successor states of former Yugoslavia. More specifically, it will discuss a specific group of phenomena, commonly referred to as universities in post-conflict societies, which developed during and in the aftermath of the violent dissolution of Yugoslavia. It aims to show how these policy developments can be understood in the broader context of transformations of the 'post-Yugoslav' space and, thus, how they are fundamentally intertwined with the processes of construction, constitution and negotiation of political communities and entities that have emerged (and continue to emerge) following the Yugoslav crisis. Before delving into the empirical terrain, however, the text will first offer a theoretical consideration of the shifting concepts of political communities relevant for the understanding of contemporary higher education.

Situating higher education in a post-national sphere

Throughout most of the modern history of Europe communities of higher education were well, if not always, explicitly defined. Early modern higher education in Europe, though in a way highly cosmopolitan (after all, there were no nation-states in the modern sense of the word), was nevertheless a strictly defined community of exclusively male scholars who lived isolated, almost monastic lives, dedicated to the pursuit of knowledge at the universities that existed at the time (for instance, Oxford, Bologna, Cambridge or Charles University in Prague). The late modern period and the rise of the nation-states brought about a closer association between universities and national projects – either through the creation of a shared cultural canon, as in the case of the German 'Humboldtian' model, or through the education of the nation's administrative and technical elite as in the case of the French 'Napoleonic' model (Neave 2000). In addition to the central 'flagship' universities, smaller regional universities started to be formed, mostly in order to aid or respond to the rapid industrialisation and support the development of the peripheries of the nation-states (cf. Ruegg 2004).

The current, postmodern period ushered in a major change in the relationship between higher education and its communities. Two aspects of this change have most frequently been the focus or object of analysis. On one hand, as a corollary to the rapid massification that followed the decades after World War II, higher education stopped being the exclusive domain of social elites; universities now included women, racial and ethnic minorities, and other people who by virtue of their background or characteristics would have earlier been excluded from higher education. Of course, this does not mean that higher education necessarily became more equitable or really reflective of the diversity of the population in Europe, but the community comprising higher education certainly became more diverse. On the other hand, the political project of European integration and its higher education equivalent, the Bologna Process, fundamentally transformed the political context of higher education (Amaral and Neave 2009, Maassen and Olsen 2007). Although nation-states still control the legislation and recognition of qualifications in higher education, the setting of agendas, priorities, models or 'examples of best practice' and indicators of success have all moved increasingly to the transnational, most frequently European, level (e.g. Olsen and Maassen 2007: 6-7, Enders 2004). This means that universities are no longer responsible only to the 'society' imagined within the boundaries of the nation-state but, increasingly, define their responsibilities and missions in relation to communities or networks of actors that span the boundaries of nation-states (Britez and Peters 2010, Enders 2004, Keating 2009).

This phenomenon needs to be seen and understood within the wider processes of the globalisation and transnationalisation of public spheres and, consequently, politics, and their transformation into what Habermas famously dubbed "the post-national constellation" (Habermas 2001). Kwiek summarises Habermas' argument as follows: "Traditionally, and especially in the postwar period, the state, society and the economy were co-extensive within national boundaries [...] What is happening today is that developments summarized under the rubric 'globalization' have put this entire constellation into question. The postnational constellation is bringing to an end the situation in which politics and the legal system intermeshed with economic cycles and national traditions within the boundaries of nation-states. The dilemma national governments face today derives from the zero-sum game into which they have been forced and is described by Habermas in the following manner: necessary economic objectives can be reached only at the expense of social and political objectives" (Kwiek 2006: 273-274).

In the Western Balkans, the transnationalisation of higher education has different facets. On one hand, it relates to the shift towards policies primarily driven by the process commonly termed 'Europeanisation'. In higher education, these policies primarily stem from the framework of the Bologna Process, but the process itself is broader, including the transformation of political and public spheres in accordance with whatever is identified as the 'European' model. On the institutional level, universities are challenging the boundaries of the nation-states primarily through strategies of 'internationalisation', primarily understood as the capacity to attract foreign (frequently fee-paying) students. To this end, universities try to offer study programmes (or at least courses) in English (or other widely-spoken languages), hire international staff (or visiting professors), and aim to present student experience as appealing to an international audience (Britez and Peters 2010; also see Zgaga, this issue). Research universities also cooperate in research projects with international consortia and other forms of research and development activities that span national boundaries.

However, transnationalisation, globalisation, and European integration are not the only relevant political processes shaping the societies of the Western Balkans today. Numerous authors have pointed to a related and parallel social process, connected to fragmentation or diversification, usually along ethnic, linguistic and other social lines. In other words, not only are political communities no longer defined by the boundaries of the nation-states, but multiple political communities exist *within* the boundaries of nation-states. Fraser (2007) has termed this the dual process of "transnationalisation and fragmentation of the public sphere". In the context of the Western Balkans, these processes are usually connected to the violent breakup of former Yugoslavia, but in many cases they both precede and follow the actual event. This means that understanding how these processes of social fragmentation shaped (and continue to shape) public policies in former Yugoslavia is a vital part of understanding the dynamics and transformations of higher education in its successor states.

Curiously enough, however, the majority of the research on higher education in the Western Balkans has focused on the processes of integration or 'Europeanisation' or, alternatively, on the national- or institutional-level *reception* and *implementation* of these processes, largely ignoring the parallel processes of fragmentation. Even the rare analyses of the conflicts and tensions generated on the intersection of different sublevels of higher education (e.g., between students and professors, or between academics and the state) have analysed them either in the context of national-level politics, or as a reflection of global trends such as the commodification of knowledge or the precarisation of the academic workforce (cf. Doolan 2012, Baćević 2010). The analytical imagination has thus hardly moved beyond the concept of 'national higher education systems', and beyond viewing these systems as the primary and most important frameworks for the interpretation of the changes in higher education.

What this article wishes to argue, however, is that, in addition to the 'post-national constellations', higher education in the Western Balkans is at least as much fundamentally influenced by the processes of fragmentation of the public sphere, especially in the context of the breakup of former Yugoslavia. Given that the discussion of these latter processes has largely remained outside of higher education research, and within the domains of politics, policy and international relations, the article will offer a brief description of the development of 'post-conflict' universities in the post-Yugoslav context, starting with Bosnia and moving on to the case studies of Kosovo, Macedonia and Sandžak. It will proceed to analyse these policy developments in relation to the social and political processes of the transformation of political communities in the aftermath of the conflict. In the conclusion, the article will discuss the implications of these processes for the understanding of the dynamics that shape higher education in the Western Balkans today.

'Fragmenting' higher education: The development of universities in the post-conflict context

Bosnia and Herzegovina

The development of 'post-conflict' higher education in the successor states of former Yugoslavia cannot be understood without at least a passing reference to Bosnia, the earliest (and probably the most familiar) instance of an institutional split along ethnic lines. Early after the start of the conflict in 1992, the Serbian staff and students at the University of Sarajevo left, establishing a separate University of East Sarajevo in the Serbian town of Pale. In Mostar, equally a multi-ethnic town with Croatian and Bosniak Muslim majorities, the Croatian part of the University of Mostar split off, forming a separate institution called Sveučiliste u Mostaru – with "*sveučiliste*" being the Croatian, but not Bosnian or Serbian word for university. The 'original' University of Mostar is today distinguished by the name "Džemal Bijedić", after a Bosnian communist politician who served as the Prime Minister of the Socialist Federative Republic of Yugoslavia between 1971 and 1977, and played a key role in the development of the university in his native town. What can be observed here is an early instance of the use of language (and institutional naming) to underline the ethnic character of the institution, simultaneously distinguishing it from other institutions in the same urban space.

The split of these two universities was very much a function of the ethnic conflict in Bosnia between 1992 and 1995. However, its consequences persisted long after the signing of the Dayton Agreement in 1995. The universities in Mostar and Sarajevo remain divided into two institutions; each of these institutions has a more or less pronounced ethnic character. This means that these universities continue to educate predominantly the members of 'their' respective ethnic groups, in this sense reproducing the ethnic divisions in Bosnian society. In the case of Bosnia and Herzegovina, the situation is rendered even more complex by the multiple and overlapping administrative layers regulating education – on the levels of the Republic, Federation / Republic of Srpska, the Brčko district and cantons. This means that in lieu of one 'national' system of higher education, Bosnia and Herzegovina actually represents 14 different systems of education. In this case, as a matter of fact, administrative fragmentation has followed the ethnic fragmentation.

Partially because of the administrative complexity, the case of Bosnia and Herzegovina remains one of the most difficult to analyse. Due to space limitations, this paper will not delve into it in detail, but will instead turn its attention to three perhaps less known, but equally (if not more) interesting cases of ethnic fragmentation in higher education: Kosovo, Macedonia and Sandžak.

Kosovo

The history of higher education in Kosovo is fundamentally intertwined with the evolution of ethnic and societal divisions that culminated, first, in the NATO intervention in 1999, and, second, the declaration of independence of Kosovo in 2008. However, the tensions surrounding the University of Prishtina reach back before the eruption of the conflict itself. The University of Prishtina was founded in 1970, largely in response to the requests of ethnic Albanians, who formed the majority in the Serbian province of Kosovo, for political autonomy (cf. Pichl and Leutloff 1999).

The communist regime of Josip Broz Tito that ruled Yugoslavia at the time was highly sensitive towards any expression of ethnic nationalism that threatened the cohesion of the Federation; however, the domains of education and culture were deemed to be sufficiently 'safe' as a vent for the tendencies that would otherwise have had a centrifugal political effect. Thus, although political autonomy was out of the question, the regime in Belgrade consented to the opening of a separate university in Kosovo in 1969. The University of Prishtina featured programmes in both Albanian and Serbo-Croatian, the official language of the SFRY. Although the goal was to make sure that Albanians spoke Serbo-Croatian, and that Serbo-Croatian speakers had at least minimum proficiency in Albanian, the reality turned out to be different. The lack of an Albanian-speaking academic elite in Yugoslavia meant that the textbooks and curricula were, up to a point, imported from neighbouring Tirana, meaning that the central government had very little control over the teaching process (Sommers and Buckland 2004). On the other hand, the Serbo-Croatian staff and students remained apart, in time leading to the development of parallel language streams – Serbian and Albanian.

The extent of this separation became evident in 1981, a year after Tito's death, when massive protests of Albanians erupted in Kosovo, with students at the University of Prishtina playing a prominent role. In response, the Serbian authorities started 'tightening' the control over the university, deemed to be the 'hotbed of Albanian nationalism'. As the situation in the province worsened, and new protests erupted in 1989, the extent of repression reached the point at which the Serbian authorities officially banned any Albanian student from enrolling in the University of Prishtina from 1990/91 onwards. In response, the Albanian students and staff withdrew into what is commonly known as the 'parallel system', a network of informal underground higher education initiatives, which were sporadically raided by the Serbian police forces. The development of parallel systems continued as the conflict exacerbated. A brief intercession happened with the Milošević-Rugova agreement in 1996, which envisaged the strict separation of Albanian and Serbian students in 'shifts', but was never implemented. The situation further deteriorated, eventually leading to the NATO intervention and the subsequent refugee crisis in 1999.

The aftermath of the intervention saw a situation that resembled a reversed mirror image of the situation before 1999 (cf. KEC 2006). Namely, while the Albanian students and staff slowly returned to the premises of the

University of Prishtina, the Serbian students and staff were scattered across makeshift facilities in Central Serbia. Attempts to introduce a 'space-sharing' arrangement at the University of Prishtina were quickly abandoned; in 2001, after the regime change in Serbia, the staff and students settled in the town of Kosovska Mitrovica, in the north of Kosovo. This meant that there now existed, technically speaking, two public universities in the territory of Kosovo, both of which could claim the name "University of Prishtina". One, consisting of the staff and students that had been part of the 'parallel system' during the role of Milošević, was housed on the premises of the University in Prishtina and run under the auspices of the international administration that was in charge of Kosovo's provisional institutions of self-government. The other consisted of predominantly Serbian students and staff that fled Prishtina after the NATO intervention, and claimed to be the legal successor of the University in Prishtina established in 1970 (Sommers and Buckland 2004). Although on the territory of Kosovo, the university was governed, financed and managed in the legislative framework of the Republic of Serbia. After 2001, the institution assumed the name "University of Prishtina temporarily located in Kosovska Mitrovica" (UPKM).

The international administration was thus faced with a problem: there were two universities claiming the same name, both of which claimed to be legal successors to the University of Prishtina. One of them catered almost exclusively to Albanian students, while the other catered exclusively to Serbian-speaking students. The international administration tried to turn the situation into an advantage; UPKM was recognised as the institution providing higher education for Serbian speakers, while the University of Prishtina (UP) was recognised as the institution of higher education for the majority Albanian population (cf. Daxner 2004). Although there were attempts to integrate minority higher education at the UP, they were quickly abandoned. Given its history as a 'parallel' institution, and the fact that most of its staff and students were involved in the fight against the dominance of the Serbian language in the institution, the expectation that the university would develop into a 'multicultural' institution was not very realistic (Den Boer and van der Borgh 2011: 74, Pupovci 2006).

During the first period of the aftermath of the conflict, both the international administration in Kosovo and the government in Serbia thus encouraged the development of two universities catering to distinct ethnic groups in Kosovo. The overall idea was to work slowly towards the integration of the UPKM into the legislative framework in Kosovo. However, these plans were interrupted with the change of government in Serbia in 2004. The new, right-wing government replaced the rector of the UPKM (who had been recognised as "cooperative" by the international community, cf. Bayerl 2006), thus contributing to the growing nationalist sentiment at the UPKM – further exacerbated by the exodus of the Serb population in Kosovo following the events of March 2004. From this moment onwards, the UPKM was ostensibly defined as an institution tasked with the 'defence of Serb national interests' in Kosovo, which also meant that it rejected most attempts at integration into Kosovar institutions initiated by the international administration. The rift, expectedly, exacerbated even further since Kosovo declared independence in 2008. The UPKM is now visibly in line with the official rhetoric of the Serbian government, which disputes the statehood and sovereignty of Kosovo. The government of Kosovo, on the other hand, despite high levels of minority rights integrated into the legal framework, did not attempt to provide higher education for Serbian speakers. Since 2010, it has integrated the teacher training programme in Bosnian into the newly established public university of Prizren, but the programme officially only targets the Bosniak ethnic minority.

The development of higher education in Kosovo is thus fundamentally intertwined with the dynamics of the political relationship between the two biggest ethnic groups – Albanians and Serbs. Although, in the early years the University of Prishtina was intended to contribute to the integration of these two groups, it quickly became a vehicle for ethnic mobilisation and, consequently, of the segregation and finally the repression of the Albanian minority. Its transformations after the conflict clearly reflected the growing social divisions between two ethnic groups. During the first period, both governments – the government of Zoran Đinđić in Serbia and the UN interim administration in Kosovo – accepted and even supported the separation of higher education institutions, limiting integration to the joint legal framework in theory and peaceful coexistence in practice. However, the political tensions beneath the surface reverberated quickly after the events in 2004, and continued to do so after 2008. Currently, rather than presenting a vehicle of integration, the two biggest public universities in the territory of Kosovo thus serve the political goal of further segregating the two biggest ethnic groups.

Macedonia

The development of higher education in the Former Yugoslav Republic of Macedonia is also fundamentally intertwined with the processes of ethnic mobilisation and fragmentation in the region that followed the breakup of former Yugoslavia and the conflicts that ensued. Minority higher education in Macedonia first became an issue after it declared independence in 1991, officially being the only republic of former Yugoslavia to secede peacefully. The secession opened questions for the biggest ethnic minority, Albanians, who feared that Macedonia, outside of the multicultural context of Yugoslavia, would develop into a 'mono-ethnic' state. One of the particularly vulnerable domains of public policy was higher education. Higher education was seen as a gateway for both positions in the public administration and social prestige and status; in former Yugoslavia, Albanians from Macedonia were able to attend higher education at the University of Prishtina but, with increased police repression and a ban on teaching in Albanian, this was no longer a possibility (cf. Czapliński 2006 and 2008). The University in Skopje had a teacher training programme in Albanian, but it was discontinued in the 1980s. Thus, access to higher education in the Albanian language became one of the most pressing issues facing the newly independent republic.

However, the Macedonian government was very slow to move on this issue, resorting to legalistic interpretations according to which higher education in public institutions could only be conducted in the state language (Macedonian). Partially in response to this, the Albanian community in Tetovo decided to move unilaterally, and founded a private institution dubbed the "University of Tetovo" (UT) in 1994. The reaction from the Macedonian state was very sharp. It deemed the institution "illegal" and "unconstitutional" and intervened during the inauguration ceremony, killing one Albanian and wounding more. This reflected the growing rift between the communities, which would eventually lead to armed conflict in 2001.

The issue, however, attracted the attention of various international organisations. The Council of Europe initiated a legislative reform programme through which it strove to include provisions for minority language higher education in the Macedonian legislation. The Organisation for Security and Cooperation in Europe (OSCE), and in particular the High Commissioner on National Minorities (HCNM), on the other hand, focused on institutional solutions. Identifying the University of Tetovo (UT) as a mono-ethnic institution whose teaching standards were at best questionable, it instead strove to develop programmes in fields deemed deficient, such as public administration and computer science (cf. Czapliński 2008). The funds were drawn from donors and international organisations, but it was only the conflict that enabled the financial construction to be completed.

The conflict in Macedonia, widely understood as originating in the 'spillover' from neighbouring Kosovo, lasted (with interruptions for ceasefire) between January and August 2001. Although lower in both scale and intensity than the conflicts in Kosovo or Bosnia and Herzegovina, it nevertheless immediately attracted the attention of the international community, which naturally feared a repetition of the scenarios of ethnic conflict in other countries of former Yugoslavia. Pressure was exerted on all sides – the Macedonian government, the ethnic Albanian political parties, and the NLA – and the peace treaty, known as the Ohrid Framework Agreement, was signed in August 2001. The treaty transformed Macedonia into a form of consociational democracy (cf. Bieber 2008, Daftary 2001), a political regime based on power-sharing between dominant ethnic groups (formulated as groups comprising over 25 percent of the population, but in reality meaning ethnic Macedonians and ethnic Albanians).

Besides altering the political power structure, the conflict also had a lasting impact on higher education. On one hand, it galvanised the international donor support necessary for completing the OSCE HCNM project; the resulting institution, named "Southeast European University" (SEEU), was officially inaugurated in Tetovo in November 2001 (Czapliński 2006). The SEEU was envisaged as a private institution providing Albanian-language higher education, but from the beginning it aimed to have a peace-building and reconciliation function; for that reason, it included teaching in Albanian, Macedonian and English. It had international leadership and developed cooperation with foreign universities and international organisations, seeking to integrate its institutional identity in the context of the European higher education area. Although the majority of its students were Albanian, the numbers of Macedonian students started rising. The idea behind the project, of course, was that the SEEU would lead to the 'phasing out' of the 'illegal' Albanian University of Tetovo (UT) and become the only institution of higher education in town, thus providing an institutional framework for the integration of the two communities (cf. Czapliński 2008).

However, this did not happen. The provisions of the Ohrid Framework Agreement that established the rules of minority representation also regulated the use of languages, opening up the possibility for a publicly financed Albanian-language institution of higher education. When the Minister of Education was appointed from one of the new ethnic Albanian parties, he interpreted these provisions as allowing a de facto legalisation of the University of Tetovo (ibid.). Thus, the State University of Tetovo (essentially, the University of Tetovo purged of its more radical nationalist elements) was established in 2004. Although the law required it to include programmes taught in Macedonian, in reality, the institution catered primarily to Albanian-speaking students.

At present, Tetovo has two universities, which arose from the same political circumstances but represent different approaches to the issue of interethnic relations. The SEEU has reflected the international community's vision of post-conflict development in Macedonia, with two communities existing side-by-side but integrated into the broader international framework (symbolised by the English language teaching) and also learning each other's languages and interacting. However, critics have noted the tendency of separation into Albanian and Macedonian language streams. The State University of Tetovo (SUT) represents another model, in which language streams are separated from the start, and the institution is recognised, at least implicitly, as primarily serving the needs of the Albanian ethnic group in Macedonia. The two universities compete for the same (or a similar) pool of students; there are indications that professors also frequently teach at both institutions and, since 2008, when the changes in education legislation allowed for the public financing of private higher education institutions, they can also compete for the same funds (cf. Farrington and Abazi 2009). There is no open hostility between the two universities such as that which exists in the case of Kosovo, but there is not a lot of cooperation either.

In sum, the configuration of higher education in Macedonia seems to closely follow the political dynamics that occurred during and following the processes of ethnic mobilisation in the region. Higher education in Tetovo is a reflection of two distinct visions of majority-minority relationships. Whether one of these will prevail in the future is an open question; what is certain is that the development of higher education will depend on the local political dynamics much more than on broader social or political concerns.

Sandžak

Among the universities that developed in the aftermath of the conflicts in the region are the two institutions of higher education in Novi Pazar, the administrative centre of Sandžak. Sandžak, covering the southwest of Serbia and a part of northern Montenegro, has for ages been a mixed region, with Bosniak Muslims constituting about 70 percent of the population. Although the region did not experience open conflict on a scale like those in Bosnia, Kosovo or Macedonia, the Muslim population was more or less severely repressed during the 1990s, both by the regime of Slobodan Milošević and the forces of the neighbouring Republic of Srpska. During the same period, it witnessed different forms of the ethnic mobilisation of Bosniak Muslims, including demands for secession from Serbia; the situation at certain points grew quite tense. The regime change in Serbia in 2000 was supposed to represent a turn in the approach to the 'Muslim question' in Sandžak. The newly elected government sought to integrate ethnic minorities into the state framework, and it was looking for reliable political partners.

During the 1990s, Sandžak became the site of political contestation between the two biggest parties representing Bosniak Muslims: the Party for Democratic Action (SDA) on the one hand, and the Sandžak Democratic Party (SDP) on the other. Although the parties departed from very similar political positions – practically, advocating autonomy for Sandžak – their mutual struggle over political power had managed to draw deep divisions among the Muslims living in Sandžak. The newly elected government in Belgrade was at pains over which party to choose as a political partner without estranging the supporters of the other. The solution was found in Mufti Zukorlić, at the time a relatively young and progressive Muslim cleric.

The Mufti convinced Prime Minister Đinđić that the political divisions are largely due to Sandžak's underdevelopment, and that founding a university in Novi Pazar would boost economic development and even do away with the tensions between the political parties. The government consented and promptly issued an operating licence to a private institution, known as the International University of Novi Pazar (IUNP). Although officially a secular institution, the IUNP was in fact owned by the Islamic Religious Community (IZ) in Serbia, and pretty soon it started framing its role as the caretaker of the interests of *Bosniak Muslims*, and not Sandžak citizens as such. Not surprisingly, this enraged other political forces in Sandžak which were fighting for the monopoly over the right to 'represent' Sandžak Bosniaks. However, they did not have to wait for long.

After Prime Minister Đinđić's assassination in 2003 and the elections in 2004, right-wing forces came to power in Serbia. In order to obtain the majority necessary to form the government, they required the support of a minority political party. Thus, an agreement was reached with the SDA – in exchange for the opening of a new university in Novi Pazar (cf. ICG 2005). The institution, which came to be known as the State University of Novi Pazar, was inaugurated in 2005. From the start, it came across as the exact opposite of the IUNP. The university was financed from the public budget, and explicitly included the "state" designation in its name. Although, in principle, it catered primarily to Bosniak students, it showed no traces of identitarian discourse related to IUNP; on the contrary, in all cases its official narratives emphasised its integration into the state network.

The two universities in Novi Pazar did not, however, attempt a peaceful coexistence that characterised those in Tetovo. From the beginning, these two institutions have been in bitter rivalry. This is not only (nor primarily) a consequence of their competition for, presumably, the same pool of students; rather, it is reflective of the rivalry over the control of Sandžak that exists between their two respective political options. For instance, the SUNP refuses to accept graduates of IUNP into master's programmes; the government has decided not to extend the licence of the IUNP even though it had promised to support it earlier. Representatives of the two universities use every opportunity to slander each other in the media and in the public in general (cf. ICG 2005). In this case, thus, the 'dual' university configuration does not reflect interethnic differences as much as the internal political divisions within a particular ethnic group. In all cases, these differences continue to 'colour' daily life in Sandžak, including its higher education.

Analysis: "Two universities under one roof"?

Although the myriad transformations of higher education during and after the conflicts in former Yugoslavia may appear too confusing for those not acquainted with the political history of the region, these diverse and, indeed, sometimes chaotic processes nevertheless share a number of characteristics. To begin with, all of the universities described above were founded and developed in the processes of ethnic mobilisation that characterised the breakup of former Yugoslavia. While some were developed by (political elites of) 'their' ethnic groups, and others were initiatives of governments or the international community, all of them were founded on the (explicitly or implicitly acknowledged) premise that it is *impossible for specific ethnic groups to obtain higher education in the framework of the existing institutions within the national higher education system.*

At times, this position was developed in the context of political repression – such as, for instance, when the Serbian authorities forbade Albanian students from enrolling in the University of Prishtina in 1990. In other instances, it was framed as a question of linguistic rights – such as the access of Albanians in the Former Yugoslav Republic of Macedonia to higher education in their mother tongue. In yet other cases, such as Sandžak, the ethnic basis for the claims was obscured by arguments related to the need for universities to provide economic development, but the 'identity-building' or 'identity-preserving' mission, at least in the case of the International University of Novi Pazar, quickly came to the forefront. Equally importantly, although specific approaches to the issue of ethnic identities in higher education vary – from the 'integrationist' model, which strove to educate members of different ethnic groups together (such as in the Southeast European University in Tetovo), to the more or less openly segregationist solutions (such as in the secession or parallel development of education institutions in Bosnia and Kosovo) – all of the described solutions seem to acknowledge or take for granted that the education of ethnic, religious and linguistic minorities *requires* separate institutions or 'special' arrangements.

Of course, it would not be impossible to see these outcomes as some sort of 'natural' result of the global processes of diversification of higher education. However, this sort of framing would fail to account for the fact that this is the most prominent, if not the only form of diversification currently happening in these countries – in all other domains, higher education seems to be homogenising rather than diversifying, with former polytechnics offering academic degrees, and multiple institutions striving to become research universities, or to attract foreign students and funding. On the other hand, critics might be inclined to see this form of fragmentation of higher education as a passing consequence of the ethnic conflicts in the region, irrelevant to the understanding of the longer-term dynamics or trends in higher education proper. However, this explanation does not take into account that violent conflicts occur in other places as well, but do not necessarily result in the ethnic or political fragmentation of higher education institutions. Even more importantly, the explanation fails to see that, in all of the above cases, education is not only a consequence of conflict, but an *instrument* of conflict.

Namely, despite the fact that armed conflicts in the region are over, the segregation of higher education embodies and perpetuates the divisions and tensions generated by the conflicts. In some cases, these divisions are ethnic, such as in Bosnia and Kosovo, with members of different ethnic groups attending different institutions. In others, such as in Macedonia and Sandžak, they predominantly run along political lines. In all cases, however, the co-existing universities are in tense relationships. This means that the development of universities in post-conflict Bosnia, Kosovo, Macedonia and Sandžak can be understood as the higher education equivalent of "two schools under one roof" (cf. Clark 2010): not only a sign of, but also an active contributor to the processes of social and political fragmentation in the region.

Students of European integration might write off this aspect of higher education as a specific feature of post-conflict development in the Western Balkans. In this context, the fragmentation of higher education is seen as a consequence of nationalist mobilisations in former Yugoslavia, and transnational processes, such as European integration, are constructed as forces that run counter to it. However, this article wishes to argue that the processes of 'integration' and 'fragmentation' are not separate, but intertwined; they present, fundamentally, two sides of the same coin. Thus, the fragmentation of higher education happening in the Western Balkans is not a separate or opposite process to the European integration. Rather, it needs to be seen as an outcome of the same set of processes shaping higher education in the rest of Europe as well. In *Empire*, Hardt and Negri present a succinct version of this argument:

> In many characterizations the problem rests on a false dichotomy between the global and the local, assuming that the global entails homogenization and undifferentiated identity whereas the local preserves heterogeneity and difference. Often implicit in such arguments is the assumption that the differences in the local are in some sense natural, or at least that their origin remains beyond question [...]. This view can easily devolve into a kind of primordialism that fixes and romanticizes social relations and identities. What needs to be addressed, instead, is precisely the *production of locality*, that is, the social machines that create and re-create the identities and differences that are understood as the local. These differences of locality are neither preexisting nor natural but rather effects of a regime of production. Globality similarly should not be understood in terms of cultural, political, or economic homogenization. Globalization, like localization, should be understood as a *regime* of the production of identity and difference, or really of homogenization and heterogenization (Hardt and Negri 2000: 44-45, original emphasis).

In other words, this article sees education policies as, fundamentally, the *regimes of the production of identity and difference*. Thus, the fragmentation of higher education in the Western Balkans is by no means a 'natural' consequence of ethnic conflict, but an outcome of political choices and actions. In this context, universities are seen as institutions that embody and mediate specific ideas on what constitutes identity (and difference), who should be educated together (and separately) and thus, finally, *what kind of society* higher education should serve.

The image of the society that the development of higher education described in this article conveyed looks quite different from what various studies of convergence of higher education would suggest (cf. Dobbins and Knill 2009). Rather than serving the purpose of developing a 'common', shared, 'European' identity, the universities analysed in this text seem to embody the idea that higher education needs to be aimed at specific social, ethnic and cultural groups. In other words, the vision of the society to which the university is responsible is one that is deeply divided along ethnic, religious and political lines. In this context, universities are constructed not as institutions that seek to overcome these differences, but take them for granted, embody them and thus, most likely, help their reproduction. This is an important lesson for understanding the role of higher education in post-conflict societies; more often than not, education is uncritically assumed to help reconciliation and post-conflict reconstruction. From these examples, it is very obvious how it can also serve different purposes.

Of course, the successor states of former Yugoslavia are neither exceptional nor isolated cases in this respect. As, among others, Delanty (2001: 142) has remarked, "One of the most striking developments in the university since the mid-1980s has been the penetration of what once was regarded as the private domain into the public domain of the university. In short, the western university became the site of major culture wars over race, ethnicity, religion and gender". Issues of identities and group belonging, in contemporary political philosophy usually appearing in the debates on liberalism, communitarianism and multiculturalism, continue to inform public policies (e.g. Dagger 2009, Gutmann 1999, Callan 1997). Unfortunately, the space here does not allow for a longer excursion into this problematic. For this reason, in the concluding part, the discussion will be limited to the implications these tendencies hold for understanding higher education policies in the Western Balkans and, by extension, in the rest of Europe.

Conclusions: What can we learn from universities in the Western Balkans?

The political and philosophical discussions of the universities' roles in 'the society' still, at least implicitly, presume a society marked by the boundaries of a unitary nation-state, of the sort that informed the university projects in the late 19th and the better part of the 20th century. However, the 'society' that the universities are supposed to 'belong' to has changed. It is no longer, nor exclusively, constrained within the boundaries of a unitary (however decentralised) or homogenised nation-state. On one hand, the processes of globalisation and transnationalisation mean that higher education policies are increasingly created by supranational bodies and organisations, with nation-states – especially those relegated to 'peripheries' – tasked primarily with the interpretation or 'implementation' of external recommendations. These processes have contributed to the greater homogenisation of higher education policies as governments and other actors speak an increasingly unified language – of efficiency, inclusiveness, employability etc. At the same time, universities as institutions span physical boundaries, with distance learning, cross-border education provision, and internationalisation all playing a substantial role.

On the other hand, the social and political framework in which universities exist has become increasingly fragmented. Universities are beginning to serve the education of one particular group – regardless of whether it is defined as Roma, Albanians, women, those from lower socio-economic backgrounds, proponents of one political party or another. This development is in fact not entirely different from the times when higher education was reserved for the members of particular social groups, that is, the elites. Of course, no one is in principle excluded from education today; however, identity-based higher education poses some problems for those who do not belong to one of the dominant groups (for instance, Gorani in Kosovo, Serbs in Macedonia, Jews in Bosnia or Roma in Sandžak), and even more for those who do not want to identify with any specific group. If education is framed in terms of group identities, all those who do not partake in this system of classification are more or less automatically excluded from it.

Of course, this text does not wish to argue that identity-specific higher education automatically leads to segregation. But, on the other hand, neither does 'Europeanised' higher education automatically lead to European integration. Following Hardt and Negri (2000), we can say that both tendencies in higher education are mechanisms for the production of identity and difference and, as such, fundamentally political (and politicised) processes. Likewise, as this text has intended to show, they are neither different nor separate; as a matter of fact, the homogenisation and fragmentation of higher education are two sides of the same process, which is not limited to the transformation of higher education in the Western Balkans within the context of European integration. Rather, it is concerned with the broader societal transformation of the former communist countries, usually referred to as a 'transition'. This process today fundamentally shapes public policies in these countries, including higher education, but also collective and group rights, linguistic policies, notions of equality etc. (cf. Offe 2004). It is this multifaceted and complex political context that is defining the field of higher education in Europe today, whether we focus on national, supranational and subnational levels (Zgaga 2007). Learning to recognise the ways in which it interacts with political structures and actors to create novel configurations of systems and institutions thus brings us a step closer to understanding both the transformations of higher education and the transformations of societies that surround and support them today.

References

Amaral, A., G. Neave, C. Musselin, P. Maassen, eds. (2009). *European Integration and the Governance of Higher Education and Research*. Dordrecht: Springer.

Baćević, J. (2010). "Masters or Servants? Power and Discourse in Serbian Higher Education Reform". *Social Anthropology*. Vol. 18. No. 1. 43-56.

Bayerl, A. (2006). "Responsibilities of the International Community for Kosovo Minority Higher Education – the Day after the Status Decision". In: *Higher Education for Minorities in Kosovo*. Prishtina: Kosovo Education Center. Available at http://www.kec-ks.org/botimet_files/education.pdf (accessed 16 July 2012).

Bieber, F. (2008). "Power-sharing and the Implementation of the Ohrid Framework Agreement". In: *Power Sharing and the Implementation of the Ohrid Framework Agreement*. Skopje: Friedrich Ebert Stiftung. 7-40.

Brennan, J. (2002). "Transformation or Reproduction? Contradictions in the Social Role of the Contemporary University". In: J. Enders, O. Fulton (eds.), *Higher Education in a Globalising World: International Trends and Mutual Observations: A Festschrift in Honour of Ulrich Teichler*. Dordrecht: Kluwer.

Britez, R., M. A. Peters (2010). "Internationalization and the Cosmopolitical University". *Policy Futures in Education*. Vol. 8. No. 2. 201-216.

Callan, E. (1997). *"Creating Citizens: Political Education and Liberal Democracy"*. Oxford: Clarendon Press.

Clark, J. N. (2010). "Education in Bosnia-Hercegovina: The Case for Root-and-Branch Reform". *Journal of Human Rights.* Vol. 9. No. 3. 344-362.

Czapliński, M. (2006). "Conflict Prevention and the Issue of Higher Education in the Mother Tongue: The Case of the Republic of Macedonia". *Security and Human Rights.* Vol. 19. No. 4. 261-272.

Czapliński, M. (2008). *Conflict Prevention and the Issue of Higher Education in the Mother Tongue: The Case of the Republic of Macedonia.* Nijmegen: Wolf Legal Publishers.

Daftary, F. (2001). "Conflict Resolution in FYR Macedonia: Power-sharing or the 'Civic Approach'?" *Helsinki Monitor.* Vol. 12. No. 4. 291-321.

Dagger, R. (2009). "Individualism and the Claims of Community". In: T. Christiano, J. Christman (eds.), *Contemporary Debates in Political Philosophy.* Oxford: Wiley-Blackwell.

Daxner, M. (2004). *Intervention on the University of Mitrovica.* Belgrade: Alternative Academic Educational Network.

Delanty, G. (2001). "Challenging Knowledge: The University in the Knowledge Society". Buckingham: Open University Press.

Den Boer, N., C. van der Borgh (2011). "International Statebuilding and Contentious Universities in Kosovo". *Journal of Intervention and Statebuilding.* Vol. 5. No. 1. 67-88.

Dobbins, M., C. Knill (2009). "Higher Education Policies in Central and Eastern Europe: Convergence toward a Common Model?" *Governance.* Vol. 22. No. 3. 397-430.

Doolan, K. (2012). "Local Voices Expressing Global Concerns: Academic Resistance in the Croatian Science and Higher Education Area". Available at www.boell.eu/downloads/HBS_KD_pd.pdf (accessed 19 July 2012).

Enders, J. (2004). "Higher Education, Internationalisation, and the Nation-state: Recent Developments and Challenges to Governance Theory". *Higher Education.* Vol. 47. No. 3. 361–382.

Farrington, D., A. Abazi (2009). "Organization and Management of Non-profit Private Higher Education in a Multi-ethnic and Multi-lingual Environment". *US-China Education Review.* Vol. 6. No. 10. 9-16.

Fraser, N. (2007). "Special Section: Transnational Public Sphere: Transnationalizing the Public Sphere: On the Legitimacy and Efficacy of Public Opinion in a Post-Westphalian World". *Theory, Culture & Society.* Vol. 24. No. 4. 7-30.

Gjurgjeala, E., S. Shala (2005). "Kosovo's over-politicised university. Institute for War and Peace Reporting". Last modified on February 21, 2005. Available at http://iwpr.net/report-news/investigation-kosovos-over-politicised-university (accessed 16 July 2012).

Gutmann, A. (1999). *Democratic education.* (Rev. edition). Princeton: Princeton University Press.

Habermas, J. (2001). *The Postnational Constellation.* Cambridge: MIT Press.

Hardt, M., A. Negri (2000). *Empire.* Cambridge and London: Harvard University Press.

International Crisis Group (ICG) (2005). *Serbia's Sandzak: Still Forgotten?* Brussels: ICG Press.

Keating, A. (2009). "Educating Europe's Citizens: Moving from National to Post-national Models of Educating for European Citizenship". *Citizenship Studies.* Vol. 13. No. 2. 135-151.

Kosovo Education Center (KEC) (2006). *Higher Education for Minorities in Kosovo. An International Discussion Held in Prishtina on 18 May 2006.* Prishtina: Kosovo Education Center. Available at http://www.kec-ks.org/botimet_files/education.pdf (accessed 16 July 2012).

Krause, K. (2009). "Interpreting Changing Academic Roles and Identities in Higher Education". In: M. Tight et al. (eds.), *The Routledge International Handbook of Higher Education.* London: Routledge. 413-426.

Kwiek, M. (2006). *The University and the State: A Study into Global Transformations.* Frankfurt: Peter Lang.

Lynch, K. (2006). "Neo-liberalism and Marketisation: The Implications for Higher Education". *European Educational Research Journal.* Vol. 5. No. 1. 1-17.

Maassen, P., J.P. Olsen, eds. (2007). *University Dynamics and European Integration.* Dordrecht: Springer.

Neave, G. (2000). "Universities' Responsibility to Society: An Historical Explanation of an Enduring Issue". In: G. Neave (ed.), *The Universities' Responsibilities to Societies: International Perspectives.* Paris: IAU. 1-28.

Offe, C. (2004). "Capitalism by Democratic Design? Democratic Theory Facing the Triple Transition in East Central Europe". *Social Research.* Vol. 71. No. 3. 501- 528.

Olsen, J., P. Maassen (2007). "European Debates on the Knowledge Institution: The Modernization of the University at the European Level". In: P. Maassen, J. Olsen (eds.), *University Dynamics and European Integration.* Dordrecht: Springer. 3-23.

Olssen, M., M. Peters (2005). "Neoliberalism, Higher Education and the Knowledge Economy: from the Free Market to Knowledge Capitalism". *Journal of education policy.* Vol. 20. No 3.

Pichl, E., C. Leutloff (1999). "The State of Education in Kosovo after the Cease-fire in June 1999". In: U. Brunnbauer (ed.), *How to Construct Civil Societies? Education and Media in Southeast Europe.* Graz: Center for Study of Balkan Societies and Cultures. 183-194.

Pupovci, D. (2006). "Dream for Multiethnic Education – Fiction and Reality in Higher Education in Kosovo today". In: *Higher Education for Minorities in Kosovo.* Prishtina: Kosovo Education Centre. Available at http://www.kec-ks.org/botimet_files/education.pdf (accessed 16 July 2012).

Readings, B. (1996). *The University in Ruins.* Cambridge, Mass.: Harvard University Press.

Ruegg, W., ed. (2004). *A History of the University in Europe.* Vol. III. Cambridge: Cambridge University Press.

Sommers, M., P. Buckland. (2004). *Parallel Worlds: Rebuilding the Education System in Kosovo.* Paris: International Institute for Educational Planning.

Tomusk, V., ed. (2007). *Creating the European Area of Higher Education: Voices from the Periphery.* Dordrecht: Springer.

Zgaga, P. (2007). *Higher Education in Transition: Reconsiderations on Higher Education in Europe at the Turn of the Millennium.* Umeå: University of Umeå.

Zgaga, P. (2009). "Higher Education and Citizenship: 'The full range of purposes'". *European Educational Research Journal.* Vol. 8. No. 2. 175-188.

The Bosnian Puzzle of Higher Education in the Perspective of the Bologna Process

Tatjana Sekulić

Abstract

This article will focus on the case study of Bosnia and Herzegovina, a country that since 2003 has been officially participating in the process of harmonising its higher education systems based on the Bologna principles (1999). The intention here is to contribute to the state-of-the-art in studies on the transformation of the higher education system(s) in this country, which seems to be relatively under-researched compared to other former Yugoslav successor countries. In the first part of the analysis we aim to reconstruct the institutional configuration of higher education in Bosnia and Herzegovina. In the following parts, the main achievements and obstacles in implementing the reform will be analysed, with references to different dimensions: political, social, economic and cultural. Finally, as Bosnia and Herzegovina has the status of "potential candidate country" to the EU accession, the impact of the European integration and enlargement process on the actual condition of Higher Education will be taken into consideration.

Key words: Bologna Process, Bosnia and Herzegovina, enlargement, European integration, harmonisation, higher education systems

Introduction

The starting point of the harmonisation of the higher education system in Bosnia and Herzegovina (B&H) with the Bologna principles coincided with the first formal step of this country towards European integration. In the same year, 2003, B&H acquired the status of a potential candidate country for EU accession (Thessaloniki European Council, June 2003) and entered the Bologna Process. It seems that from the very beginning the reform of the higher education system has been perceived by both academics and the general public as part of a 'package' imposed by the European Commission through claims related to the *acquis communautaire*, a "powerful non-negotiable condition of accession" and "rock hard principle" of the enlargement road map (Jørgensen 1999), although from the outset the Bologna Process was not directly linked to EU integration. In spite of all initial and current resistance, cultural and political, most universities within B&H have implemented the "3+2+3" or "4+1+3" system in 2005–2006, and currently the reformed doctorate-level studies commence at first enrolment.

As in many other national cases, the reform seems to be perceived as highly problematic and its critical aspects were pointed out by the interviewees in a way quite similar to some of the first conclusions of recent research results on the reform in other European countries.[1] Yet, B&H is unique in its state and institutional composition and complexity, as an ex-Yugoslav post-communist country in transition that is with great difficulty attempting to shed its war heritage (1992–1995). The establishment of a scientific community that should take part in the creation of the European Higher Education Area (EHEA) may be considered one of the pillars of the re-building of political, social and cultural institutions and of re-weaving the devastated social texture of a country which in April 2012 celebrated the 20th anniversary of its contested independence.

Our intention here is, first, to design a map of the main academic institutions and others related to the higher education system(s) in B&H on all levels (state, entity, cantonal and Brčko district), analysing their mutual interaction. Then we will try to identify the most important positive and negative aspects of the implementation of the Bologna Process as it pertains to this specific context, with the help of an explorative pilot research based on in-depth interviews with academic representatives of the University of Sarajevo and of the University of East Sarajevo.[2] The impact of EU integration-related conditions on the process of Bologna implementation will only be examined partially. As for the voice of students, it will be postponed until the second step of this research. A more critical analysis of the Bologna Process itself will also be left for another occasion.

The methodological approach employed in this research was mainly descriptive and analytical; the qualitative inquiry based on in-depth interviews offered some important reference points, but cannot be considered fully significant and exhaustive for this case study.

---

1   See Neave 2002 and 2005, Moscati 2010, Moscati, Regini, and Rostan 2010, Vaira 2011, Pechar 2012.

2   The interviews were conducted in January 2012 with: Rector and Deputy Rector for International Cooperation of the University of East Sarajevo; Deputy Rector of the University of Sarajevo; Dean of the Faculty of Political Sciences, Sarajevo; Head of the Department of Sociology, Faculty of Political Sciences Sarajevo; Vice-Dean for International Cooperation of the Faculty for Natural Sciences and Mathematics; Vice-Dean for International Cooperation of the Faculty of Philosophy, Sarajevo.

Short historical overview of the development of higher education institutions in Bosnia and Herzegovina

The first modern higher education institutions of B&H were formed during and after World War II, with the creation of the Agriculture Faculty (1940), the Medical Faculty (1944), the Law Faculty and the Higher School for Educational Sciences (1946), followed by the establishment of the University of Sarajevo in 1949. It remained for several decades the only Bosnian university until 1976, when three other universities were established in Banja Luka, Mostar and Tuzla. In the past, several institutions that could be considered at the higher education level were situated in the city of Sarajevo, such as the Higher School of Sufi Philosophy founded in 1531 by Gazi Husrev Beg, the Shariah Law Higher School from 1887 or the Sarajevo Seminary founded in 1882, which is considered the first Serbian high school in B&H. Bosnian youngsters also used to continue their studies at the nearby universities with a longer tradition such as the University of Zagreb founded in 1669, or the University of Belgrade founded in 1905, or elsewhere, if possible, such as in Vienna or Istanbul.

A further development would wait until the 1990s and a time of war (1992–1995) during which the territory and institutions of the former Socialist Republic of Bosnia and Herzegovina were split along new dividing lines based foremost on the nationality of the three constituent 'peoples' of this country: Bošnjaks (former Bosnian Muslims), Bosnian Croats and Bosnian Serbs (Sekulić 2002). The Washington Agreement of February 1994 between the political and military élites of Bošnjaks and Bosnian Croats conceived the Federation of Bosnia and Herzegovina and determined its future cantonal structure, while the new form of state was decided by the Dayton Peace Agreement signed in November 1995: one state composed of two entities, the Federation of B&H and the Republic of Srpska, plus the Brčko District with a special status. The Federation was subdivided into ten Cantons with a high degree of autonomy, especially in relation to the culture and education spheres. All institutional levels of state power(s) act with limited sovereignty since all important political decisions have had to obtain the approval of the High Representative of the International Community. The Office of the High Representative (OHR) was also established by the Dayton Peace Agreement, with all ambiguities related to the meaning and contextualisation of what should be an 'International Community'.

At the very beginning of the conflict in April 1992, two of four Bosnian universities were divided: the University of Sarajevo obtained its counterpart in the University of East Sarajevo, and the Džemal Bijedić University of Mostar in the University of Mostar (*Sveučilište u Mostaru*). The analysis of the role and responsibility of the intellectuals and academic teaching staff in the creation and perpetration of the ethno-nationalist ideology, with its associated 'language of hatred', but also of significant examples of democratic and liberal patterns of resistance to it, goes beyond the purpose of this work. Yet what should be briefly mentioned is the immeasurable damage caused by the killing of teachers and students. The main victims of the war in B&H (1992–1995), above all other dimensions of division – ethno-national belonging, the question of guilt and responsibility, the definition of the war etc. – were youngsters, as demonstrated by the Research and Documentation Centre Sarajevo: almost 42 percent of the war victims belonged to the age group 18–35.[3] The material damage is difficult to count: university buildings, research laboratories and libraries were destroyed, such as the University Library of Sarajevo that was burned down by Republic of Srpska military and paramilitary forces in late August 1992. There are no available statistics about the brain-drain of university professors, researchers and students during and after the war, but in 2009 two-thirds (66.5 percent) of those in the age group 18–35 expressed their wish to live in another country, if possible (UNDP 2010: 12 and 122). Among other reasons, just one can be mentioned: in June 2012, the actual unemployment rate of those under 25 years of age was almost 58 percent (European Commission 2012).

The legacy of war has heavily influenced the post-war development of higher education institutions in this country, especially during the first years after the war and before B&H entered the process of EU integration. As often stressed by the interviewees, some of these basic systemic deficiencies make the general improvement very slow and difficult to achieve. Government(s) instability – "political gridlock" was the expression used in the formal documents of the OHR, along with a fragile civil society and other serious economic and social issues, are problems shared with other countries in transition. Then, the weak central state power and lack of will by political élites on the entity and cantonal levels to cooperate on a process to build common institutions are features that more specifically describe the

---

3   See www.idc.org.ba.

Bosnian case. Together with the issue of memories of war and the questionable reconciliation process, all dimensions of the context complexity emerge quite clearly.

At present, the public higher education system in B&H consists of eight state universities, two in the Republic of Srpska (Sarajevo East and Banja Luka), six in the territory of the Federation (Sarajevo, Zenica, Tuzla, two in Mostar, Bihać), and two independent institutes of higher education. On the other hand, B&H is facing the phenomenon of the proliferation or 'mushrooming' of private universities as has already happened in the other countries in transition, with particular regard to those in the Western Balkans area (Zgaga 2010). Seventeen HE institutions (universities, colleges and higher schools) were established in the territory of Republic of Srpska, thirteen in Federation and three in Brčko District.

The fragmentation of the universities, especially the private ones, together with the political and administrative division of the state universities, constantly increases the difficulties of academic practices. In the following chapters we will try to identify the most important obstacles to implementation of the Bologna reform, starting from the EHEA basic priorities – new legislation, new university governance of the "re-integrated university", quality assurance mechanisms, the European credit transfer and accumulation system (ECTS), curriculum renewal, democratic and ethical standards and the recognition of multi-ethnicity (Zgaga 2003).

Structural characteristics of higher education system(s) in Bosnia and Herzegovina

The structural dimension of the higher education system in B&H seems to be one of the most decisive variables in implementation of the reform. The historical heritage of the higher education system of former Yugoslavia, as the basic field of the Bologna reform implementation, can hardly be defined by the usual analytical terms such as the Napoleonic *or* Humboldtian model. The university systems in socialist regimes were of course well divorced from the ideal of an 'ivory tower', although it might be argued that certain autonomy of the academic community was achieved in the Yugoslav case. It may be easier to find some similarities with the Napoleonic ideal of a state-control model, radicalised by the post-totalitarian political dominion over all other spheres of society, education and science included. Savić (1998: 12-

14), for example, described the socialist system of education as a "polygon for practicing the official ideology" of the regime, framed within two metaphors: "locomotive" and "prison" (*Lepoglava*),[4] where the question of "academic liberties" was seen even more radically as "abstaining from politics" – isolation was a price for a certain degree of autonomy and freedom within the community of peers.

Nevertheless, we agree with Turajlić (2009: 16-17) when she asserts that the former Yugoslav higher education system had some specific characteristics regarding some other socialist regimes, adding that certain aspects of the Yugoslav experience (or experiment) should not simply be rubbished together with other pieces from the communist heritage. Specifically, she spoke about the introduction of a *self-government* model in all faculties in the mid-1960s, and of a certain level of gradual decrease of state control, "particularly within the faculties of natural sciences, bio-medical sciences and engineering". In some cases, the degree and quality of academic autonomy, especially at faculty level, improved with the introduction of this new concept at all institutional levels and university faculties. In the mid-1970s, all institutions were re-structured as '*organisations of associated labour*', with a *workers' assembly* as a major decision-making body, and that increased the process of modelling the entire society as a (socialist) enterprise, providing new kinds of governance challenges to the university administration.

In any case, the tradition of a specific kind of relationship between individual faculties and the university, in other words, very strong and independent faculties and quite weak universities as a "loose confederation of the faculties", still persists in the post-communist and after-war period (Zgaga 2010). This pattern created a kind of paradox: while the higher education system of the former Yugoslavia was under straight political control of the Federal and Republic Ministries of Education, notwithstanding the rhetoric of top-down-imposed self-management, its internal organisation was completely decentralised (Tiplić 2008). Yet that does not mean the system as such could be considered fragmented in a

---

4   The *Lepoglava* prison, situated near the city of Varaždin in northern Croatia, became
     famous during the period of the Kingdom of Yugoslavia since many communist
     leaders, Josip Broz Tito *in primis*, were incarcerated in it. The myth of this prison as
     an 'excellence school of Marxism' was created by the communist regime after World
     War II.

negative sense: decentralisation sometimes produced more liberal practices within independent faculties, as was stressed by one of the interviewees:

> For certain aspects the lack of integration was not negative for several reform procedures, a number of processes could be smothered if we would insist on integration without structural and informatics support. Financial autonomy of the faculties was welcome concerning the actual situation of the economy, so that they had more possibility to interact with the economic and social institutions and earn proper funds that the Ministries or Government were not able to assure (Deputy Rector of the University of Sarajevo).

However, today the higher education system in B&H primarily manifests its transitional structure. The oldest institution, the University of Sarajevo, is still decentralised in almost all important aspects, probably because it is more difficult to reform a profoundly grass rooted model of governance, although some important steps have been taken in the last few years:

> We are going toward the integration, that process has never been blocked. Many functions that are not strictly academic are already integrated. [...] Our approach is maybe too slow, but it is systematic and it really needs structured informatics support, with specific software imposed (Deputy Rector of the University of Sarajevo).

The construction of the re-integrated model of university governance seems to depend on its size, with smaller universities being much easier to manage, and on age, with 'younger' universities embracing the Bologna and EHEA Principles with fewer administrative problems. The first university restructured in this sense was the University of Tuzla (2000), followed by those of Zenica, Banja Luka, East Sarajevo (2008–2009), and Bihać (2010), although all of them still consider themselves in the process of transition. The two Universities of Mostar are still at the beginning of the process of integration due among other reasons to the absence of a Cantonal Law in accordance with the Framework Law on Higher Education. In any case, the university integration process seems to be accepted by all stakeholders, both academics and political, and is slowly proceeding, notwithstanding different kinds of obstacles.

Yet the political structure of the state remains the most important variable considering the specific Bosnian context. As mentioned, there is no Ministry for University and/or Education on the state level, just a Sector for Science and Education as part of the Ministry for Civil Affairs, as was reported by the Commission of the Sector in 2011:

> Organisation of the education system in B&H is founded by the Constitution so that the sphere of education is under the complete and undivided jurisdiction of the Entity of the Republic of Srpska, of the Cantons (10) of the Federation B&H and of the District of Brčko. Every one of these twelve administrative units has its own Ministry of Education, laws regarding the sphere of education, a budget, the right to decide the policy of education; all of them have rights and duties related to the mandate of the respective government, responsible for the organisation and functioning of education in its own field of responsibility (Ministry of Civil Affairs 2011: 2).

This institution has no power of governance, only for counselling and coordination. The B&H Federation's main consultative body is the Council of Ministers, formed by ten Cantonal Ministries of Education combining different names and responsibilities – Culture, Education, Science and Sport. The Republic of Srpska has a Ministry of Culture and Education, where centralised power facilitates the decision-making process. Finally, the Brčko District has a Sector for Education and Culture.

If what Savić (1998: 12) wrote more than ten years ago is still acceptable – that "the main part of the former East European regimes did not permit the emancipation of their universities from its founder State" and that the "bureaucratic delegitimisation of the university institution is still controlled by State ministries of Education", the absurdity of the Bosnian fragmented context could become more transparent. The same authoritarian control pattern, applied on the level of these 'statelets', continuously slows down and obstructs the decision-making process at both the single university and on the state level.

Consequently, regarding legislation, B&H only adopted the Framework Law on Higher Education in 2007 after many years of discussion, even if it was not binding. Every single decision of state importance has to be first made with a consensus of the ten Cantonal ministries, the Ministry of the Republic of Srpska and of the Brčko district. One can easily imagine how this decision-making process is exposed to the negative synergy and short-sightedness of local political powers. This situation is problematic especially regarding the Federation B&H, such as in the case of giving a licence for the creation of a new university. Since all decisions are taken on the Cantonal level, the quality assurance procedures are exposed to the will of the local political elite, which has negative effects on mutual institutional trust on the state, regional and European levels.

Ethno-nationalist rhetoric is still present in academic practices, as a pattern of a "return to the times of national universities" (Zgaga 2010: 7), starting from the self-representation of the universities on their site's home-pages that, in some cases, seems to invoke the logic of the "invention of tradition" (Hobsbawm and Ranger 1986). Notwithstanding this, some important positive perspectives on the changes and challenges emerged from the interviews with the institutional representatives.

Towards full implementation of the Bologna principles: 'An Obstacle Course'

From 2007 onwards, after the adoption of the Framework Law of Higher Education, B&H formally accepted the European strategic targets for development of the higher education system based on the Bologna Declaration. A parallel transformation process started. On one side there was the institutional and legislative reconstruction of the system as a whole and, on the other, there was tedious work on the structural renewal of the curriculum, together with the creation of a new evaluation system and accreditation patterns with quality assurance mechanisms, allied with reconsiderations of the relationship between the university and labour market, the real mobility of teachers and students on the European and international levels and the (re)construction of the fundaments for scientific research.

The Framework Law defined the legislative basis for the foundation of several institutions that permitted and promoted cooperation in this area at the state level. The Conference of Ministers of Education and the Rector's Conference of Bosnia and Herzegovina were both established in 2008. The first is considered the highest permanent counselling body although it has no competence to interfere in any constitutive or legislative power of the government(s) at any level; in B&H it is made up of 14 ministries responsible for educational issues. The second one, the Rector's Conference, is also a counselling institution, dealing concretely with implementation of the university reform. This institution still has quite a weak political impact regarding issues of educational policy, but its power is growing, as was underlined by our interlocutors, and is becoming a significant pressure group amongst local and state political élites, and more and more capable of influencing their decisions. Still, it has no autonomous financial resources, not even a secretary office or database. In order to operate in a more consistent way, the Rector's Conference founded the Commission for Monitoring the Bologna Process in December 2010.

The Framework Law (2008) also established two independent state agencies in the area of Higher Education: the Agency for the Development of Higher Education and Quality Assurance, and the Centre for Information and Recognition of Qualifications in Higher Education. Both of these are members of European and international networks. The Agency is a member of INQAAHE, an associate member of ENQA and a full member of the CEEN Network, while the Centre participates in the work of ENIC/NARIC.

According to the Report on the Condition of Higher Education in Bosnia and Herzegovina published in September 2011 by the Ministry of Civil Affairs, the main legislative framework has been established and the road map for the development of all segments of the higher education system is well defined by the Strategy of the Development of Education in B&H 2008–2015, adopted in 2007.

The basic elements of the Bologna model have been formally implemented in all higher education institutions. Faculties are traditionally structured in several departments, each of them responsible for organising three cycles of degree courses: undergraduate (three or four years), postgraduate – master's degree (two or one year) and a three-year PhD. The ECTS is fully operative although with several negative characteristics, similar to other European experiences. The significance of the credits has to be better defined as their application is still quite formal, with more coordination among academics and teaching staff on the renewal of the curriculum needed.

Most university courses are at the undergraduate level. In July 2011, 624 courses were being conducted in both public and private universities, this figure decreased to 477 for the second-degree-level courses. The third-level courses were offered only in seven universities – four private and three public – in 2010–2011 there were 61 active PhD courses based on Bologna principles. The Report indicates a lack of finance, insufficient numbers of highly qualified teaching staff, together with infrastructural deficiencies as the main causes of these negative aspects. The impact of this situation needs to be further contextualised. Despite the lack of statistical reporting on education, a number of quite indicative data is available: only 5 percent of B&H citizens have a university degree, which is extremely low compared to the European standard of 25 percent. B&H is at the bottom of the EU scale regarding university enrolment for those aged between 19–24 years. Only 20 percent of youth are actually enrolled in some higher education institution with a dropout rate about 13 percent, and the average time spent in university is between 5 and 7 years. The number of students is approximately 142,000 (2010–2011), while the number of teaching staff amounts to about 4,000, in other words, one professor for every 35 students.[5]

Although all universities have introduced the ECTS system of evaluation since 2005–2006, there are still huge difficulties regarding the recognition of the credits and diplomas obtained, not only from abroad but also inside the country; notwithstanding these shortcomings, diploma supplements are regularly offered by almost 85 percent of the universities.

Another great problem is the formal regulation of university qualifications and the definition of professions which is still under discussion at the state level. While universities in the territory of the Republic of Srpska harmonised their laws with the Lisbon Recognition Convention (2003), in many cases Cantonal Laws on Higher Education are not yet harmonised with the Framework Law (which is not compulsory!), so that some universities still apply the degree recognition procedure based on the 1988 Law. In all these cases, that currently concern seven out of ten cantons, instead of legislation, counselling bodies produce recommendations with which the local academic and political powers arbitrarily comply. The participation of students and researchers in mobility and exchange programmes proposed at the EU level, like Erasmus Mundus or Jean Monnet, is made even more difficult by all these issues, coupled with the general political situation in the country that often slows down the process of including B&H students and teachers in European flows of knowledge and research. For example, as the state of B&H did not adopt a decentralised structure of the system for administering pre-accession EC funds before the deadline, as it had been requested, the last evaluation of the Commission (European Commission 2012) on this issue was negative, with the indirect consequence that the country again remained with a restricted right to participate in programmes of scientific exchange. This is a very good illustration of the interrelation between the reform of the higher education institutions and the demands of the EU pre-accession process.

While the Centre for Information and Recognition of Qualifications tries to solve this kind of problems, the Agency has been facing some other important issues. From 2008 on, the Agency produced all the basic documents and acts essential for its functioning: *Criteria for the accreditation of higher education institutions in B&H* (2010), *Criteria for*

---

5   All data were provided by the B&H Ministry of Civil Affairs.

the selection of domestic and international experts for evaluation and revision of the quality of HE institutions and courses (2009)*, and Standards for the quality assurance in the higher education system of B&H* (2007)*.* The list of experts was formed by 334 persons belonging to different categories: academic staff, stakeholders from the labour market, students and international experts; the training of local experts has been promoted. The Agency helped organise an internal system of quality assurance in almost all public and some private institutions which then initiated a standard model of self-evaluation.

To date, a few universities have introduced self-evaluated reports and declared themselves ready to enter the process of external evaluation, such as the University of Sarajevo. Although all these procedures were respected, the basic work of the Agency, which concerns the accreditation of higher education institutions and courses, is still far from over. Article 61 of the Framework Law gave temporary accreditation to all higher education institutions in B&H, setting for them an initial deadline of two years, then four, to end the accreditation procedure for every single course, based on the standards and criteria defined by documents of the Agency. The deadline expired on August 2011, and by October 2012 there had only been six cases of higher education institutions applying for the accreditation, and for which commissions of experts were established. Just one of them is situated in the territory of Federation, the University of Zenica, while the other five are private universities and high schools of the Republic of Srpska.

The consequence of this situation is that no higher education institution in the country can formally be considered accredited in terms of the Framework Law. It is again the domain of politics that is responsible if the job has not been done yet, as the ministries had a duty to define a legal framework for the accreditation procedure in the form of a Law on Higher Education, or another kind of legal regulation of this issue. Until October 2012, just three out of ten cantons had produced an appropriate legislative basis for these procedures.

Another important question concerns the financial aspect: the European standards and recommendations (ENQA 2005) indicate that the procedure should be financed by public institutions, but not by the responsible ministry or the higher education institution involved, as the quality assurance and accreditation need to be performed by autonomous subjects. In this specific context, it seems quite difficult to provide convincing arguments for the importance of the accreditation procedure in order to add it to the agenda of political priorities of both the ministries and civil society actors.

Finally, according to almost all of the interviewees, the impact of the European integration process on the harmonisation of the higher education system in B&H has been crucial, despite there being no direct and formal connection between the Bologna Process and EU educational and research policy. The political pressure of EU institutions acts through the accession road map promoted by the European Commission, in accordance with the B&H orientation to the integration. Financial support for the structural reform projects has also been essential as the country itself is still unable to produce the material basis for deep changes. The main sources are funds that promote the process of institution building, such as the Instrument for Pre-Accession Assistance (IPA) funds and Tempus programmes, in particular Tempus III (Modernisation of Higher Education in Countries surrounding the EU, 2000–2006) and Tempus IV (Reform of Higher Education through International University Cooperation, 2007–2013).

Any major integration of B&H into the EU's research programmes, that should allow for an improvement to the current poor condition of research, is still waiting for political, economic and social reforms that will help the country achieve the status of a candidate for the EU (Sekulić 2011), although the EC Progress Report for 2012 indicated some "slight increase" in the number of submissions under the Seventh EU Research Framework Programme (FP7). Again, the Republic of Srpska has adopted the Law on Scientific Research Activities and Technology for 2012–2016, while the Federation is still waiting for the harmonisation of the legislation on cantonal level to adopt the Law on the Science and Research and Development System and Policy. "Insufficient communication and coordination between science Ministries and Entities", denounced by the Progress Report 2012, remains both the cause and consequence of this vicious circle (European Commission 2012).

Conclusion

The condition of the higher education system in B&H, almost ten years after its formal access to the Bologna Process, leaves little room for optimism. The European Commission Progress Report for 2012 again used relatively negative expressions to describe the actual situation in the field of education:

"some progress", "slight increase", "no harmonised procedures yet", although it seems to be a little more generous than the previous report (European Commission 2011). If we compare this to the basic Bologna principles adopted within the EHEA – quality, mobility, diversity and openness – it would be really easy to find arguments confirming the statements of the Progress Report, as this brief analysis has demonstrated. In fact, obstacles and missing results are much more visible than any other dimension.

Nevertheless, most of the interviewed actors involved in the process itself sustained with a firm conviction, although with a critical distance, the importance of the Bologna Process for institution- and education-building practices in a country with such a recent heritage of war and its consequences. No state in the region has had the same starting point and needed so much effort in every single step. Maybe in this case another scientific endeavour is needed, capable of identifying those aspects that have been improved as regards international mobility, the autonomy of the universities, student participation in the governance of higher education, public responsibility for higher education, the social dimension of the Bologna Process *notwithstanding* economic difficulties, and cultural resistance or political obstruction from a certain part of local and regional élites.

As one of the interviewees said:

> The reform based on Bologna principles is the best thing that could have happened to Bosnia and Herzegovina. I know that it is quite a controversial statement, but I'm very glad to repeat it in public. It is almost the only European project that has been giving a certain kind of results, although it seems, looking from outside, that they are not sufficient or still too slim (Deputy Rector of the University of Sarajevo).

References

ENQA (2005). *Standards and Guidelines for Quality Assurance in the European Higher Education Area*. Helsinki.

European Commission (2011). "Bosnia and Herzegovina 2011 Progress Report, October 2011". Available at http://ec.europa.eu/enlargement/index_en.htm (accessed 22 October 2012).

European Commission (2012). "Bosnia and Herzegovina 2012 Progress Report, October 2012". Available at http://ec.europa.eu/enlargement/index_en.htm (accessed 22 October 2012).

Framework Law on Higher Education in Bosnia and Herzegovina (Okvirni zakon o visokom obrazovanju u Bosni i Hercegovini). *Official Gazette of Bosnia and Herzegovina*. No. 59/2007.

Hobsbawm, E., T. Ranger (1983). *The Invention of Tradition*. Cambridge: Cambridge University Press.

Jørgensen, K. E. (1999). "The Social Construction of the Acquis Communautaire: A Cornerstone of the European Edifice". *European Integration Online Papers (EIoP)*. Vol. 3. No. 5. Available at http://eiop.or.at/eiop/texte/1999-005a.htm (accessed 22 October 2012).

Law on Higher Education (Zakon o visokom obrazovanju). *Official Gazette of Republic of Srpska*. No. 28/1994.

Ministry of Civil Affairs – Bosnia and Herzegovina (2011). Report on the Condition of the Higher Education and on the Realization of the Framework Law on Higher Education in Bosnia and Herzegovina (Izvještaj o stanju u području visokog obrazovanja i izvršenju Okvirnog zakona o visokom obrazovanju u Bosni i Hercegovini). September 2011.

Moscati, R., ed. (2010). *Come e perché cambiano le università in Italia e in Europa: Nuove politiche dell'istruzione superiore e resistenza al cambiamento*. Napoli: Liguori Editore.

Moscati, R., M. Regini, M. Rostan, eds. (2010). *Torri d'avorio in frantumi? Dove vanno le università europee*. Bologna: il Mulino.

Neave, G. (2002). "Anything Goes: or, How the Accommodation of European Integration an Inspiring Number of Contradictions". *Tertiary Education and Management*. Vol. 8. No. 3. 181-197.

Neave, G. (2005). "Euro-Philiacs, Euro-Sceptics and Europhobics: Higher Education Policy, Values and Institutional Research". *Tertiary Education and Management*. Vol. 11. No. 2. 113-129.

Pechar, H. (2012). "The Decline of an Academic Oligarchy. The Bologna Process and 'Humboldt's Last Warriors'". In: A. Curaj et al. (eds.), *European Higher Education at the Crossroads: Between Bologna Process and National Reforms*. Dordrech: Springer. 613-630.

Savić, O. (1998). "Da li je univerzitet subjekt znanja?". *Beogradski krug / Belgrade Circle*. No. 3-4 1997, 1-2 1998. 9-16.

Sekulić, T. (2002). *Violenza etnica. I Balcani tra il nazionalismo e la democrazia*. Roma: Carocci.

Strategy of the Development of Education in B&H 2008-2015 (2007). Council of Ministers of Bosnia and Herzegovina.

The Gallup Organization (2009). "Views on European Union Enlargement". Analytical Report. *Flash Eurobarometer*. No. 257.

Tiplić, D. (2008). Managing Organizational Change during Institutional Upheaval: Bosnia-Herzegovina's Higher Education in Transition. BI Norwegian School of Management Oslo, Series of Dissertation, 5/2008.

Turajlić, S. (2009). "From Tug-of-War towards a Study of Policy". In: M. Vukasović (ed.), *Financing Higher Education in South-Eastern Europe: Albania, Croatia, Montenegro, Serbia, Slovenia*. Belgrade: Centre for Education Policy.

UNDP (2010). *Early Warning System*. Report on B&H. Sarajevo.

Vaira, M. (2011). *La costruzione della riforma universitaria e della riforma didattica. Idee, norme, pratiche, attori*. Milano: LED.

Zgaga, P. (2003). "The External Dimension of the Bologna Process. Higher Education in South East Europe and the European Higher Education Area in a Global World: Reforming the Universities of South East Europe in view of the Bologna Process". *Higher Education in Europe*. Vol. 28. No. 3. 251-258.

Zgaga, P. (2010). "The Role of Higher Education in National Development. South-Eastern Europe and Reconstruction of the Western Balkans". In: *The Europa World of Learning 2011*. London: Routledge. 19-24. Available at http://bit.ly/rf4MpT (accessed 22 October 2012).

Web sources

Agency for Development of Higher Education and Quality Assurance: www.hea.gov.ba

Centre for Information and Recognition of Qualifications, Bosnia and Herzegovina: www.cip.gov.ba

Ministry for Civil Affairs, Bosnia and Herzegovina: www.mcp.gov.ba

European Commission, Department for Enlargement, Bosnia and Herzegovina: www.delB&H.ec.europa.eu

National Tempus Office in B&H: www.tempusB&H.com

University of Sarajevo: www.unsa.ba

University of East Sarajevo: www.ues.rs.ba

Centre for Research and Documentation Sarajevo: www.idc.org.ba

Reclaiming the Role of Higher Education in Croatia: Dominant and Oppositional Framings

Danijela Dolenec and Karin Doolan

Abstract

Framed within a critical theory perspective that draws on Fraser's (2000 and 2003) concept of justice, this chapter outlines the development of the neoliberal doctrine in higher education and analyses how it influenced the official discourse in Croatia with respect to the concepts of development, and the role of the state and higher education in particular. The analysis shows that the official rhetoric primarily advanced a marketised conception of higher education whose role is to service the labour market and contribute to economic growth. This dominant framing of the role of higher education is contrasted to the oppositional discursive framing by the Independent Student Initiative, a student protest movement in Zagreb that has rejected neoliberal reforms of higher education. The movement framed higher education as a public good and emphasised the role of the state in shielding public services from privatisation and commodification. The oppositional discourse of the Independent Student Initiative is interpreted as a transformative struggle against socio-economic injustice which has extended the spectrum of the political Left in Croatia.

Key words: student protest movement, critical theory, neoliberal doctrine, higher education policy, Croatia

Introduction

Critical reflections on the 'neoliberal turn' have in recent times taken on dramatic overtones (Giroux 2011, Saunders 2010, Lynch 2006). Neoliberalism has been described as "the most dangerous ideology of the current historical moment" (Giroux 2011: 1), which not only seeks to annul the contradictions between democratic values and market fundamentalism, but also weakens any viable political agency. Social movements that have opposed neoliberal politics initially spread under the anti-globalisation umbrella in the late 1990s, signalling the start of a "ferocious contest over people's interpretations and understandings of the supposed benefits of neoliberal economic policies" (Ayres 2004: 11). However, since at that time many Western states were experiencing periods of seeming prosperity, the contested framings of the effects of neoliberal policies were fighting an uphill battle. This situation has changed substantially since the start of the economic crisis in 2008 which, according to authors such as Streeck (2011), has exposed the ugly underbelly of neoliberal policies through a succession of growing public deficits and private indebtedness. After the global financial system meltdown, governments have sought to restore their respective economies by rescuing banks, and then passing the bill onto the average citizen who is paying for this rescue with their private savings, as well as suffering cuts in reduced public services and higher taxation (ibid.). The prospects of ordinary citizens today are now frequently discussed within the context of a 'Lost Decade', so it is no wonder that the effects of the economic policies implemented since the early 1990s are undergoing a renewed wave of criticism.

The renewed struggle over how we understand the effects of neoliberal policies is happening within the field of higher education as well, and not only in Western Europe. Since 2008 student protest movements have emerged across Europe, in the United States and Canada, as well as in Chile, Mexico and other Latin American states. The Independent Student Initiative that was formed in 2008 at the University of Zagreb joined these movements in an affirmation of education as a public good based on democratic principles and the values of freedom and equality (Academic Solidarity 2012). This chapter focuses on this student protest movement as a case study of an oppositional discursive framing that rejected neoliberal reforms in higher education. After critically reviewing the genesis and development of neoliberal policies in higher education and introducing Nancy Fraser's conceptualisation of social justice, the chapter analyses ways in which the dominant neoliberal discourse has found its expression in government documents, as well as how this has been challenged through the emergence of the student protest movement in Zagreb.

The basic argument is that whereas constructions of higher education in official state documents predominantly reflect the neoliberal model, the student protests in Croatia construct higher education along the counter-hegemonic humanist tradition. It is argued that the protest movement in Croatia advanced a critique of capitalism and the neoliberal model of marketised education and, in Fraser's (2003) terms, a transformative struggle against injustice. The chapter suggests that the protest movement is a 'new subject' on the political playing field that has extended the spectrum of the political Left in Croatia, using equality as the main yardstick for judgements against neoliberalism as an "ideology of inequality" (Negri 1989: 55).

The neoliberal doctrine in higher education

Neoliberalism is a diverse set of ideas, discursive representations, public policies and practices which have three core beliefs in common: the benevolence of the free market, minimal state intervention, and the individual as a rational economic actor (Saunders 2010). It represents the belief that market-led growth will trickle down to benefit all members of society, as well as the belief that the market is intrinsically more efficient than government (Self 1999). The political ascendancy of neoliberal policies is attributed to Thatcher's and Reagan's terms in office in the early 1980s, from where they spread across Europe and globally. This was a time when the concept of the welfare state was coming under "sustained intellectual attack" (Le Grand and Robinson 1984). The belief that many of the economic, social and political problems of the period were attributable to the continuing growth of the welfare state was established as a dominant doctrine (Pierson 1998). The public sector was accused as the main culprit for the sluggishness of Europe's economies and, as a result, government budgets sustained strong cutbacks (Le Grand and Robinson 1984, Thesiens 2004). Thatcher's and Reagan's governments broke the post-war consensus according to which the state intervened in the market to provide security, prosperity and greater equality (Judt 2010), and instead pushed for the liberalisation of trade and investment, tax cuts and cuts to public spending, deregulation and privatisation of state-owned industries (Ayres 2004).

The implementation of these policies led to a dismantling of the post-war settlement between labour and capital, which used to be based on a strong welfare state, unionised workers, the political objective of full-employment and Keynesian economic policies (Streeck 2011). The result was, according to authors such as Bourdieu (2003: 35), a steady erosion of the welfare state and the loosening of safeguards in "the interests of the dominated, the culturally and economically dispossessed, women, [and] stigmatised ethnic groups". According to Brown (2005: 42), the new role of the state became facilitating competition and free trade, while the cost-benefit calculus was to become "the measure of all state practices". Such a conception reduces the citizen to a consumer, an individual constantly in pursuit of ways to increase his/her human capital (Saunders 2010, Brown 2005).

These neoliberal economic policies were taken up by the European Union in its reforms during the 1990s (Judt 2010). The EU's Lisbon

Strategy was adopted in 2000 with the objective of boosting growth and competitiveness in Europe. This was a turning point in terms of the role of the state in EU policy discourse whereby the welfare state became colonised by economic policy-making. In other words, while in the 1980s the EU discourse on social policy was couched within the concept of the European welfare state, since the Lisbon Strategy the EU's discourse on social policy has become much more economically-oriented (Dolenec 2007). Chalmers and Lodge (2003) trace it as being born out of the shadows of the Stability and Growth Pact, whereby the new politics of the welfare state were designed within the constraints of the procedures guarding macroeconomic performance which prohibit excessive government deficits and public debt. The Maastricht criteria from 1992 and the Stability and Growth Pact from 1998 effectively closed a number of policy options available for pursuing social objectives which has made it difficult to extract more resources for social policy (Green et al. 2000, Esping Andersen 2001). As a result, the EU's policy prescriptions since the 1990s and the 2000s started to increasingly resemble those of international financial organisations such as the IMF and the World Bank (Guillen and Palier 2004). In a deliberate emulation of the US model of development, the Washington consensus on deregulation, the minimal state and low taxation travelled to Europe (Judt 2010).

In higher education the neoliberal doctrine is manifested as the construction of higher education as a private good to be purchased through tuition fees, through cuts in state funding, via the notion that the primary role of higher education is to drive economic progress, in the increase of adjunct labour, or through the focus on individual achievement (Giroux 2011, Saunders 2010). At their core, neoliberal policies in higher education represent a reduced reliance on public funding and a reorientation towards private investment both in the form of increasing student tuition fees and third-party investments. They also encompass the introduction of management practices from private sector enterprises which include the professionalisation of university management and the separation of academic from management functions, the introduction of quantified targets, regular assessments that are tied to funding and, finally, the progressive implementation of output-based public financing. In addition, the application of market logic to universities and learning emphasises the utility of knowledge and its relationship to the labour market (Olssen and Peters 2005). According to Brown (2011), a number of writers expound what they see as the benefits of this marketised higher education system compared to a government-controlled non-market system: increased efficiency, responsiveness to 'customers', and innovation and revenue diversification. Apple emphasises how in a period of crisis "We are told by neoliberals that only by turning our schools, teachers, and children over to the competitive market will we find a solution" (Apple 2001: 409).

Perhaps the key shift towards the neoliberal doctrine in higher education has been the assertion that its primary role is to drive economic progress and realise national economic interests (Jessop 2008). Indeed, since the 1990s public funding for universities has been made contingent upon a more direct contribution to the economy (ibid.). For obvious reasons, this rationale has particularly devastating consequences in the field of the humanities and liberal arts, as has been thoroughly documented (Nussbaum 2010, Giroux 2011, Collini 2012). In addition, by advancing the assumption of individuals guided by self-interest, the neoliberal doctrine has shifted the definition of citizenship towards one of 'consumer citizen' whereby the individual is supposedly free to choose, but is in exchange held responsible for his/her own well-being (Lynch 2006).

The strengthening of the neoliberal doctrine within the higher education field has led to significant changes in the policies on public spending. Until the 1980s higher education was free or almost free for students across Europe, while today most countries charge some amount of tuition fees (Eicher 2000). On a similar note, while before the 1980s governments provided support for students' living costs mainly in the form of grants, since then there has been a shift towards the increased provision of loans for living costs. All of these reforms have signalled the privatisation of higher education – the shifting of the cost of higher education from public to private sources (Tilak 2005).

This change can also be observed in the Croatian higher education landscape: since the mid-1990s the growth of the student population has been based on the growing number of self-financed students (Matković 2009). While in the 1993/1994 academic year only 11.8 percent of students were paying tuition fees (Matković 2009), by 2010/2011 this share had increased to 60 percent (Cvitan et al. 2011). At the same time, the amount of tuition fees paid by undergraduate students grew over 50 percent from the mid-1990s, while fees for graduate studies increased even more substantially. Some indications of a reversal of this trend have been visible since September 2012, with the decision of the current centre-left government to fund tuition fees for all students at the point of enrolment and throughout the study course for students who acquire the required ECTS points. In addition, the newly introduced funding agreements with universities include social criteria such as increasing the enrolment of mature students, supporting students from low socio-economic backgrounds and students with disabilities, as well as increasing retention. These recent policies may be interpreted as tactical concessions which reflect the influence of the Independent Student Initiative, but their actual impact regarding the proportion of students paying tuition fees as well as their broader implications for access to higher education and social mobility in Croatia have yet to be established.

Critical educational theory and Fraser's conception of justice

Already in the mid-1970s, in their seminal study on education and capitalism Bowles and Gintis (1976) argued that if we are to understand what drives policy change the field of education must be analysed within a political economy framework. How education is financed and regulated depends on political decisions, which are in turn guided by ideas about what education is for, as well as by broader worldviews regarding societal well-being, social mobility and emancipation (Gradstein, Justman, and Meier 2004). Within the political economy of education, critical educational theory focuses on how education is shaped by structures and processes of power in society, as well as ways in which education is a powerful force for shaping people's perceptions, beliefs and behaviours. While the dominant neoliberal doctrine repeatedly demands that we consider how education serves the needs of the economy, a critical perspective asks what needs does the economy serve: does it enable us to do things we consider really important (Collini 2012)? The economy should not be understood as an autonomous system to which societies must yield – instead, societies should control and direct the economy to meet our individual and collective needs (Polany 1944).

Critical educational theory is therefore used to confront neoliberal policies in education with counter-hegemonic discourses that evoke popular power and collaborative governance (Brown 2005). It advances concepts of justice, ethics and equality, the autonomy of academic labour, the right to education, the university as a public sphere and the role played by the liberal arts and humanities in fostering a culture premised on the practice of freedom and mutual empowerment (Saunders 2010, Nussbaum 2010, Giroux 2011). While aiming to revive the idea of the Humboldtian university, this critique has been careful not to fall prey to nostalgia, aware that universities have always been sites of social reproduction and elitism (Ash 2008). In this conception, the university is above all a place to think rather than a place to prepare students to be competitive in the global market place. For authors such as Nussbaum (2010), the role of education cannot be reduced to supplying human capital to the market – it must nurture critical thought, a daring imagination and an understanding of the complexity of the world we live in.

In large part the literature on the spread of neoliberal policies, as well as on resistances that have followed it, focuses on the Anglo-American context and continental Europe – with few analyses of complementary developments in the post-communist context of the Western Balkans. We use Nancy Fraser's concept of justice (2000 and 2003) to interpret the student protest movement in Croatia as the initial site of resistance to the spread of the neoliberal doctrine. Fraser's (2000) concept of justice refers to both class and status forms of injustice and the struggles for redistribution and recognition. Redistributive struggles relate to the socio-economic axis of injustice such as poverty, economic exploitation, inequality and class differentials, where the focus is on the demand for a fair distribution of resources (ibid.). However, a socially just society should also resolve concerns comprising the cultural axis of injustice – disrespect, cultural imperialism and status hierarchy (ibid.). The focus of this axis is misrecognition, status subordination and inequalities relating to issues of gender and sexuality, ethnicity, religion and nationality. As the following analysis shows, the language of the protest movement is primarily crouched in the critique of capitalism and the concepts of redistribution and socio-economic justice.

When discussing ways of overcoming injustice, Fraser (2000 and 2003) distinguishes affirmative from transformative strategies. The key distinction lies in the contrast between the underlying social structures and social outcomes that they generate. Affirmative strategies for redressing injustice aim to correct inequitable outcomes of social arrangements without disturbing the underlying social structures that generate these outcomes. In contrast, transformative strategies aim to correct unjust outcomes by restructuring the underlying generative framework. The problem with applying affirmative remedies to identified injustices is that such strategies tend to reify collective identities, discourage innovation or dissidence – in a nutshell, they homogenise the group in question while at the same time reifying it (ibid.). Transformative remedies have opposite effects. Since they employ strategies of deconstruction, interaction and non-conformism, they effect a growth in solidarity without creating stigmatised groups. For Fraser, transformative strategies are more desirable, but they are at the same time more difficult to execute since they are highly vulnerable to collective action problems and feasible only in highly unusual circumstances. Practical political actions usually fit somewhere along the continuum of the two identified poles of affirmative and transformative strategies. Applying this distinction, we interpret the student protest movement in Croatia as a transformative struggle focused on the socio-economic axis of injustice.

Empirical Strategy

The central question guiding the analysis was how development, the role of the state and of higher education are framed in government documents and in the documents of the student protest movement. Discourse analysis was used for its understanding of discourse as constituting social reality and providing legitimacy to actions, guiding actors in their actions and providing images through which we understand ourselves and our surroundings (Nokkala 2008). In other words, discourse analysis enables the exploration of background assumptions of the analysed texts by relying on specific assumptions about society (Denscombe 1998: 309). As our introductory review has shown, we adopt a critical stance towards the neoliberal doctrine and the effects its policies have had in the field of higher education. Given that we were involved in the protest movement, a critical discourse analysis seems to be the most appropriate research strategy since it assumes an advocacy role on the part of the researcher (Meyer 2001).This method is fundamentally concerned with analysing structural relationships of dominance, power and control as manifested in language (Wodak 2001). It focuses on investigating inequality as expressed and legitimised by discourse, and it is 'critical' in that it takes an explicit political stance (ibid.).

The analysed official government documents are from the period from 2003 to 2007, when a centre-right government led by the Croatian

Democratic Union was in power. The three key government policy documents which define societal development and the role of higher education within it are included in the analysis. The first is the Strategic Development Framework as the umbrella political document defining government objectives for the 2006–2013 period. The second is the Education Sector Development Plan 2005–2010 as the official document outlining the strategy of the development of the education sector for the period up to 2010, and the third is the Science and Technology Strategy (2006–2010), which outlines the government's research policy.

The oppositional discourse is reconstructed from the texts of the student protest movement led by the Independent Student Initiative for the Right to Free Education. The event that marked the emergence of the student protest movement at the Faculty of Humanities and Social Sciences of the University of Zagreb was a public demonstration for free education that was held on 5 November 2008 and attended by 1,500 people (Independent Student Initiative 2009a). However, the defining moment for the movement was the blockade of the Faculty of Humanities and Social Sciences, which started on 20 April 2009 and lasted for 35 days. The blockade was in part a reaction to the disappointment that students felt at their demands being ignored while using conventional methods for expressing grievances, which radicalised the movement. Against the backdrop of more severe austerity politics that had unfolded since 2008, the continuous growth of tuition fees served as the immediate tipping point for the emergence of the student protest movement within the higher education field in Croatia. When it comes to the texts by the protest movement, the selection for our analysis was difficult since the movement produced many collectively authored programmatic texts as well as authored papers. We decided to focus on the texts produced at the very beginning of the student protest movement since this was the moment when the movement constituted itself as a new political actor and when it became an agenda setter in the public debate in Croatia. We analyse the first issue of the pamphlet *Skripta* containing the manifesto of the Independent Student Initiative, the following four issues of the pamphlet, and the *Blokadna Kuharica* booklet which documented the Faculty blockade in 2009.

The next section discusses how development and the role of the state are constructed in the dominant and oppositional discourses, followed by a section that outlines how the role of higher education is constructed in the two discourses.

The struggle over defining development, the role of the state and the role of higher education

The role of the state and development

With the implementation of the Lisbon Strategy, the European Social Model, originally coined by Jacques Delors to signify an alternative to the American form of pure-market capitalism (Jepsen and Pascual 2005), underwent an important re-semantisation in an effort to adjust it to new circumstances. Making Europe the most competitive economy of the world required reforming the labour market and social policy (Sapir 2006). The emphasis shifted from the state as a safeguard for the unemployed, sick, elderly and other groups at risk to the state as an enhancer of individual chances, a state that focuses on fostering employment, improving the business environment and maintaining macroeconomic stability (Dolenec 2007). After the role of the state is redefined in these terms, social policies are designed to "level the playing field" through education, skills and improved employability on one hand, while targeting social assistance to the most disadvantaged in order to reduce poverty and social exclusion (ibid.). In other words, the original meaning behind the concept of the European social model, which used to refer to a generous welfare state (Scharpf 2002), was to a large extent abandoned. Can we trace the influence of the Lisbon Strategy regarding the framing of development and the role of the state in Croatian official discourse?

The Introduction to Croatia's Strategic Development Framework (SDF) reveals somewhat of a balancing act in how it envisions development. The main strategic goal is defined as "growth and employment in a competitive market economy acting within a European welfare state of the 21st century" while the results of the measures it proposes, if applied, would lead to "an average increase of about 5% in the rate of economic growth in the period up to 2010, and above 7% after 2010". The formulation of the main strategic goal and the means by which its attainment will be measured reveals a strong focus on economic growth as the primary societal objective. At the same time, the second part of the formulation referring to growth "within a European welfare state of the 21st century" seems to signal the safeguarding of social and economic rights. Throughout the document, the reference to the European welfare state appears either with the prefix "modern" or the suffix "of the 21st century", and never on its own. It seems that the writers wanted to simultaneously communicate some guarantee of existing social and economic rights and a necessity to redefine what a welfare state entails. A search through the document reveals no clear indication of what this change might be, apart from referring to the European welfare state "adjusted to the conditions of the 21st century" (Government of Croatia 2006: 6). This qualifier seems to send out a warning sign.

While the SDF does not explicitly formulate what a European welfare state for the 21st century encapsulates, its discussion of social policy and of the changed role of the state (a chapter in the document is entitled *The New Role of the State*) testifies to the strong discursive influence of the Lisbon Strategy, which is cited on three occasions in the document. Already in the Introduction, the SDF mentions "the new role of the state" and stresses the need to change "the traditional role of the state", followed by a formulation according to which the state should be transformed into "an efficient and effective service acting for its citizens and entrepreneurs" (ibid.: 12). In this "new, open world" of "efficiency" and "effectiveness" the state is no longer an instrument of social intervention, but of social mediation. The state is no longer the "creator, leader and executor of change" (ibid.), but works together with the private sector on a partnership basis in search of the best development solutions. Even though Croatian citizens exhibit an egalitarian political culture as well as high expectations from the state in the provision of social services (Županov 1969, Štulhofer 1997 and 2000), the SDF diagnoses that

> "Although the effects of egalitarianism that was promoted for decades and the expectations that the state will take care of the individual still exist, such beliefs are slowly disappearing. New generations are maturing and realising that their greatest support in life is in the results of their work." (Government of Croatia 2006: 13).

The use of the word "maturing" is particularly telling since immaturity seems to stand for not realising the value of self-reliance and individualism.

The chapter *The New Role of the State* completes this redefinition by focusing on the need to reduce the public sector as well as make it a more efficient service provider. More specifically, the reform should start from "the basic principle that the state should relinquish to the market all those activities which the market performs more efficiently and intervene only in correcting market failures" (ibid.: 64). At the same time, the "institutional and administrative competencies of the state must also be enhanced to create a stable, predictable and transparent business environment" (ibid.). Therefore, even though on the surface the SDF seems to balance the 'social' and the 'market', its discussion of objectives, priorities and measures reveals a strong belief in the market and a preference for the retrenchment of the state. This retrenchment is particularly acute in terms of distancing from the previous regime, framed in terms of the need to nurture the will to succeed and take on personal responsibility, which are presented as values which had been "for decades supressed in socialism" (ibid.: 13). It is interesting to note that, although the SDF pronounces clearly which political and economic set up it is against (socialism), there is no explicit mention in the document of capitalism. The adoption of capitalism is thus revealed as fully naturalised; an unquestioned state of affairs to which there is no alternative.

The government discourse in the SDF mirrors the Lisbon Strategy discourse on development, centring on economic growth and a retrenchment of the welfare state. Entrepreneurship is a key concept within this framework and a chapter in the SDF focuses exclusively on this. The SDF argues that Croatia should put science, technology, innovation, a large part of the state administration and the education system "at the service" of entrepreneurship: the positive effect on entrepreneurship "must become one of the basic criteria to assess all activities of the state and all forms of spending taxpayers' money" (ibid.: 56). Along these lines, the SDF states that "wherever there is competition there are better results" (ibid.: 23). Similarly, privatisation is advocated as a superior strategy of allocating resources since "private ownership has clearly proven to be far more successful than state ownership" (ibid.: 59). In other words, the key ingredients for Croatia's development are a retrenchment of the welfare state, entrepreneurship, privatisation and competition – the central components of the neoliberal doctrine. Similarly to Nokkala's (2008) observations about the narrative construction of Finland as a "small country" in official documents, the SDF also constructs Croatia as a "small economy" (Government of Croatia 2006: 11 and 46) and "small country" (ibid.: 16 and 56) whose survival depends on these ingredients. The proposed reforms are presented as unavoidable, with no room left for alternatives.

Although the manifest of the student protest movement (Independent Student Initiative 2009b) largely focuses on higher education, like other student movements globally, the movement had more ambitious objectives. Callinicos' (2006) remark with respect to the UK student protest movement according to which "preserving and developing what is valuable in existing universities cannot be separated from the broader struggle against capitalism itself" may as well have been applied in the case of the Independent Student

Initiative in Zagreb. The manifest is quite explicit in this respect: "The stock markets have crashed as a result of a neoliberal capitalist doctrine which promotes private business, whose main aim is maximising profit, being understood as untouchable [...] our long-term goal is to end the neoliberalisation of this society". In addition, the *Blokadna Kuharica* (Independent Student Initiative 2009a: 71) makes it clear that "the student fight for free education needs to be understood as part of a more encompassing fight for defending the interests of the majority, and not particularistic and selfish [...] as some media and politicians try to present it".

Regarding the role of the state, the manifest notes that its role in terms of providing social services is being labelled as socialist; "a word which in the media context is the equivalent of complete disqualification", whereas the offered alternative is Social Darwinism "in which individual consumption and shopping malls should compensate for the loss of social security and collective solidarity". The *Blokadna Kuharica* describes this as "a neoliberal attack on social rights". In other words, the protest movement develops a far-reaching and systemic criticism of the existing economic relations and policy priorities, emphasising development in terms of public goods and collective solidarity. In Fraser's (2003) terms, the movement does not adopt an affirmative approach which would focus narrowly on furthering their interests and social position, but a transformative approach which challenges the neoliberal order and emphasises the redistributive role of the state. The following quote illustrates this:

> Private capital is the fundamental pillar of the neoliberal capitalist order and it is therefore unrealistic to expect that private investors will willingly give up the control of their private playgrounds that we naïve people call states. If we go back just a little bit, it becomes evident that the money that states used to avoid bankruptcy of banks is the money of tax payers – that is, our money. Private capital remains protected and it always gets another chance of accumulating new profit. Metaphorically speaking, the people are scraping leftovers from an already empty mug after the capitalists have skimmed all the cream. There is money, but it is the people who make this money that should decide what to do with it, and force the state to distribute it more justly (through pressure from below) (Independent Student Initiative 2009b, FAQ section, our translation).

Unlike the SDF document which critiques socialism and does not mention capitalism, the student manifesto aims to rehabilitate the socialist tradition and offers a scourging critique of the capitalist economy as benefiting the privileged elites at the expense of the citizens. The discourse of the manifesto, their relationship with respect to the former regime, as well as the intellectual tradition which they invoke (e.g. David Harvey, Slavoj Žižek etc.) position the student protest movement within the neo-Marxist political tradition. The fact that they were disparaged by the mainstream media as Yugo-nostalgic and communist further supports the conclusion that they were successful in positioning themselves as a political actor of the radical Left. It seems that the SDF's idea of 'maturity' was turned on its head by this generation of student activists.

The role of (higher) education

When it comes to discussing the role of education more specifically, it features prominently in the SDF, which aims to develop and transform Croatian society and the economy into a "knowledge society". This concept is a direct transfer of the language of the Lisbon Strategy, which committed the EU to becoming "the most dynamic and competitive *knowledge-based economy* in the world" (our italics). The knowledge society narrative emphasises the importance of higher education for the competitiveness of nation-states, regions and individuals (Nokkala 2008). This orientation is especially prominent in the goals formulated in Chapter 2 of the SDF (Government of Croatia 2006), *People and Knowledge*: a better balancing of labour force supply and demand, reducing long-term employment, promoting lifelong learning, modernising vocational education, extending compulsory education, increasing the share of people with higher education in the total population, increasing total allocations to education but also the efficiency of spending, and finally stimulating the participation of the private sector in the financing of regular education and in-service training (ibid.: 20). This formulation of objectives reveals the education sector as conceived primarily in terms of its economic impact, i.e. the better functioning of the labour market and ways in which it can increase economic competitiveness. The following extracts further illustrate this:

> One of the key features of the Croatian labour market is the relatively weak link between educational results and market needs, that is, insufficient influence of the labour-force market (i.e. the needs of the labour market) on the features of the educational system (ibid.: 19);

> Introducing measures to encourage the commercialisation of academic research – with the aim of efficient cooperation between the university and research institutions with business structures (ibid.: 26).

When discussing education and research, the SDF states that "the role of the state and the public sector in encouraging the transfer of knowledge and technology is necessary and justified, because innovation and the dissemination of knowledge and technologies create important positive social effects. State investments are necessary in creating the conditions for research and higher education, because these are areas where shifts in financing may produce significant positive results" (ibid.: 25. Unfortunately, this objective of increased public investment in higher education and especially in research and development has not been implemented. The current government's legislative proposal from early 2012 refers to Croatia's investment in research and development as being at 36.5 percent of the EU average, while Croatia's public investment in higher education is at 83 percent of the EU average (Academic Solidarity 2012). This reflects an international trend whereby "higher education is expected to play [a role] in advancing global competitiveness within a context of constrained public spending" (Robertson 2010: 201). Supposedly to make up for the shortfall in public spending, the SDF notes the importance of private investments, illustrating the faith in private initiative and competition:

> It is necessary to stimulate private initiatives in education (at the same time respecting high quality standards), as well as partnerships with the private sector. It is crucial to develop public private partnerships through the inclusion of the private sector in improving the material conditions and infrastructure of the educational system (Government of Croatia 2006: 23).

Like the SDF, which presents a failed attempt at balancing societal development and market allocation by dominantly framing higher education as a mechanism of economic growth, the Education Sector Development Plan 2005–2010 (ESDP; Ministry of Science, Education and Sports 2005) also tries to balance social and economic priorities. For instance, in its definition of the role of education it evokes concepts such as equal opportunities and the common good:

> The role of the education system is to create and develop intellectual, professionally competent and humanistic-oriented human capital that will benefit the country and the common good. Education has a crucial role in equipping all children, young people and adults with equal opportunities when entering society and the labour market, regardless of their social background (ibid.: 5).

Although this document draws on terms such as the common good or equal opportunities, the role of education is again firmly couched within the context of the Lisbon Strategy and the knowledge economy. The ESDP directly mentions the Lisbon Strategy as the foundation of its principles and goals, and evokes the need to modernise education systems "to allow the EU to become the most competitive and dynamic knowledge-based economy in the world" (ibid.: 9). In addition, the education system needs to respond to labour market needs by improving efficiency and including the adult population in education, thereby contributing to a reduction of the unemployment rate.

The ESDP formulated four overall priorities for the education sector: improving the quality and effectiveness of education; improving teacher education; improving management and efficiency of the education system; and promoting education for social cohesion and economic growth and development. In terms of the fourth objective of education for social cohesion and economic growth, the ESDP primarily has in mind the development of lifelong learning. As it specifies: "Due to the increasing pace of social and economic change, it is necessary to improve the flexibility of the education system, so that individuals have greater opportunities to change their education/training, in line with the changing needs of the labour market and the concept of lifelong learning" (ibid.: 21). This conception of the individual as taking on the risks in an ever-changing market through constant education (Nokkala 2008) is a close reflection of the role of education as conceptualised in the Lisbon Strategy. Jessop (2008: 14) labels this as the "subordination of information, knowledge and learning to the demands of the expanded reproduction of the globalising knowledge economy". Further examples of this in the ESDP include: "adapting the enrolment policy to meet labour market demands in the Republic of Croatia" (Ministry of Science, Education and Sports 2005: 34).

The Science and Technology Policy of the Republic of Croatia 2006–2010 (STP; Ministry of Science, Education and Sports 2006) reveals the same strong reliance on the Lisbon Strategy in conceptualising objectives for Croatia's research and technology policy, as well as the context of globalisation, European integration and the imperatives of knowledge economies. The Foreword invokes the Lisbon Strategy's goals and invites Croatian citizens to be prepared for permanent education as "a factor of self-improvement and social advancement [that] should become a way of life" (Foreword). The overall objective is to "stimulate scientific excellence and enable the transfer of knowledge and results of scientific discoveries to industry and business in order to increase competitiveness and generate sustainable growth and productivity" (ibid.: 12). Again the rhetoric of "self-improvement", "competitiveness" and "excellence" dominates.

In summarising all three documents we may say that, although competing narratives are present whereby social cohesion is married to competitiveness, as well as sustainability to economic growth, when these contradictory objectives are forced into a showdown, the neoliberal objectives of employability, economic growth and competitiveness repeatedly carry the day. Social cohesion is revealed as a secondary objective, almost a necessary internal stabiliser for the market mechanism at work.

In opposition to the concern for economic growth and the economic role of higher education and research, the main concern of the Independent Student Initiative is the education system as a public good and the idea of social justice. The manifesto states opposition to the "privatisation of higher education", to higher education institutions becoming profit-making, and to market logic in terms of hiring which "can be especially detrimental for the academic world". The framings in the manifesto enable a characterisation of this protest as a transformative struggle against socio-economic injustice. Firstly, there is a strong and repeated emphasis on the economic status of individuals and the fact that economic status should not be a barrier to accessing higher education. Access to higher education is framed as a right, with references to the UN's Universal Declaration of Human Rights, while attempts to restrict this right are characterised as socially destructive and polarising. The following quotes illustrate this:

> In light of the fact that the right to education is a right that belongs to everyone, regardless of the economic status of the individual, our action is a sign of protest against the reckless and socially insensitive taking away of that right.

> We are taking our part of the responsibility to defend general social interests from the socially destructive processes of commercialisation and social polarisation based on economic status.

> We demand the abolition of tuition fees on all levels: undergraduate, graduate and postgraduate. The taxes that we are paying must be sufficient to guarantee elementary rights and institutions of social justice and equality (Independent Student Initiative 2009b).

In addition, there is a rejection of the argument according to which there 'simply is not enough money in the public purse', whereby the claim made is that the taxes paid by ordinary citizens must suffice to guarantee the right to higher education. This discussion according to which there simply is not enough public funding for higher education as not an objective necessity but a matter of political priorities is elaborated in the FAQ section of the first pamphlet *Skripta* and it is revisited again in the *Blokadna kuharica* document that came out several months later. The Independent Student Initiative rejects the justification based on the budget deficit as an objective necessity and opens up the question of progressive tax policies directed at banks and large corporations as a source of additional funding for education. All the identified elements of the manifesto point to a socio-economic conceptualisation of injustice, whereby the redressing of injustice is seen in redistributive measures that would guarantee a right to education. Moreover, the movements' objectives are clearly formulated as a transformative struggle since they do not aim to affirm the rights and privileges of one social group but instead point to the underlying societal framework, and the injustices that are generated by neoliberal policies across diverse social domains.

Conclusion

Since the mid-2000s the official discourse in Croatia has been uncritically copying the Lisbon Strategy policy objectives as a set of ideas directed towards increasing the competitiveness of European knowledge-based economies. The current economic crisis has revealed that, instead of the prosperity of all, the implementation of these policies has led to increasing inequality, rising unemployment and reduced social mobility across Europe. However, even if one remains a staunch believer in free markets in the face of the current crisis, there is still the question of whether in Croatia the objective of creating a globally competitive knowledge economy was ever intended to be actually implemented. As we have shown, in Croatia levels of public investment in R&D and higher education are substantially lower than the EU average. Perhaps in Croatia the Lisbon rhetoric of competitiveness has instead been used to downplay the responsibility of the government for the higher education sector and for societal well-being more broadly. Since the economic crisis, the competitiveness rhetoric seems to have been primarily used to justify reduced public spending on higher education and research and to camouflage an increasingly insecure future for universities.

As our analysis has shown, the discursive split regarding the role of the state and higher education between the official discourse in Croatia and that of the student protest movement is stark. The official discourse during the 2003–2007 period of a centre-right government dominantly advanced a narrow conception of higher education whose role is to contribute to a skilled workforce for the economy. The commodification of higher education was constructed as a necessity for economic growth, a developmental path to which there was no alternative. A critical perspective that challenged this view emerged at the University of Zagreb during 2008 and 2009. The Independent Student Initiative rejected this dominant framing of higher education by demanding that the state protects public goods against privatisation and commodification. It has drawn attention to the fact that Croatia has been witnessing cuts in public spending and a changed role of the state not only in the field of higher education, but across diverse social domains from healthcare to pensions. Employing Fraser's (2000 and 2003) concept of social justice, the protest movement was characterised as a transformative struggle against socio-economic injustice which challenged the implementation of neoliberal policies. Finally, we have hinted at recent developments which suggest that the protest movement has extended the spectrum of the political Left by introducing topics pertaining to socio-economic inequalities into the public debate. These developments surely merit analytical attention and charter further avenues for research.

References

Academic Solidarity (2012). *Deklaracija o visokom obrazovanju i znanosti.* Zagreb: Akademska Solidarnost.

Apple, M. (2001). "Comparing Neo-liberal Projects and Inequality in Education". *Comparative Education.* Vol. 37. No. 4. 409-423.

Ayres, Y. M. (2004). "Framing Collective Action Against Neoliberalism: The Case of the 'Anti-Globalization' Movement". *Journal of World-systems Research.* Vol. 10. No. 1. 11–34.

Ash, M. G. (2008). "From 'Humboldt' to 'Bologna': History as Discourse in Higher Education Reform Debates in German-speaking Europe". In: B. Jessop, N. Fairclough, R. Wodak (eds.), *Education and the Knowledge-based Economy in Europe.* Rotterdam: Sense Publishers. 41-61.

Bourdieu, P. (2003). *Firing Back. Against the Tyranny of the Market 2.* London: Verso.

Bowles, S., H. Gintis (1976). *Schooling in Capitalist America. Educational Reform and the Contradictions of Economic Life.* New York: Basic Books.

Brown, W. (2005). *Critical Essays on Knowledge and Politics.* Princeton and Oxford: Princeton University Press.

Brown, R., ed. (2011). *Higher Education and the Market.* New York: Routledge.

Callinicos, A. (2006). *Universities in a Neoliberal World*. London: Bookmarks Publications.

Chalmers, D., M. Lodge (2003). "The Open Method of Co-ordination and the European Welfare State". *LSE CARR Discussion Paper*. No. 11. Available at http://eprints.lse.ac.uk/35993/1/Disspaper11.pdf (accessed 18 October 2012).

Collini, S. (2012). *What Are Universities For?* London: Penguin.

Cvitan, M., K. Doolan, T. Farnell, T. Matković (2011). *Eurostudent Report for Croatia*. Zagreb: Institute for the Development of Education.

Denscombe, M. (1998). *The Good Research Guide for Small Scale Social Research Projects*. Buckingham: Open University Press.

Dolenec, D. (2007). Does the European Social Model Matter? An Analysis of Social Policy Change in Croatia 1996-2007. (Unpublished master's thesis). Zagreb: Faculty of Political Science.

Eicher, J-C. (2000). "The Financing of Education: an Economic Issue?" *European Journal of Education*. Vol. 35. No. 1. 33-44.

Esping Andersen (2001). "A welfare state for the 21st Century". In: A. Giddens, *The Global Third Way Debate*. Oxford: Polity Press. 134-156.

Fraser, N. (2000). "Rethinking recognition". *New Left Review*. No. 3. 107-120.

Fraser, N. (2003). "Social Justice in the Age of Identity Politics: Redistribution, Recognition and Participation". In: N. Fraser, A. Honneth (eds.), *Redistribution or Recognition: A Political-Philosophical Exchange*. London: Verso.

Giroux, H. A. (2011). "Beyond the Swindle of the Corporate University: Higher Education in the Service of Democracy". Available at http://www.henryagiroux.com/online_articles.htm (accessed 18 October 2012).

Government of Croatia (2006). Strategic Development Framework of the Republic of Croatia. Available at http://www.mrrfeu.hr/userDocsImages/Publikacije/Strateski_okvir_za_razvoj_2006_2013.pdf (accessed 18 October 2012).

Gradstein, M., M. Justman, V. Meier (2004). *The Political Economy of Education*. Boston: MIT Press.

Green, A., A. Wolf, T. Leney (2000). *Convergence and Divergence in European Education and Training Systems*. London: Institute of Education, Bedford Way Papers.

Guillen, A., B. Palier (2004). "Introduction: Does Europe Matter? Accession to EU and Social Policy Developments in Recent and New Member States". *Journal of European Social Policy*. Vol. 14. No. 3. 203-209.

Independent Student Initiative (2009a). "Blokadna kuharica". Available at http://www.slobodnifilozofski.com/2009/11/dostupna-blokadna-kuharica-u-pdf.html (accessed 18 October 2012).

Independent Student Initiative (2009b). "Skripta 1". Available at http://www.slobodnifilozofski.com/2009/04/arhiva-skripta.html (accessed 18 October 2012).

Jepsen, M., A. S. Pascual (2005). "The European Social Model: An Exercise in Deconstruction". *Journal of European Social Policy*. Vol. 15. No. 3. 231-245.

Jessop, B. (2008). "A Cultural Political Economy of Competitiveness and its Implications for Higher Education". In: B. Jessop, N. Fairclough, R. Wodak (eds.), *Education and the Knowledge-based Economy in Europe*. Rotterdam: Sense. 13-39.

Judt, T. (2010). *Ill Fares the Land*. London: Penguin.

Le Grand, J., R. Robinson, eds. (1984). *Privatization and the Welfare State*. London: George Allen and Unwin.

Lynch, K. (2006). "Neo-liberalism and Marketisation: The Implications for Higher Education". *European Educational Research Journal*. Vol. 5. No. 1. 1-17.

Matković, T. (2009). "Pregled statističkih pokazatelja participacije, prolaznosti i režima plaćanja studija u Republici Hrvatskoj 1991.-2007". *Revija za socijalnu politiku*. Vol. 16. No 2. 239-250.

Meyer, M. (2001). "Between Theory, Method and Politics: Positioning of the Approaches to CDA". In: R. Wodak, M. Meyer (eds.), *Methods of Critical Discourse Analysis*. London: Sage.

Ministry of Science, Education and Sports (2005). *Education Sector Development Plan of the Republic of Croatia*. Available at http://public.mzos.hr/Default.aspx?sec=3144 (accessed 18 October 2012).

Ministry of Science, Education and Sports (2006). "Science and Technology Policy of the Republic of Croatia". Available at http://public.mzos.hr/Default.aspx?sec=3144 (accessed 18 October 2012).

Negri, A. (1989). *The Politics of Subversion. A Manifesto for the Twenty-First Century*. Cambridge: Polity Press.

Nokkala, T. (2008). "Finland is a Small Country. Narrative Construction of the Internationalisation of Higher Education". In: B. Jessop, N. Fairclough, R. Wodak (eds.), *Education and the Knowledge-based Economy in Europe*. Rotterdam: Sense. 171-190.

Nussbaum, M. (2010). *Not for Profit: Why Democracy Needs The Humanities*. Princeton and Oxford: Princeton University Press.

Olssen, M., M. A. Peters (2005). "Neoliberalism, Higher Education and the Knowledge Economy: From the Free Market to Knowledge Capitalism". *Journal of Education Policy*. Vol. 20. No. 3. 313-345.

Pierson, C. (1998). *Beyond the Welfare State*. Cambridge: Polity Press.

Polany, K. (1944). *The Great Transformation*. Boston: Beacon Press

Robertson, S. (2010). "Corporatisation, Competitiveness, Commercialisation: New Logics in the Globalising of UK Higher Education". *Globalisation, Societies and Education*. Vol. 8. No. 2. 191-203.

Sapir, A. (2005). "Globalisation and the Reform of the European Social Models". Bruegel Background Document (prepared for ECOFIN informal meeting in Manchester).

Saunders, D. B. (2010). "Neoliberal Ideology and Public Higher Education in the United States". *Journal for Critical Education Policy Studies*. Vol. 8. No. 1. 41-77.

Scharpf, F. W. (2002). "The European Social Model: Coping With the Challenges of Diversity". *Journal of Common Market Studies*. Vol. 40. No. 4. 645-670.

Self, P. (1999). *Rolling Back the Market: Economic Dogma and Political Choice*. New York: St. Martin's Press.

Streeck, W. (2011). "The Crises of Democratic Capitalism". *New Left Review*. No. 71. 5-29.

Štulhofer, A. (1997). "Kulturna inercija i razvoj gospodarstva". *Erasmus*. No. 19. 64-70.

Štulhofer, A. (2000). *Nevidljiva ruka tranzicije: ogledi iz sociologije*. Zagreb: Biblioteka časopisa Socijalne ekologije – Razvoj i okoliš.

Theisens, H. (2004.) *The State of Change. Analysing Policy Change in Dutch and English Higher Education*. Enschede: Center for Higher Education and Policy Studies (CHEPS).

Tilak, J. B. G. (2005). "Global Trends in the Funding of Higher Education". *IAU Horizons*. Vol. 11. No. 1.

Wodak, R. (2001). "What CDA Is About – A Summary of Its History, Important Concepts and Its Developments". In: R. Wodak, M. Meyer (eds.), *Methods of Critical Discourse Analysis*. London: Sage.

Županov, J. (1969). "Industrijalizam i egalitarizam". *Sociologija*. Vol. 12. No. 1. 5-43.

Reconsidering Higher Education Reforms in the Western Balkans: 'Policy Colonies' or 'Policy Autarchies'?

Pavel Zgaga

Abstract

The principal aim of this paper is to consider the higher education reforms in eight countries of the Western Balkans (Albania, Bosnia and Herzegovina, Croatia, Kosovo, Macedonia, Montenegro, Serbia as well as Slovenia) in the perspective of the last two decades. The guiding question is what the main characteristics of higher education reforms in these countries have been since the 1990s until the present and how they relate to the international policy processes and developments. In particular, we will focus on the politicisation and privatisation of higher education, implementation of the Bologna Process and the dichotomy of international norms and local identities. At this point, we will address the issue of the 'centres' and 'peripheries' relationship in the regional higher education policy context. On this basis, we will finally discuss and dispute the view that 'peripheral countries' simply play the role of a kind of 'policy colony' within the contemporary Western Balkans higher education reforms.

Key words: higher education policy, higher education reforms, centres and peripheries, internationalisation, Bologna Process, former Yugoslavia, Western Balkans

Introduction

It is necessary to start with the very notion of the Western Balkans: *what are the Western Balkans*? The term is quite new. Before 1990, the region consisted of two countries – and therefore just two national higher education systems: the Socialist Federative Republic of Yugoslavia (six republics; two autonomous regions) and the Socialist People's Republic of Albania. None of them was part of the 'Eastern Bloc' (each of them represented another kind of 'revisionism' from the Soviet point of view) but the border between them was hermetically closed and there was practically no bilateral cooperation in higher education and research. After 1990, this hermetic border disappeared and Albania has opened its borders widely but, following a decade of regional wars and conflicts, new borders – including a 'Schengen' one – have been developed between the seven new countries which have emerged on the territory of former Yugoslavia.

During this period, a time of 'transition', the notion of the Western Balkans was born in Western Europe; it began to be used in the new Euro-language as a seemingly neutral term for a region that remained outside the first (2004) and second (2007) waves of EU enlargement – and which cannot easily be put over a common denominator. First of all, this is not the whole of the Balkans (i.e., two new EU member states, Bulgaria and Romania, are not included). Secondly, this is also not the whole of the Western Balkans (if we speak in strictly geographical terms, Slovenia, another new EU member state, is also not included, at least in terms of a part of its territory). It is a modern geopolitical term; its formal and popular definition is usually grasped in the formula 'ex-YU countries – Slovenia + Albania'.

Albania does not share a common heritage in higher education development before 1990 (and after the end of World War II) with the seven other countries, while Slovenia, which does share this common heritage, has been 'excluded' from the concept of the Western Balkans. Yet it is important to stress that the former socialist Yugoslavia was open to the West, its education system was decentralised (due to the different languages, educational and cultural traditions etc.) and there were common as well as quite diverse elements among the six previous republics (that made up the federation). During the two decades of 'the transition', the new nation-states have developed their systems in different ways and the previous common elements have become less evident. On the other hand, Albania has moved far away from its autarchic past and firmly positioned itself within the (new) regional framework (Zgaga 2010).

Post-1990 developments: Massification, expansion, legislating

Yet, the dynamics of higher education in this region with a population of almost 25 million unfortunately still remain on the margins of contemporary higher education studies. The region has never been in the centre of research; there is both a lack of data and a lack of prior studies. In addition, this area of research is determined by a controversial logic of the common and the different, the uniform and the diverse. This is not only in our case – i.e., when discussing higher education – but also when studying other segments of societies in the region. It is important to pay attention to differences in the region, but within the limits of this article we cannot draw a complete picture. Here, we will mainly focus on common characteristics of the region which we identified in our survey, although we will also try to point out certain differences. In doing so, we will lean on the results of a regional study recently performed by our centre (CEPS 2012). First, we will highlight three of the most noticeable trends and then we will analyse the interviews we conducted as part of our field research.

On the surface, the most visible feature of the regional higher education systems is *massification*. In former Yugoslavia, there was a boom in participation rates already in the 1970s, but in the 1980s and particularly closer to 1990 this trend slowed down considerably. For example, in Slovenia which was treated as the most economically developed part of the federation, after a rapid increase in the late 1970s the total undergraduate enrolment in 1988 (the last year before the peak of the crisis and the start of the common state falling apart) was only slightly higher (31,055) than in 1985 (29,601) and in 1981 (26,207) while the total number of graduates even dropped from 5,621 in 1985 to 5,467 in 1988 (Zgaga 2004). In general, participation rates in higher education were still quite low; in more developed republics, around 15 percent of a cohort studied while in less developed parts and in Albania this figure was much lower.

At the turn of the decade and in the early 1990s, these numbers began to climb rapidly. This rise depended on specific economic and political circumstances in individual countries. There were several reasons: from a change in cultural patterns and social ambitions via unemployment and migrations to new national policies addressing the 'upcoming knowledge society' etc. Of course, the situation was quite different in those territories affected by wars and conflicts, in particular in Bosnia and Herzegovina and Kosovo. General emigration flows as well as liberalised border crossings also led many young people to study abroad. Until 2000, in most parts of the region enrolment levels doubled or tripled and this trend has been continuing in the last decade.

Another easily visible feature of the developments is *the growth in the number of higher education institutions* – public and in particular private. With a few exceptions, there is no long university tradition in the region. Upon the disintegration of the federal Yugoslavia in 1990, there were 19 universities serving a country of 21 million people. Three of them were established in the late 19th and early 20th century and two of them immediately after World War II. Almost all the others were established during the boom period of self-management socialism in the late 1960s and 1970s to support decentralised economic development. In Albania, the first university was founded in 1957 and it was the only university there up until 1990, although some new institutes or their branches were also established in this period (Uvalić Trumbić 1990, Šoljan 1991, Zgaga 2011).

Therefore, in 1990 there were altogether 20 public universities in the region; today, there are 47 (almost all of them crowded with students) as well as about 250 private universities and other higher education institutions[1] with a relatively small number of students (in all countries almost as a rule below 15 percent of the total). The expansion of higher education in the region has been enabled and accelerated by amendments made to legislation after 1990 but it has also been a result of the limited funds available to public universities and perhaps unreasonably high expectations with regard to private initiative in higher education. Altogether, this trend has led to an almost uncontrollable situation. Of course, within this general trend significant specific features are evident from country to country.

We can conditionally speak about *three waves of legislating* in the region. Some elements of a common logic can also be found in approaches to the legislative regulation of higher education. At the beginning of and during the 1990s, legislators chiefly focused on the general framework which had been profoundly challenged everywhere by the overturn of the political system and by the economic conditions. For example, so-called 'non-budget' or self-paying students were introduced at public universities along with 'budget-funded' ones and private institutions were legally allowed at this stage.

In the background of this *first wave of legislating*, the existing 'philosophy' of higher education remained largely the same. There were a few attempts to regulate 'spontaneity' in the field of higher education which erupted after 1990 but, in general, there were predominantly only technical adaptations of the traditional system – in both legal and value terms – adaptations to the new political and economic order. As large parts of the region were affected by wars and conflicts, it would be unrealistic to expect any frontal and substantial conceptual shifts and the development of new strategies and policies during this period.

---

1   It is quite difficult to obtain an exact figure; yet it is clearly higher than lower.

Due to the complex circumstances, the first wave of legislating was delayed by about a decade in some countries, e.g. in Bosnia and Herzegovina, Kosovo, (the Former Yugoslav Republic of)[2] Macedonia and Montenegro. In contrast, only Slovenia – which remained outside the armed conflicts after the summer of 1991 – was lucky enough to be able to address some fundamental conceptual issues already during this stage: e.g. the issue of a 'fragmented' university system with strong faculties and a weak central university administration (the Law on Higher Education of 1993 declared that only the "University is a legal personality" but the implementation of this provision took several years); the issue of the quality as well as the accreditation and evaluation of institutions; the issue of Europeanisation and internationalisation (it joined the European Commission's Tempus programme in 1991 as the first country in the region, and the Erasmus programme in 1999) etc. (Zgaga 1998). Another very specific – and in fact contradictory to the Slovenian case – situation occurred in Serbia where Milošević's government imposed a legal amendment in 1998 which strongly interfered with the traditional autonomy of universities and provoked a mass protest movement of students and teachers. This movement created an inspirational space for developing strategic ideas on higher education which were partly instrumentalised at the beginning of the 2000s by Zoran Đinđić's new democratic government (In Defence... 1997, In Defence... 1998, Turajlić 2004).

The *second wave of legislating* occurred at the beginning of the 2000s or – in some countries – a little later. On one hand, it was an obvious task of the 'post-conflict' period and 'reintegration into Europe'; on the other hand, it was directly connected to Europeanisation processes and in particular to the Bologna Process (Scott 2006, Zgaga 2003). Slovenia joined it already in 1999, Croatia in 2001 and the other five countries in 2003; only Kosovo has not joined it yet due to its political status. The legislating agenda of the second wave was 'stronger', at least at first sight: the common European Higher Education Area (EHEA) has provided the conceptual basis for the modernisation of higher education – the basis that had been lacking before in most countries of the region. However, there is much evidence that the desire to 'Europeanise' the system overnight too often resulted in 'cosmetic changes'

---

2   The name of the country is still disputed with Greece and in the diplomatically correct language its name is the Former Yugoslav Republic of Macedonia (FYROM). This is yet another aspect of tensions in the broader region.

and not in a substantial and strategic conversion. Of course, this is a general problem (Freyburg and Richter 2010) and not only a higher education one.

There is also much evidence that, at least at the beginning of this period, bottom-up incentives to modernise either curricula or governance models at the level of institutions were particularly strong. These incentives were furthered by increasing multilateral cooperation among institutions; Tempus which all the countries of the region had gradually joined by the early 2000s was particularly influential in this respect. In some countries, elements of the first and second waves appeared simultaneously, e.g. in Macedonia where, after the ethnic conflict of 2001, private universities were allowed under a legal amendment which also provided some incentives leading towards the system's greater openness and internationalisation.

As the Bologna Process has been progressing and as the gap between the improvised 'cosmetic changes' and real challenges at the national level has been widening, more amendments have been adopted in all countries since 2005. This is the *third wave of legislating*. Yet, at this stage of the reforms another common problem in the policy making process has become evident: on one hand, the successive and often contradictory amendments have been approved following governmental 'swinging' (i.e., conservative governments felt a need to change the previous liberal legislation and vice versa). This practice has led to stagnation with regard to long-term national strategic targets. On the other hand, this has also led to specific regional (mis)interpretations of the Bologna Process. Last but not least, this has not been only negative: all of this has contributed to the revival of a debate about the role of higher education first of all in the national but also European context as well as its future.

Higher education reforms of the last decade: Key issues and concerns

In our regional survey (CEPS 2012), we focused on the reforms of the last decade and tried to delineate their specific logic in specific national contexts. Here, we will highlight three themes assisted by the words of our interviewees[3] and responses to the questionnaire:[4] (1) reforms in general; (2)

---

3   Altogether, 77 interviews with academics (rectors and vice-rectors, deans and vice-deans) at 16 universities in eight countries as well as with representatives from

implementation of the Bologna Process; and (3) the international policy impact in the region. The views and positions in the interviews will be quoted anonymously (as agreed with the interviewees), only the code of an interviewee (two digits) and the date the interview was conducted are given in brackets. The majority of interviews were conducted in local languages; in these cases, we provide our English translation.

Reforms of higher education: Politicisation and privatisation as the biggest concerns

The large majority of our interviewees agrees that "real changes started only after 2000" (28; 9/3/12), that "in the early 1990s there were no substantial reforms; we only started thinking more independently" (29; 9/3/12), that the most important changes of the contemporary period are *"linked to the* adoption of the *Bologna Declaration – then* the *reforms of the last 10 years started"* (15; 29/2/12) etc.

This understanding prevails among academics, while ministerial representatives usually add that even the earlier period was not totally 'passive', at least not in all countries of the region, e.g. in Croatia:

> There were three important changes: the first one in 1996 when a binary system was introduced; then in 2000 when the state relinquished control of universities; the state got out of direct control and influence after the constitutional court took some decisions regarding autonomy. The third reform was in 2003 when the Bologna Process was legally introduced and implemented in 2005 (34; 16/3/12).

The interviewees like to stress the weight of the (traditional) 'mentality' which is understood as a significant obstacle to necessary changes in the region and which urges for (new) 'awareness-raising'. This is particularly expressed when reforms at the institutional level are in focus:

> The reform [at our university] meant, first of all, working on changing the awareness of people, the awareness of the university teachers; changing the awareness that a university teacher and assistant are not the Law, that the teacher is not someone who nobody can supervise, that he is someone who is only subject to science and that the rest should behave as he says. This mentality has been present in the heads of many teachers at our university. [...] The most

---

ministries and quality assurance agencies and with independent experts were recorded between February and April 2012.

4   Altogether, there were 2,019 respondents (professors, lecturers and assistants) from 16 universities in eight countries. The poll was conducted between March and May 2012.

difficult task was to change the teachers, to make them understand that they are no longer in the centre of the process but that now the students are in the centre (66; 27/3/12).

The reforms were generally initiated by the responsible ministries. At least in some countries, academics felt they had been introduced into these initiatives and took part in them: "*Universities have had a fairly large impact on shaping higher education policy*", e.g. in the process of developing the national master plan for higher education in Slovenia (as proven by 37; 11/4/12). In Macedonia, on the other hand, political negotiations after the slowdown of ethnic conflicts (ended by the Ohrid Agreement of 2001 which also includes some provisions on education for ethnic groups which were adopted in a legal amendment), provided "*a possibility to start changing the traditional law on higher education*" (01; 8/2/12). This political approach was interpreted at the institutional level as the proper context to speed up the modernisation of higher education.

However, some interviewees give an impression that even in those countries where this cooperation existed in previous times it has been eroded by today. Of course, gradual disillusionment in the 'new era' has probably been contributing to the darker picture today. The just quoted interviewee added: "*I do not know if this is still true. Now, the university is under the main pressure from politics*" (37; 11/4/12). Another one stated:

Twenty years ago, higher education played a significantly more important role in national politics, not only in terms of funding, but also the amenities of support. Today, higher education and research are not priorities (39; 10/4/12).

There is no real evidence that politics directly interferes in everyday academic matters or interferes 'in the old way'; nevertheless, there is evidence that politics has been penetrating higher education in an indirect and often quite harmful way. Some of the interviewees' statements are quite direct here, e.g.:

The university is absolutely a political body. This is not the junction where we are one profession, one body we have; it is by the political line. Ideally, a professor at a university is a non-political entity. But here, a complete replacement of the thesis has occurred: politics is all in shreds (27; 1/3/12).

Who shapes higher education policy at the national level? Four to five individuals. All these people have established private universities, faculties. [...] We are shutting our eyes if we believe that the university, faculties and experts are shaping higher education policy. [With us today,] higher education has become 'politics.com' (42; 27/2/12).

The politicisation of higher education is particularly connected to issues concerning private institutions; they were almost everywhere legally allowed already during the first wave of legislating but this sector really started to grow only after 2000. In one interview, a complaint is made that:

> the latest legislative proposals from two years ago were aiming at the privatisation of higher education and the goal was to destroy [our] University [...]. This was the aim of politics for reasons of personal gain. The idea is that the university would be cut into several smaller ones and the declared reason was said to be international comparison – that 'this is being done elsewhere in Europe' (29; 9/3/12).

Similar ideas have also been heard in another country where the 'old', 'capitol' public university was in danger of being divided into several universities while new ones, often private and with political support, have already been set up. Counter-arguments that in many European countries smaller universities are being combined to form larger ones today usually cannot be heard in the region.

In this context, one expert succinctly noted: *"State universities will be sacrificed in favour of private universities"* (27; 1/3/12). Reforms of higher education not only target 'modernisation' in order to 'better serve the needs of the nation' etc. They have encroached deeply into areas where conflicts of elites are taking place but they are also associated with the *'tycoonisation'* of higher education if we may borrow a popular word from the region at this point. *"The private sector did not bring investment into higher education"*, says one interviewee working at a quality assurance agency. *"It is my impression that most of these institutions have been established on the principle 'take the money and run'"* (76; 26/3/12). In the interviews concerns were also heard from a ministerial representative, e.g.:

> Furthermore, at some private universities, the boss, the founder, has a strong influence on university governance; this bothers us at the Ministry. We wouldn't want the founder to have anything do with the university governance except for the arrangement of certain internal relations. This is connected to the issue of autonomy and, therefore, it bothers us (07; 8/2/12).

The privatisation of higher education is obviously a Pandora's box in the Western Balkans. There has been a growing belief throughout the region that 'only competition can assure quality'. A consensus has been built around the thesis that traditional universities are working inefficiently and they need competition and such competition may come only from new institutions. It would be quite difficult to defend them against this criticism;

after a decade of political, economic and societal crisis they have been widely criticised for their 'unresponsiveness' and 'ossification', but they are also often academically depleted. However, until now there has been no proof that private institutions offer a real alternative. Interviewees at the 'old' universities liked to stress that the new institutions are by no means competitors to them; they see their competitors as existing abroad.

The following words by an academic from a university established in the 1970s summarise the essence of the problem simply but optimally:

> I think that in these lands of ours [orig. "na ovim našim prostorima"] private initiative has been allowed too soon – not only on the higher education level, but also on other levels of [pre-tertiary] education. It was too early, too early. [...] The situation in the aftermath of the war is good grounds for various *malfeasances* and we, in these lands, Balkans lands, are susceptible to *malfeasance*, unfortunately. When we get the right to establish a private faculty or university we will do this not for the sake of the prosperity of our community [...] as a whole, but because we need money for our own pockets. The private institutions – not only [with us] but in the broader region – are in the first place commercially oriented. This means they are established in order to sell. [...] Not only have I thought that this is not good, it is completely sure that this is not good. *What we have let happen with education* in these our lands – namely by opening up the private sector of education – is the biggest enemy [of our country] (66; 27/3/12).

Has the privatisation of higher education progressed due to international influences? Using more offensive words (and applying a discourse well known from the region's traditions): are 'these lands of ours' threatened from 'the outside'? The question is not merely rhetorical. Through a period of 'transition' the region 'has learned' how to behave 'to catch up with Europe'. And so, *"some people thought let it be, let the market decide and so on"*. Yet, today *"I simply think it was too liberal a policy. Without going back into the reasons I think it was very harmful"* (63; 21/3/12).

The problems discussed here trigger another question: what is the real impact of the international trends and international policies on domestic reforms? The international and particularly European higher education space in usually estimated very highly everywhere in the region and joining the Bologna Process has often been proudly portrayed as a success at the national as well as institutional level. However, it looks as if there is a lack of a balance between a desire for integration into the international space and the necessary reforms which should be implemented at home. *"I need to stress, and I agree more with that one hypothesis that there is a stronger desire to be involved in these international trends than we really wanted to reform our national system according to our taste"* (36; 22/2/12). This problem has led to changes which occurred *"in formal rather than substantive terms"* (27; 1/3/12). This is perhaps the crucial issue when it comes to implementing the Bologna Process in the region.

Between Bologna and 'Bologna'

Our interviewees were practically unanimous that the most important lever and the key impetus for national reforms has been the Bologna Process (in this context, the interviewees very rarely mention other international organisations or fora). However, this statement is far from being simply enthusiastic. One cannot overlook the great work that has been done particularly at the institutional level, for example in modernising curricula, and to which the respondents often expressed a positive attitude; on the other hand, one can also not overlook the many critical comments.

In our so-called *Questionnaire A,* respondents – academic staff ranging from professors to assistants – were asked (Q-13) if the Bologna Process has contributed importantly to the quality of their institutions. We searched for 'fans' and 'opponents'; for this reason, the answers were evaluated on a scale from +2 (strongly agree) to –2 (strongly disagree), while neutral answers (i.e., those who responded "neither agree nor disagree" or "no opinion") were eliminated from the calculations. (We must add here that some respondents pointed out in their comments that there has been an impact on quality, but a negative one, which may mean that the overall results should be interpreted somewhat more towards the negative end of the scale.)

The mean score for the region is *negative*: –0.45. It is particularly negative in Croatia (–1.05) and Bosnia and Herzegovina (–1.02), while it is positive only in Kosovo (+0.48). The positive and negative 'votes' from Albania (+0.01) and Slovenia (–0.01) neutralised each other: this speaks of two opposing blocks of approximately equal strength. The remaining three countries (Macedonia, Montenegro and Serbia) are very close to the regional mean. Within individual countries, there are a few visible inconsistencies between the two universities included in our sample. Thus, for example, the score for the 'capitol' university in Albania is negative (–0.26), whereas the score for the 'regional' one is positive (+0.45). It is similar in Montenegro (–0.91 vs. +0.63) and much less explicit in Macedonia (–0.56 vs. –0.18); yet in both cases the second university is a private (non-profit) one. Generally speaking, the 'capitol' or 'traditional' universities are more prone to a negative assessment than the 'new' and private ones. Only in the case of Slovenia is this relationship reversed, but the difference between both universities is negligible (0.00 vs. –0.04). To understand these data better, it is also important to check the share of undecided (i.e., neutral answers) respondents by countries and universities: there are only 13.61 percent of such respondents in Albania while in Macedonia this share is the highest, 32.69 percent. In other countries, it is between one-fifth and one-quarter of the total.

Therefore, with a few exceptions respondents in the region do not perceive the Bologna Process is contributing importantly to the quality of their institutions. This matches with the findings from the interviews which, of course, give a more detailed insight into the issue and related problems. Many interviewees think it is necessary to distinguish between criticisms of the Bologna Process on one side and criticisms of the domestic higher education system and its failures on the other. We will consider some of the details of this soon.

We mentioned that most countries in the region only officially joined the Bologna Process in 2003. This does not mean that until then the universities were completely cut off from the Process. On the contrary, almost everywhere there were 'avant-garde' institutions (or semi-organised circles within them) which started before their minister signed the Declaration. Bilateral and multilateral inter-university cooperation projects seem to have been the strongest levers in these cases. We can call this phase of accession to Bologna *the bottom-up phase*; it is mainly evidenced in project work. A dean of a technical faculty from the region interpreted this stage as follows:

> Here we said that if there had been no Bologna we would have invented Bologna. We were actually headed in that direction before our minister signed the Declaration. The Faculty of Technical Sciences is very complex – there are 12,000 students; we are a technical university so to say – and many of our professors were in the world. So we initiated some processes ourselves – and we welcomed Bologna. Bologna entered faculties via the university and through national institutions and even a few NGOs had some influence (11; 22/2/12).

Later, after the official accession, ministries launched legislative changes mostly through amendments to relevant laws. This was *the top-down phase* which was accelerated practically everywhere due to its 'urgency' – and this has gradually led to more and more criticism among the academic, student and broad publics. In many countries, substantial formal changes took place so to say overnight; while reading the documents and interviews we cannot escape the impression that the main actors often wanted to be recognised as 'the best student in class' and they immediately legally regulated the national system, as 'requested by Europe'.

Among several complaints expressed or reported in the interviews, we identified a '*file rouge*': a lack of coordination of institutions at the national level and a lack of necessary resources to run reforms. There were further weak points, like e.g. a lack of 'information campaigns'; preparatory activities have been usually limited to the circle of governmental and academic decision-makers while the everyday academic, senior or junior, and student remained in an information shadow. "*Information was kept inside* [the Ministry]; *the academic community was not very aware about the real changes* [in the European context]. *Usually, the top management of universities and top officials in the Ministry are much better informed about the need for change internationally. They are the drivers of change*" (01; 8/2/12).

The interviewees are almost unanimous again: the 'Bologna agenda' itself has not presented a problem in their countries and their institutions; the problem is the implementation of the reforms. Here are some particularly interesting statements about this:

> In 2003 there was the introduction of the Bologna system that has a lot of good points; however, it has been introduced with a little force, hastily and we needed plenty of years [to heal] the childhood diseases, to correct much of this. My opinion is that a large number of people looked a bit too one-sided and dogmatically at all the regulations. [...] These are all people from the previous system, who are entrenched there, so they thought that the adoption of rules, regulations and laws is changing society, changing education. And it is not so. [First] you need to create the conditions (29; 9/3/12).

> With us there is the situation that whatever the Bologna Process proposes the legislators or government officials quickly put into law. There is an impression that it is simply going too fast. For instance, in PhD studies there should be [by law] 180 credits [ECTS] while even in Europe it has not yet been agreed on whether these studies have credits or not. Another example: there must be 40 percent electives [by law]. All recommendations of the Bologna Process very quickly enter the regulations. [...] An impression emerges that we are doing something that someone else told us to (04; 23/3/12).

> The legislation prescribed by Bologna was fully respected, but the way of working at faculties has not changed. It is necessary to reduce the number of students in groups and to increase the number of professors as well as to make

communication among them more direct. Better computer infrastructure is needed; libraries should be better equipped and working conditions improved (22; 1/3/12).

The elderly two universities are such strong and static institutions that they respond to these changes in their own way. Thus, it is not even possible to dramatically impose something on *large institutions. My assessment* is not *impartial because I was involved in these things first within* [an 'old'] *university* and *then because I helped* to *co-found a new institution: this reform was channelled with a bun in the pocket, or slightly in half, so that as little as possible could be changed,* and then they *complained how wrong it all is. There has been no problem in the spirit of the Bologna Process, which is very advanced; the problem is in its implementation* (46; 10/4/12).

Thus, it is not unexpected that the current reputation of the Bologna Process "is very bad. But you know: many things are attributed to Bologna and Bologna is dragged down, but Bologna is not at fault for this. Bologna does not impose this system of evaluation or another one. [...] Everyone who wanted to change something, to introduce a personal idea, said – 'Ah, Bologna requires it and we need to change it now because of Bologna'. [...] That was the general climate" (33; 22/2/12). The interviewees sometimes refer to problems of 'understanding' Bologna; we could say that problems with implementation actually start with problems of interpreting what, in fact, European Ministers have agreed upon in their declarations and communiqués. This is not exclusively a Western Balkans issue; however, the region has obviously contributed its own special interpretation or perhaps a few of them. Even in one of our interviews we found a concrete example of such an 'original' interpretation: "According to Bologna, there can only be 7 exams per year and 24 hours in the classroom" (48; 13/3/12). Of course, nothing like this has been required within the bodies of the Bologna Process.

Several interviewees are obviously well aware of this problem and some also openly and critically reflect on both (mis)interpretations as well as their criticisms, like for example the following academic who works in the position of Vice Rector:

What actually is the idea of Bologna? Which are the elements we are not happy with? Do they result from Bologna or not? [...] A lot of consequences of the transformation in society and the diseases we have had during this transformation are seen as a consequence of Bologna leading to a critical attitude which is actually not a critical attitude to Bologna but a critical look at the consequences of the problems in [our] society. For example, there is reduced funding for higher education, an increasing number of candidates for general studies [i.e., not professional ones] because industry has collapsed etc. The easiest way is to say: 'Oh, that's because Bologna insists on 3+2'. My opinion is that this critical attitude is unduly sharp (04; 23/3/12).

Sometimes, it is possible to also find a similar approach among interviewees from ministries; one of them noted a specific lethargy within universities which contributes to the problems of 'understanding Bologna' as well as its implementation:

As a government representative I am personally very disappointed about the lack of initiative and inactivity of our higher education institutions. We have a system where institutions initiate change [...]. For us, it is the opposite: everything is initiated from the level of the Ministry – and then institutions feel this as an imposition from the top. [...] I am seeing a few national debates for the first time now, with criticisms of Bologna. But I expected more; they stopped fast. Given the scepticism with which [our] higher education space accepted Bologna, I would have expected [...] that there would really be a lot of suggestions and national debates, e.g. why it is unacceptable, how it will be adapted to the national context etc. But we are more Papal than the Pope and we have implemented Bologna in legislation almost literally, which again indicates the absence of debate (43; 16/2/12).

In discussions over the previous decade, the difference between the responsibility 'of' higher education (institutions) and the responsibility 'for' higher education (by its stakeholders, starting with the government) has been highlighted several times and this can again be helpful at this point. In this context, a warning was uttered that the "lack of involvement as well as over-involvement, or badly conceived policies, will harm the sector" (Weber and Bergan 2005: 8). There has obviously been an abundance of both in the region. On one hand, there has been a small academic 'avant-garde' pushing towards modernisation mainly through project work (i.e., not on a system level) but surrounded by a sceptical or passive (here we leave aside the reasons) academic majority while, on the other, there has been a substantial re-regulation of legal systems which has even been 'swinging' from one concept to the opposite following changes in the political composition of a government.

The composition of the two new cycles, bachelor and master, has occupied the very centre of regional disputes. *Either '3+2' or '4+1'?* This has been the key dilemma of legislators, academics and students. This dilemma has been reinforced by the fact that the new two-cycle structure has no tradition in the region and that it has therefore been incomprehensible to many. Within this context, there has been a hot debate on what the relationship should be between the 'new' degrees (Bachelor and Master) and the 'old' Diploma. The 'avant-garde' started by redesigning the old curricula (most often four years but in some cases like medicine, engineering etc. also longer) into new three-year ones. There was resistance at universities and around 2005 in some countries an interpretation gained supremacy whereby the 'old' Diploma should be recognised as equal to the 'new' Master (Zgaga and Miklavič 2011, Kurelić and Rodin 2012). The old 'research-based' Master's disappeared. In some cases, this was immediately put into law; in the most direct and problematic way in Slovenia and Croatia (2006).

This was crucial for 'understanding' Bologna and its 'adjustment to local circumstances'. Thus, an 'avant-garde' dean reports how the reforms were 'swinging' at their faculty:

> We started with a plan to reduce a four-year study programme to three years, as it was conceived, and we conceptualised the master's programme as research-based [...] Then there was madness in the then Ministry [...] and study programmes were extended. [Now,] we have an undergraduate study programme which lasts five years. Total madness. At the same time, we wiped out the master's programme. [...] Today, people study with us for five years to get the same title [i.e., a degree] which was previously awarded after four years of study. Someone is making fun of us (42; 27/2/12).

This was an extreme case which has been producing problems and dilemmas up until today; some other countries have avoided such a solution and remained 'more liberal' regarding the '3+2' or '4+1' dispute but they have also had some time to learn about the consequences of this kind of 'interpretation'. In any case, this has probably been the centre of polemics and criticisms which still persist in the region. As I show in more detail elsewhere (Zgaga 2010), these criticisms may be divided at least into 'conservative' and 'progressive' ones. The first group recommends e.g. boycotting changes (but in a more 'political' than 'research' language), while the latter recommends to "distinguish between the *idea* of the reform with the potentials that it unlocks, from the *reality* of its imperfect implementation with disappointments that it brings" (Gregorić 2010).

Between international norms and local values and identities

There has been an inspiring discussion on these issues in a Croatian social sciences journal where 'progressives' proposed drawing "a distinction between the harmonisation of higher education in Europe (the Bologna Process) and the attempt to introduce the Bologna Process into our country ('Bologna')" which is "a distortion of the original idea" and "an example of a failed reform and an example of unwilling Europeanisation". Further, 'Bologna' "understands the Bologna Process in a way which makes its implementation in Croatia impossible". Relying on Kuhn's concept of "paradigm change" and Feyerabend's "interaction of traditions", it has been shown "that 'Bologna' is an undesired mixture of our old tradition and the model introduced by the Bologna Declaration" (Kurelić 2010: 9 and 11).

Further discussion pointed out what we have partly already heard in the interviews above: "Implementation of the Bologna reform in Croatia is a failure. In essence, the majority of higher education establishments have extended their original four-year degree programmes into five-year ones. At the same time, such extended programmes were mechanically split in two parts in order to satisfy the formal requirement of 3+2 or 4+1". Further on, "master programs did not develop in direction of diversity and multi-disciplinarity but, as a rule, remained mono-disciplinary and substantively related to the first Bologna cycle" (Rodin 2010: 30 and 26). Unfortunately, in other countries there was much less discussion of this type; this is also a reflex of the state of higher education studies in the region.

It can be concluded that the central problem of the higher education reforms and their implementation in the region is that the reception of the Bologna Process has chiefly been held in discourses dominated by a traditional value code. The normative dimension of the system has been changed fundamentally while the axiological dimension has remained largely unchanged. At this point, the 'international' and the 'global' meet the 'native', or vice versa. This conclusion requires further consideration of the internationalisation and Europeanisation processes or, better, the international impact on regional higher education systems.

The situation regarding internationalisation in the region has been quite diverse. Slovenia started its integration and accession processes already at the beginning of the 1990s, followed at the end of that decade by Croatia which was previously on hold because of the war. Macedonia, as the second country of the ex-YU region which avoided the wars of the 1990s, but not a violent ethnic conflict in 2001, was in this regard in a really unfavourable geopolitical situation. Albania passed through a politically very turbulent decade and had no real tradition in international academic co-operation; it needed to ensure the basic conditions for international cooperation first. Other countries were involved in wars and conflicts; Serbia and Montenegro (until its separation from Serbia) were also under international sanctions. Only since the beginning of the 2000s has the whole region been open and ready for international – as well as regional – academic cooperation. As a result, the level of internationalisation of higher education is today quite different among the different countries.

The isolation and marginalisation of the 1990s is often felt in the central and southern parts of the region (not in Croatia and in particular not in Slovenia). Our interviewees from this part are almost unanimous about the great benefit of the international influence. We several times heard words like these: *"For too many years we were a very closed society, in a very bad condition, and* [...] *for us, any experience coming from the international* [space] *is very good.* [...] *It is very important to see where we are and where they are. This exchange of experience is very welcome for all of us"* (58; 23/3/12). As a particular case, international quality evaluators were mentioned, e.g.: *"Through these external evaluators we are pushing toward this internationalisation process. Rightly so"* (63; 21/3/12).

We also often heard that joint international projects are very helpful and valuable for capacity-building and overall development at home universities; however, we also registered complaints regarding the sustainability of the project outcomes, e.g. about the continuity of the established new study programmes. Further on, the European and international promotion of the modernisation of universities is highly conditioned; this conditionality is by no means unproblematic as it can create a tension and even a conflict between 'international norms' and 'local values and identities'. *"I would say that it* [i.e., international influence] *is largely connected with the financial support that they offer. You know ... here is the recommendation, here is the idea, here is the priority that we are setting – and here is the money. You either take it or leave it"* (64; 19/3/12).

On the other hand, accelerated international (i.e. Western) influences create a new kind of one-dimensional thinking: *"You can find a lot of* xenomania *in higher education: whatever is produced in the West is good;* [...] *whatever is not produced in the West, e.g. in China or Russia, is not 'science'. In our law, let me say, to be Doctor of Science you have to publish at least two articles in a* Western *journal"* (49; 16/3/12). This kind of thinking may only deepen the tension between the 'local' and 'international'. This can be seen in every-day culture as well as in higher education.

The experience of international assistance in the reconstruction and modernisation of higher education in those parts of the region, where the aid has been substantial, is leading to some doubts today. In the following interview, this particularly came to the fore:

> This vague attitude of the European institutions has a whole series of consequences at the national level. This reserved attitude is OK: we will not interfere much, you have freedom, you can do so taking into account your specifics etc. But others do not understand it this way. Here, for example: Balkan people are accustomed to working according to a recipe. [...] They haven't become accustomed to this: 'Make it as you wish but, nevertheless, take care to be similar to the others or to be able to communicate with the others.' There was slavery here, when someone told us what to be. Or socialism, when they announced from the centre: 'It will be like this!' This does not change overnight. [...] These European initiatives, they are good, but they are not entirely clear to make them understood by the people. [...] They [i.e., European institutions] should be more transparent; they should be more direct (09; 22/3/12).

We recently read that a conceptual differentiation between "identity convergence" and "identity divergence" may help "explain the different trajectories of Europeanisation in otherwise similar states" of South-East Europe (Subotić 2011: 310). This general statement can also be applied to higher education. At a similarly general level, addressing EU political conditionality in the Western Balkans, Freyburg and Richter have raised "serious doubts" about the prospects of the external democracy promotion via political conditionality in the region (Freyburg and Richter 2010: 263). Their "article has sought to show that national identity significantly influences the effectiveness of external democratization by political conditionality" and that "[n]ational identity plays a crucial role by 'filtering out' issues that are beyond the scope of appropriate government action" (ibid.: 275).

In greater detail, they argue: "Conditionality as an incentive-based instrument is only under certain preconditions suitable for catalysing substantial change in countries characterized by legacies of ethnic conflict. [...] our study confirms that in cases where conditions correspond to a prevailing national identity, external incentives may well trigger democratization. However, if conditionality criteria contradict a nation's self-conception, states will not comply or – in case of identity conflict – do so only inconsistently. Democratic change is then only possible in the course of a profound identity change" (ibid.:

276). We only need to change the word "state" with "university" and this thesis can also be applied to higher education in the region.

In conclusion, Freyburg and Richter quote Vladimir Tismaneanu, a Romanian and American political scientist, who claims the "good news is that the ongoing transitions take place simultaneously with the reinvention of Europe, and that the ideal of a united Europe is one of the most contagious and magnetic models these countries have ever dealt with" (ibid.). Yet the problem with 'good news' today (late 2012) is that the very 'ideal of a united Europe' is in a deep crisis. This is not a problem only for the 'united Europe' but also for its peripheral parts. This is well known to all countries of the region. Last but not least: the region borders Greece. At this point, countries of the region are again at a crossroads.

Conclusion: 'Policy colonies' or 'policy autarchies'?

There is a common belief (whether justified or not is not so important here) that in today's highly internationalised and/or globalised higher education policies 'peripheral countries' play the role of a kind of 'policy colony'. Higher education policy 'visions' come to these countries from 'centres'; foreign answers are given for domestic troubles. Is this true? At the end of our analysis of higher education reforms in the Western Balkans, we posit a provisional hypothesis (to be considered in detail next time) that this is only an 'outside' appearance while from the 'inside' we are dealing with 'policy autarchies'.

Three decades ago, Philip Altbach realised that "the centre-periphery concept has been applied to various societal relations but only recently to education" (Altbach 1998: 30). This application took place predominantly within the context of neo-colonialism which "consists of the policies of the industrialized nations that attempt to maintain their domination over the Third World", he added (ibid.: 31). Three decades later, the discussion on globalism overshadowed the discussion on neo-colonialism; yet it seems that the application of the centre-periphery concept to education has not progressed. However, this concept could be put to good use when analysing the emerging EHEA and, in particular, the Western Balkans.

Another article – it is 10 years old – helped us with conceptualising this issue also in the context of the Western Balkans: Marginson's analysis of "nation-building universities in a global environment" (Marginson 2002). He analysed the development of the Australian university system of the second half of the previous century and offers some comments which also appear to be important in our context. At the turn of the millennium when the discussion on globalisation in higher education had reached its peak, he warned us not to forget the *national* dimension: "Institutional identity is constituted by more than global systems: it is a product of history and retains national, local and disciplinary roots. The global dimension does *not* subsume the whole of the national dimension which enabled the modern university. [...] The old nation-building project has not disappeared, it has been refocused on position and strategy in a global context. [...] In the global era, with its shorter timelines and one externally-administered shock after another there is a new urgency to the nation-building role of governments and universities" (ibid.: 413-414).

A new "global/national world" is rotating around "global centres" and giving a particular challenge to countries on the periphery: "when nations on the periphery compete with institutions of the 'core' on the terms of the core, the outcome is not global success but weak imitation" (ibid.: 415). This is particularly painful in higher education. It was known already to Altbach that Third World "universities that are clearly peripheral in an international context are central nationally in terms of training and sometimes in terms of applied research and knowledge" (Altbach 1998: 41). He named this "a curious paradox" (ibid.: 32).

Yet the post-neocolonialist, globalist period from the turn of the millennium brings even harder challenges with it; in the Australian case Marginson articulates them as follows: "Once seen as an investment in the nation, Australian universities are now seen primarily as a source of fiscal savings used to retire debt and sustain the nation's global credit rating. According to the neo-liberal world-view, this does not matter: the national-public character of the universities is obsolete; if they are to survive and prosper they must re-fashion themselves as self-supporting global corporations" (Marginson 2002: 419).

Let us return from Australia to the opposite side of the planet – the Western Balkans. Political developments of the last 25 years led to the decay of the Yugoslav socialist federation which was open to the West much more than any other socialist country as well as to the decay of the autarchic socialist system in Albania. As a result, instead of these two 'utopias' there are eight nation-states in the region, joining the European Union or aiming to join it. Despite the nation-building traditions which each country is proud of, they are *nation-states in the making* – occurring in really troublesome conditions. The problem is dual: not only are the Western Balkans a European 'periphery'; the centre-periphery relationship can also be identified within it – in 'soft', e.g. value-based, terms as well as in 'hard' ones, e.g. economic facts.

A common problem of universities in the region is that they operate within nationally weak environments (small and young nation-states, weak economies, identities in the making etc.) and that they feel internationally largely 'unrecognised' (only one of them has been appearing on the Shanghai ranking list during the last decade and its position has usually been between 400 and 500). Their situation is further complicated by the fact that they are drawn into conflicts among national elites and the 'ideological struggle', which co-generate new private institutions that contribute to the reduction of the former academic criteria, the dominance of political considerations in the assessment of academic affairs, and the like. In a period when these universities should be recognised as one of the main pillars of building the new nation-state, new citizenship as well as 'integration in Europe' and cross-border cooperation, their role has been turned into the neoliberal "source of fiscal savings" as Marginson says. This is in particular obvious in the new wave of Slovenian reforms (2012) which are literally destroying the public higher education system with the argument of saving public funds in 'a period of a deep financial and economic crisis'.[5]

In the given circumstances, reforming higher education in the Western Balkans is truly a troublesome process. Also in our interviews we often encountered a feeling that the wheels of the reforms are spinning in neutral: strategic questions for universities as well as nation-states remain unanswered. Let us consider four more characteristic statements:

> Always we were starting anew. [...] Since the 1990s, we have been elaborating new strategic documents every four years again (09; 22/3/12).

> In our country we may have too much concentration on ourselves. [...] For the last few years we have concentrated too much on what our problems are, but not what is the global scene. At the state level, the global picture is a bit neglected (04; 23/3/12).

> [International impacts on national reforms] are certainly not marginal impacts; however, at the entrance these impacts can be identified at a high level but then, in a situation of 'softening', they are dropped (15; 29/3/12).

> We copy in a rather formal way the Bologna papers and make appropriate laws and regulations – not thinking at all why it should be. [...] There is a belief that

---

5   At the end of 2012 Marginson's words sound in Slovenia 'prophetic': by pledging allegiance to the 'lean state' and urgent fiscal savings, the Government's budget cut for 2013 has been proportionally the highest in the higher education and research area.

'we are fantastic' and that anyone who doesn't admit it actually hates us. Thus, PISA is a 'conspiracy of the West' (18; 29/3/12).

The thesis that 'smaller', 'transitional', 'underdeveloped', 'peripheral' etc. countries are simply playing the role of a 'passive territory' and that they are merely a 'policy colony' for the implementation of ready-made ideas from international and/or transnational policy circles seems to be far too short; at least in the case of the Western Balkans. However, these countries are not 'policy autarchies' either. The European and global discourses penetrate them – but after the implementation phase they are either 'softened' or 'dropped'. 'Peripheral' countries – and their higher education systems – differ from 'central' ones; political conditionality with ready-made formulas and solutions imported from the outside do not solve the problem; on the contrary. Of course, they should not be left on their own – so to say, pushing them into autarchy. More than in the 'centre' countries, a balance between the general and the particular is called for. A balance which holds important policy implications.

Acknowledgments

The author gratefully acknowledges the support of the Slovenian National Agency for Research through its grant DEP-08-EuroHESC-OP-016.

References

Altbach, Ph. (1998). *Comparative Higher Education Knowledge, the University and Development.* Boston: CIHE, Boston College.

CEPS (2012). Differentiation, Equity, Productivity: The social and economic consequences of expanded and differentiated higher education systems – internationalisation aspects (DEP-08-EuroHESC-OP-016). The Western Balkans Survey (January 2012 – June 2012). First results. Internal materials. Ljubljana: August 2012.

Freyburg, T., S. Richter (2010). "National Identity Matters: The Limited Impact of EU Political Conditionality in the Western Balkans". *Journal of European Public Policy.* Vol. 17. No. 2. 263-281.

Gregorić, P. (2010). "Achievements and Failures of the Bologna Process to Date". Round Table 'Processing the Bologna Process: Current Losses and Future Gains'. University of Zagreb, UNESCO Chair for Governance and Management of Higher Education. Zagreb, 5-6 March 2010.

In Defence of the University (1997; 1998). *Beogradski krug / Belgrade Circle.* No. 1-2 and 3-4.

Kurelić, Z. (2009). "How Not to Defend Your Tradition of Higher Education". In: *Politička misao / Croatian Political Science Review.* Vol. 46. No. 5. 9-20.

Kurelić, Z., S. Rodin (2012). "Failure of the Croatian Higher Education Reform". *CEPS Journal*. Vol. 2. No. 4. 29-52.

Marginson, S. (2002). "Nation-building Universities in a Global Environment: The Case of Australia". *Higher Education.* Vol. 43. No. 3. 409-428.

Rodin, S. (2009). "Higher Education Reform in Search of Bologna". In: *Politička misao / Croatian Political Science Review*. Vol. 46. No. 5. 21-38.

Scott, P. (2002). "Reflections on the Reform of Higher Education in Central and Eastern Europe". *Higher Education in Europe*. Vol. 27. No. 1-2. 137-152.

Scott, P. (2006). "Higher Education in Central and Eastern Europe". In: J. F. Forest, Ph. G. Altbach (eds.), *International Handbook of Higher Education*. Part Two: Regions and Countries. Dordrecht: Springer. 423-441.

Subotic, J. (2011). "Europe is a State of Mind: Identity and Europeanization in the Balkans". *International Studies Quarterly*. Vol. 55. No. 2. 309-330.

Šoljan, N. N. (1991). "The Saga of Higher Education in Yugoslavia: Beyond the Myths of a Self-Management Socialist Society". *Comparative Education Review*. Vol. 35. No. 1. 131-153.

Turajlić, S. (2004). *Visoko obrazovanje u Srbiji*. Beograd: Alternativna akademska obrazovna mreža.

Uvalić Trumbić, S. (1990). "New Trends in Higher Education in Yugoslavia?" *European Journal of Education*. Vol. 25. No. 4. 399-407.

Vukasović, M. (2005). "Visoko obrazovanje na putu ka Evropi: četiri godine kasnije" [Higher Education on the Road to Europe: Four Years Later]. In: *Visoko obrazovanje na putu ka Evropi: četiri godine kasnije*. Zbornik radova. Beograd: Alternativna akademska obrazovna mreža. 400-407.

Weber, L., S. Bergan, eds. (2005). *The public responsibility for higher education and research*. Strasbourg: Council of Europe Publishing.

Zgaga, P., ed. (1998). *Development of Higher Education in Slovenia*. Ljubljana: Ministry of Education and Sport.

Zgaga, P. (2003). "Reforming the Universities of South East Europe in View of the Bologna Process". *Higher Education in Europe*. Vol. 28. No. 3. 251-258.

Zgaga, P. (2004). *Analiza gibanj v strukturi študentov in diplomantov v terciarnem izobraževanju (1981 – 2004)* [Analysis of trends in the structure of students and graduates in tertiary education]. Ljubljana: CEPS.

Zgaga, P. (2007). *Higher Education in Transition. Reconsiderations on Higher Education in Europe at the Turn of the Millennium*. Umeå: Umeå University.

Zgaga, P. (2010). "The Role of Higher Education in National Development. South-Eastern Europe and Reconstruction of the Western Balkans". In: *The Europa World of Learning 2011*. London: Routledge. 19-24. Available at http://bit.ly/rf4MpT (accessed 15 November 2012).

Zgaga, P., K. Miklavič (2011). "Reforming Higher Education in Transition. Between National and International Reform Initiatives: The Case of Slovenia". *European Education*. Vol. 43. No. 3. 13-25.

Editors

John Brennan is Emeritus Professor of Higher Education Research at the Open University and a Visiting Professor at the University of Bath and London Metropolitan University. His interests lie broadly in the area of higher education and social change. For nearly 20 years, he directed the Centre for Higher Education Research and Information at the Open University where he led and participated in many national and international projects on topics such as graduate employment, quality assurance, the academic profession, and universities and social transformation. He has published several books and many reports and articles on higher education and its changing relationship with society and has spoken at countless conferences on higher education in the UK and many other parts of the world. Before joining the Open University in 1992, he had been Director of Quality Support at the Council for National Academic Awards and had held academic posts at Lancaster University and Teesside Polytechnic.

Contact: john.brennan@open.ac.uk

Ulrich Teichler has been a Professor at the International Centre for Higher Education Research (INCHER-Kassel), University of Kassel, Germany, since 1978 and a director of the Centre for 16 years. Born in 1942, he studied sociology, receiving a PhD from the University of Bremen in 1975. He was a researcher at the Max Planck Institute for Educational Research, Berlin (1968–1978), did a dissertation on higher education and social selection in Japan, and was vice president of the University of Kassel (1980–1982). His work visits to about 80 countries include: visiting scholar in Japan (1970–1972) and the Netherlands (1985–1986); part-time, short-term or visiting professorships at Northwestern University, Evanston/Illinois (1986–1992), College of Europe, Bruges (1994–1996), Hiroshima University (2004) and Open University, UK (2007–2012). He is the author or editor of more than 1,000 academic publications on the following key research areas: higher education and the world of work, international comparison of higher education systems, international cooperation and mobility; in addition: education and social selection, the academic profession, access and admission, continuing professional education, and evaluation in higher education. He is a member (with coordination functions) of the International Academy of Education and the Academia

Europaea; founding chairman of the Consortium of Higher Education Researchers (CHER) and former president and distinguished member of EAIR; doctor honoris causa of the University of Turku (Finland); and sponsor of the Ulrich-Teichler Prize for the best doctoral and master theses at German-speaking universities on higher education.

Contact: teichler@incher.uni-kassel.de

Pavel Zgaga is Professor of Philosophy of Education and Education Policy at the University of Ljubljana, Slovenia where he started his academic career in 1978. In the 1990s, during the period of social and political transition in Slovenia he was State Secretary for Higher Education as well as Minister of Education and Sport. After his return to academe, he served as a Dean of the Faculty of Education. In 2001 he co-founded the Centre for Educational Policy Studies (CEPS) and has been and continues to be its director. He has held several research grants and directed national and international projects mainly concerned with the development of higher education in the European context. In these areas, he has also been cooperating with relevant agencies of the European Commission and several international organisations, e.g. the Council of Europe, UNESCO, the OECD etc.; he has also been an invited speaker in a number of countries. He was engaged in the early years of the Bologna Process. He has published several books, reports and articles on (higher) education and (higher) education policy and is doctor honoris causa of the University of Umeå (Sweden).

Contact: pavel.zgaga@guest.arnes.si

Contributors

Jana Baćević is currently visiting professor at the Central European University in Budapest. She has a PhD (2008) in Social Anthropology from the University of Belgrade; between 2007 and 2008 she was OSI/FCO Chevening Scholar at the University of Oxford and, between 2010 and 2011, visiting research fellow at the Central European University, Budapest. Previously she taught at the University of Belgrade and Singidunum University and worked with the Centre for Education Policy in Belgrade as well as a consultant for a number of non-governmental and international organisations, focusing on higher education for minorities, development and social integration. Her research interests lie at the intersection between sociology, anthropology, politics and philosophy of knowledge, with a special focus on universities as institutions.

Contact: jana.bacevic@magd.oxon.org

Leon Cremonini has been a researcher at the *Centre for Higher Education Policy Studies* since 2006. He graduated in Political Science from the University of Bologna, Italy, in 2000 and has since worked both in Europe and with the RAND Corporation in the USA. His interests concentrate on the internationalisation of higher education, quality assessment at the institutional and programme level, selection and access, and on the study of university and programme rankings. In 2007–2009 Leon was a fellow of the "Global Policy Fellowship Programme" launched by the *Institute for Higher Education Policy* (USA) and designed to share ideas and experiences on equity and access policies for historically disadvantaged populations in tertiary education around the world. Leon has presented papers and published on these topics and been involved in a number of international projects concerned with the development of quality assurance and accreditation systems in several countries in Africa, the Middle East and South-East Asia. In the Netherlands, Leon has collaborated with the Dutch Ministry of Education, Culture and Science, contributing to the debates on "word-class universities" and selection as well as the financing of higher education.

Contact: l.cremonini@utwente.nl

Danijela Dolenec works at the Faculty of Political Science of the University of Zagreb, teaching comparative politics and social science methodology. She received her master's from the LSE (2005), and her doctorate in political science from ETH Zürich (2012). Her primary interest in post-communist democratisation evolved during her time at Harvard University as a Fulbright scholar (2007/2008). Danijela has written on the commodification of European systems of higher education and the Europeanisation of post-communist party systems, while most recently she authored *Democratic Institutions and Authoritarian Rule in Southeast Europe* (ECPR Press, forthcoming in 2013) and co-authored *We Need to Change*, a study on sustainable development in Croatia (Domazet, Dolenec and Ančić 2012).

Contact: ddolenec@fpzg.hr

Karin Doolan is Assistant Professor at the Department of Sociology, University of Zadar in Croatia, lecturing in sociology of education, cultural theory and research design. Before taking up this position, she worked at the Institute for Social Research in Zagreb as a researcher and consultant on various projects with a prominent social justice agenda (e.g. higher education participation, gender equity in compulsory schooling). She has also contributed as a policy analyst to developmental projects in both Croatia and the UK. She holds a PhD (2010) and MPhil (2003) in sociology of education from the University of Cambridge. Her academic interests include higher education policy research, theorisations of social reproduction across different political and economic contexts (with a particular interest in Bourdieu's conceptual tools), theorisations of social justice, as well as the ways in which societies and educational institutions can be organised to further it.

Contact: kdoolan@unizd.hr

Mari Elken is employed as a PhD research fellow in the Department of Educational Research at the University of Oslo, as well as being enrolled in NATED (National Graduate School in Education). She belongs to the HEIK (Higher Education: Institutional Dynamics and Knowledge Cultures) research group. Her main research interests are linked to higher education policy and governance, and the construction of a Europe of Knowledge. Her doctoral project focuses on the development of the European Qualifications Framework. She currently also runs the Hedda blog on higher education (http://uv-net.uio.no/wpmu/hedda/). From September to December 2012 she was a visiting fellow with the CHEPS (Centre for Higher Education Policy Studies) at University of Twente.

Contact: mari.elken@ped.uio.no

Elsa Hackl, Master's Degree in Law, Doctoral Degree in Politics, has worked in occupational/educational research and as a civil servant in a senior position (director at the Austrian Ministry for Higher Education and Research). She was Visiting Fellow at the University of British Columbia, Canada and at the European University Institute, Florence; she also worked as an expert for the OECD, the Council of Europe and the Salzburg Seminar. She was a member of the OECD/CERI Governing Board 2004–2010 and after 2006 External Advisor for ESCP – Europe Course Board. Now, she is working at the Department of Political Science, University of Vienna. Her research topics include education policy, public administration, Europeanisation and internationalisation.

Contact: elsa.hackl@univie.ac.at

Ellen Hazelkorn is Vice President of Research and Enterprise, and Dean of the Graduate Research School, Dublin Institute of Technology, Ireland; she also leads the Higher Education Policy Research Unit. She works closely with the International Association of Universities (IAU), and has been a consultant to the OECD. She is a member of the Higher Education Authority (Ireland). Ellen has been/is a member various governmental and international review teams, and has worked/is working with universities and university associations around the world. She is a member of various editorial boards: *Higher Education Policy*, *International Journal for Researcher Development*, and *Higher Education Management and Policy*. She is a member of the International Committee for the American Education Research Association (2012–2015). Her research and commentary has been reported by *The New York Times*, *International Herald Tribune*, *The Economist*, the *Times Higher Education*, *U.S. News & World Report*, the *Chronicle of Higher Education*, *The Australian* and others. She writes a regular blog for the *Chronicle of Higher Education*. *Developing Research in*

New Institutions was published by OECD (2005), and *Rankings and the Reshaping of Higher Education: The Battle for World-Class Excellence* by Palgrave Macmillan (2011).

Contact: ellen.hazelkorn@dit.ie

Manja Klemenčič is a postdoctoral researcher at the Centre for Educational Policy Studies of the Faculty of Education, University of Ljubljana where she is involved in the project *Differentiation, Equity, Productivity: The Social and Economic Consequences of Expanded and Differentiated Higher Education Systems – Internationalisation Aspects* (DEP-08-EuroHESC-OP-016). She is also a Postdoctoral Fellow in Education at the Harvard Graduate School of Education working on the monograph *Student Power in Europe*. Manja obtained a PhD in International Studies and an M.Phil in European Studies from the University of Cambridge. She has held several research fellowships at: the Centre for Social Science Research in Berlin (2011/12), the Center for International Higher Education at Boston College (2010/2011); the Minda de Gunzburg Center for European Studies at Harvard (2007/2008), the Center for Business and Government at Harvard Kennedy School (2004/2005), and the Centre for European Policy Studies in Brussels (2004). From 2013, she will be Managing Editor of the *European Journal of Higher Education*.

Contact: manja.klemencic@gmail.com

Janja Komljenovič is an assistant researcher at the Centre for Educational Policy Studies, University of Ljubljana. She has been working in the field of higher education for several years, beginning as a student representative in 2003 when she was involved in national and European higher education policy making, especially in the Bologna Process and quality assurance. In 2007 she worked for the European University Association and between 2009 and 2011 she was advisor to the Slovenian Minister of Higher Education, Science and Technology; since 2011 she has been working at the University of Ljubljana. Her research interests mainly encompass the roles of universities in contemporary societies, the changing circumstances of higher education and university autonomy.

Contact: janja.komljenovic@guest.arnes.si

Klemen Miklavič is an assistant researcher at the Centre for Educational Policy Studies, University of Ljubljana. He obtained both a university diploma and a research degree in social sciences from the University of Ljubljana. His work has been devoted to the field of higher education policy for more than a decade, dating back to his student activism. After graduation, he continued to work as a consultant, expert or freelance researcher for a number of NGOs, intergovernmental organisations and research centres such as the Council of Europe, the Centre for Education Policy in Belgrade etc. During 2008–2009 he was employed at the OSCE Mission in Kosovo as a senior adviser responsible for higher education and ethnic minority issues. He has continued since then to nurture his interests in the role of higher education in society, especially in (post)conflict settings.

Contact: klemen.miklavic@guest.arnes.si

Marek Kwiek, Full Professor and Director, Centre for Public Policy Studies (since 2002), and Chairholder, UNESCO Chair in Institutional Research and Higher Education Policy, University of Poznan, Poland. His research interests include university governance, welfare state and public sector reforms, the academic profession, and academic entrepreneurialism. He has published 110 papers and 8 monographs, most recently *Knowledge Production in European Universities. States, Markets, and Academic Entrepreneurialism* (2013) and *The University and the State: A Study into Global Transformation* (2006). A higher education policy expert to the European Commission, USAID, the OECD, the World Bank, UNESCO, the OSCE, and the Council of Europe. He has participated in 20 global and European research projects and 20 international higher education policy projects in the last ten years. He serves as an editorial board member of the *Higher Education Quarterly*, *European Educational Research Journal*, and *European Journal of Higher Education*.

Contact: kwiekm@amu.edu.pl

Susan Robertson is Professor of Sociology of Education, Graduate School of Education, University of Bristol. Susan has been engaged in researching the privatising of education more generally – and written on the emergence of new governing strategies within the education sector more generally. She has also written extensively and critically on higher education and its role in the development of competitive knowledge-based economies. Susan is currently founding editor of the journal *Globalisation, Societies and Education*.

Contact: s.l.robertson@bristol.ac.uk

Martin Ryan joined the Higher Education Policy Research Unit at the Dublin Institute of Technology (DIT) after submitting his PhD thesis to the University College Dublin (UCD) School of Economics in spring 2012. In his doctoral research (supported by the Irish Research Council for the Humanities and Social Sciences), Martin examined the determinants of study behaviours and student achievement; and the production of scientific output by early-career researchers. Prior to starting his PhD, Martin worked as a research assistant at the Geary Institute (UCD), and submitted an M.Phil. dissertation to DIT in 2007; his master's research was on the transition from school to higher education. Martin holds a postgraduate diploma in economic science (UCD, 2005), a bachelor's degree in business studies (DIT, 2004), and he has taken courses in econometrics at the London School of Economics (2007), the Barcelona Graduate School of Economics (2008) and the University of Michigan (2009).

Contact: martin.ryan@dit.ie

Tatjana Sekulić, PhD in Sociology at the University of Milan, is an Assistant Professor of Sociology at the University of Milan-Bicocca where she teaches Political Sociology of Europe and Sociology of Education. The main fields of her research are: European integration in a polycentric perspective; new wars and contemporary conflicts, crimes of war and genocide studies; democratic transition of post-totalitarian regimes and new forms of totalitarianism; higher education structural and institutional transformation. She has published several studies such as *Violenza etnica. I Balcani tra democrazia e etnonazionalismo* (Roma: Carocci 2002); "L'università e le integrazioni europee: le nuove sfide dell'agire accademico" in Boffo S., Rebeggiani E., *La Minerva ferita. Crisi e prospettive dell'università in Italia*, Napoli: Liguori editore 2011; Leccardi C., Feixa C., Kovacheva S., Reiter H., Sekulić T., *Young People and Social Change after the Fall of the Berlin Wall*, Council of Europe Publishing, Strasbourg 2011.

Contact: tanja.sekulic@unimib.it

Voldemar Tomusk, PhD, is a teacher, moralist and social commentator of Estonian origin, living in Mitcham, Surrey in England. He is the Director for Institutional Support of the International Higher Education Support Programme of the Open Society Foundations. Voldemar has taught physics and psychology, and served in the Estonian Ministry of Education. He completed his doctoral work in sociology of education "Blinding Darkness of the Enlightenment: Towards the Understanding of Post State-Socialist Higher Education in Eastern Europe" in 2001 under a fellow finno-ugric social philosopher Prof Osmo Kivinen at the University of Turku, Finland. He has written extensively about higher education reforms in Central and Eastern European countries and published criticisms and lamentations on the European Higher Education Area project, most recently in a forthcoming paper "European Higher Education after Gellner, Malinowski and Wittgenstein".

Contact: voldemar.tomusk@opensocietyfoundations.org

Martina Vukasović works as a PhD research fellow at the Department of Educational Research at the University of Oslo, also belonging to the NATED (National Graduate School in Education) and HEIK (Higher Education: Institutional Dynamics and Knowledge Cultures) research groups. She focuses on higher education policy and organisational change and her PhD is about institutional change in three flagship universities from former Yugoslavia. She is a member of the Council of the Magna Charta Observatory and the Governing Board of the Centre for Education Policy in Serbia (where she previously worked as a researcher and director). From September to December 2012 she was a visiting scholar at Scancor (Scandinavian Consortium for Organisational Research) at Stanford University.

Contact: martina.vukasovic@ped.uio.no

Index

Abazi, A. 299
Abbas, A. 196
Academic freedom 29, 44, 106, 277, 314
Access 7, 8, 12, 21, 22, 83, 91, 95, 117,
    124, 134, 141-144, 146-148, 151,
    152, 154, 156, 165, 166, 168, 172,
    175-178, 194, 201-204, 209, 211-
    216, 219, 223-227, 233-245, 249,
    253, 263, 280, 297, 302, 321, 330,
    341
Adelman, C. 83, 87
Aghion, P. 82
Albania 19, 117, 119, 121, 122, 126-130,
    132-134, 293, 294, 299, 302, 305,
    347-350, 357, 358, 364, 367
Alexander, J.C. 250
Altbach, P. G. 203, 235, 251, 366, 367,
    369
Amaral, A.12, 262, 288, 290
Apple, M. 329
Archer, L. 245, 247
Aru, H. 276
Arum, R. 142, 152-154, 235, 239, 242,
    244
Ash, M.G. 331
Ashwin, P. 196
Attewell, P. 235, 251
Attwood, R. 177
Autonomy 16, 18, 29, 41, 42, 44, 45, 49,
    84, 88, 106, 109, 110, 276, 277,
    279, 293, 294, 300, 311, 313-315,
    322, 330, 351, 353, 355
Avis, G. 264
Ayres, Y.M. 325, 327

Baćević, J. 24, 25, 291
Barr, N. 94, 173
Barrera-Osorio, F. 174
Bartlett, W. 236
Batory, A. 38, 46
Bayerl, A. 296
Beerkens, E. 265, 266

Beerkens-Soo, M. 202, 223
Bekhradnia, B. 93, 94, 150
Bennett, D. 175
Bergan, S. 361
Bernstein, B. 155, 156
Bertrams, K. 103
Bialecki, I. 235-237, 242
Bieber, F. 298
Bienefeld, St. 102, 111
Birnbaum, R. 102
Bleiklie, I. 45
Boffey, D. 179
Bologna 8, 14, 24, 83, 122, 123, 129,
    131, 264, 266-268, 282, 289, 315,
    357, 358, 360, 363
Bologna Declaration 12, 37, 56, 66, 83,
    265, 275, 278, 279, 282, 317, 353,
    363
Bologna Process 14, 16, 19, 24, 25, 27,
    29, 33, 37, 38, 46, 59, 61, 63, 66,
    69, 76, 83, 87, 90, 103, 108, 111,
    120, 122, 123, 126, 131, 146, 179,
    225, 261, 262, 265, 266, 269, 271,
    273-282, 290, 309, 310, 313, 317,
    318, 321, 322, 347, 351-353, 356,
    357-363, 368
Bomberg, E. 267, 268
Börzel, T. 120, 121, 133, 261, 268, 269
Bosnia and Herzegovina 25, 271, 292,
    293, 298, 309, 311, 313, 317, 318,
    322, 347, 349, 351, 357
Bourdieu, P. 195, 202, 327
Bowles, S. 245, 330
Brady, N. 92
Branković, J. 278
Breen, R. 247
Brehony, K. 92
Breneman, D. 166
Brennan, J. 11, 21, 104, 190, 191, 193,
    197, 288
Britez, R. 288-291
Brown, P. 194

Brown, R. 94, 168, 170, 328
Brown, W. 327, 330
Browne, J. 93, 95, 168-170, 172
Buckland, P. 294, 295
Burawoy, M. 146, 150, 152, 153
Bürger, S. 63, 71
Burgess, T. 103
Butler, N. 82, 84

Calhoun, C. 30, 148, 152, 154
Callan, E. 304
Callinicos, A. 336
Canada 44, 326
Capano, G. 123
Capitalism 326, 330, 331, 334, 336, 337
Carpentier, V. 161
Cartmel, F. 241, 245, 253
Causa, O. 245, 246
Centre(s) 7, 9, 11, 14, 26, 28, 38, 41, 61,
     86, 88, 106, 123, 125, 127, 128,
     130, 134, 205, 208, 220, 223, 224,
     275, 276, 280, 300, 312, 318, 319,
     329, 332, 343, 347-349, 354, 365-
     369
Chalmers, D. 328
Chambers, M. 91
Change - social ch. 7, 13, 23, 30, 185,
     250
- policy ch. → Policy
Citizen(s) 62, 64, 93, 155, 158, 171, 207,
     279, 300, 318, 326, 327, 329, 335,
     337, 340, 341
Citizenship 55, 58, 61, 62, 65, 75, 329,
     368
Clark, B.R. 146-149, 152, 186
Clark, J.N. 303
Clarke, J. 112
Clegg, C. 153-157
Codling, A. 118, 119, 130
Collini, S. 329, 330
Commercialisation 168, 338, 341
Communism 23, 141, 158, 233, 234, 237,
     240, 242

Competitiveness 12, 15, 16, 18, 28, 36,
     38, 39, 43, 45, 48, 49, 84-86, 94,
     95, 104, 110-113, 123, 128, 328,
     338-342
Conditionality 133, 134, 269, 364, 365,
     369
Conflict 25-27, 102, 202, 203, 216, 226,
     289, 292-300, 302-304, 312, 351,
     352, 363, 365, 377
Convergence 9, 11-13, 15, 16, 24, 38, 45,
     48, 49, 83, 118, 121, 123, 261-263,
     265-271, 282, 283, 304, 365
Cooling-out 146-149, 152, 155
Corbett, A. 37, 83, 87, 265
Cremonini, L. 22, 202, 203
Crises 156, 174
Croatia 19, 24, 26, 27, 117, 119, 121,
     126-129, 130, 133, 134, 261-265,
     271-274, 281-283, 292, 294, 314,
     325, 326, 329-343, 347, 351, 353,
     357, 362-364
Cvitan, M. 329
Czapliński, M. 297, 298

Daftary, F. 298
Dagger, R. 304
Dale, R. 84
Davies, L. 89
Daxner, M. 295
De Lourdes Machado, M. 103
De Wit, H. 57
Deem, R. 92, 168
Delanty, G. 288, 304
Demographics 22, 233-235, 243, 244,
     252-254
Dempsey, N. 79
Den Boer, N. 295
Denscombe, M. 332
DeShano da Silva, C. 245
Difference 12, 13, 59, 74, 80, 108, 120,
     142, 156, 186, 189, 218, 219, 237,
     240, 243, 303, 304, 306, 358, 361
Differentiation 9, 18, 19, 21-23, 43, 95,
     101-104, 112, 122, 135, 186-198,

233, 234, 239, 241, 242, 250, 253, 254, 365

Diversification 7, 10, 18, 19, 25, 43, 44, 49, 101-113, 117-135, 143, 236, 291, 302, 329

Diversity 9, 11-13, 15, 18, 19, 23, 62, 86, 95, 102-105, 113, 117-120, 122-126, 128, 130, 134, 135, 191, 196, 223, 266, 290, 322, 363

Dobbins, M. 235, 262, 304

Dolenec, D. 26, 27, 328, 334

Dolowitz, D. 268

Domanski, H. 240, 249

Doolan, K. 26, 27, 291

Duczmal, W. 235, 241, 242, 252

Dufner, B. 90

Duvekot, R. 205-209

Easterlin, R. A. 251

Eicher, J.-C. 329

Elite 20, 21, 92, 95, 103, 111, 142-148, 150, 154, 174-177, 186, 190, 191, 193, 195, 197, 205, 236, 237, 239-243, 289, 294, 316

Elken, M. 24, 122

Enders, J. 243, 290

Enlargement 309
- European e. 348

Enserink, M. 90

Equity 7-10, 19, 21, 22, 28, 117, 122, 148, 166, 178, 185, 190, 193, 197, 201-204, 206, 209, 219, 225

Estermann, T. 276

Ethnicity 304, 313, 331

Europe 7-13, 15-17, 19, 22, 23, 29, 30, 36-39, 43-45, 55-57, 59, 60, 62-66, 72, 73, 75, 79-87, 89, 94, 96, 102, 104, 111, 113, 123, 125, 135, 146, 150, 161, 162, 164, 165, 177, 188, 190, 203, 205, 207, 233-235, 237, 239, 240, 244, 248, 251, 252, 262, 265, 266, 268, 270, 276, 282, 289, 290, 297, 303, 304, 306, 326-329,

331, 334, 342, 348, 351, 355, 356, 359, 363, 365, 366, 368
- European enlargement → *Enlargement*
- European integration → *Integration*

European Higher Education Area (EHEA) 13-15, 46, 64, 84, 85, 103, 123, 150, 270, 274, 276, 298, 310, 313, 315, 322, 351, 366

Europeanisation 11-14, 18, 24-27, 33, 34, 38, 46, 102, 117, 120, 122, 133, 261-263, 265, 267-271, 281-283, 290, 291, 351, 363, 365

Fairclough, N. 35, 36, 46

Farrington, D. 299

Faulks, S. 153

Featherstone, K. 261

Ferencz, I. 62, 63

Fielden, J. 165

Financing 42, 89, 128, 132, 133, 153, 244, 252, 287, 299, 328, 338, 339
- education f. 128, 133, 244, 252, 299, 328, 338, 339

Fligstein, N. 163

France 17, 64, 69, 70, 82, 87-90, 92, 94, 95, 195, 250, 251, 277

Frances, C. 250, 251

Frank, D.J. 104

Fraser, N. 27, 291, 325, 326, 330-332, 337, 343

Freyburg, T. 352, 365, 366

Furlong, A. 241, 245, 253

Gamoran, A. 239

Garben, S. 267

Geiger, R. L. 240, 243, 250

Gellner, E. 142

Germany 17, 64, 69, 70, 82, 87, 88, 90-92, 94, 95, 103, 107, 130, 227, 247, 248, 251

Gill, S. 163

Gintis, H. 330

Giroux, H.A. 325, 328, 329, 331

Glaeser, A. 158

Globalisation 7, 9, 11-14, 24, 25, 27, 85,
    86, 104, 290, 291, 305, 325, 340,
    367
Globalism 366
Goedegebuure, L. 239, 250
Gornitzka, A. 38, 42, 46, 48, 84, 121,
    123, 261, 266, 269
Governance 18, 24, 26, 33, 38, 42, 44,
    45, 49, 84, 90, 92, 108, 109, 112,
    123, 128, 132, 133, 163, 165, 226,
    265-268, 270, 275-279, 287, 313-
    316, 322, 330, 352, 355
Grabert, M. 87
Gradstein, M. 330
Graduate 7, 21, 41, 43, 55, 67, 68, 69, 71,
    76, 91, 145, 152, 153, 166, 173,
    190, 214, 329, 341
- g. surveys 55, 68, 69, 71, 76
Graziano, P. 362
Green, A. 328
Gregorić, P. 362
Guaqeta, J. 174
Guillen, A. 328
Guillot, M. 250
Guri-Rosenblit, S. 119, 123
Gutmann, A. 304

Habermas, J. 171, 290
Hackl, E. 18, 112
Hardt, M. 303, 305
Harmonisation 83, 103, 267, 309, 321,
    363
Hartmann, E. 45, 46, 48
Harvey, D. 44, 338
Hazelkorn, E. 17, 80, 92
Heinze, T. 262, 265, 267, 268
Hentschke, G. 166
Héritier, A. 262, 276, 282
Heuveline, P. 250
Higher education
- h.e. contraction 22, 233, 235-239, 241-
    244, 250-254
- h.e. governance → Governance
- h.e. policy(ies) 15-17, 19, 20, 24, 26,
    37, 38, 46, 48, 56, 79, 82, 83, 90,
    92, 94-96, 102, 121, 122, 123, 130,
    141, 152, 158, 161, 162, 169, 179,
    180, 262, 265, 267, 268, 270, 279,
    281, 282, 304, 305, 347, 354, 366
- h.e. reform(s) 9, 10, 24, 27, 46, 85, 106,
    113, 119, 121, 123, 133, 261, 347,
    352, 363, 366
- h.e. statistics 59-65, 72, 75, 213, 233,
    234, 241, 312
- massified h.e. 19-21, 33, 102, 103, 119,
    143-148, 152, 157, 185, 186, 190,
    191, 194, 197, 202, 226, 235, 238,
    240, 242, 274, 289, 294, 348, 349,
    351
- national h.e. 9, 12, 13, 117, 118, 122,
    165, 235, 249, 265, 291, 302
- pathways to h.e. 203, 213, 223, 225
- private h.e. 19, 128, 165, 233, 234, 236,
    240, 243, 252, 253, 279, 281, 299
- public h.e. 128, 165, 166, 240, 313, 368
- the role(s) of h.e. 25-27, 40, 123, 154,
    176, 288, 304, 325, 328, 333, 334,
    341, 352
Hill, D. 44, 45
Hobsbawm, E. 317
Holsinger, D.B. 245
Hood, C. 163, 168
Huisman, G. 122, 123
Huisman, J. 102, 111, 118, 239, 267

Identity 25, 158, 191, 298, 302-306, 365,
    367
Inequality 21, 151, 155, 185, 187, 188,
    196, 201, 203, 205, 209, 223, 226,
    234, 239, 244, 245, 249-251, 253,
    254, 326, 331, 332, 342
Institutionalism 35, 269
Integration 25, 37, 41, 48, 50, 124, 130,
    134, 164, 227, 265, 267, 273, 274,
    278, 279, 281-283, 287, 288, 290,
    291, 296, 298, 301, 305, 309, 310,
    312, 315, 321, 340, 356, 363, 368

- European i. 25, 37, 41, 48, 50, 265, 267, 268, 279, 283, 287, 290, 291, 303, 306, 309, 312, 321, 340, 363, 368
Internationalisation 8, 9, 11, 13, 27, 71, 74, 122, 129, 249, 269, 270, 291, 305, 347, 351, 352, 363, 364

Jacob, J. 245
Jahr, V. 69
Janson, K. 71, 75
Japan 44, 68, 81, 203, 242
Jepsen, M. 334
Jessop, B. 35, 36, 163, 329, 340
Johansson, A. 245, 246
Jongbloed, B. 235, 241-243
Jørgensen, K.E. 309
Judt, T. 327, 328
Justice 27, 241, 253, 325, 326, 330, 331, 341, 343
Justman, M. 330

Kant, I. 102, 104
Karseth, B. 267
Keating, A. 290
Kehm, B. 92, 122, 261
Kelo, M. 61
Kelsey, J. 166
King, R. 235
Kinser, K. 161, 166
Kivinen, O. 239
Klemenčič, M. 18, 19, 128
Knight, J. 236, 241
Knill, C. 262, 265, 267, 268, 304
Knowing self 141, 157
Knowledge 15, 16, 19-23, 28-30, 33, 36-42, 45, 56, 73, 74, 80, 83, 85, 86, 131, 141-146, 152-158, 176, 178, 196, 197, 202, 203, 207, 210, 211, 218, 223, 241, 268, 289, 291, 319, 328, 339, 340, 367
- k. economy 15, 16, 28, 29, 33, 36-38, 42, 45, 48, 49, 79, 83, 118, 134, 143, 146, 149, 150, 156, 168, 179, 180, 206, 235, 244, 254, 287, 338, 340, 342
- k. society 20, 23, 29, 39, 45, 68, 118, 143, 149, 158, 185, 206, 338, 349
Kogan, I. 237, 247
Komljenovič, J. 15
Konrad, J. 205, 206
Kosovo 25, 272, 287, 292-296, 298-300, 302, 303, 305, 347, 349, 351, 357
Krause, K. 287
Krzyżanowski, M. 35
Kurelić, Z. 362, 363
Kwiek, M. 22, 235, 237, 242, 249, 252, 290
Kyvik, S. 264

Lambert, R. 82, 168
Landry, C. 88, 89
Lange S. 45
Lanzendorf, U. 61, 71
Larsen, K. 166
Lauder, H. 158, 194
Le Grand, J. 327
Lechuga, V. 166
Legislating 348, 350-352, 355
Leutloff, C. 293
Levy, D. 161
Levy, D. C. 243, 244, 250, 252
Lifelong learning 41, 121, 149, 206-208, 211, 266, 269, 338, 340
Lindstrom, N. 38, 46
Lodge, M. 328
Loprieno, A. 108, 109
Lucas, S. R. 205
Lukas, T. 275, 276
Lynch, K. 287, 325, 329

Maassen, P. 82, 87, 242, 262, 265, 288, 290
Macedonia 25, 271, 287, 292, 293, 297-300, 302, 3030, 305, 347, 351, 352, 354, 357, 358, 363
Marginson, S. 366-368

Market 13, 20-22, 29, 36, 37, 41, 43, 47-
    49, 92, 93, 103, 104, 106, 107, 118,
    128, 149, 156, 157, 161-164, 166-
    168, 170-174, 176-180, 188, 190,
    191, 194, 208, 210, 211, 219, 221,
    236, 241-243, 245, 254, 280, 317,
    320, 325, 327-329, 331, 334-336,
    338-341, 356
Marketisation 20, 161, 180, 234
Marsh, D. 268
Marshal, J. 90
Martin, T. 17, 20, 142, 143, 146, 194
Massification 119, 144, 145, 147, 202,
    240, 242, 274, 289, 348, 349
Matković, T. 329
Mayer, J. W. 104
McGettigan, A. 169, 170, 172, 173, 176
McLean, M. 196
Meek, L. 117-119, 130, 239
Meier, V. 330
Meritocracy 21, 185, 186, 190, 194-197
Meyer, J.W. 103,
Meyer, M. 332
Middlehurst, R. 165
Middleton, C. 93
Miklavič, K. 15, 279, 280, 362
Mobility 7, 15-17, 21, 22, 34, 37, 55-76,
    83, 91, 123, 146, 148, 151-153,
    166, 171, 176, 187, 188, 194, 197,
    205, 233, 234, 245-249, 267, 317,
    319, 322, 330, 342
- social m. 21, 28, 141, 147, 148, 151-
    153, 171, 179, 187, 188, 194, 197,
    201, 233, 234, 245-249, 330, 342
- student m. 15-16, 55-76, 146
Moore, R. 197
Morgan, J. 93, 175
Moscati, R. 310
Murdock, J. 61
Musselin, C. 262, 265, 268, 269
Myklebust, J. P. 86

Naidoo, R. 197
Nation-state 33, 290, 305, 368

Neave, G. 103, 118, 288-290, 310
Negri, A. 303, 305, 326
Neoliberal doctrine 26, 27, 325, 327-332,
    336
Neoliberalism 163, 325-327
Newman, J. 112
Newman, K. S. 235
Nokkala, T. 39, 276, 332, 338, 340
Nussbaum, M. 329, 331

Offe, C. 306
Okri, B. 157
Olsen, J. P. 12, 44, 261, 267, 288, 290
Olssen, M. 36, 287, 328
Opportunity 55, 92, 112, 147, 155, 170,
    171, 201, 251, 266, 301
- educational opportunities 142, 188, 202,
    279
Orosz, A. 273, 274
Orr, D. 67
Oswald, A. 92

Pabian, P.
Palfreyman, D. 240
Palier, B. 328
Parsons, T. 202
Pascual, A. S. 334
Patel, K. 191, 193
Patrinos, H. 174
Pechar, H. 107, 310
Peck, J. 163
Pépin, L. 37
Periphery (-ies) 9, 11, 14, 119, 240, 243,
    289, 305, 347, 366-369
Peters, M. A. 36, 287, 288, 290, 291, 328
Peterson, J. 267, 268
Pfeffer, J. 242
Piattoni, S. 123
Pichl, E. 293
Pierson, C. 327
Poland 7, 22, 23, 64, 69, 70, 233-237,
    239, 240, 242, 244, 245-254
Polany, K. 330
Polanyi, K. 161, 162

Policy
- educational p. 15-17, 19, 20, 24, 26, 33, 37, 38, 46, 48, 56, 79, 82, 83, 90, 92, 94-96, 102, 107, 121-123, 130, 133, 134, 141, 152, 158, 161, 162, 169, 179, 180, 262, 265, 267, 268, 270, 279, 281, 282, 288, 304, 305, 317, 347, 354, 366
- European (EU) policy 7, 14, 16, 18, 55, 65, 67, 76, 83, 84, 101, 102, 105, 112, 122, 269, 282
- higher education p. → *Higher education*
- national p. 14, 18, 24, 27, 95, 117, 120, 123, 126, 131, 238, 254, 261, 265, 266, 269, 271, 274, 280-283, 347, 239, 353, 356, 369
- p. changes 24, 262, 263, 265, 271, 274, 278, 281, 283
- p. transfer 7, 24, 27, 29, 261-263, 265, 267-271, 277, 281, 283
Politics 20, 45, 168, 177, 180, 268, 287, 290-292, 314, 320, 325, 328, 333, 354, 355
Pollack, M. A. 266
Post-Communism 141
Post-conflict 25-27, 289, 292, 299, 303, 304, 351
Post-national 24, 287, 289, 290, 292
Pratt, J. 103
Prest, M. 89
Preston, S. H. 250
Privatisation 20, 27, 161, 180, 325, 327, 329, 336, 341, 343, 347, 353, 355, 356
Profit 20, 156, 161, 164-168, 170, 174, 175, 178, 202, 337, 341, 357
Protest 27, 325, 326, 331-333, 336-336, 341, 343, 351
Pupovci, D. 295
Pusser, B. 166

Quality 7, 13-15, 17, 19, 21, 43, 46, 47, 49, 63, 71, 83-86, 91, 105, 106, 108, 111, 112, 119, 123, 125, 128-132, 152, 155, 163, 168, 170, 171, 174, 175, 188, 190, 196, 197, 201, 204, 205, 209, 210-212, 221, 223-226, 236, 237, 239, 245, 267, 270, 271, 273-282, 288, 313-318, 320-322, 339, 340, 351, 353, 355, 357, 358, 364

Radaelli, C. M. 35, 261, 267, 268
Randle, K. 92
Ranger, T. 317
Rankings 17, 43, 79, 80, 82-84, 86-88, 90-96, 102, 110, 126, 127, 130, 146, 150, 189, 196, 201, 203, 212, 225, 226
Rauhvargers, A. 80
Ravinet, P. 38, 46, 266
Recognition 21, 22, 37, 43, 49, 56, 66, 73, 93, 107, 128, 165, 166, 171, 178, 203, 206, 207, 210, 241, 265, 267, 270, 273, 275, 277, 279-281, 290, 313, 319, 331
- r. of degrees 37, 49, 56, 66, 107, 128, 265, 280, 281, 290, 319
- r. of prior learning (RPL) 21, 22, 66, 203, 206, 207, 210
Regini, M. 103, 310
Reichert, S. 83, 118
Rhodes, R. A. W. 163
Rhoten, D. 30, 154
Richter, S. 352, 365
Richters, E. 62
Rinne, R. 239
Risse, T. 120, 121,133, 261, 268, 269
Ritzen, J. 81, 82
Robertson, S. L. 20, 21, 35, 36, 164, 166, 169, 178, 339
Robinson, R. 327
Rodin, S. 362, 363
Roksa, J. 142, 152-154
Rostan, M. 310
Ruegg, W. 289

Sainsbury, L. 168
Salancik, G. R. 242
Salmi, J. 203, 226
Santiago, P. 235, 244
Sapir, A. 334
Saunders, D.B. 325, 327, 328, 331
Savić, O. 313, 316
Scharpf, F. W. 334
Scherrer, C. 48
Schmidt, V. A. 35
Schofer, E. 103
Scott, P. 103, 240, 351
Searle, J. R. 154
Sebök, M. 110
Sedelmeier, U. 269
Sekulić, T. 26, 321
Selectivity 56, 104, 162, 163, 177, 233,
    240, 242, 243, 251
Self, P. 327
Serbia 19, 24, 25, 117, 119-122, 126,
    127, 129, 130, 133, 134, 261-265,
    271, 272, 274, 277, 278, 281-283,
    295, 296, 300, 301, 347, 351, 357,
    364
Shavit, Y. 201, 202, 239
Skulasson, J. 36
Slantcheva-Durst, S. 252
Slater, D. 162
Slovenia 7, 19, 24, 117, 119, 121, 126,
    127-131, 133, 134, 236, 239, 248,
    261-265, 271-274, 279-283, 347-
    349, 351, 354, 357, 358, 362-364,
    368
Socialism 23, 24, 158, 336, 337, 350, 365
Solbrekke, T. D. 267
Sommers, M. 294, 295
Sorokin, P. 146
Steinel, M. 276
Stensaker, B. 82, 87
Stone, D. 267
Streeck, W. 326, 327
Subotic, J. 365
Szczepanski, J. 240

Šoljan, N. 263, 350
Štulhofer, A. 335

Tapper, T.
Taylor, C.
Teichler, U. 11, 16, 56, 57, 61-63, 68, 69,
    71, 72, 75, 104, 117, 118, 186, 190,
    236
the Netherlands 7, 21, 69, 70, 201, 203-
    205, 208-213, 218-226
Theory 41, 119, 213, 226, 296, 325, 330
- critical th. 325, 330
Thomas, E. 205
Thompson, J. 93, 94
Tierney, W. 166
Tilak, J.B.G. 329
Tina, A. 329
Tiplić, D. 314
Tomusk, V. 20, 288
Tonkiss, F. 162
Toynbee, P. 187, 195
Tracking 43, 204, 212
Trondal, J. 267
Trow, M. 20, 102, 142-148, 150, 152,
    186
Turajlić, S. 314, 351
Turner, S. 166

Udam, M. 276
United Kingdom 7, 17, 20, 21, 48, 61, 64,
    65, 69, 70, 82, 87, 88, 92-95, 103,
    142, 150, 158, 162, 164, 165, 167,
    173, 180, 185-198, 247, 336
Universities
- modernisation of u. 18, 41, 42, 87, 109,
    120, 121, 123, 351, 354, 355, 364,
    365
- private u. 109, 313, 318, 320, 350, 352,
    354, 355
- public u. 109, 236, 237, 239-241, 243,
    252, 295, 296, 350, 355
- state u. 236, 299, 301, 313, 355
- nation-building u. 366
University

- South East European U. Tetovo 297-
   299, 302
- U. of Belgrade 263, 277, 278, 311
- U. of Buckingham 165
- U. of California 146, 147
- U. of Džemal Bjedić (Mostar) 292,
   293, 311, 312, 313, 315
- U. of East Sarajevo 292, 310, 312, 315
- U. of Kassel 7, 61
- U. of Ljubljana 7, 8, 263, 279, 280
- U. of London 7, 165, 190
- U. of Mostar 292, 293, 311-313, 315
- U. of Novi Pazar 300-302
- U. of Prishtina 293-297, 302
- U. of Prizren 296
- U. of Sarajevo 292, 293, 310, 311-313,
   315, 320, 322
- U. of Tartu 264
- U. of Tuzla 311, 313, 315
- U. of Vienna 105, 106, 110, 111, 311
- U. of Zagreb 263, 311, 326, 333, 343
- U. of Zenica 313, 315, 320
USA 36, 44, 80, 81, 84, 143, 166, 202,
   203
Uvalić Trumbić, S. 350

Vaira, M. 310
van den Dungen, M. 210, 221-223, 225
van der Borgh, C. 295
van der Hijden, P. 56
van Elk, R. 204
van Vught, F. A. 86, 102, 123, 239, 242,
   250
Vedder, R. 175
Verger, A. 166
Vickers, P. 150
Vincent-Lancrin, S. 104, 235, 251
Vink, M. P. 261
Voegtle, E. 262, 267
Vossensteyn, H. 202, 223
Vukasović, M. 24, 120, 121, 128, 129,
   268

Wächter, B. 56, 61-63
Walker, D. 187, 195
Wang, Y. 158
Weber, L. 361
Westerheijden, D. F. 123, 262, 266
Western Balkans 19, 23-27, 29, 118, 122,
   131, 135, 290-292, 303-306, 313,
   331, 347, 348, 355, 360, 365-369
Whittaker, R. 206
Whittaker, S. 206
Willetts, D. 167, 170, 173
Witte, J. 83, 262, 265
Wodak, R. 35, 36, 46, 332
Wood, F. 118

Young, M. 21, 156, 185, 186, 235, 241,
   251
Yugoslavia 24-26, 262, 263, 272, 287-
   289, 291-294, 297, 298, 301, 303,
   304, 313, 314, 347-349

Zgaga, P. 15, 27, 28, 119, 129, 279, 280,
   288, 291, 306, 313, 314, 316, 348-
   351, 362
Ziegele, F. 86

Županov, J. 335

Higher Education Research and Policy (HERP)

Edited by Marek Kwiek

Vol. 1   Marek Kwiek / Andrzej Kurkiewicz (eds.): The Modernisation of European Universities. Cross-National Academic Perspectives. 2012.

Vol. 2   Marek Kwiek / Peter Maassen (Eds.): National Higher Education Reforms in a European Context. Comparative Reflections on Poland and Norway. 2012.

Vol. 3   Marek Kwiek: Knowledge Production in European Universities. States, Markets, and Academic Entrepreneurialism. 2013.

Vol. 4   Pavel Zgaga / Ulrich Teichler / John Brennan (eds.): The Globalisation Challenge for European Higher Education. Convergence and Diversity, Centres and Peripheries. Second Revised Edition. 2016.

Vol. 5   Jelena Branković / Maja Kovačević / Peter Maassen / Bjørn Stensaker / Martina Vukasović (eds.): The Re-Institutionalization of Higher Education in the Western Balkans. The Interplay between European Ideas, Domestic Policies, and Institutional Practices. 2014.

Vol. 6   Hamish Coates (ed.): Higher Education Learning Outcomes Assessment. International Perspectives. 2014.

Vol. 7   Gabriella Pusztai: Pathways to Success in Higher Education. Rethinking the Social Capital Theory in the Light of Institutional Diversity. 2015.

Vol. 8   Pavel Zgaga / Ulrich Teichler / Hans G. Schuetze / Andrä Wolter (eds.): Higher Education Reform: Looking Back – Looking Forward. 2015.

www.peterlang.com